Light—Science & Magic

An Introduction to Photographic Lighting

Second Edition

Fil Hunter
Paul Fuqua

Focal Press
An Imprint of Elsevier

Boston Oxford Johannesburg
Melbourne New Delhi Singapore

Focal Press is an imprint of Elsevier.

Copyright © 1997 by Fil Hunter and Paul Fuqua

No part of this publication may be reproduced, stored in a retrieval system, or transmitted in any form or by any means, electronic, mechanical, photocopying, recording, or otherwise, without the prior written permission of the publisher.

Permissions may be sought directly from Elsevier's Science & Technology Rights Department in Oxford, UK: phone: (+44) 1865 843830, fax: (+44) 1865 853333, e-mail: permissions@elsevier.co.uk. You may also complete your request on-line via the Elsevier Science homepage (http://www.elsevier.com), by selecting 'Customer Support' and then 'Obtaining Permissions'.

∞ This book is printed on acid-free paper.

Library of Congress Cataloging-in-Publication Data

Hunter, Fil.

Light-science and magic: an introduction to photographic lighting/Fil Hunter, Paul Fuqua – 2nd ed.

p. cm.

Rev. ed. Of: Light-science & magic. C 1990

Includes index.

ISBN-13: 978-0-240-80275-6 ISBN-10: 0-240-80275-6

1. Photography-Lighting. I. Fuqua, Paul. II. Hunter, Fil. Light-science & magic. III. Title

TR590. H84 1997

778. 7'2—dc21 96-48403

CIP

British Library Cataloging-in-Publication Date

A catalogue record for this book is available from the British Library.

The publisher offers special discounts on bulk orders of this book.
For information, please contact:
Manager of Special Sales
Elsevier
200 Wheeler Road
Burlington, MA 01803
Tel: 781-313-4700
Fax: 781-313-4802

ISBN-13: 978-0-240-80275-6
ISBN-10: 0-240-80275-6

For information on all Focal Press publications available, contact our World Wide Web homepage at http://www.focalpress.com

10

Printed in the United States of America

To Ross Scroggs and Robert Yarbrough,
teachers who taught.

Contents

Preface

"Reason and magic," said he, "may meet and become one in that which one calls wisdom, initiation; in belief in the stars, in numbers."

–Thomas Mann, Doctor Faustus

How photography has changed since the first edition of *Light – Science & Magic!* Transmitting pictures electronically was a secret craft understood only by a few in the news business. Film was a *requirement* for shooting a picture. If a client needed a black-and-white brochure, we actually had to make *prints*.

In a world of digital image acquisition, desktop electronic retouching, and World Wide Web publishing, how much can a new edition of *any* photographic text resemble its seven-year-old ancestor?

As it turns out, quite a bit.

A lot of photographic books are obsolete. We have even written some of them. But *Light – Science & Magic* is not one of them.

Sure, we made a few mistakes. We implied that HMI lights would never see common usage, and we told people bluntly that a good flash meter could never be a good continuous light meter! By and large, however, the principles in *Light – Science & Magic* are just as new — and just as old — as they were the first day the book was printed.

Styles of photographic lighting have changed, and they will change again. *Light – Science & Magic* does not go out of style because it was not and is not based on style. This book is based on the behavior of light. These principles will not change until fundamental physics does.

Seven years ago we said:

> *The purpose of this book is to introduce a logical theory of photographic lighting as fundamental as those we use for the other aspects of photography - theory that enables beginning photographers to predict results* before *setting up lights; allows a professional photographer of one specialty to easily see how a photographer with a different type of expertise might have produced a given picture...*
>
> *Contrary to the impression you may get from briefly thumbing through this book, it is not about lighting a selection of classic subjects. It is simply about lighting.*
>
> *We hope this is not primarily a "how-to" book. For example, we show three basic ways of lighting a flat piece of metal. Only one of these three makes a good picture and that one by itself would be good enough for a "how-to." However, all three show* principles, *and those principles are likely to be useful even if you never light a piece of metal.*

This book was the first to outline what we consider to be the basic principles of lighting so that those principles could easily be transferred to any subject matter and to any equipment. Of course, this is the opinion of the authors. We admit our bias, but here are a few anecdotes that our bias cannot influence:

- A successful portrait photographer claims to have learned more about portraiture from the chapter on lighting a box than in all of his portraiture books and classes together.
- A wedding photographer attempted his first product shot and won first place in a state *professional* competition with that picture after reading this book. (No, *not* good news. He beat one of the authors in the process!)
- A junior college adopted this material for its class on studio lighting. In the first year, assignments done for that class won more awards in the student art competition than in all of the other classes in the Art Department combined.

Use this book as a cookbook, if you like. There are certainly some excellent lighting recipes here. However, we think our discussion of how each ingredient works matters more than the recipes that use them. Alter the proportions, adjust the time, and add or delete elements to suit your own taste.

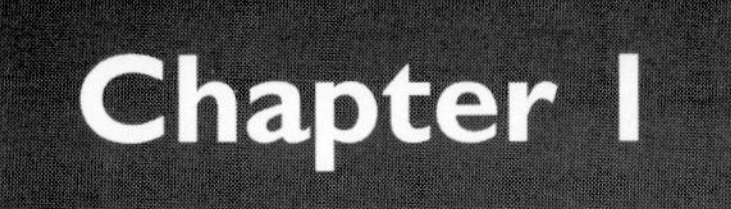

Chapter 1

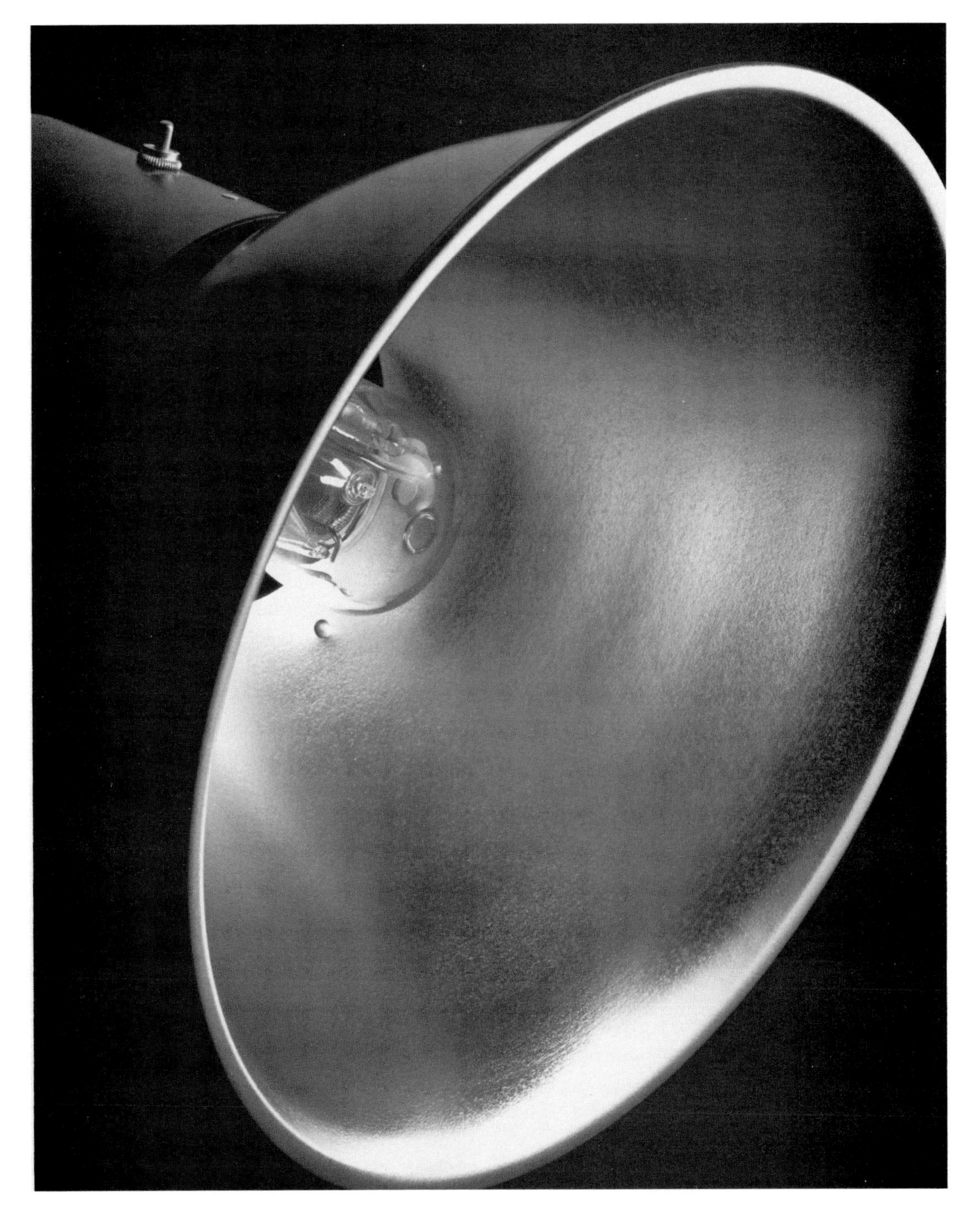

How to Learn Lighting

We know things about lighting that you would like to learn. Otherwise, you would not have bought this book. Nevertheless, *Light–Science & Magic* is a discussion, not a lecture. You bring to this discussion your own opinions about art, beauty, and aesthetics. We do not intend to change those opinions and may not even influence them very much. We will be more bored than flattered if reading this book causes you to make pictures that look like ours. For better or worse, you have to build your own pictures on your own vision.

What we *do* have to offer you is a set of tools. This book is about technology. Science. Brass tacks. Information for you to use when you please, if you please, and how you please.

This does not mean that this book is not about *ideas*, because it is. The basic tools of lighting are principles, not hardware.

Shakespeare's tool was the Elizabethan English language, not a quill pen. Photographers without mastery of lighting are like a Shakespeare who could speak only the language of the people in the Globe Theater pit. Being Shakespeare, he still might have come up with a decent play. But it would have certainly taken a lot more work and, very likely, more blind luck than most people are entitled to expect.

Light is the language of photography. Patterns of light convey information just as surely as spoken words. The information that light conveys is clear and specific. It includes definite statements, such as "the bark of this tree is rough" or "this utensil is made of stainless steel, but that one is sterling."

Light, like any other language, has a grammar and a vocabulary. Good photographers need to learn that grammar and vocabulary. Fortunately, photographic lighting is a lot easier to master than a foreign language. This is because physics, not societal whim, makes the rules.

The tools in this book are the grammar and vocabulary of light. Whatever we say about specific technique is important only to the extent that it proves the principles. *Do not memorize the lighting diagrams in this book.* It is entirely possible to put a light in exactly the same spot shown in the diagram and, still, make a bad picture—especially if the subject is not identical to the one in the diagram. But if you learn the principle you may see several other good ways to light the same subject that we never mention, and maybe never thought of.

WHAT ARE "THE PRINCIPLES"?

To photographers, the important principles of light are those that predict how it will behave. Some of these principles are especially powerful. You will probably be surprised to find how few they are, how simple they are to learn, and how much they explain.

We discuss these key principles in detail in Chapters 2 and 3. They are the tools we use for everything else. In later chapters we put them to work to light a wide range of different subjects. At this point we will simply list them.

1. The effective size of the light source is the single most important decision in lighting a photograph. It determines what types of shadows are produced and may affect the type of reflection.
2. There are three types of reflection possible from any surface. They determine why any surface looks the way it does.
3. Some of these reflections occur only if light strikes the surface from within a limited family of angles. After we decide what type of reflection is important, the family of angles determines where the light should or should not be.

These are the most important concepts in this book. If you pay close attention to them whenever they come up, you will find they will usually account for any other details you may overlook or we may omit.

WHY ARE THE PRINCIPLES IMPORTANT?

The three principles we have just given are statements of physical laws that have not changed since the beginning of the universe. They have nothing to do with style, taste, or fad. The timelessness of these principles is exactly what makes them so useful. Consider, for example, how they apply to portrait style. A representative 1949 portrait does not look like most portraits made in 1899 or 1999. But a photographer who understands light could execute any of them.

Chapter 8 shows a good way to light a portrait, but some photographers will not want to use it, and even fewer will do so in twenty years. (Granted, Shakespeare is good, but who wants to write like him today?) Frankly, we do not care whether you use our portrait arrangement or not. However, we very much *do* care that you understand exactly how and why we did what we did. The answers to those "hows" and "whys" allow you to produce your own pictures your own way. Good tools do not limit creative freedom. They make it possible.

Good photographs take planning, and lighting is an essential part of that planning. For this reason, the most important part of good lighting happens before we turn on the first lights. This planning can take many days or it can happen a fraction of a second before pressing the shutter release. It does not matter when you plan or how long it takes, as long as you get the planning done. The more you accomplish with your head, the less work you have to do with your hands—and you can think faster than you can move.

Understanding the principles enables us to decide what lights need to be where before we begin to place them. This is the important part. The rest is just fine tuning.

HOW WERE THE EXAMPLE SUBJECTS CHOSEN FOR THIS BOOK?

The portrait is only one of the seven basic photographic subjects we discuss. We chose each subject to prove something about the basic principles. We also lit the subject to show the principle, regardless of whether there might be other good ways to light the same thing. If you know the principles, you will discover the other ways without any help from us.

This means that you should give at least some attention to every representative subject. Even if you have no interest in a particular subject, it probably relates to something you do want to photograph.

We also chose many of the subjects because they are rumored to be supremely difficult. Those rumors are spread by people who lack the tools to deal with such subjects. We intend to dispel the rumors.

Additionally, we tried to use studio examples whenever possible. This does not mean *Light–Science & Magic* is *only* a book about studio lighting. Light behaves the same way everywhere, whether it is controlled by the photographer, by the building designer, or by God. But you can set up indoor experiments like ours at any hour of any day regardless of the weather. Later, when you see the same lighting in a landscape, on a public building, or at a press conference, you will recognize it, because you will have seen it before.

Finally, we chose each example to be as simple as possible. If you are learning photography, you will not have to leave the setup in your living room or in your employer's studio for days at a time to master it. If you teach photography you will find that you can do any of these demonstrations in a single class session.

DO I NEED TO DO THESE EXERCISES?

If you are learning photography without any formal instruction, we suggest you try all of the basic examples in this book. Do not simply read about them. What happens in your head is the most important part of lighting, but the eye and the hand are still essential. Guided experience coordinates the three.

When we talk about soft shadows or polarized direct reflections, for example, you already know how they look. They happen in the world, and you see them every day. But you will know them and see them still better once you have made them happen.

If you are a student, your class assignments will keep you busy enough without any further demands from us. Your teacher may use the exercises here or invent new ones. Either way, you will learn the principles in the book because they are basic. They happen in all lighting.

If you are a professional photographer trying to expand your areas of expertise, your judgment about what exercises you need is better than ours. Generally, these will be those that are least like the things you are already photographing. You may find our basic examples to be too simple to be an entertaining challenge. Try complicating things a bit. Add an unexpected prop, an unusual viewpoint, or a special effect to our basic example. You might as well get a striking portfolio piece out of the effort while you are at it.

If you are a highly experienced photographer, you have already seen most of our examples in your own work. Use our organization of the material to reevaluate why your lighting works. Most of us have a few basic lighting setups that we use and reuse to the point of habit. Looking at our work through other photographers' philosophies reveals those habits and shows fresh approaches. If anything we say helps you to do this, please let us know so that we might use the example in our next book. Or let us know about your own new book so we can read it!

WHAT KIND OF CAMERA DO I NEED?

Experienced photographers consider this a silly question. But we have taught this material, we know how many perfectly intelligent students ask it, and we have to answer it. There are two good answers, and they contradict one another slightly. The weight we place on each answer matters more than the answers themselves.

If you do these exercises as we recommend them, with mostly static subjects, a large format view camera is technically capable of results superior to anything else. However, successful photographs depend on the photographer more than the equipment. Inexperienced photographers work best with the camera with which they are familiar. Experienced photographers work best with the camera they like. These human factors sometimes have more to do with the success of a photograph than the purely technical principles.

If you want to try a new type of camera, we encourage you to do so, but not at the same time you are trying new lighting techniques. "Sufficient unto each day is the evil thereof." Learn the lighting well enough to get good results with familiar tools. If those results are not good enough, then consider another camera.

When you do consider another camera, remember that the camera also influences other equipment needs. Larger cameras require more light and smaller cameras require more lenses. Larger images have less depth of field, so larger cameras need to be used at smaller apertures. This means using more light if we want to keep comparable exposure times. Forgetting this can lead to inferior results from a superior new camera.

Available lenses determine your camera viewpoint. A good selection of lenses allows the freedom to pick the best viewpoint. If the camera has the best possible viewpoint, view-camera type adjustments may be unnecessary. However, if you have a view camera, the adjustments allow you to find a good viewpoint for almost any subject using only one lens. Well-equipped photographers using view cameras usually have only about half as many lenses as comparably equipped 35mm users have.

None of this needs to worry you if someone can loan you equipment for your experiments or if you already have a fully equipped studio. However, if you are one of the majority of photographers, you buy equipment one piece at a time and less often than you would like. Try to adjust your timing and select a price bracket that allows you to back up each new piece of equipment with the accessory equipment to use it effectively.

WHAT LIGHTING EQUIPMENT DO I NEED?

We expect you to ask this question, so we have a precise and definitive answer ready. We do not want to leave out any details, so this will be another two-part answer:

1. No photographer has enough lighting equipment to do every assignment as well as possible.
2. Most photographers have enough equipment to do almost every assignment well.

No matter how much lighting equipment you have, there will be times when you want more. Suppose, for example, you can illuminate a large set to expose a slow film at f/180 for 1/1000 second. (Please call the fire department before turning on this apparatus.) You will probably then find that you want still more light in a particular shadow, or you may find that you need to light a still larger area to fit the required composition.

Even if you have no lighting equipment at all, you may be able to get the job done. Can the subject be photographed outdoors? If not, sunlight through a window may be a good light source. Inexpensive tools, such as white cloth, black paper, and aluminum foil, can allow you to control sunlight as effectively as the best manufactured equipment.

Good lighting equipment is a great convenience. Doing without it may require a faster film or a longer shutter speed. If the sun moves too far across the sky before you are ready to expose the film, you may have to wait until it returns the next day and hope there is no more and no less cloud cover the second time around. Professional photographers know that convenience becomes necessity when they have to photograph what the client wants when the client wants.

But this message is not aimed at professionals. They already know how to do whatever is needed with whatever is available. We are more interested in encouraging students now. You have advantages that professionals do not. Within broad limits, you can select the size of your subject.

Small scenes require less light. You may not have a 3 x 4-meter soft box, but a desk lamp with a 60-watt bulb with a tracing paper diffuser can light a small subject identically. Within broad limits, you can also select the best time to shoot the picture. Getting an assignment done sometime before class at 10:00 on Thursday is less demanding than having an appointment to do the job between 9:00 and 10:00 on Thursday.

All of this applies slightly more to still photographers than to people doing motion pictures and video. If you are one of the latter, you lack one important control that still photographers have. If you are shooting moving images, you cannot use a longer shutter speed to compensate for lower light levels. But you can, at least, use a wider aperture than still photographers. Your smaller image makes it easier to get adequate depth of field. Be glad.

Lack of equipment is a handicap. You know it and we know it. But the lack is not an insurmountable obstacle. Creativity can overcome it. Just remember that creative lighting occurs primarily in planning the lighting. Part of that creativity means anticipating the limitations and deciding how to work with them.

WHAT ELSE DO I NEED TO KNOW TO USE THIS BOOK?

We assume you know basic photography. You know how to determine a reasonable exposure, at least close enough that bracketing can cover errors. You understand depth of field. You have mastered the mechanical operation of your camera.

That is all. We have no intention of being ruthless in our examination of your background credentials. Just to be safe, however, we suggest you keep a good basic photography book on hand when you read this one. (We did when we wrote it.) We do not want you to find easy material difficult just because we unknowingly use a technical term you have not seen before.

You also need an outline of the basic lighting equipment we will be using throughout this book. We provide such an outline in the appendices at the end of this book. If you are not already familiar with lighting equipment, we recommend you turn there next (especially "Risk Management" on pages 301–303). If you are already reasonably familiar with the equipment, move on to the next chapter. Refer to the appendices any time we talk about an unfamiliar tool.

WHAT IS THE "MAGIC" PART OF THIS BOOK?

Learn about the light and the science. The magic will happen.

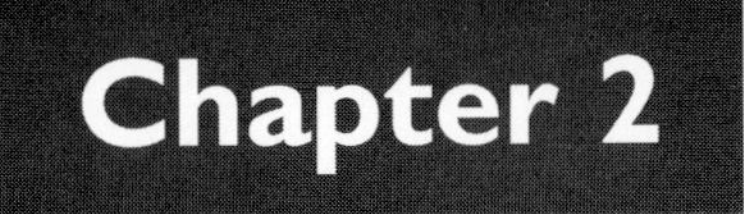

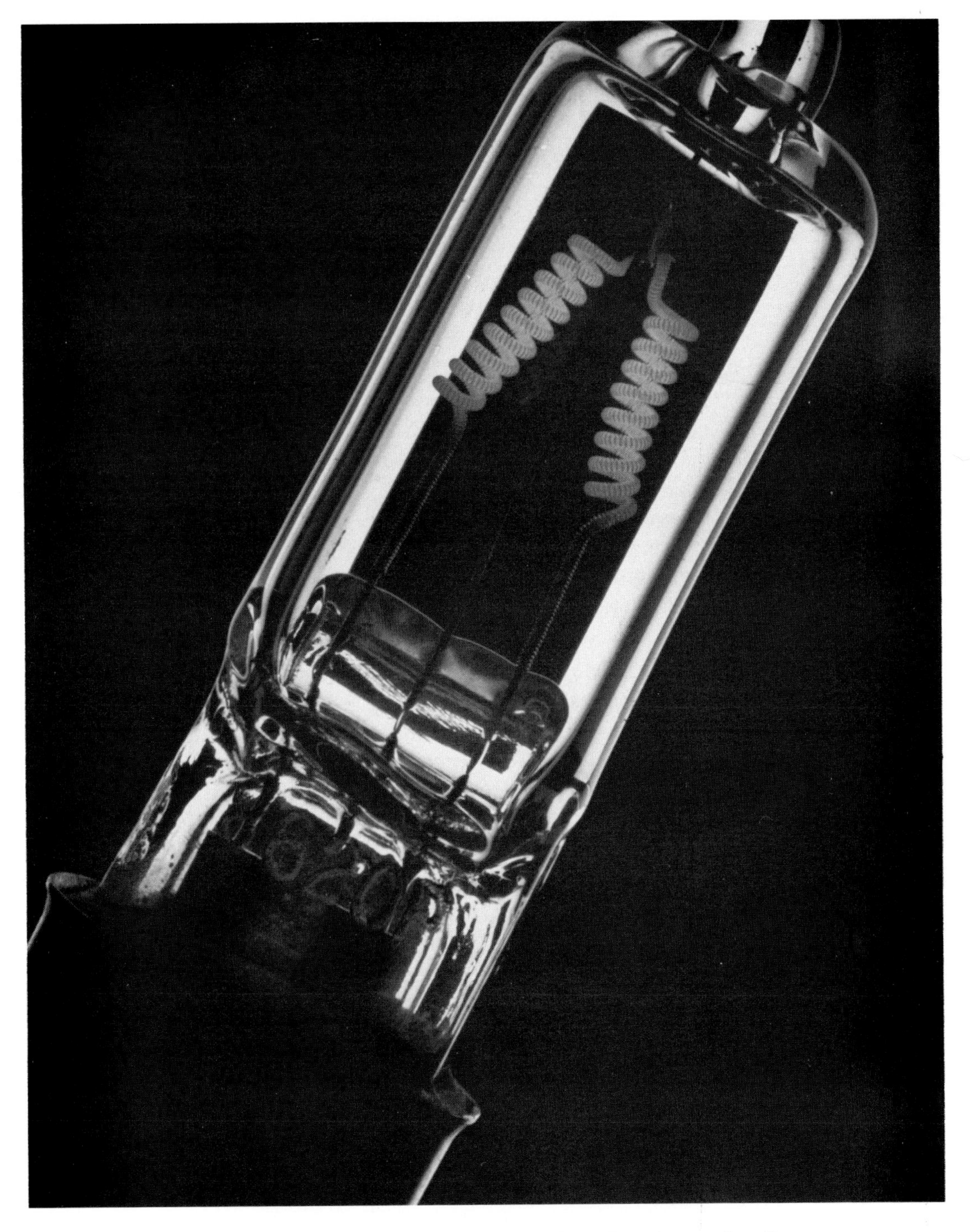

Light: The Raw Material of Photography

In some ways photographers resemble musicians more than painters, sculptors, and other visual artists. This is because photographers, like musicians, are more interested in the manipulation of energy than of matter.

Light is the raw material of photography, just as sound waves are the raw material for music. A piece of film or a video cassette recorder circuit might be necessary, but it is secondary. We can replace one photographic medium with another just as we can substitute a banjo for a clarinet. Timbre changes, but the essential melody remains intact.

Photography begins the moment light is emitted from a source. It climaxes with still more light reflecting from a print, passing through a transparency, or beaming from a television picture tube and striking a human eye. All steps between manipulate light, whether to control it, to record it, or, ultimately, to present it to a viewer.

Photography *is* the manipulation of light. Whether those manipulations serve artistic or technical purposes hardly matters; the two are often synonymous. Whether the manipulations are physical, chemical, electrical, or electronic, they are all motivated by the same mission and guided by the same understanding of how light behaves.

In this chapter we are going to talk about light, the raw material from which we make pictures. You, the reader, are already familiar with most of the ideas we will discuss. This is because you have been learning to see since the day you were born. Even if you happen to be a novice photographer, the occipital lobe of your brain has enough information about the behavior of light for you to be a master.

We want to attach words and labels to some of this unconscious and semiconscious information. This will make it easier for us to talk about light with other photographers, just as musicians find it easier to say "b flat" or "4/4 time" instead of humming a scale or tapping a rhythm.

This is the most theoretical chapter in this book. It is also the most important because it is the foundation for all that follows.

WHAT IS LIGHT?

A complete definition of the nature of light is quite complex. In fact, several Nobel Prizes have been awarded for various contributions to the working definition we use today. We will simplify our discussion by using a definition adequate for applied photography. If you are still curious after reading this, see any basic physics text.

Light is a type of energy called *electromagnetic radiation.* Electromagnetic radiation travels through space in tiny "bundles" called *photons*. A photon is pure energy and has no mass. A box of photons the size of an elephant weighs nothing.

The energy of the photon produces an electromagnetic field around the photon. A field is invisible and cannot be detected unless there is a material object in the field on which it can exert a force. This sounds pretty mysterious, until we realize that one common example of a field is the magnetic field surrounding an ordinary magnet. We cannot tell the field exists unless we move a nail close enough for the magnet to attract it. Then the effect of the field is apparent: The nail jumps to the magnet.

Unlike the field around the magnet, however, the electromagnetic field around the photon is not constant in strength. Instead, it fluctuates as the photon travels. If we could see this change in the strength of the field it would look something like Figure 2.1.

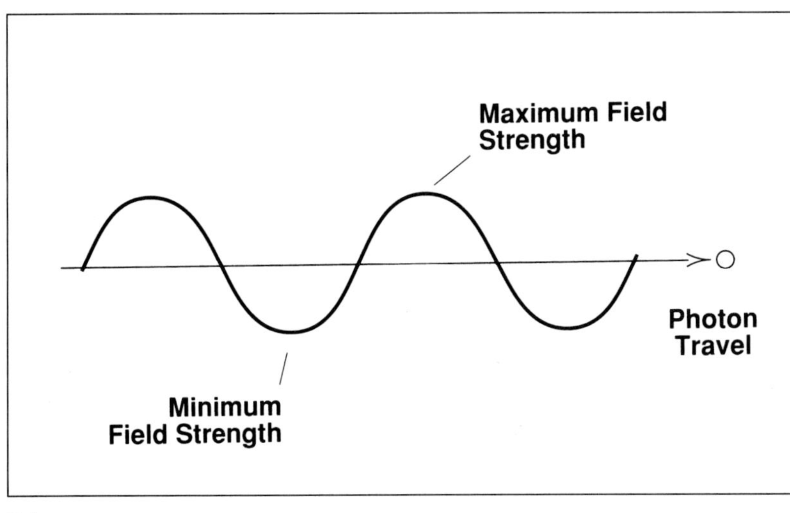

2.1

◀ *The magnetic field around a photon fluctuates from its maximum to its minimum strength as the photon travels.*

Notice that the strength of the field moves from zero to its maximum positive strengths then back to zero, and then repeats the pattern in the negative direction. This is why the field around a beam of light does not attract metal like an iron magnet does. The field around a photon of light is positive half of the time and negative the rest of the time. The average charge of the two states is zero.

As the term implies, an *electromagnetic field* has both an electrical component and a magnetic one. Each component has the same pattern of fluctuation: zero to positive, to zero, to negative, and back to zero again. The electrical component is perpendicular to the magnetic one. The relationship between these two components is easier to see if we assume that Figure 2.1 represents just the electrical component. Then, if you turn this book so that the edge of the page is toward you, the same diagram will represent the electrical field.

All photons travel through space at the same speed, but the electromagnetic field of some photons fluctuates faster than that of others. The more energy a photon has, the faster the fluctuation. Human eyes can see the effect of this difference in photon energy levels and of this difference in the rate of field fluctuation. We call the effect *color* (Figure 2.2). Red light, for example, has less energy than blue light, so the rate of its electromagnetic field fluctuation is only about two thirds as fast.

We call the rate of fluctuation of the electromagnetic field its *frequency,* and we measure it with the unit called *hertz*. Hertz is the number of complete wavelengths that pass a point in space each second. Visible light is only one narrow range out of all the many possible electromagnetic frequencies.

 *The rate at which the electromagnetic field fluctuates varies. We perceive this variation as different colors.*

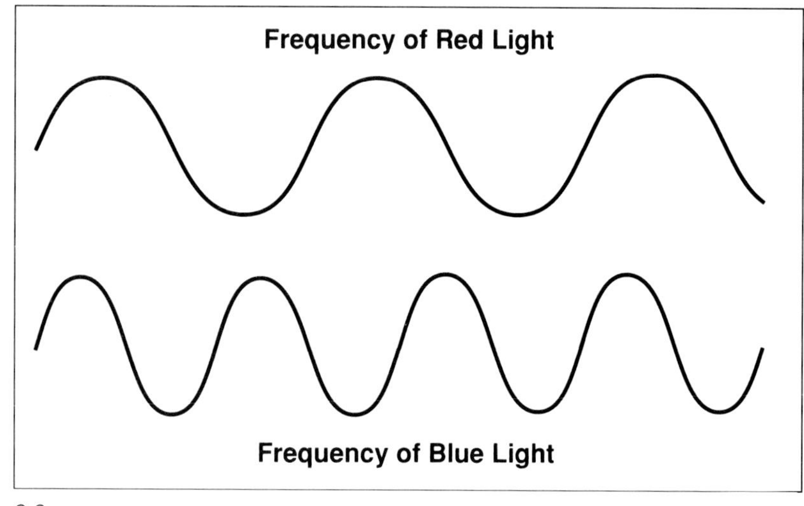

2.2

Electromagnetic radiation can travel through a vacuum and through some forms of matter. We know that light, for example, can pass through transparent glass. Electromagnetic radiation is not closely related to mechanically transmitted energy, such as sound or heat, which can *only* travel through matter. (Infrared radiation and heat are often popularly confused because they tend to accompany one another.) Electromagnetic radiation exerts a force in a vacuum, analogous to the gravitational force extending through space between earth and its moon.

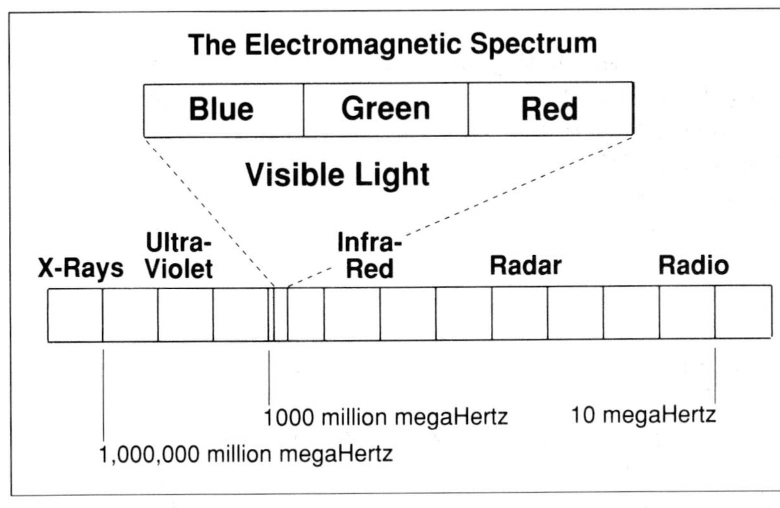

2.3

◀ *This diagram shows the electromagnetic spectrum. Notice that visible light is only one small part of it.*

Most film is sensitive to a much wider range of electromagnetic frequencies than the human eye can perceive (Figure 2.3). This is why a picture can be degraded by ultraviolet light, which we cannot see in a landscape, or by x-rays, which we cannot see emitted by a machine at an airport.

HOW PHOTOGRAPHERS DESCRIBE LIGHT

Even if we confine our attention to the visible portion of the electromagnetic spectrum, everyone knows that the effect of one group of photons may be radically different from that of another! Examining our album of mental images, we all see the difference between an autumn sunset, a welder's arc, and an early morning fog. Even in a standard office location, the decision to install fluorescent tubes, tungsten spots, or large skylights can have a major effect on the decor (as well as on the mood and the productivity of the occupants).

Photographers, however, are interested in more than just the mental images of a given lighting effect. They need technical descriptions of the effect. Being able to describe the light is the first step in being able to control it. Or if the light is not controllable, as it is not in a landscape or an architectural picture, describing the light implies seeing the light well enough to know whether to shoot or to wait until conditions improve.

As photographers, we are primarily concerned with the brightness, color, and contrast of the light. In the following several pages, we will take a brief look at each.

Brightness

To a photographer, the single most important quality of a light source is its brightness. A brighter light is almost always a better light.

At the most basic level, if the light is not bright enough, we cannot get a picture. If the light is brighter than the minimum we must have, then we can probably get a better picture.

Photographers who use film can use a smaller aperture or a faster shutter speed if they have more light. If they do not need, or want, a smaller lens opening or a shorter exposure time, then more light allows using a slower, finer grained film. Either way, the image quality improves.

Even if film is irrelevant, the brightness of the light source still is important. Videographers prefer a smaller aperture for most shots, as do still and motion picture photographers. Furthermore, adequate illumination allows a videographer to forego boosting the gain on the camera. This produces sharper pictures on the screen with better color saturation and less video noise.

Usually photographers prefer dimmer light only when there is an aesthetic improvement in one of the other qualities of light—the color or the contrast.

Color

We can use light of any color we please, and very strongly colored lights frequently make an artistic contribution to the photograph. Nevertheless, most pictures are made with white light. However, even "white" light comes in a range of colors. Photographers consider light to be "white" when it contains a roughly even mix of the three primary colors: red, blue, and green. Human beings perceive this combination of light colors to be colorless.

The proportions of the color mixture may vary to a great extent, and people still cannot perceive any difference, unless they have the different light sources side by side for comparison. The eye can detect a very slight change in the color mixture, but the brain refuses to admit the difference. As long as there is a reasonable amount of each primary color, the brain says "this light is white."

Film cannot make the automatic adjustment to color that the brain does. Photographers must therefore pay attention to the differences between various white light sources. In order to classify variations in the color of white light, photographers borrow the color temperature scale from physicists. The color temperature scale is based on the fact that if we heat a material in a vacuum hot enough, it will glow. The color of this glow depends on how much we heat the material. We measure *color temperature* in degrees on the Kelvin temperature scale. The measurement unit, *degrees Kelvin,* is simply abbreviated "K."

Interestingly enough, light with a *high* color temperature is composed of a disproportionate amount of those colors artists call *cool.* For example, 10,000K light has a great deal of blue in it. Similarly, what physicists tell us is a *low* temperature source has much of those colors artists call *warm.* Thus, a 2000K light tends toward the red to yellow family of colors. (None of this is surprising. Any welder can tell us that the blue-white welding arc is hotter than a piece of red-hot metal being welded.)

There are three standard light color temperatures used by photographers. One of these is 5500K and is called *daylight*. There are two *tungsten* color temperature standards, 3200K and 3400K. The last two are close enough together that sometimes the difference between them does not matter.

Photographers can buy film that is *color balanced* for any of these three light color standards. Video cameras usually have colored filters inside the camera. Selecting the appropriate filter balances either daylight or tungsten illumination to the optimum color for the video tube in the camera.

Contrast

The third important characteristic of a photographic light is its contrast. A light source has *high contrast* if its rays all strike the subject from nearly the same angle. Light rays from a *low-contrast* source strike the subject from many different angles. Sunlight on a clear day is a common example of a high-contrast light source. Notice that the rays of sunlight in Figure 2.4 are parallel to one another. They all strike the subject at the same angle.

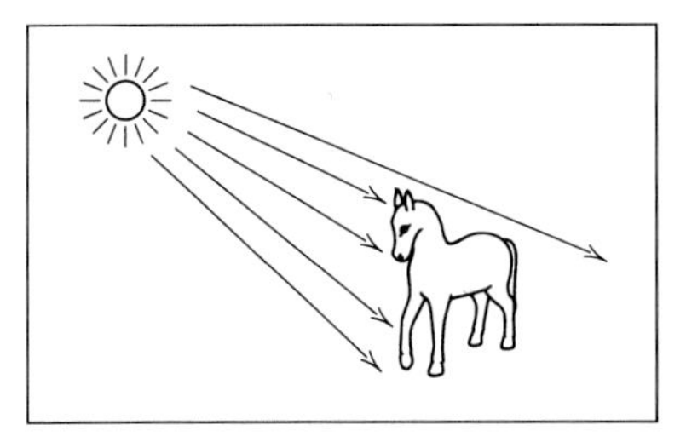

2.4

◀ *The rays from a small, high-contrast light source all strike a subject at approximately the same angle, producing a hard-edged shadow.*

The easiest way to recognize a high-contrast light source is the appearance of the shadows. In the diagram, we see that no light enters the shadow area. This causes the edge of the shadow to be sharp and clearly defined. We made Figure 2.5 with such a light source. Notice the crisp, hard-edged shadow of the horse.

► *Hard-edged shadows are characteristically produced by small light sources.*

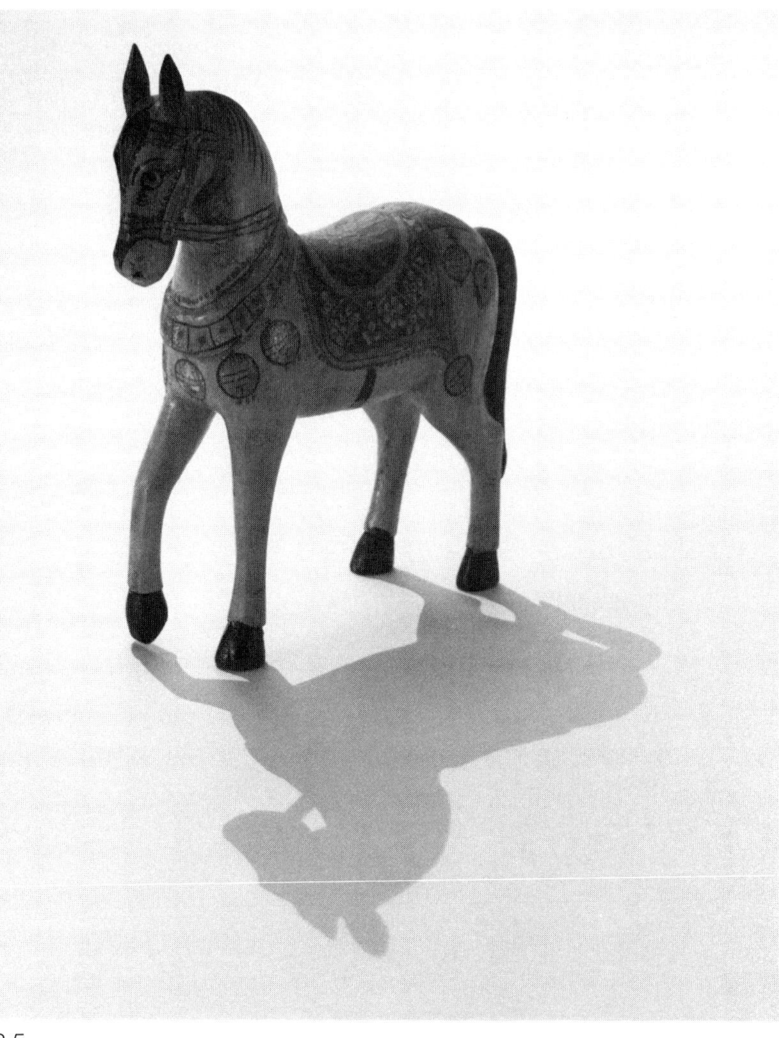

2.5

A shadow with sharply defined edges is called a *hard shadow.* For this reason, high-contrast light sources are also said to be *hard*.

Now let us imagine what happens when cloud cover obscures the sun. Look at Figure 2.6. The sunlight scatters as it passes through the cloud. Consequently, the light that passes through the clouds strikes the subject from many different angles. Therefore, on an overcast day sunlight becomes a low-contrast light source.

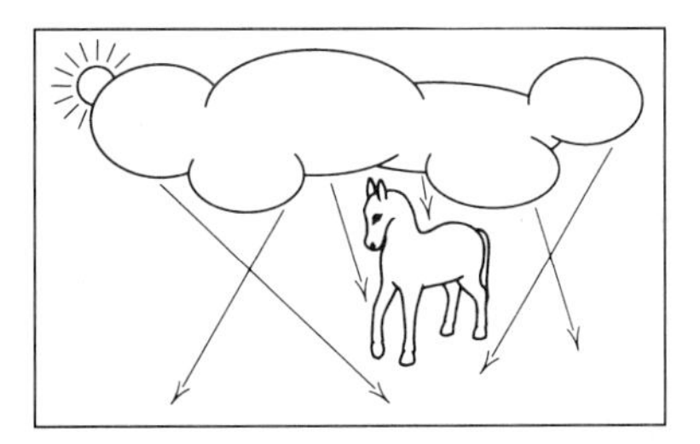

◀ *The cloud scatters the sun's light rays, causing them to strike the subject from many different angles. This produces the soft shadow characteristic of large lights.*

2.6

Again, the contrast of the light source is revealed by the appearance of the shadow. Some of the rays of light partly illuminate the shadow, especially at its edge. This difference is apparent in Figure 2.7.

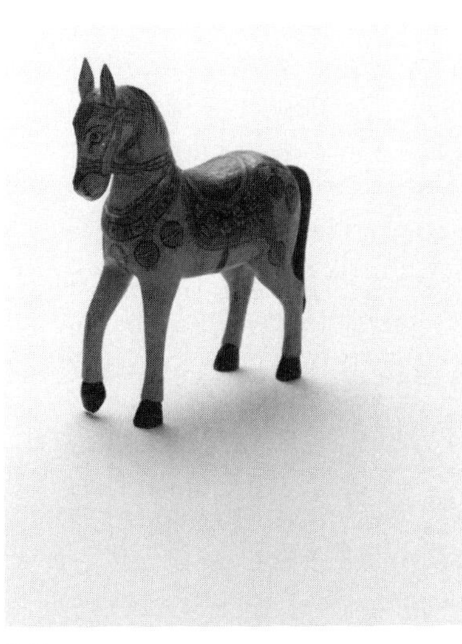

◀ *A shadow so soft that it is just barely visible is the result of a very large light source.*

2.7

In the photograph using low-contrast light, the shadow of the horse is no longer clearly defined. It is no longer hard. The viewer cannot decide exactly what part of the table top is in shadow and what is not. A shadow such as this one, with no clearly defined edge, is called a *soft shadow*, and the light producing it is called a *soft* light.

Notice that we are using the words *hard* and *soft only* to describe how sharply the edge of a shadow is defined. We are *not* using these terms to describe how light or dark the shadow is. Notice that the *center* of each horse shadow is about the same gray in each picture. A soft shadow may be either light or dark, just as a hard shadow may be either light or dark.

For single light sources, the *size* of that source is the primary factor influencing its contrast. A small light source is always a hard light source, and most large sources are soft ones. We see that the sun in Figure 2.4 occupies little area in the diagram, so it is a small light source. The cloud covers a greater area in Figure 2.6, making it a large source.

Notice that the physical size of a light does not completely determine its effective size as a photographic light source. We know that the sun is more than a million kilometers in diameter. However, it is far enough away to act as a small source for a photographic subject on earth.

If we could move the sun close enough to us, it would become an extremely large light source. We could then make softly lit photographs in sunlight, even without any cloud cover, assuming we could find a solution to the heat problem! Another extreme example has a more practical use: A small lamp on a laboratory workbench can be an effectively large source if we put it close enough to an insect specimen.

Be aware, however, that the correlation between the size of a light source and its contrast is just a generality, not an absolute. Remember that we can optically alter a light with special attachments. Appendix 2 describes some of them. For example, a spot attachment can focus the light rays of a strobe head, and a grid blocks the rays from all but a narrow range of angles. In neither case can the light strike the subject from many different angles. This makes a light equipped with such a device hard, regardless of its size.

The Contrast of a Photograph

The contrast of the light is only one of the influences on the contrast of a photograph. If you are an experienced photographer, you know that you can find high contrast in an image with low-contrast light and vice versa.

Contrast is also determined by subject matter composition, exposure, and development. Everyone knows a scene that includes black and white subjects is likely to have more contrast than one with entirely gray objects; but increasing the film development can produce high contrast, even in an entirely gray scene in very low-contrast lighting.

The relationship between exposure and contrast is a bit more complex. Increased and decreased exposure can both reduce contrast in an average scene. However, increasing exposure will increase contrast in a dark subject, while decreasing exposure may increase contrast in a light-gray scene!

We will talk about the relationship between lighting and contrast throughout this book, and we will show how exposure affects contrast in Chapter 9.

LIGHT VERSUS LIGHTING

We have talked about the brightness, color, and contrast of light. These are all of the important characteristics of light. However, we have said very little about *lighting.* Indeed, the little we have said about lighting has more to do with the absence of light, the shadows, than with the light itself!

Shadow is the part of the scene that the light does not strike. *Highlight* is the area illuminated. We want to talk about highlight, but we are not quite ready for it. If you look at the two horse pictures, you will see why. The two photographs have very different lighting, but there is very little difference in the highlight on the horse's back.

Is it possible that lighting determines the appearance of the shadow, but not the highlight? Figures 2.8 and 2.9 prove otherwise.

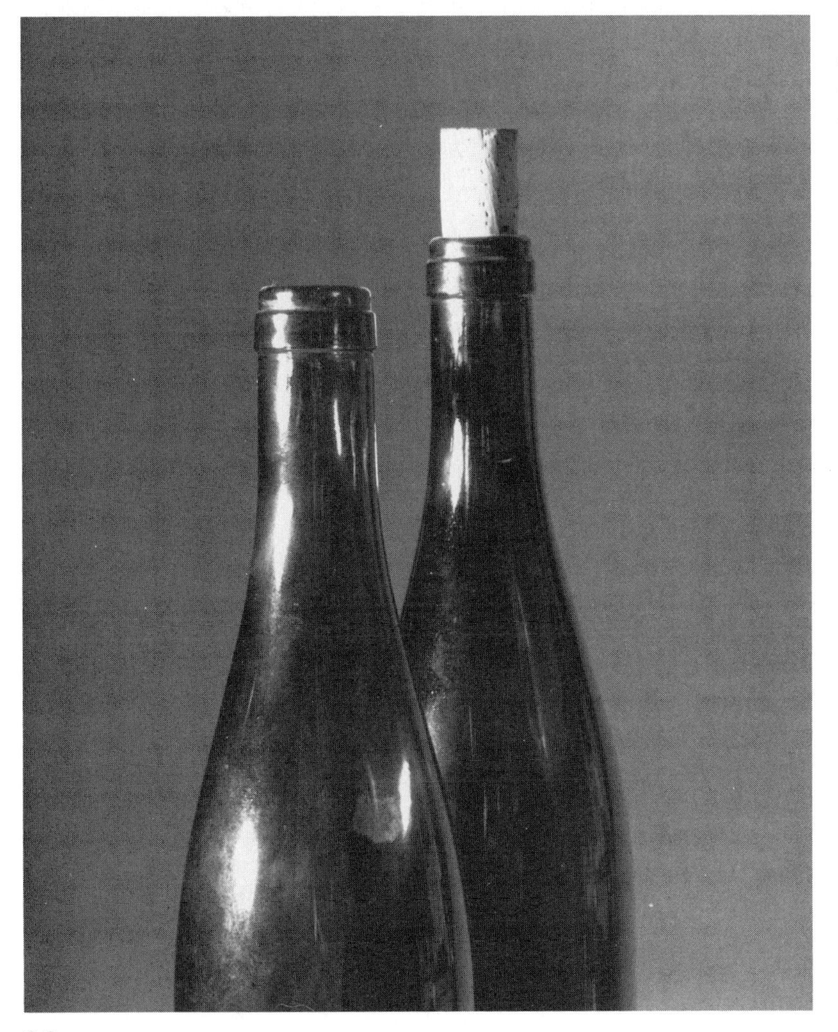

2.8

◀ *A small light source produces small, hard highlights on these glass bottles. Compare these with the highlights in the following photograph.*

► *We produced these large highlights on the bottles by using a large light source.*

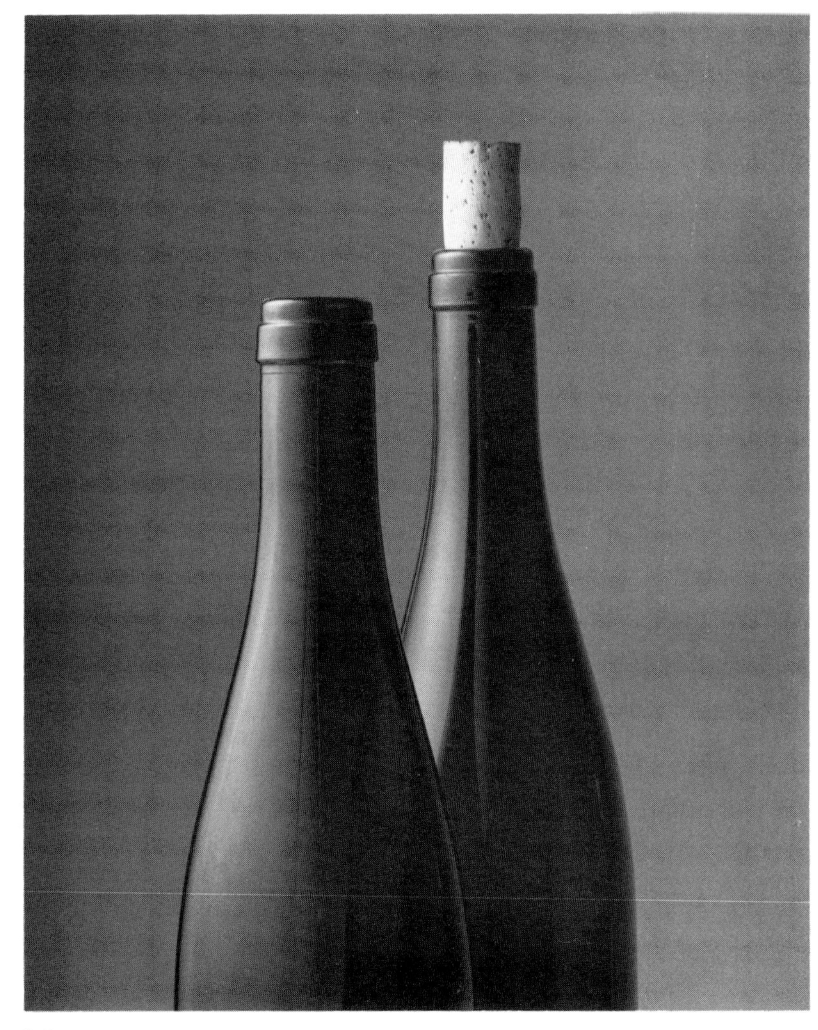

2.9

The glass bottle in Figure 2.8 was illuminated by a small, high-contrast light source. Figure 2.9 is the result of a large, soft source. Now the difference in the highlights is obvious. Why does the contrast of the light have such a dramatic effect on the appearance of the highlight on the bottle but almost no effect on the horse? As you look at the examples, you already know that the difference in the lighting is caused by the subject itself.

Photographic lighting is more than just light. Lighting is a relationship between the light, the subject, and the viewer. If we want to say any more about lighting, we must talk about the subject.

HOW THE SUBJECT AFFECTS THE LIGHTING

Photons move. Photographic subjects often sit still. This is why we tend to consider light to be the "active" player in the photographic event. Such a mental orientation handicaps our ability to "see" a scene.

Two identical photons striking two different surfaces can appear dramatically different to the eye and to the camera. The subject changes the light and different subjects change the light in different ways. The subject plays an active role, just as the photon does. To perceive or to control lighting, we have to understand how the subject does that.

The subject can do three things to a photon that strikes it: it can transmit, absorb, or reflect that photon.

Transmission

Light that passes through the subject, as in Figure 2.10, is said to be *transmitted*. Clean air and clear glass are examples of common materials that transmit light.

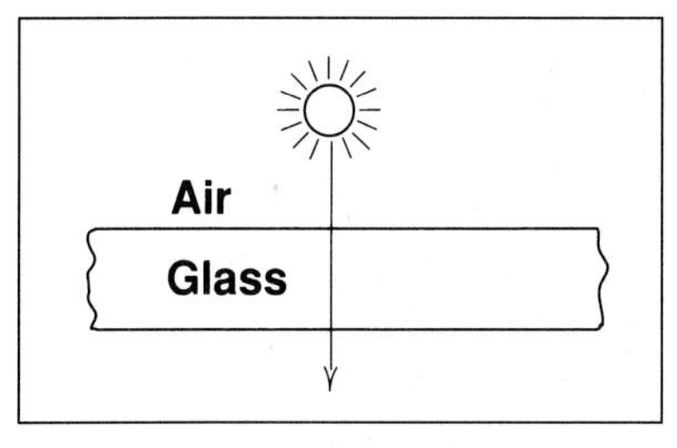

◀ Transmitted light. Clear glass and clean air are common materials that transmit visible light well.

2.10

Showing you a photograph of transmitted light would be useless. A subject that *only* transmits the light cannot be seen. The subject that does not alter the light in some way is invisible! Of the three basic interactions between the light and the subject, simple transmission is the least significant in a discussion of photographic lighting.

However, the simple transmission shown in Figure 2.10 can occur *only* if the light strikes the surface at an angle perpendicular to it. At any other angle, the transmission of the light has accompanying refraction. *Refraction* is the bending of rays of light as they are transmitted from one material to another. Some materials refract light more than others. Air, for example, refracts light very little, while the glass used in a camera lens refracts it a great deal. Figure 2.11 illustrates the phenomenon.

► *A light ray striking a light-transmitting material at any angle bends. This bending is called refraction. Dense glass, such as that used for camera lenses, refracts light especially strongly.*

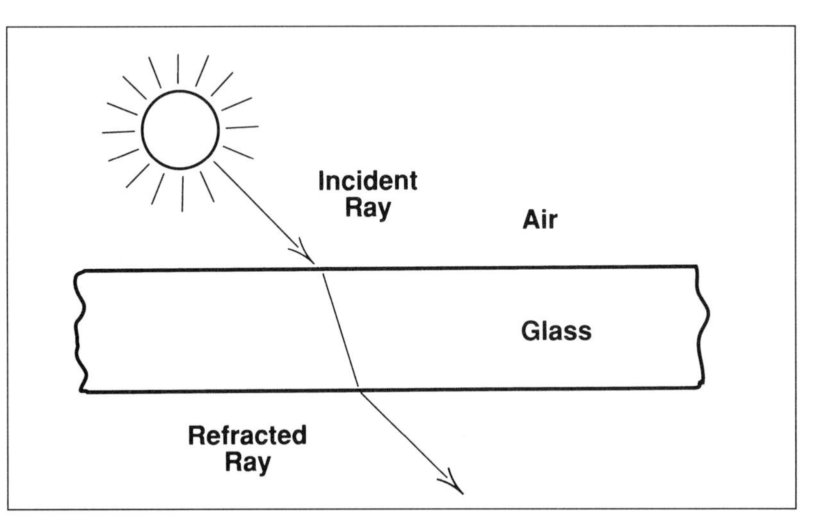

2.11

Refraction is caused by a variation in the speed of light caused by the material through which it is transmitted. (The speed of light is constant *in a vacuum.*) The light in Figure 2.11 is slowed as it enters the denser glass. The photons that strike the glass first are the first to have their speed reduced. The other photons, still in air, race ahead, causing a bending of the ray. Then the ray bends a second time, but in the opposite direction, as each photon regains its speed upon exiting back into the air.

Unlike simple transmission, refraction can be photographed. This is one of the reasons that completely transparent subjects are not invisible. Refraction causes the wavy edge of the glass flask in Figure 2.12.

► *The foreground glass flask refracts the image of the flask in the back.*

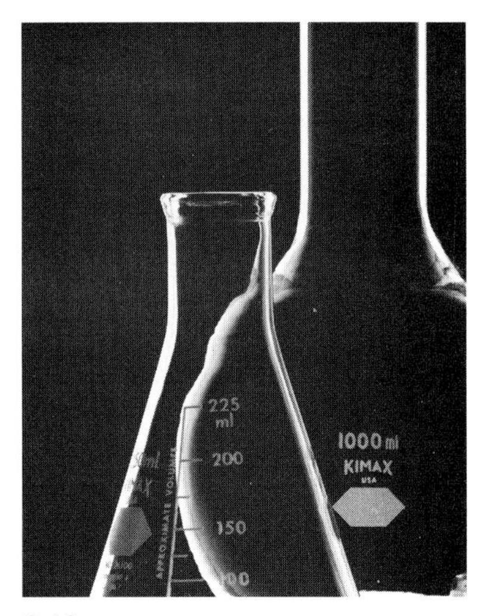

2.12

Direct and Diffuse Transmission

So far we have talked about *direct transmission,* in which light passes through a material in a predictable path. Materials such as white glass and thin paper scatter the light rays in many random, unpredictable directions as they pass through. This is called *diffuse transmission* (Figure 2.13).

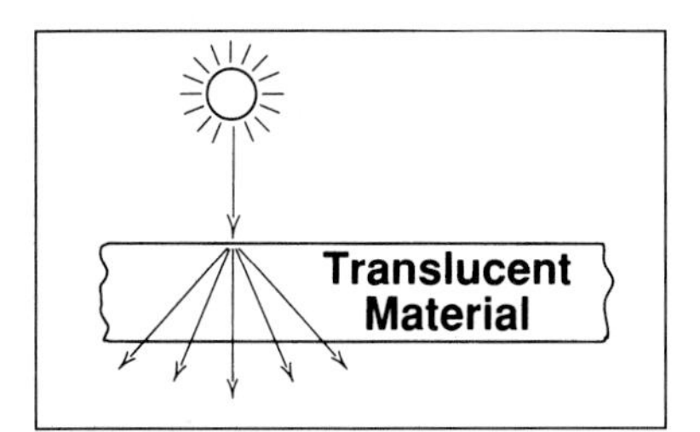

2.13

◀ *Diffuse transmission is the scattering of light passing through a translucent material.*

Materials that produce diffuse transmission are called *translucent* to distinguish them from *transparent* materials, such as clear glass, which do not significantly diffuse the light.

Diffuse transmission is more important when we talk about light *sources* than in discussing photographic *subjects*. Covering a small light with a large translucent material is one way to increase its size and, therefore, to soften it. A diffusion sheet in front of a strobe and the clouds covering the sun, as in Figure 2.4, are examples of translucent materials serving such a function.

Translucent *subjects* are of little special importance to photographers because their translucence usually requires no special lighting consideration. This is because they always absorb some of the light and reflect some of the light, in addition to transmitting it. Absorption and reflection are both more major influences on photographic lighting. We will deal with these next.

Absorption

Light that is *absorbed* by the subject is never again seen as visible light. The absorbed energy still exists, but it is emitted by the subject in an invisible form, usually heat (Figure 2.14).

► *Absorbed light turns to heat. We can feel it, but it is no longer visible to the camera.*

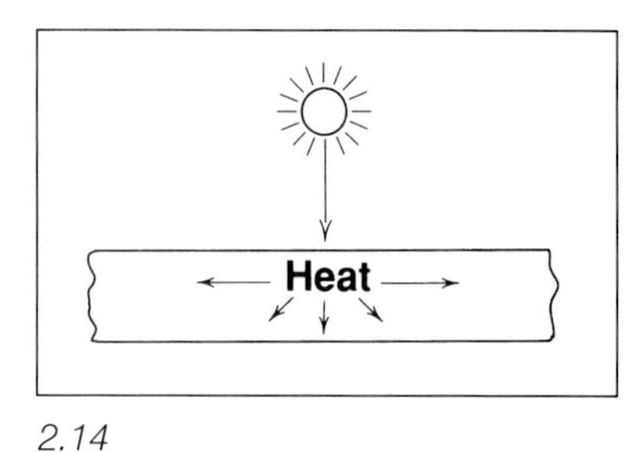

2.14

Like transmission, simple absorption cannot be photographed. It is "visible" only when we compare it to other light in the scene that is not absorbed. This is why highly light-absorbing subjects, such as black velvet or black fur, are among the most difficult things to photograph.

Most subjects absorb part, but not all, of the light striking them. This partial absorption of light is one of the factors determining whether we see a given subject as black, white, or some intermediate gray. Any particular subject will also absorb some frequencies of light more than others. Such selective absorption of certain light frequencies is one of the factors determining the color of a subject.

Reflection

Reflection is light striking a subject and bouncing off. You know that and need no further explanation from us. The concept is easy because we use it daily. Reflection makes vision possible. We do not see objects, we see light. Since most objects produce no light, their visibility depends entirely on light reflected from them. We do not need to show you a photograph of reflection. Almost any picture you have on hand will serve the purpose.

However, the familiarity of reflection does not mean that it needs no further discussion. On the contrary, the importance of reflection demands that we devote most of the next chapter to it.

Chapter 3

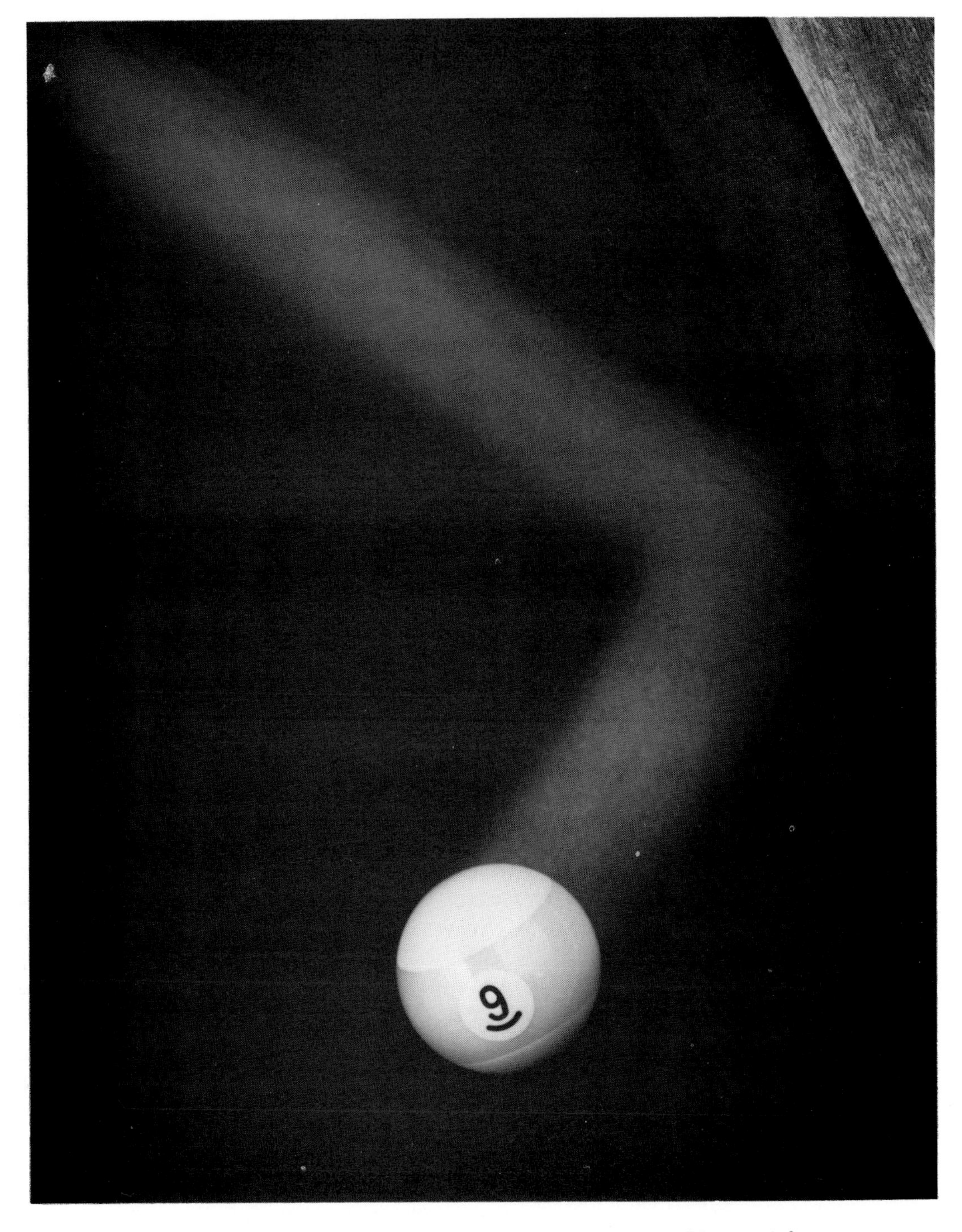

The Management of Reflection and the Family of Angles

In the last chapter we took a close look at light and how it behaves. We saw that the three most important qualities of any light source are its brightness, color, and contrast. We also saw that the subject, not just the light, has a major influence on lighting. A subject can transmit, absorb, or reflect the light that strikes it.

Of the three ways the subject can affect the lighting, reflection is the most visible. Highly transparent subjects have minimal effect on light, so tend to be invisible. Highly absorbent subjects may also be invisible because they convert light into other forms of energy, such as heat, which we cannot see.

Photographic lighting, therefore, is primarily an exercise in reflection management. Understanding and managing reflection, for the result the photographer wants, is good lighting. In this section, we will look at how subjects reflect light and how to capitalize on those reflections to your advantage.

We will begin our discussion of reflection with a "thought experiment." We would like you to create three different images in your mind. First, on a desk top, imagine a piece of very thick, perfectly smooth, gray paper. The gray should be a medium one, light enough to write on, but dark enough that no one would confuse it with white. Next, visualize a piece of metal of the same size as the paper. We suggest old pewter. The metal should also be smooth and exactly the same gray as the paper. Third, make a mental ceramic tile, very glossy and the same shade of gray as the other two subjects. Finally, put the three mental images together on the same desk and examine the differences you see in the three subjects.

Notice that none of the subjects transmits any light. (That is why we made the paper thick.) Furthermore, they all appear to absorb the same amount of light (because they are all the same gray). Yet, the difference in the three subjects is apparent. You have seen it. (If not, try again, and you will, now that you know we expect you to do so!)

The reason that these subjects, with identical transmission and absorption, appear different is that *the subjects reflect the light differently*. The reason you can see the differences without looking at examples on this page is that they are part of that visual knowledge you already have in the occipital lobe of your brain!

In this chapter, we are not going to tell you very many things your brain does not already know. We will, however, put some of that knowledge into words. This will make it easy for us to talk about reflection for the rest of this book.

TYPES OF REFLECTION

Light can reflect from a subject as either *diffuse reflection, direct reflection,* or *glare*. Most surfaces cause some of each of these three types. The proportions of each type of reflection vary with the subject, and it is the proportion of each reflection in the mix that makes one surface look different from another.

We are going to examine each of these types of reflections in some detail. In each case, we will assume that the reflection is a perfect example, uncontaminated by either of the other two. This will make it easier to analyze each of them. (Events in nature sometimes offer nearly perfect examples, but not quite.)

For now, we do not care what type of light source might be producing any of the following examples. Only the reflecting surface matters. Any sort of light could work.

DIFFUSE REFLECTION

Diffuse reflections are the same brightness regardless of the angle from which we view them. This is because the light from the sources is reflected equally in all directions by the surface it strikes. Figure 3.1 shows a diffuse reflection. In it we see light falling on a small white card. Three people are pointing their cameras at it.

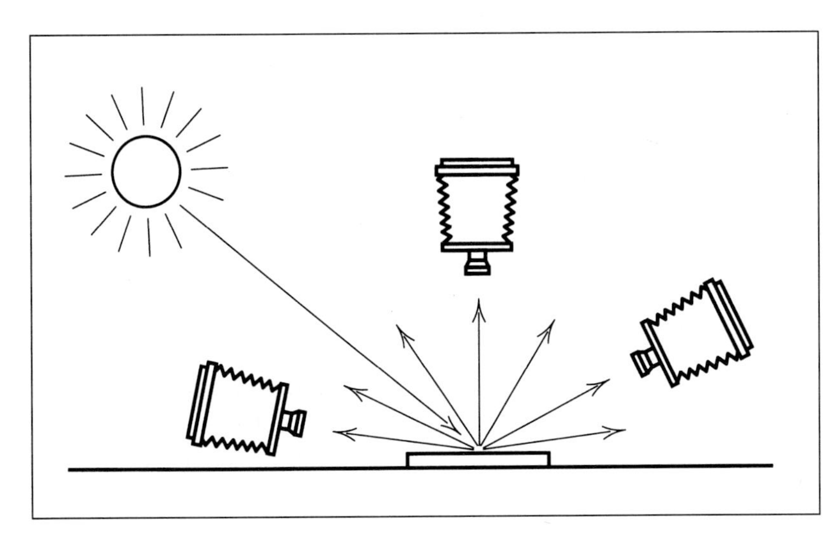

3.1

◀ *A white card gives off almost nothing but diffuse reflection. Because diffuse reflection from a light source is reflected equally in all directions from the surface, all three cameras see the card as having the same brightness.*

If each of these individuals were to photograph the white card, each of their pictures would record the subject as the *same* brightness. The image of the card would have the same density in each negative. Neither the angle of illumination of the light source nor the camera's angle of view would affect the brightness of the subject in such a picture.

Other than in lighting textbooks, no surfaces reflect light in a perfectly diffuse manner. However, white paper sometimes approximates such a surface. Now look at Figure 3.2. Notice that the scene contains a mostly white sheet of newspaper.

► *The newspaper in this scene gives off primarily diffuse reflection. It would appear white from any angle.*

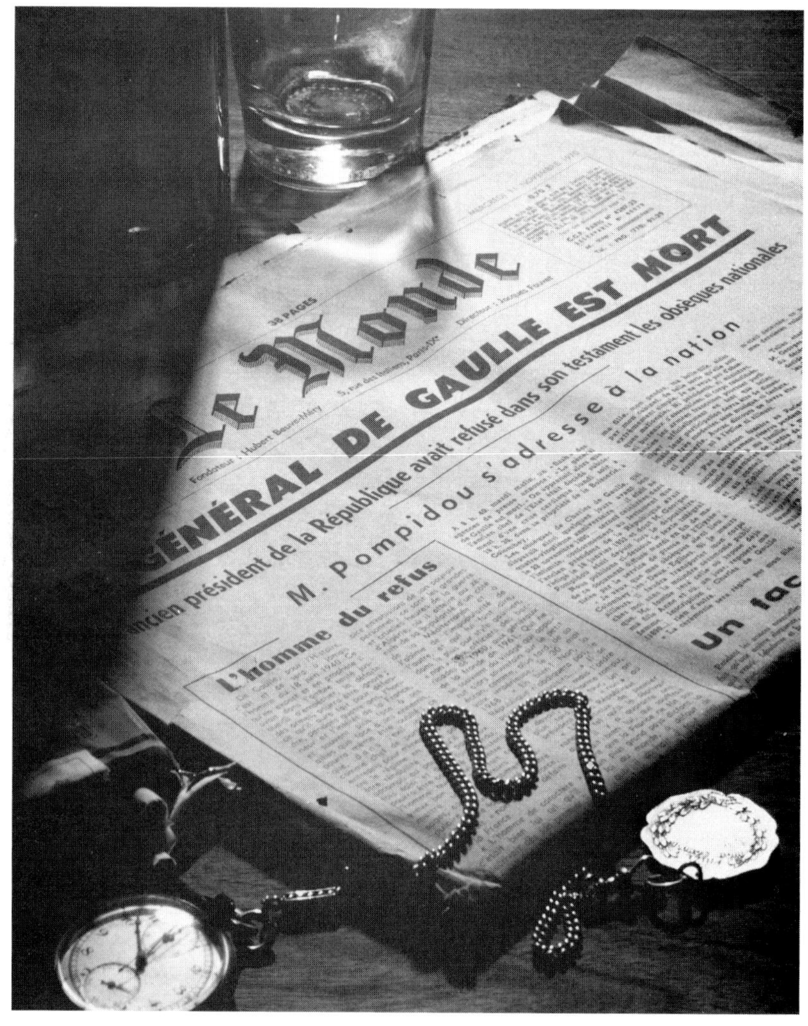

3.2

There is a reason that we choose to put the white newsprint in this particular example. All white things produce a great deal of diffuse reflection. We know this because they appear white regardless of the angle from which we view them. (Walk around the room you are in now. Look at the white objects and the black objects from different angles. Notice that the apparent brightness of the black objects may change with viewpoint, but the white objects stay about the same!)

Diffusion Confusion

In Appendix 1, we discuss diffusion of the light source by reflecting the light from an umbrella or by covering it with a translucent material. We call light passing through translucent material *diffuse transmission*. Now we speak of *diffuse reflection.* The two concepts have enough in common that we should pay special attention to the differences between them.

Diffusing the light source has no effect on whether the reflection is diffuse. Remember that small light sources are always "hard" (undiffused) and that large light sources are almost always "soft" (diffused). Then notice that Figures 3.2 and 3.3 show diffuse reflections produced by both diffused and undiffused light sources. Similarly, Figures 3.5 and 3.6 show direct reflections produced by diffused and undiffused light sources.

The word *diffusion* is a good one because its meaning is perfectly consistent in both uses. In each case, it means a scattering of the light. But *what* does the scattering, the light or the subject? The source determines the type of light and the surface determines the type of reflection. Any light can produce any reflection, depending on the subject.

The contrast of the light source does not affect the appearance of a diffuse reflection. It is worth proving this with one more picture of the same scene. The earlier photograph was lit by a small light. We could see that by the hard shadows cast by the objects in it. Now look at Figure 3.3 to see what happens when we use a large light instead.

► *The soft shadows prove we used a large light. The highlights in the newspaper look the same because the size of the light source does not alter the appearance of diffuse reflection.*

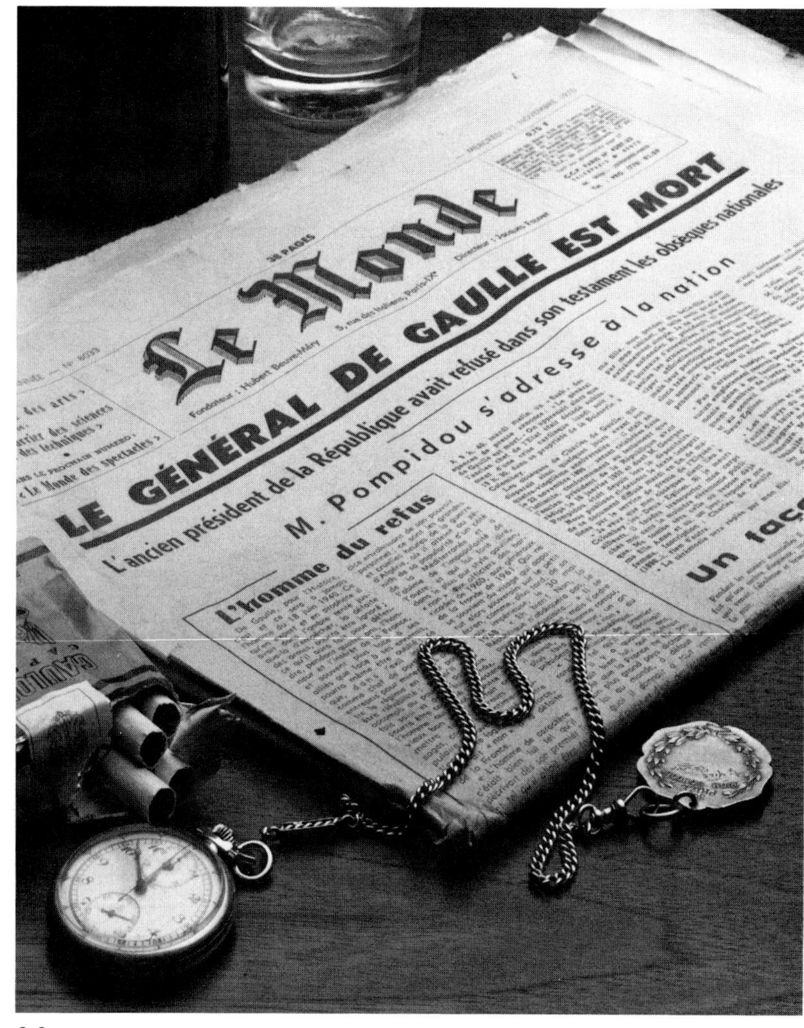

3.3

Predictably, the large light source has softened the shadows in the scene. But notice that the highlights on the paper look about the same. The diffuse reflection from the surface of the paper is identical to that in Figure 3.2.

So we now have seen that neither the angle nor the size of the light source affects the appearance of a diffuse reflection. However, the distance from the light to the surface of the subject does matter. The closer the light gets to the subject, the brighter the subject becomes and, at a given exposure setting, the lighter the subject appears in the finished picture.

Specular Reflection and Specular Light

Photographers sometimes call direct reflection *specular reflection*. As a synonym for direct reflection this is a perfectly good term. If you use the word *specular* in this way, please feel free to substitute the words as you read *direct*.

However, some photographers also use *specular* to mean smaller, brighter highlights within a large one; others mean highlights created by a small light source. *Direct reflection* does not necessarily imply either of these. Because *specular reflection* has different meanings to different people, we will not use the term in this book.

Modern usage adds further inconsistency. Originally *specular* was used *only* to describe the reflection, not the source of the light. (The Greek root means "mirror.") Today, some photographers use specular light as a synonym for hard light, but a "specular" light source does not necessarily produce a "specular" reflection! A hard light is always hard, but the way it reflects depends on the surface of the subject. So we will always call specular lights *hard* in order to make it clear that we are talking about the light, not the reflection.

The Inverse Square Law

A diffuse reflection gets brighter if we move the light source closer to the subject. If we needed, we could calculate this change in brightness with the *inverse square law*. The inverse square law says that intensity is inversely proportional to the square of the distance. Thus, a light at any particular distance from the subject will light the subject with an intensity four times as bright as the same light twice as far away. Similarly, a light will have nine times the intensity of the same light moved three times as far from the subject. As the intensity of the light falling on the subject varies, so does that of the diffuse reflection.

Ignoring the math, this simply means that reflection from a surface gets brighter if we move the light closer and dimmer if we move the light farther away. Intuitively, this seems immediately obvious. Why even bother to mention it? Because such intuition is often misleading. Some subjects, as we shall soon see, do not produce brighter reflections as the light moves closer to them!

DIRECT REFLECTION

Direct reflections are a mirror image of the light source that produces them. They are also called *specular reflections.*

Figure 3.4 is similar to Figure 3.1, but this time we have replaced the white card with a small mirror. Both the light source and the observers are in the same positions as they were earlier.

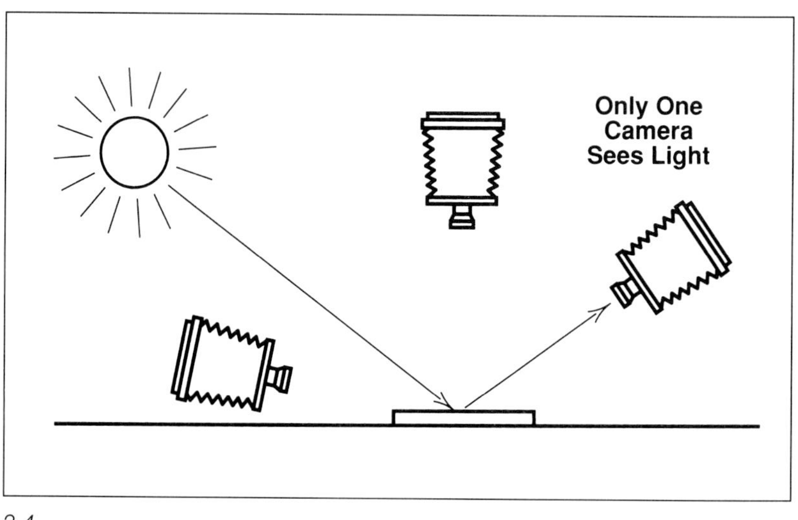

3.4

► *Direct reflection. Looking at the mirror, one of the cameras sees a blinding reflection of the light source, while the others see no reflection at all.*

Notice what happens. This time one of the three cameras now sees a blindingly bright reflection, while the others see no reflection at all in the mirror.

This diagram illustrates the direct reflection produced when a light is directed at a polished surface such as glass. The light rays bounce from the smooth surface at the same angle at which they hit it. More precisely stated: *the angle of incidence equals the angle of reflectance.* This means that the point at which direct reflections can be seen is exactly determined by the angles between the light source, the subject, and the camera viewpoint.

So, with all that in mind, it is easy to see why the three cameras see such a difference in the brightness of the mirror. Those positioned on each side receive no reflected light rays. From their viewpoint the mirror appears black. None of the rays from the light source is reflected in their direction because they are not viewing the mirror from the one (and *only*) angle in which the direct reflection of the light source can happen.

However, the camera that is directly in line with the reflection sees a spot in the mirror as bright as the light source itself. That is because the angle from its position to the glass surface is the same as the angle from the light source to the glass surface. Again, no real subject produces a perfect direct reflection. But brightly polished metal, water, or glass may nearly do so.

Breaking the Inverse Square Law?

Did it alarm you to read that the camera that sees the direct reflection will record an image "as bright as the light source"? How do we know how bright the direct reflection will be if we do not even know how far away the light source is?

We do not need to know how far away the source is. The brightness of the image of a direct reflection is the same regardless of the distance from the source. This principle seems to stand in flagrant defiance of the inverse square law, but an easy experiment will show why it does not.

You can prove this to yourself, if you like, by positioning a mirror so that you can see a lamp reflected in it. If you move the mirror closer to the lamp, it will be apparent to your eye that the brightness of the lamp remains constant.

Notice, however, that the *size* of the reflection of the lamp *does* change. This change in size keeps the inverse square law from being violated. If we move the lamp to half the distance, the mirror will reflect four times as much light, just as the inverse square law predicts. But the *image* of the reflection covers four times the film area. So that image still has the same density on the negative. In plainer words, if we spread four times the butter on a piece of bread of four times the area, the thickness of the butter stays the same.

Now we will look at a photograph of the scene in the previous diagram. Once again, we will begin with a high-contrast light source. Figure 3.5 has a mirror in place of the earlier newspaper. Here we see two indications that the light source is small. Once again, the shadows are hard. Also, we can tell that the source is small because we can see it! It is reflected in the mirror. Because the image of the light source is visible, we can easily anticipate the effect of an increase in the size of the light. This allows us to plan the size of the highlights on polished surfaces.

► *Two clues tell us this picture was made with a small light source: hard shadows and the size of the reflection in the mirror.*

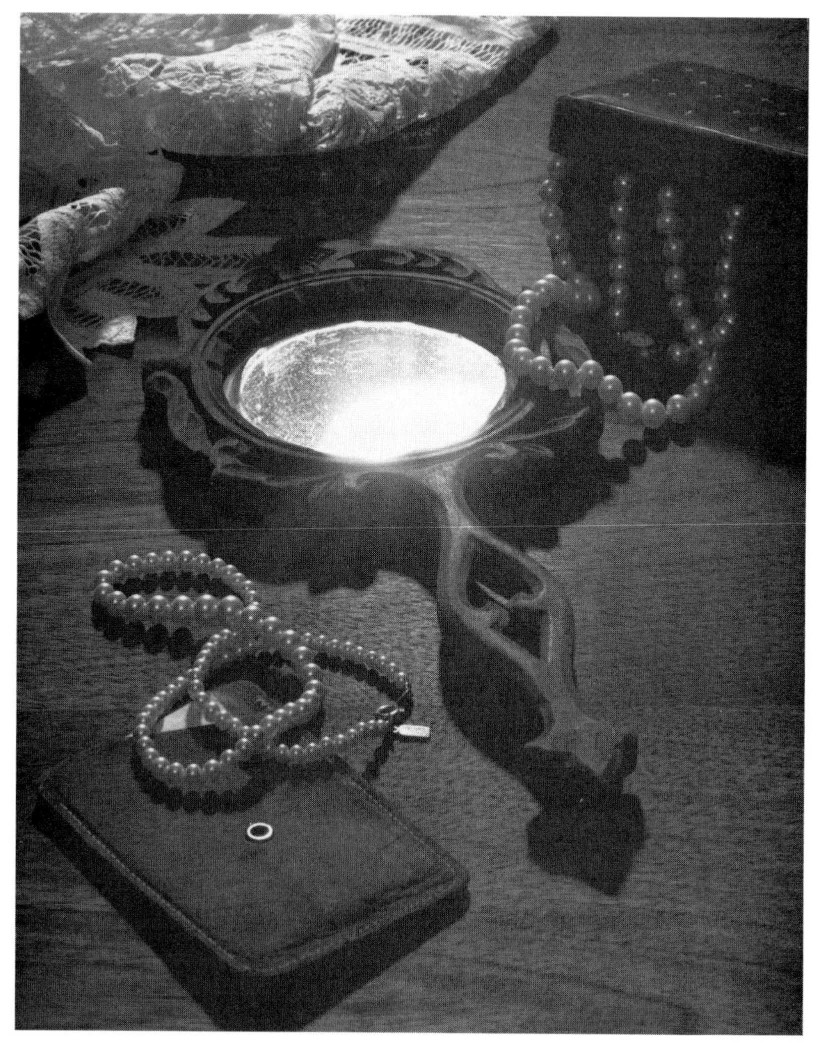

3.5

Now look at Figure 3.6. Once again, the large, low-contrast light source produces softer shadows. The picture is more pleasing, but that is not the important aspect. More important is the fact the reflected image of the large light source completely fills the mirror. In other words, the larger light source *fills the family of angles that cause direct reflection.* This family of angles is one of the most useful concepts in photographic lighting. We will discuss that family in detail.

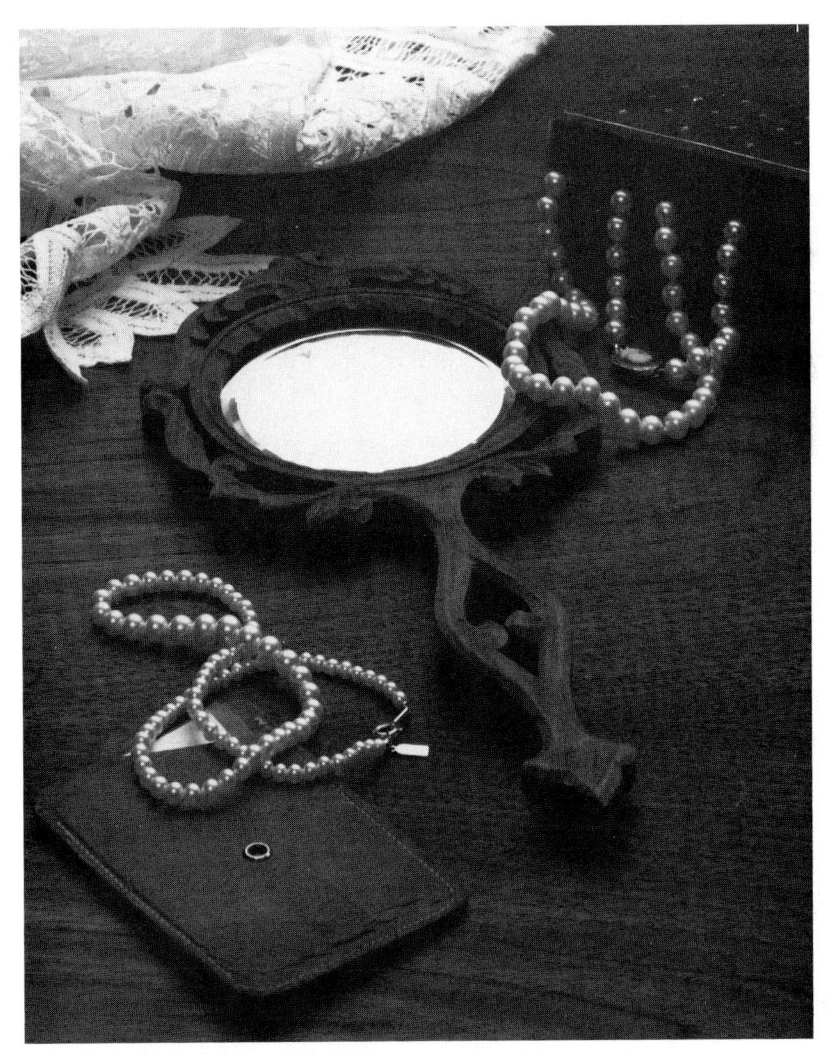

◀ *A larger light softens the shadow. More importantly, the reflection of the light now completely fills the mirror. This is because the light we used this time was large enough to fill the family of angles that causes direct reflection.*

3.6

THE FAMILY OF ANGLES

Our previous diagrams have been concerned with only a single point on a reflective surface. In reality, however, each surface is made up of an infinite number of points. A viewer looking at a surface sees each of these points at a slightly different angle. Taken together, these different angles make up the *family of angles that produce direct reflection.*

In theory, we could also talk about the family of angles that produce diffuse reflection. However, such an idea would be meaningless because diffuse reflection can come from a light source at *any* angle. Therefore, when we use the phrase *family of angles* we always mean those angles that produce direct reflection.

This family of angles is important to photographers because it determines where we should place our lights. We know that light rays will always reflect from a polished surface, such as metal or glass, at the *same* angle as that at which they strike it. So we can easily determine where the family of angles is located, relative to the camera and the light source. This allows us to control if and where any direct reflection will appear in our picture.

Figure 3.7 shows the effect of lights located both inside and outside this family of angles.

► *Light* **A,** *positioned within the family of angles, will produce a direct reflection. Light* **B**, *outside the family of angles, will not.*

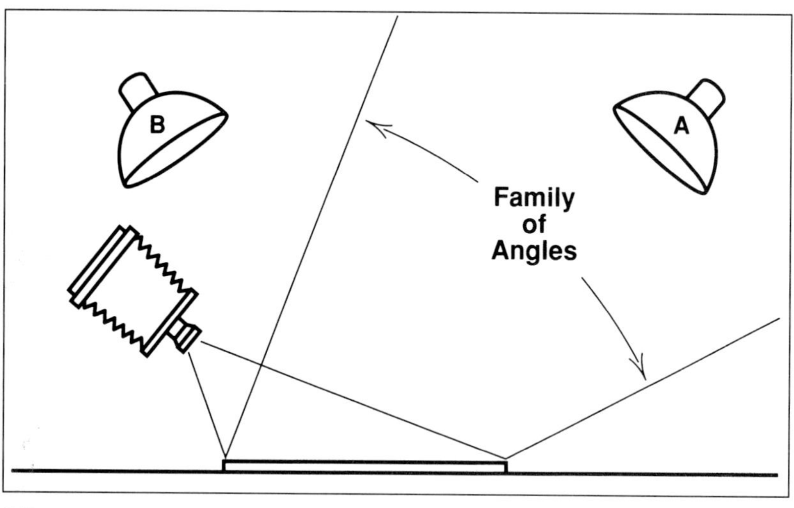

3.7

As you can see from Figure 3.7, any light positioned *within* the family of angles *will* produce a direct reflection. A light placed anywhere else will not. Consequently, any light positioned *outside* of the family of angles *will not* light a mirror-like subject at all, at least as far as the camera knows.

Photographers sometimes want to see direct reflection from most of the surface of a mirror-like subject. This requires that they use (or find in nature) a light large enough to fill the family of angles. In other scenes, they do not want to see any direct reflection at all on the subject. In those instances, they must place both the camera and the light so that the light source is not located within the family of angles. We will use this principle repeatedly in the coming chapters.

GLARE REFLECTION

A *glare reflection* is a *polarized* direct reflection. In every other way, it is so similar to an ordinary direct reflection that we could treat them as the same. However, polarization of glare reflections gives photographers several specialized techniques and tools for dealing with them.

Like the direct reflection, only one viewer in Figure 3.8 will see the reflection. Unlike the direct reflection, an image of the glare is always substantially dimmer than a photograph of the light source itself. A *perfectly* polarized direct reflection is exactly half as bright as an unpolarized one (provided the light source itself is not polarized). However, since polarization is inevitably accompanied by absorption, the reflections we see in the scene are more likely to be much dimmer than that. To see why polarized reflection cannot be as bright as an unpolarized direct reflection, we need to know a bit about polarized light.

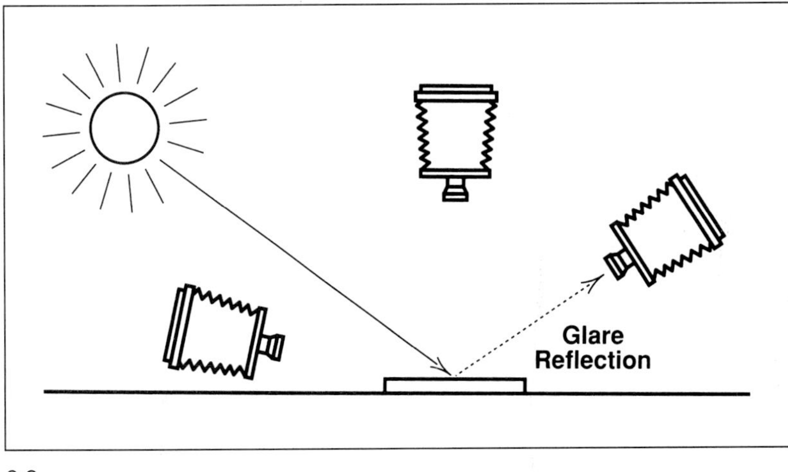

3.8

◀ *Polarized direct reflection is called glare reflection, or glare for short. It looks like unpolarized direct reflection, only dimmer.*

We have seen that the electromagnetic field fluctuates around a moving photon. In Figure 3.9 we have represented this fluctuating field as a jump rope being swung between two children. One child is spinning the rope while the other simply holds it.

► *The oscillating electromagnetic field around a photon represented as a jump rope. The child on the left is spinning the rope while the one on the right holds on.*

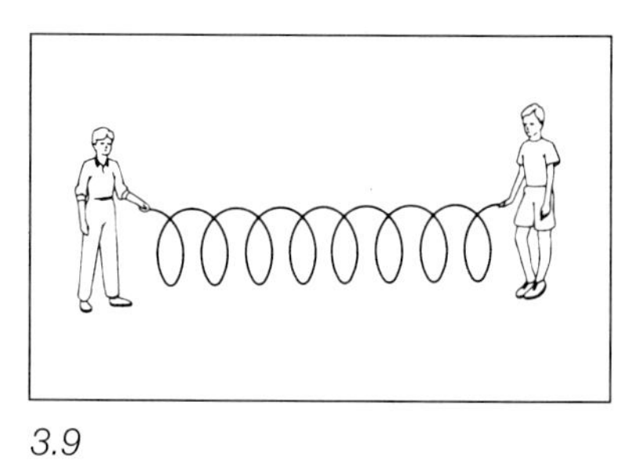

3.9

Now, let us imagine that a neighbor quickly puts up a picket fence between the children, as shown in Figure 3.10. The rope now bounces up and down instead of swinging in an arc. This bouncing rope resembles the electromagnetic field along the path of a photon of polarized light.

► *When the children are forced to spin the rope through the picket fence, it bounces up and down instead of spinning in an arc. A polarizing filter blocks the oscillation of light energy the same way.*

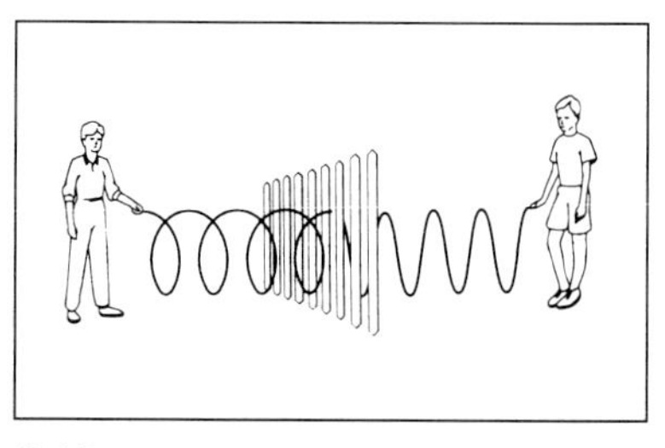

3.10

Molecules in a *polarizing filter* block the oscillation of the light energy in one direction, just as the picket fence does to the oscillating energy of the jump rope. The molecular structure of some reflecting surfaces also blocks part of the energy of the photon in the same manner. We see such a photon as a polarized reflection or glare.

Now suppose the same neighbor, not satisfied with eliminating just a part of the children's play, installs a horizontal fence in front of the first, as shown in Figure 3.11.

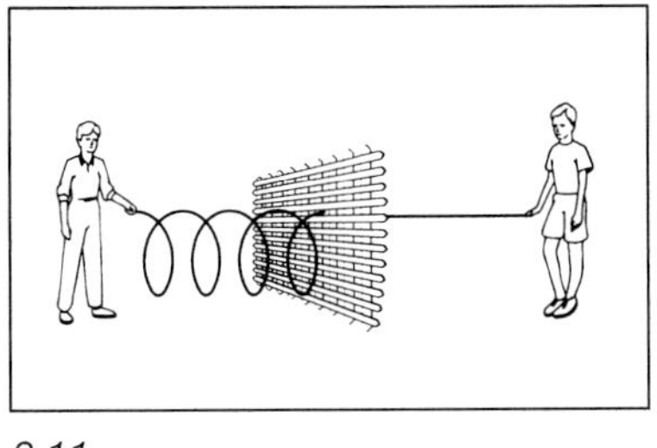

3.11

◀ This time the nasty neighbor has ruined the children's play by adding a horizontal fence to the first. Now, if one child spins the rope, the other will see no movement.

Now, with the second fence in place, if one child spins the rope, the other sees no rope movement at all. The crossed picket fences block the transmission of energy from one end of the rope to the other. Crossing the axes of two polarizing filters blocks the transmission of light, just as the two picket fences do with rope energy. Figure 3.12 shows the result. Where the polarizers overlap with their axes perpendicular, none of the type is visible on the page. The transmission of light reflected from the page to the camera has been completely blocked.

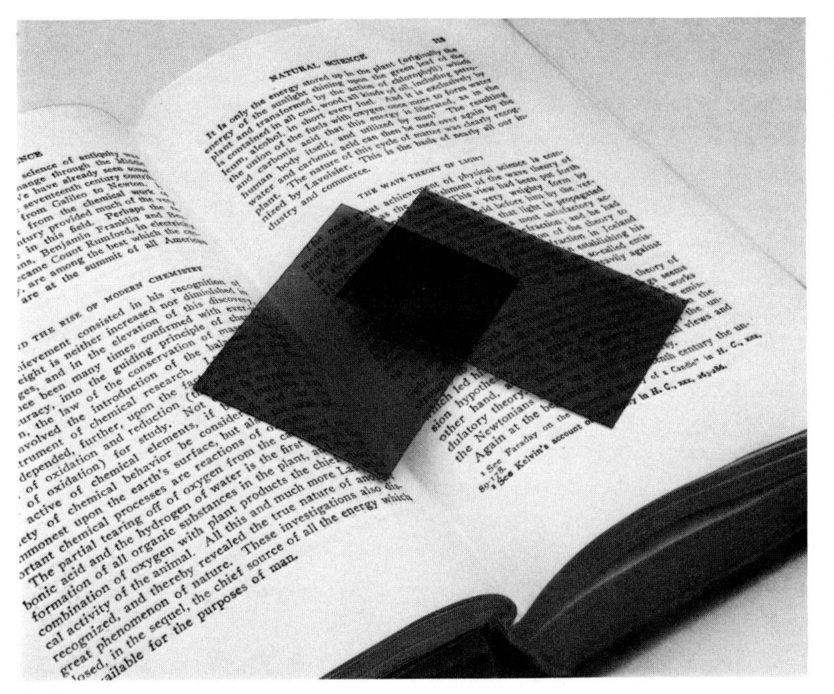

3.12

◀ The two overlapping polarizers have their axes perpendicular. They block light just as the two fences did with the energy of the jump rope.

A lake, painted metal, glossy wood, or plastic can all produce glare reflection. Like the other types of reflection, the glare is not perfect. Some diffuse reflection and some unpolarized direct reflection are mixed with the glare. Glossy subjects produce the most glare.

Glare is more likely to be visible if the subject is black or transparent. Black and transparent subjects do not necessarily *produce* stronger direct reflections than white ones. Instead, they produce weaker diffuse reflection, making it easier to see the direct reflection. This is why you saw the change in apparent brightness of the black objects, but not of the white ones, when you walked around your room a while ago.

Glossy black plastic can show us enough glare reflection to make a good example. The scene in Figure 3.13 includes a black plastic mask and a feather. They are placed on a sheet of glossy black plastic. We used the same camera and light position as in the pictures of the newspaper and the makeup mirror. However, this time we begin with a large light source rather than a small one.

► *The glossy black plastic sheet and mask give off almost nothing but polarized direct reflection. The feather gives off almost nothing but diffuse reflection.*

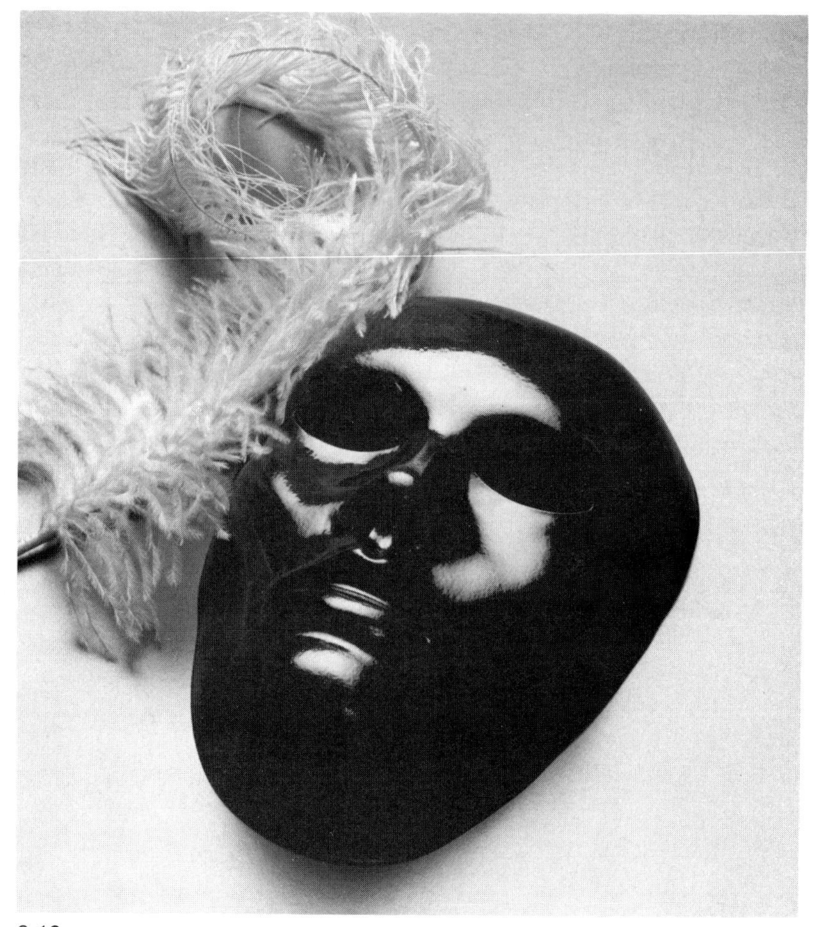

3.13

Both the mask and the plastic sheet produce nearly perfect glare reflection. From this angle, glossy plastic produces almost no unpolarized direct reflection; and black things never produce much diffuse reflection. However, the feather behaves quite differently. It produces almost nothing but diffuse reflection.

The light source was large enough to fill the family of angles defined by the plastic sheet, creating glare over the entire surface. The same light was large enough to fill only part of the family of angles defined by the mask. We know this because of the highlights we see only on the front of the mask. Predictably, the glare reflection in this picture looks like unpolarized direct reflection, but it is far less bright.

Now look at Figure 3.14. We made it with the same setup we used with the previous picture, only this time we placed a polarizing filter over the camera lens. Since glare was almost the only reflection from the black plastic in Figure 3.14, and since the polarizing filter blocks glare, little of the light reflected from them reached the film. As a result, the plastic now looks black.

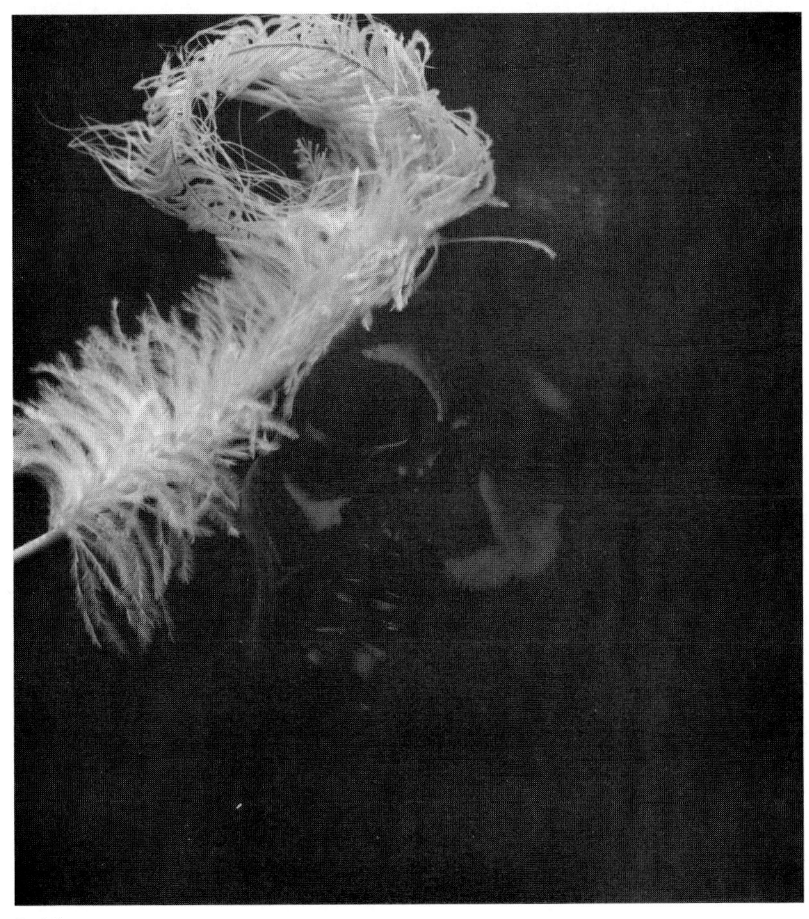

◀ *A polarizer over the camera lens blocks the polarized direct reflection. Only the feather, which gives off diffuse reflection, is easily visible.*

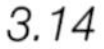

3.14

We did have to open our aperture by about two stops to compensate for the neutral density of the polarizing filter. How do you know that we did not accidentally miscalculate the exposure? (Maybe we did so deliberately, just to get the image dark enough to prove our point?) The feather proves that we did not. The diffuse reflection from the feather was *not* blocked by the polarizer. So, with accurate exposure compensation, the feather is about the same gray in both pictures.

Is It Glare or Ordinary Direct Reflection?

Polarized and unpolarized direct reflections often have similar appearance. Photographers, out of need or curiosity, may want to distinguish one from the other.

We know that direct reflection appears as bright as the light source, while glare reflection appears dimmer. However, brightness alone will not tell us which is which. Remember that real subjects produce a mixture of reflection types. A surface that seems to have glare may actually have weak direct, plus some diffuse, reflection.

Here are a few guidelines that tend to tell us whether a direct reflection is polarized:

- If the surface is made of a material that conducts electricity (metal is the most common example), its reflection is likely to be unpolarized. Electrical insulators, for example, plastic, glass, and ceramics, are more likely to produce polarized reflection.
- If the surface *looks* like a mirror, for example, bright metal, the reflection is likely to be simple direct reflection, not glare.
- If the surface does not have a mirror-like appearance, for example, polished wood or leather, the reflection is more likely to be glare if the camera is seeing it at an angle of forty to fifty degrees. (The exact angle depends on the subject material.) At other angles, the reflection is more likely to be unpolarized direct reflection.
- The conclusive test, however, is the appearance of the subject through a polarizing filter. If the polarizer eliminates the reflection, then it is glare. If, on the other hand, the polarizer has no effect on the suspect reflection, then it is ordinary direct reflection. If the polarizer reduces the reflection but does not eliminate it, then it is a mixed reflection.

Increasing Glare

Most photographers know that polarizers can eliminate glare they do not want. But in some scenes we may like the glare and even want more of it. In such cases we can use the polarizer to effectively *increase* glare. We do this by rotating the polarizing filter ninety degrees from the orientation that reduces glare. The glare then passes through easily.

It is important to understand that a polarizer always blocks some unpolarized light. By doing this, in effect, it becomes a neutral density filter that affects everything except direct reflection. Thus, when we increase the exposure to compensate for the neutral density, the direct reflection is increased even more.

Turning Ordinary Direct Reflection into Glare

Photographers often prefer that a reflection be glare so that they can manage it with a polarizing filter mounted on their camera lens. If the reflection is not glare, the polarizer on the lens will have no effect except to add neutral density.

However, placing a polarizing filter over the *light source* will turn a direct reflection into glare. A polarizer on the camera lens can then manage the reflection quite nicely.

Outdoor photographers who lack the luxury of studio lighting find that the open sky often serves as a beautifully functional polarized light source. Facing the subject from an angle that reflects the most polarized part of the sky can make the lens polarizing filter effective. This is why photographers sometimes find polarizing filters useful on subjects such as bright metal, even when the filter manufacturer has told them that polarizers have no effect on such subjects. In those cases, the subject is reflecting a polarized source.

APPLYING THE THEORY

Excellent recording of a subject requires more than focusing the camera properly and exposing the film accurately. The subject and the light have a relationship with each other. In a good photograph, the light is appropriate to the subject and the subject is appropriate to the light.

The meaning of *appropriate* is the creative decision of the photographer. Any decision the photographer makes is likely to be appropriate if it is guided by understanding and awareness of how the subject and the light *together* produce an image.

We must decide what type of reflection is important to the subject and then capitalize on it. In the studio, this means *manipulating* the light. Outside the studio, it often means getting the camera position, anticipating the movement of the sun and clouds, waiting for the right time of day, or otherwise *finding* the light that works. In either case, the job is easier for the photographer who has learned to see what the light is doing and to imagine what it could do.

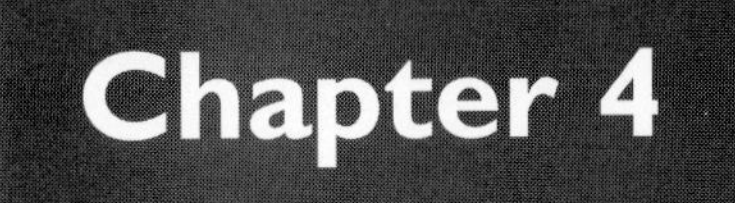

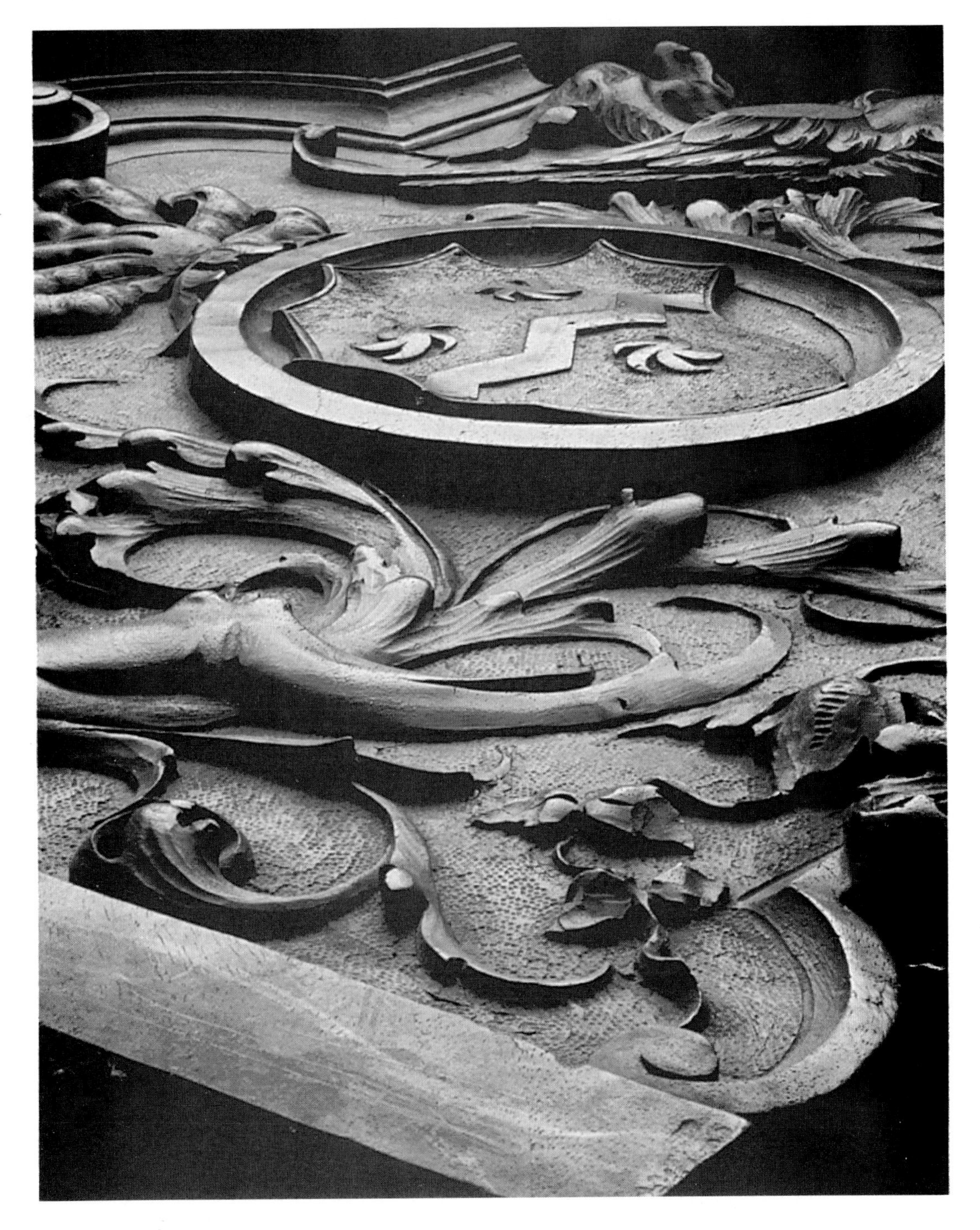

Surface Appearances

All surfaces produce diffuse, direct, and glare reflections in varying degrees. We see all of these reflections, but we are not always conscious of all of them.

Years of programming enable our brains to edit the image of the scene. This editing minimizes reflection that is distracting or trivial to the subject. At the same time, it maximizes the importance of whatever light is essential to our comprehension of the scene. The psychological image in the brain may be quite different from the photochemical one the eye sees.

A reflection in a shop window may be many times the brightness of the goods displayed inside. Nevertheless, if we are interested in the merchandise, then that is what we see, not the interfering reflection.

But the brain cannot edit an image of an image so effectively. If we photograph the same shop window, without eliminating the surface reflection, then a viewer looking at the picture may not be able to see through the glass at all!

Psychologists have not completely explained why this difference exists. Movement certainly has something to do with it, but not everything. Some visual defects are less disturbing in a motion picture film or videotape than they might be in a still photograph, but not much.

Photographers know that the brain cannot edit an image of the scene as well as the scene itself. We discovered the fact when we learned how quickly we could spot defects in our images, even though we could not see them at all when we carefully examined the original scene. Unconscious parts of our brain did us the "service" of editing the scene to delete extraneous and contradictory data. But the viewer becomes fully conscious of the same details on seeing the picture.

How do pictures reveal things we might never otherwise notice? That is a question for another book. This book is about what we need to do about that fact and how to take advantage of it. When we make a picture we have to consciously do some of the editing that other observers do unconsciously.

THE PHOTOGRAPHER AS EDITOR

Photographic lighting deals mainly with the extremes: the highlights and the shadows. When we are happy with the appearance of these two, we are likely to be pleased with the middle range also. Highlight and shadow together reveal form, shape, and depth. But *highlight alone* is usually enough to reveal what the *surface* of an object is like. In this chapter we will concern ourselves primarily with highlight and surface. Most of our example subjects will be flat and two dimensional, or nearly so. In Chapter 5 we will complicate matters a bit with three-dimensional subjects and a more detailed discussion of shadow.

In the last chapter, we saw that all surfaces produce both diffuse and direct reflections, and that some of the direct reflections are polarized. But most surfaces do not produce an even mix of these three types of reflections. Some surfaces produce a great deal more of one than another. The difference in the amounts of each of these reflections determines what makes one surface look different from another.

One of the first steps in consciously editing the photographic image is to look at the subject and decide what kind of reflection causes the subject to appear the way it does. The next step is to position the light, the subject, and the camera to make the photograph capitalize on that type of reflection and minimize the others.

When we do this we *decide* what kind of reflection we want the viewers to see. Then we engineer the shot to make sure they see that reflection and not others.

"Position the light" and "engineer the shot" imply moving light stands around a studio, but we do not necessarily mean that. We do much the same thing when we pick the camera viewpoint, day, and time outside the studio. We will use studio examples in this chapter simply because they are easy for us to control to demonstrate the specifics clearly. The principles apply to any type of photography.

In the rest of this chapter, we will see some examples of subjects that require us to capitalize on each of the basic kinds of reflections. We will also see what happens when we photograph reflections that are inappropriate to those subjects.

CAPITALIZING ON DIFFUSE REFLECTION

Photographers are sometimes asked to photograph paintings, illustrations, or antique photographs. Such *copy work* is one simple example of a circumstance in which we usually want *only* diffuse, and not direct, reflection.

Since this is the first concrete demonstration of lighting technique in this book, we will discuss it in great detail. The example shows how an experienced photographer thinks through *any* lighting arrangement. Beginners will be surprised at the amount of thinking involved in even such simple lighting, but they should not be dismayed by it. Much of this thinking is identical from one picture to the next, and it quickly becomes so habitual that it takes almost no time or effort. You will see this as we progress, and we will omit some of the detail in future discussions.

Diffuse reflection gives us the information about how black or how white the subject is. The printed pages of this book have blacks and whites. These are determined by areas that produce a great deal of diffuse reflection (the paper) and those that produce little diffuse reflection (the ink).

Because diffuse reflection can reflect light frequencies selectively, it also carries most of the color information about the subject. If we were not concerned about your eye strain, we might have printed this page with magenta ink on blue paper. You would then know that we had done such a thing because the diffuse reflection from the page would tell you.

Notice that diffuse reflection does not tell us very much about what the surface is made of. Had we printed this page on smooth leather or glossy plastic instead of paper, the diffuse reflection would still look about the same. (You *could,* however, tell the difference in material by the direct reflection.)

When we copy a painting or another photograph, we are usually not interested in the type of surface on which it was produced but in the colors and values in the original image. Look at any of the photographs in this book. Can you tell whether we made the original print on glossy paper? Of course not. This is because when the book printers copied the photographs, they capitalized only on the diffuse reflection.

The Angle of Light

What sort of lighting might accomplish this? To answer that question, let us begin by looking at a standard copy setup and at the family of angles that produces direct reflection.

Figure 4.1 shows a standard copy camera arrangement. The camera is on a stand and is aimed at the original art on a copy board beneath it. This particular camera has a lens whose image on the film encompasses a forty-degree horizontal angle of view, typical of normal lenses. Assume that the height of the camera is set so that the image of the original art exactly fills the film area.

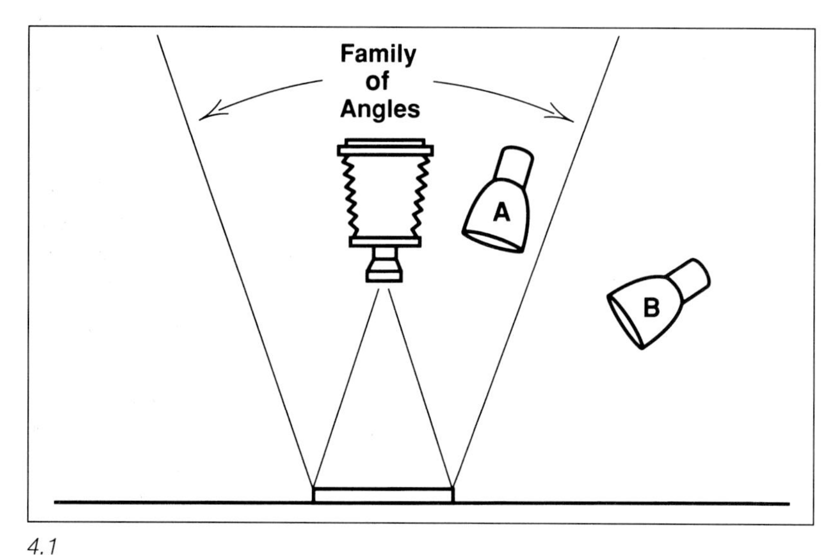

► *The family of angles that produces direct reflections in a "copy" lighting setup. Light* **A** *will produce direct reflection,* **B** *will not. There is a similar family of angles on each side of the camera.*

4.1

We have drawn the family of angles from which a light, or lights, can produce direct reflection. Most copy arrangements use a light on each side of the camera. We need only one light to see the principle.

Such a diagram makes it easy to light the setup. Once again, any light within the family of angles will produce direct reflection, and a light located outside that family will not. We also know from Chapter 3 that a light can produce diffuse reflection from *any* angle. Since we want *only* diffuse reflection, we place the light anywhere outside the family of angles.

Figure 4.2 is a painted fan, photographed with the light placed outside of the family of angles. We see only diffuse reflection from the surface, and the tone values in the photograph closely approximate the original.

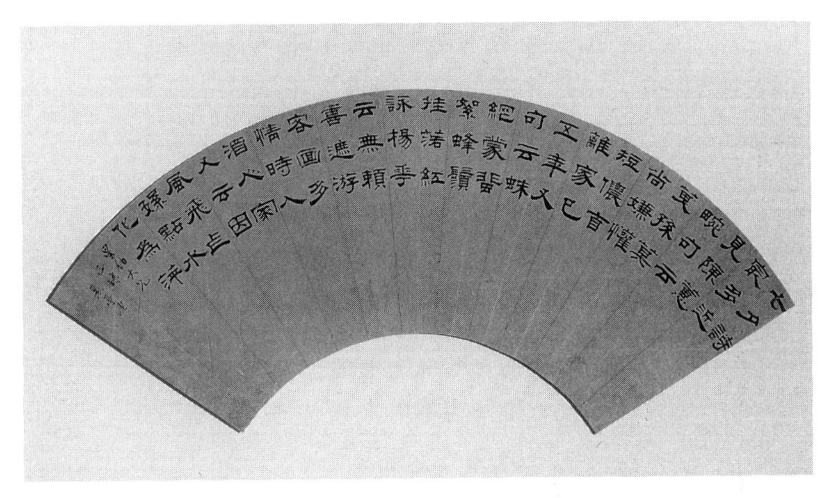

4.2

◀ *In a good picture, the antique Chinese fan we see has nothing but diffuse reflections and the tones closely resemble those in the original.*

By way of contrast, in Figure 4.3 the light was inside the family of angles. The resulting direct reflection causes an unacceptable "hot spot" on the glass covering the fan.

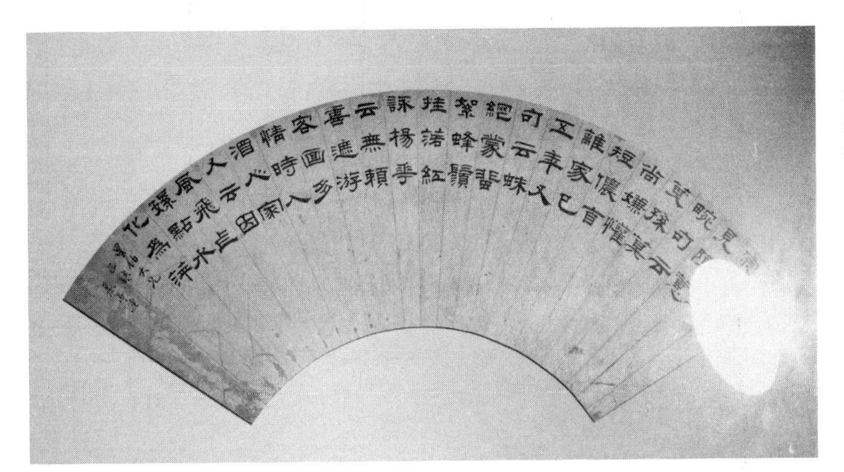

4.3

◀ *Placing the light inside the family of angles caused an unacceptable hot spot and obscured some of the detail.*

This is all straightforward in the studio or the laboratory. However, photographers are also asked to photograph large paintings in museums or other locations from which they cannot be removed. Any one who has ever done this knows that museum curators *always* place display cases or pedestals *exactly* where we want to put the camera. In such situations, we need to place the camera closer to the subject than we might otherwise. We then switch to a wide-angle lens to get the whole subject to fit the film area.

Figure 4.4 is a bird's-eye view of our museum setup. Now the camera has a very wide-angle lens with a ninety-degree horizontal angle of view.

► *The family of angles has grown much larger in this arrangement using a wide-angle lens. The result is a small range of acceptable lighting angles. Only lights outside the family of angles, such as* **B,** *will produce satisfactory results.*

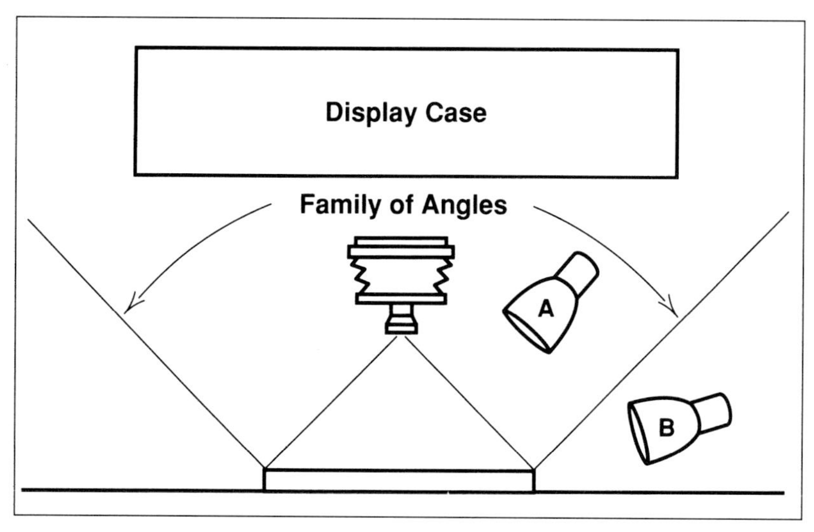

4.4

Look what has happened to our family of angles! The family of angles causing direct reflection has grown much larger, and the range of acceptable angles for copy lighting is much smaller. The light now needs to be much farther to the side to avoid unacceptable direct reflections.

Shooting a copy with the camera in this position would yield drastically inferior results if we kept the light where we had it in Figure 4.1. The same lighting angle that works well when the camera is farther away can cause direct reflection if the camera is closer. In this case, we would have to move the light farther to the side.

Finally, notice that in some museum-like situations, the shape of the room may make the placement of the lights more difficult than that of the camera. If it seems impossible to position the lights to avoid direct reflection, we can sometimes solve the problem just by moving the camera farther away from the subject (and using a correspondingly longer lens to obtain a large enough image size).

In Figure 4.5, the room is too narrow to allow easy light placement, but it is deep enough to allow the camera to be placed at almost any distance. We see that when the camera is farther from the subject, the family of angles that produces direct reflection is small. Now it is easy to find a lighting angle that avoids direct reflection.

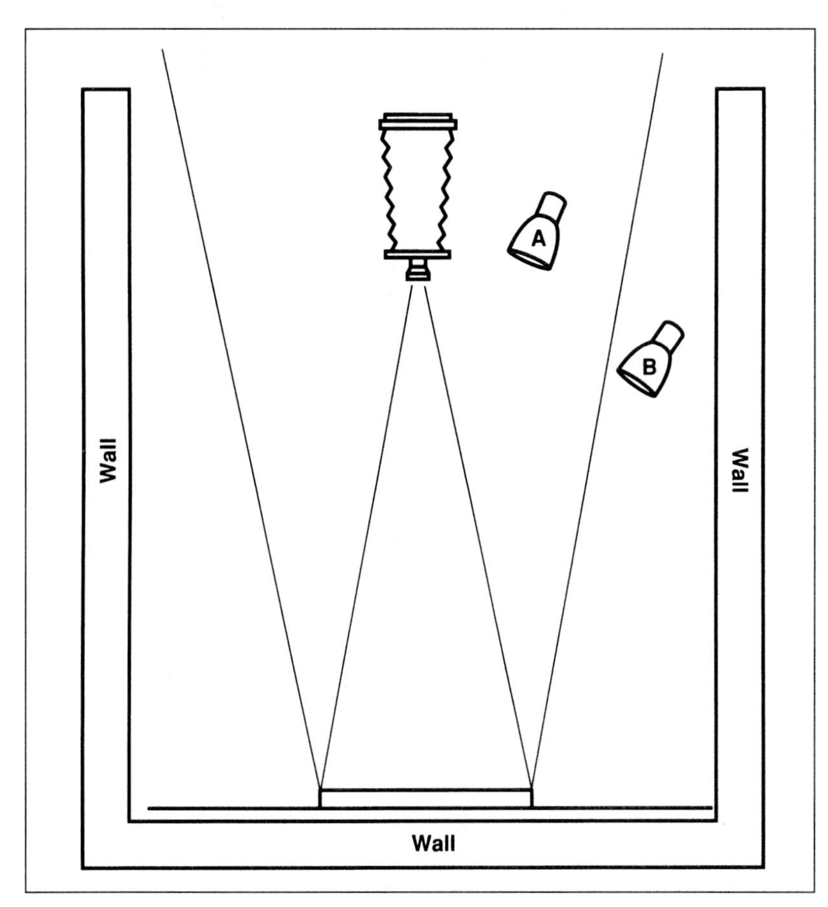

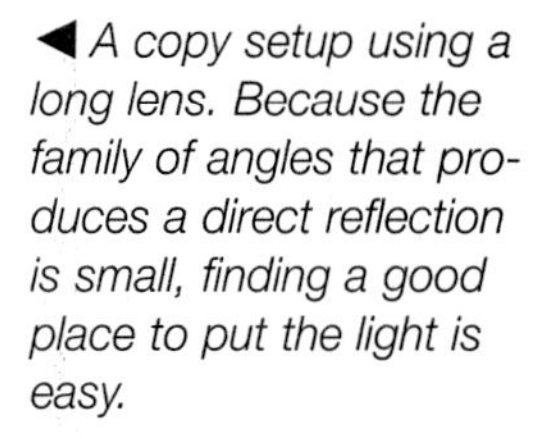
◀ *A copy setup using a long lens. Because the family of angles that produces a direct reflection is small, finding a good place to put the light is easy.*

4.5

The Success and Failure of the Rule of Thumb

Texts that attempt simply to demonstrate basic copy work (as opposed to general lighting principles) often use a diagram like Figure 4.6 to represent a standard copy setup.

▶ *The "standard" copy setup sometimes produces good results and sometimes does not. A usable lighting angle depends also on the distance between the camera and subject, and the choice of lens focal length.*

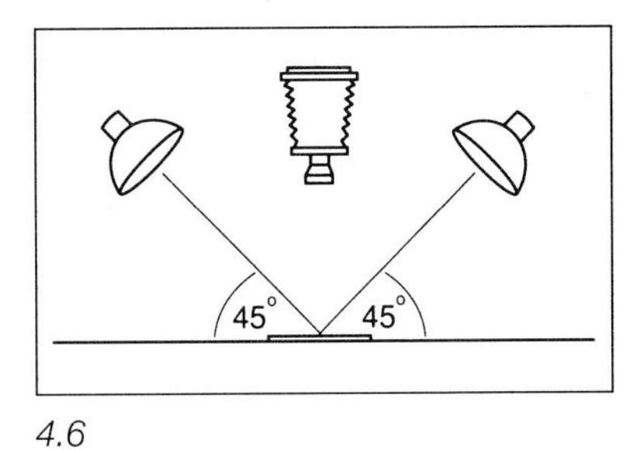

4.6

Notice that the light is at a forty-five-degree angle to the original. There is nothing magic about such an angle. It is a rule of thumb that usually works, but not always. As we saw in the previous example, a usable lighting angle depends on the distance between the camera and the subject, and the resulting choice of lens focal length.

More importantly, we need to notice that this rule may fail to produce good lighting if we do not give attention to the distance between the light and the subject. To see why, we will superimpose Figure 4.1 over Figure 4.6.

In Figure 4.7, we see two possible light positions. Both lights are at a forty-five-degree angle to the subject, but only one of them will produce acceptable lighting. The light that is closer to the subject is within the family of angles that produces direct reflection and will cause a hot spot on the surface. The other light is far enough away to be outside the family of angles and will illuminate the surface nicely.

▶ *The importance of the distance between the light and the subject. Both of the lights shown are at forty-five degrees to the center of the subject, but only **B** is satisfactory. Light **A**, inside the family of angles, will produce direct reflections.*

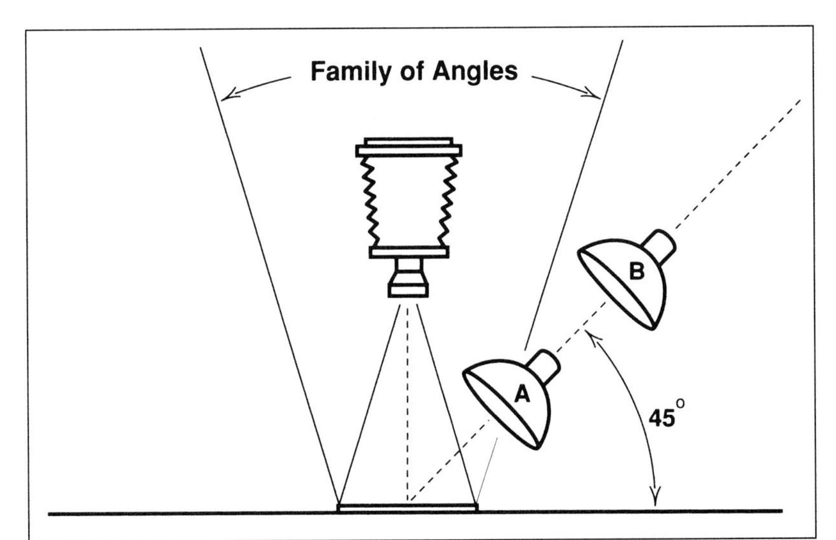

4.7

So we see that the forty-five-degree rule will work fine if the photographer gets the lights far enough away from the subject surface. In fact, the rule does often serve well because photographers generally do move the lights farther away from the subject for yet another reason, to obtain even illumination.

The Distance of Light

Another thing we know about diffuse reflections is that they get brighter as the light gets closer to the reflecting surface. Figure 4.8 shows an example of how this increased brightness can cause problems.

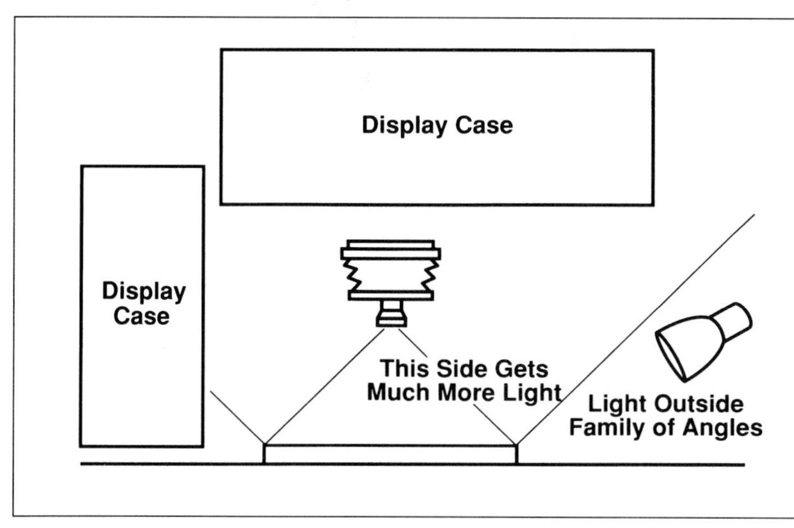

4.8

◀ *The positions of the museum display cases force the use of a short focal-length lens. The light must be at a shallow angle to be outside the family of angles, so it must be farther away to get even illumination.*

Once again, we are using a wide-angle lens to photograph the subject. Remembering that such situations leave a very small range of angles of illumination that do not cause direct reflection, we have positioned the light at a very shallow angle to the surface. But the edge of the subject that is closer to the light receives so much more light than the edge farther away that uniform exposure of the film is impossible.

Figure 4.9 shows the resulting exposure. The shallow lighting angle avoids direct reflection, but the diffuse reflection on one side of the image is so bright that the consequences are almost as bad.

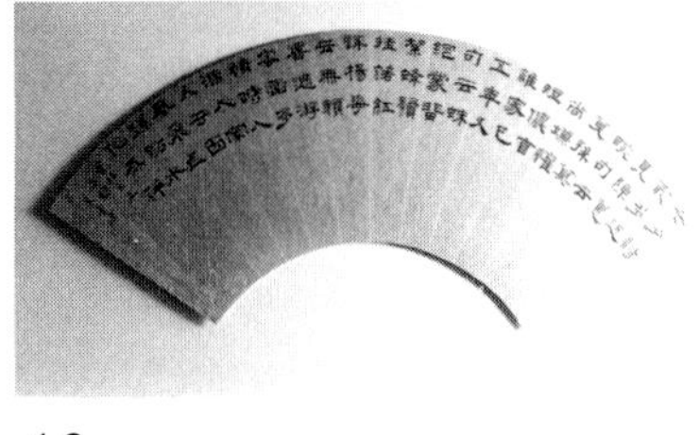

4.9

► *A possible consequence of the situation shown in Figure 4.8. Although the light placement avoided direct reflection, the illumination is too uneven to preserve detail on both the left and right sides.*

Obviously, a second light on the other side of the subject would help to provide more even illumination. (This is exactly why most copy setups do, indeed, use two lights.) But with extremely shallow lighting angles, the second light still does not provide uniform exposure of the film. We simply get two overexposed areas instead of one, with a dark area in the center.

One solution to this problem is to move the light closer to the camera. (An extreme example of this is a flash mounted directly on the camera.) Then the light is roughly the same distance from all points on the surface, and the illumination is more even. But this solution is also likely to place the light in the family of angles that cause direct reflection, and that is a worse problem.

The only solution to this problem that always works is to move the light farther away from the subject. In theory, a light that is an infinite distance away will produce equally bright diffuse reflections at all points on the surface, even at the most shallow angle. Unfortunately, a light an infinite distance away is also likely to be infinitely dim. (We will not even begin to deal with the problems of finding a light stand that high.)

In practice, we do not usually need to get the light quite that far away to obtain satisfactory results. We just need to get the light far enough from the subject to produce *acceptably* even illumination, but keep it close enough for acceptably short exposure times.

We could offer you mathematical formulas to calculate an acceptable distance between the light and the subject at any given angle (and for any given acceptable side-to-side exposure error), but you would not use the formulas because you do not need them. The human eye is good at judging the acceptable compromise distance, provided the photographer is aware of the potential problem from the start. And double-checking that judgment by measuring various points on the surface with a light meter, or making a test Polaroid, is faster than calculating.

Doing the Impossible

The preceding examples tell us that even illumination and glare-free illumination can be mutually exclusive goals. The closer the light source is to the camera, the more directly it lights the subject and the more even the illumination becomes. On the other hand, the farther the light is to the side, the less likely it is to be within the family of angles that causes direct reflection.

We have also seen that the usual solution to this dilemma requires more working space in any direction. Here is why:

- Moving the lights closer to the camera axis, for example, means moving the camera farther away from the subject (and using a correspondingly longer lens to get a similar image size). This creates a smaller family of angles that cause direct reflections and allow more freedom in choosing the angle to light the subject.
- Conversely, if circumstances dictate that the camera be very close to the subject, then we must light the subject at a very shallow angle to keep the light source outside the family of angles. We must then place the lights much farther from the subject to achieve even illumination.

Unfortunately, we sometimes lack the working space we need for either of these solutions. A photographer may have to photograph a rare document in a storage area so filled with filing cabinets that there is almost no room to work. Even in a gallery area, there may not be enough floor space to properly light a really large painting.

Figure 4.10 shows such an "impossible" lighting problem. The camera could be on a tripod aimed at a document on the floor, the obstacles on the sides could be filing cabinets, and the ceiling could set the restriction on camera height. Or the camera could be focused on an 8 x 10-foot painting on a wall with other walls or display cases presenting the obstacles. Either way, we cannot position the camera and lights to provide illumination that is both uniform and glare-free.

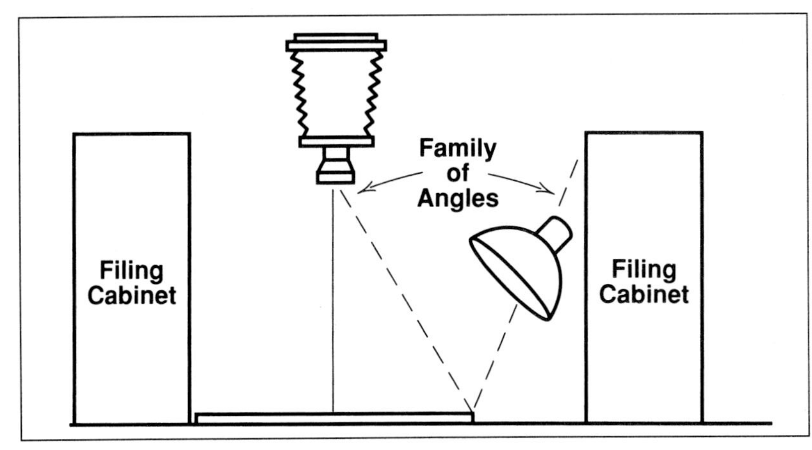

4.10

◀ *An "impossible" lighting situation: We cannot position the camera and lights to provide uniform, glare-free illumination.*

At a glance we predict that the photograph made with such an arrangement is useless. Figure 4.11 confirms the prediction.

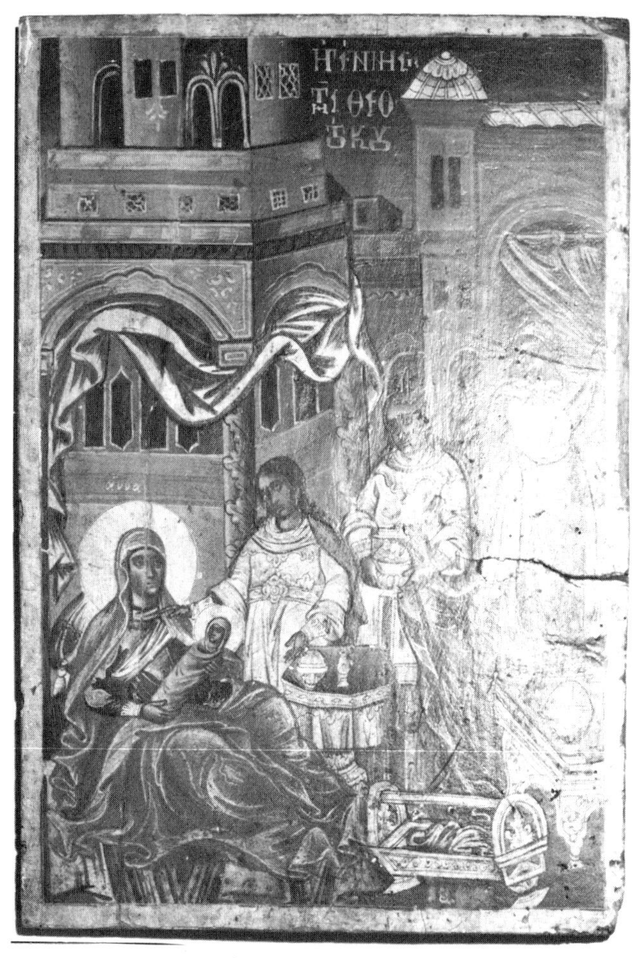

4.11

► *One result of the "impossible" situation shown in Figure 4.10. This picture is, as you can clearly see, useless. Because of the way in which we were forced to set up our lights, the original was partially obliterated by the direct reflection from its surface.*

The solution is easy when we remember (a) the "glare" we see on the surface of the original is a mixture of direct and diffuse reflection, and (b) a polarizing filter on the lens can eliminate *polarized* direct reflection.

Figure 4.12 shows how. We first position the lights for even illumination, without concern about whether we are creating direct reflection. Then we place polarizing filters over the lights with their axes oriented toward the camera. This assures us that the direct reflection is polarized. Next, a polarizing filter on the camera, with its axis oriented ninety degrees to those on the lights, eliminates that polarized direct reflection.

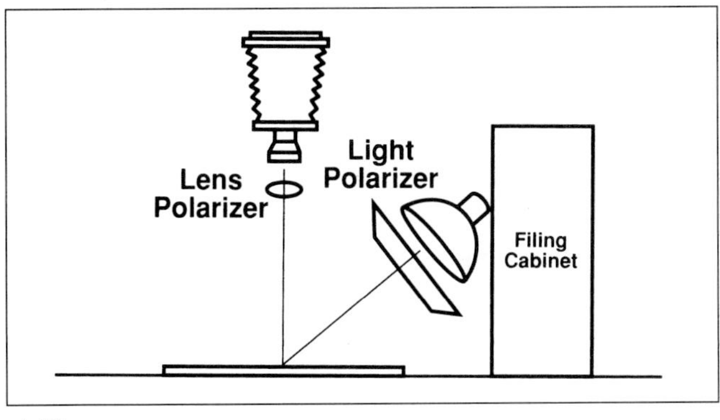

4.12

◀ *The solution to the "impossible" lighting requires placing the lights for even illumination and using polarizers to prevent glare.*

In theory, this arrangement allows the camera to see only the diffuse reflection. In practice, we may still see some glare because no polarizing filter is perfect. However, the defect is negligible in all but the worst cases. Figure 4.13 proves it. Neither the camera nor the light has been moved, but the improvement is dramatic.

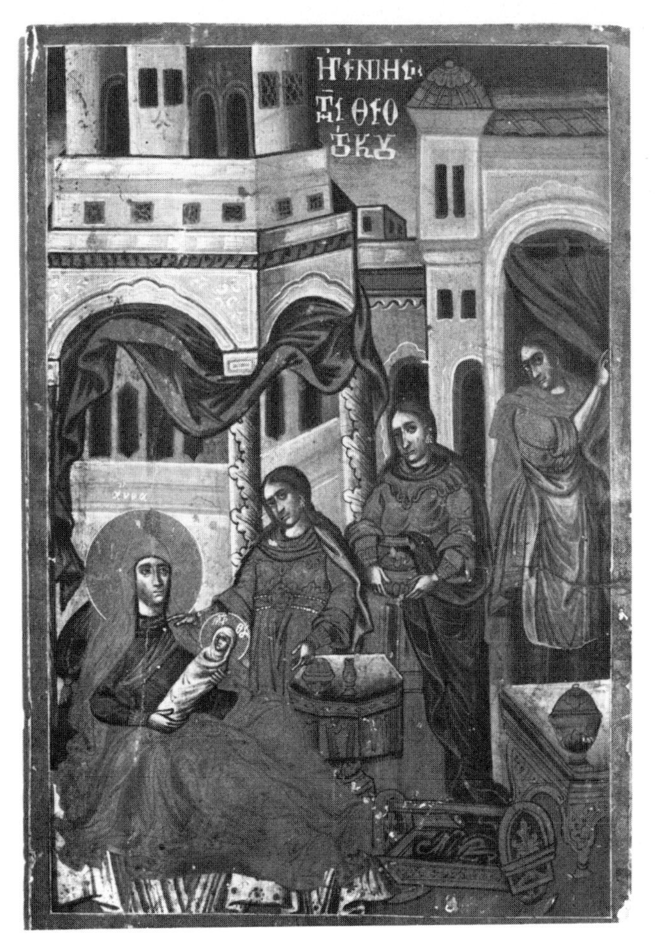

4.13

◀ *A good photograph despite "impossible" circumstances, using the solution from Figure 4.12.*

Using Diffuse Reflection and Shadow to Reveal Texture

In any discussion of surface definition, we must talk about texture. (This is why we promised at the beginning of this chapter that all examples would be *nearly* two dimensional.) We will first look at a photograph that fails to reveal the texture of the subject. This will help us to analyze the problem and to come up with a better solution.

We photographed textured white cloth in Figure 4.14 with a portable strobe mounted on the camera. If the object is to show texture, the picture is decidedly unsatisfactory.

► *Needlework photographed with the light mounted on the camera. With no contrasting highlights and shadows, much detail is invisible.*

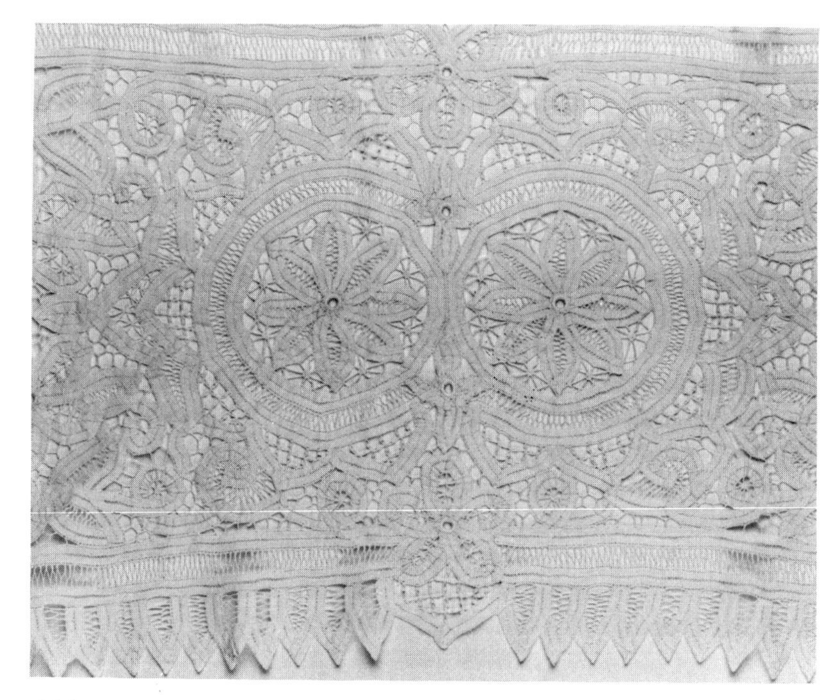

4.14

The whiteness of the cloth contributes to the problem. We know that *all* white subjects produce diffuse reflections, and we know that the brightness of a perfect diffuse reflection does not depend on the angle of illumination. For this reason, light striking the side of a particle of texture reflects back to the camera almost as brightly as light striking the top of the particle.

Using Light-Polarizing Filters

Polarizing the light source has serious drawbacks and is a solution to avoid whenever possible. Fortunately, understanding and controlling the size and angle of the light source makes polarizing the light source itself unnecessary in most situations. Some photographers go for years without needing to use light-polarizing filters.

We have deliberately conceived the "impossible" copy problem to be one of those rare cases in which polarizing the light is the *only* solution to the problem. Photographers whose specialty routinely requires highly controlled lighting will occasionally encounter these cases. Since awareness of a problem is the first step toward the solution of the problem, we want to list the possible difficulties now.

In theory, the combined effect of a "perfect" polarizing filter on the light and another on the lens should cost a total of two stops of exposure. But real polarizers are far from perfect. In practice, because polarizers have a lot of neutral density, the actual exposure reduction is likely to be four to six stops.

The problem gets even worse in noncopy situations, where we are likely to lose additional light through diffusion materials. The consequent aperture may be too wide to maintain adequate depth of field. Or the exposure may be so long that reciprocity failure becomes difficult to calculate and camera or subject movement is increasingly difficult to avoid.

The ideal solution to this problem is to use the most powerful lights that our budget and the available electrical current allow. If that is not enough, we treat the problem like any other low-light-level scene: We use a camera support as sturdy as possible and focus the camera as carefully as possible to make maximum use of what little depth of field we have.

The second problem is that polarizing filters are vulnerable to damage by heat. Remember that the light absorbed by the polarizers does not simply disappear. It turns into heat and threatens to cook things!

Photographers using strobes often leave the polarizers off the lights until they are ready to shoot. They turn off the modeling lights before attaching the polarizing filters. The brief flash of the flash tube presents minimal heat danger.

Polarizing filters used with incandescent lights need to be attached to a bracket or a separate light stand a distance away from the light. The exact distance depends on the wattage and the reflector design of the light. It is worth cutting a small piece of the polarizing material and deliberately burning it in front of the light to determine a safe distance.

Finally, we must remember that polarizing filters can have a minor effect on color balance. If the color in the photograph must closely match the color of the subject, it is wise to shoot and process a color test and adjust the color-compensating (CC) filtration before exposing the final film.

The solution is to move the light to a very shallow angle to the surface so that it skims across, as seen in Figure 4.15. This gives each particle of texture a highlight side and a shadow side.

► *A small light at a very low angle to the subject produces the contrasting highlights and shadows needed to reveal texture in medium- and light-toned subjects.*

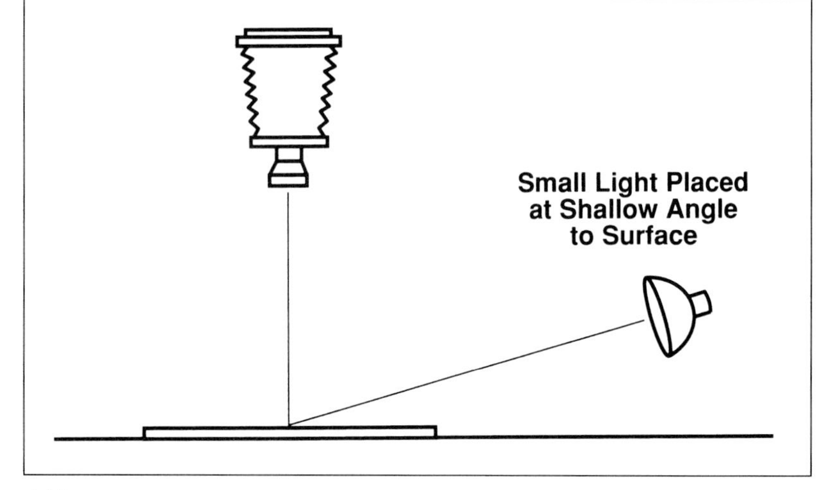

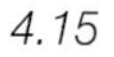

4.15

Notice that this arrangement may produce uneven illumination, just as it did when we moved the light to a shallow angle in the copy setup in Figure 4.8. The solution is the same: Move the light farther from the subject.

The texture in this type of surface can be helped still more if we use as small a light source as possible. This is because small light sources produce sharply defined shadows. If the particles of texture are tiny, their image on film may be too small to resolve sharply. If the shadow itself is as sharp as possible, then the image of the shadow is more likely to survive the limitations imposed by the optics and the film. See Figure 4.16.

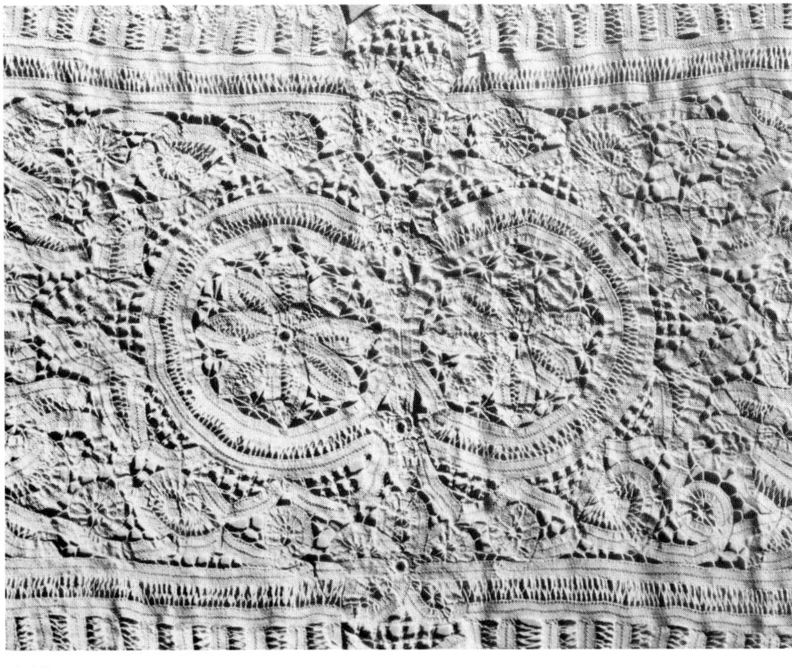

4.16

◀ *The same needlework used in Figure 4.14, this time photographed with raking light like that used in Figure 4.15.*

Lighting for texture in this manner is so easy to understand that it is almost intuitive. Even if you happen to be a novice photographer, we are sure you would have discovered the technique without our help. We are not trying to point out the obvious. Instead, we want to contrast the lighting of this piece of cloth with another, less obvious, example in which the same technique does not work at all.

CAPITALIZING ON DIRECT REFLECTION

Figure 4.17 has the same lighting as the successful photograph of the cloth texture. It shows how applying a good technique at the wrong time can produce a bad picture. We would reasonably expect the coarser texture in the leather to be easier to photograph. But the lighting that revealed the texture so well in the cloth loses almost all detail in the leather. You have to take our word that the texture exists.

▶ *The same lighting that revealed texture in the white needlework loses most detail in the black leather Bible.*

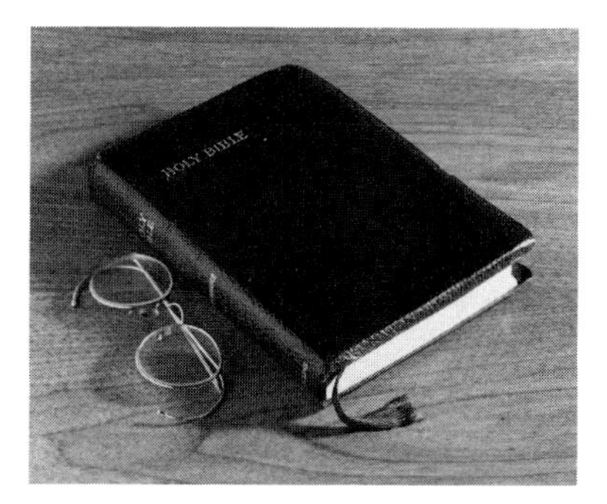

4.17

The raking light we used on the white cloth revealed detail by placing a shadow on one side of each particle of texture *and* a diffuse highlight on the other side. The same shadow exists on one side of each particle of texture in the black leather (although you cannot see it). But the diffuse highlight on the other side of each particle is gone. The problem with this photograph is caused by the subject itself. It is black, and black subjects, by definition, produce little diffuse reflection.

We know that increasing exposure would enable the weak diffuse reflections on the leather to record on film, but an exposure increase is rarely an available option because important light-toned areas also exist in most scenes. If we increased the exposure, the highlight detail in the lighter subject matter might be hopelessly lost. Besides, this is a book about lighting, not about the zone system, and because of that, we feel honor-bound to deal with the problems without exposure modification, using lighting technique alone.

If we cannot get significant diffuse reflection from the leather surface, we will try to produce direct reflection instead. This seems to be our only remaining option. Since direct reflection can only be produced by light coming from a limited family of angles, our first step is to see where that family of angles might be.

Figure 4.18 shows where the light *must* be if the camera is to see direct reflection on the surface. Furthermore, to produce direct reflection across the *entire* surface, the light must be large enough to *completely fill* this family of angles. Therefore, we need a light of at least the size and in the position shown in the diagram. The light source for this picture could be an overcast sky, a soft box, a reflector card illuminated by still another light source, or any of the other tools described in Appendix 2. All that matters is that the light be the right size and in the right place.

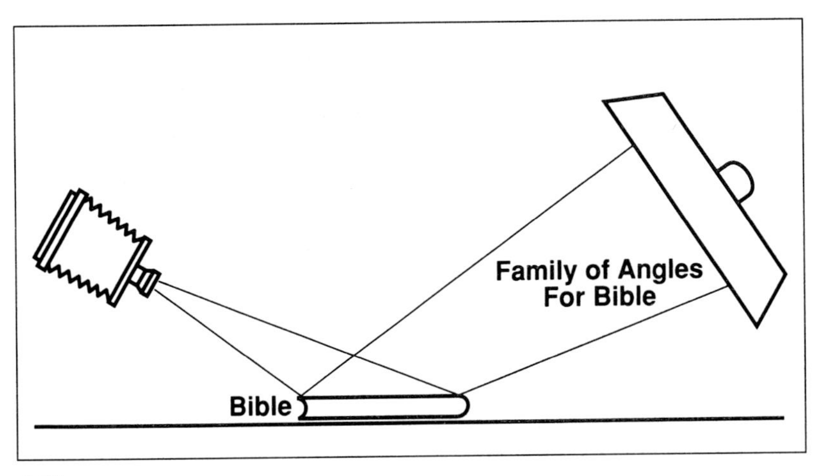

4.18

◀ *A light filling the family of angles defined by the black leather Bible.*

Notice that this arrangement could not be more different from the one that worked well for the white cloth. Instead of raking the light from the side, we have put it above the subject. This nearly eliminates the small shadows that defined the cloth texture. Instead of a small light source, we have a large one. This means that whatever slight shadows do remain in the texture will be too soft to define the texture clearly.

In other words, the theory that predicts the best way to light the cloth also says that our new lighting arrangement is the worst possible way to light the leather! This apparent contradiction is caused by the earlier theory neglecting one consideration—direct reflection.

The large light near the camera produces the magnificent texture visible in Figure 4.19. No exposure increase was necessary. The amount of light falling on the leather is the same as that in Figure 4.17. Nevertheless, the highlight in the leather texture has moved up the tonal scale from near black to middle gray.

► *Using the lighting diagrammed in Figure 4.18 maximizes direct reflection and reveals texture in the leather.*

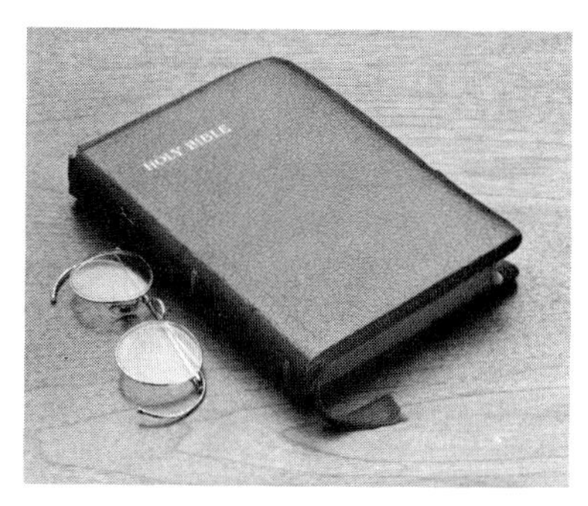

4.19

The apparent increase in illumination comes from good reflection management. The leather surface can produce little diffuse reflection, but a great deal of direct reflection. By capitalizing on the type of reflection appropriate to the surface, we have recorded the subject as well as possible.

COMPETING SURFACES

Photographers would have less gray hair, and less income, if all work were as easy as the examples we have seen so far in this chapter. Some surfaces are rendered better by capitalizing on diffuse reflection, others by capitalizing on direct reflection. However, the best lighting for one can be the worst for the other. When we have both in a single scene, our job gets harder.

Too often, however, to be completely legible, some parts of the scene require diffuse reflection while others need direct reflection. In many of these cases, we can simply deal with the more important part of the scene. If we get that right, viewers do not notice minor defects in the lighting of the rest of the surface. But on other occasions several entirely different parts of the surface are all important, and those different parts of the picture absolutely must have different lighting.

This does not require any new principles. It does mean that we have to apply more than one principle to light a single scene. As we saw in the photographs of the white cloth and the black leather, the technique that produces one effect often excludes another. In extreme cases, this means that the problems presented by competing surfaces are not solvable. When that happens, a photographer needs a good understanding of light, not just to make the picture, but also to give the client a convincing explanation of why retouching is essential.

Commercial photographers sometimes work out the composition of a photograph before beginning to perfect the lighting. After all, if the relationship of the angles between the light, the subject, and the camera are critical, it makes no sense to carefully position the light before knowing the orientation of the subject.

Figure 4.20 is one such preliminary composition. One small light to the right of the camera illuminates this collection of surfaces. The position of the light is similar to the single-light copy setup shown in Figure 4.1. For now, the only purpose of that light is to light the subject well enough to see it in the camera.

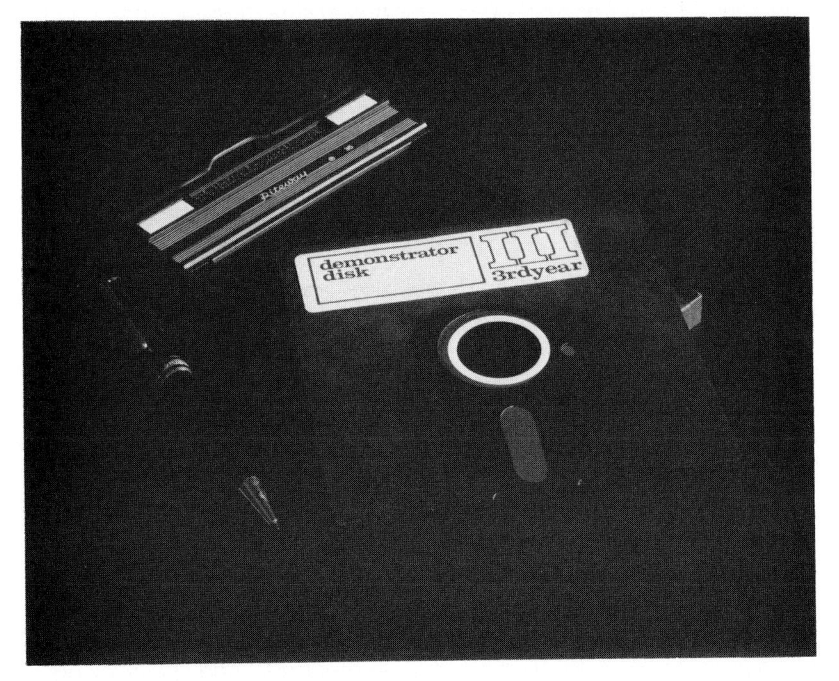

◀ *Lit by one small light to the right of the camera, this photograph was exposed only by diffuse reflection.*

4.20

Before lighting a scene well, we have to decide what is important in it. This picture is intended to sell specialized computer software to professional photographers. Almost any advertising image needs to carry the message as strongly as possible and as independently of the text as possible. (A reader may continue turning pages without bothering to read the copy if the photograph, by itself, does not create enough interest in the product.)

With that in mind, this photograph must make the floppy disk immediately visible: That tells the reader that software is involved. The film holder is also important to let the reader know that the software has something to do with photography. Finally, but not least, the label is essential to identify the product.

Of the three important surfaces, only the type on the label is adequately recorded in the first photograph. We would expect that, because the lighting resembles copy lighting, and there is no technical difference between photographing a label and copying a painting. But the black disk on the black film holder does not have enough shadow detail to survive even the reasonably good reproduction in this book. Had this shot been used for the intended ad in a trade newsletter, on newsprint paper, the result would have been even worse.

Since the test shot suffers from the same problems we saw in the black leather, we decided to try the same solution diagrammed earlier in Figure 4.18. We used a light large enough and positioned to maximize the direct reflection on the black surfaces.

Figure 4.21 is the result. Predictably, the detail in the black disk and film holder are quite good. Equally predictable, the direct reflection that brightens the black plastic has the same effect on the black type in the label. The type is too weak to look good. Unless your eyes are good, it is not even legible.

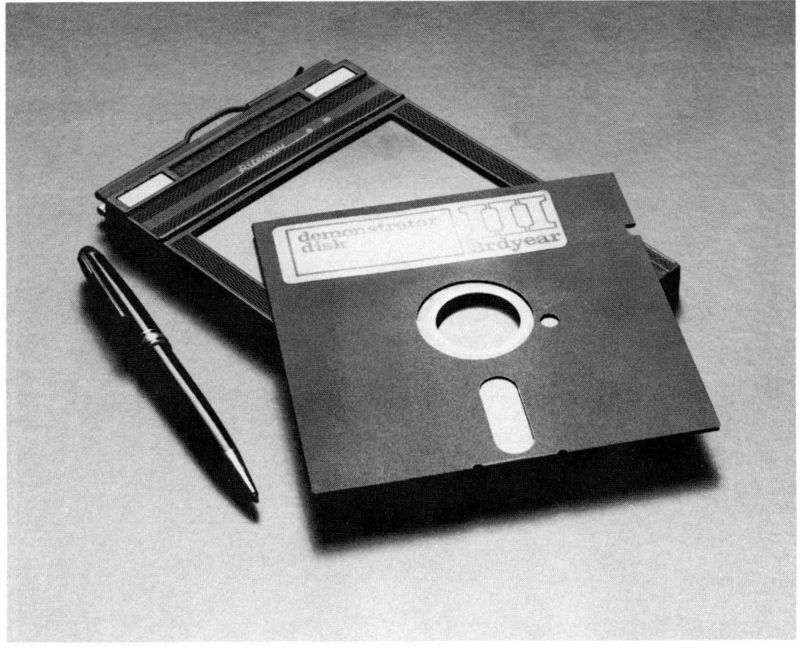

◀ *Direct reflection alone produces good detail in the black film holder and computer disk, but the black type on the label is too weak.*

4.21

Thus, each basic lighting is good for one type of surface but bad for the other. Nevertheless, both surfaces are important. This complicates life considerably. Fortunately, there are several possible solutions available. We will present four of the more promising ones.

Try a Lens Polarizing Filter

On some surfaces, the direct reflection we do not want will turn out to be glare (polarized direct reflection). If this is the case, we can eliminate the offending reflection with a polarizing filter on the lens. If we are lucky, the direct reflection we want to keep will be unpolarized and will not be significantly affected by the filter.

More likely, however, the direct reflection will be polarized on both surfaces or on neither. So if the polarizer eliminates the undesirable reflection, it also filters out the direct reflection we do like. Although the lens polarizing filter often fails to solve this kind of problem, it is still the best solution to try first because it is so quick and easy.

Use a Still Larger Light

Figure 4.22 shows a light large enough to fill the family of angles causing direct reflection, plus a large range of angles that do not.

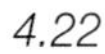 *This light source is much larger than that needed to fill the family of angles that causes direct reflection on the disk and film holder.*

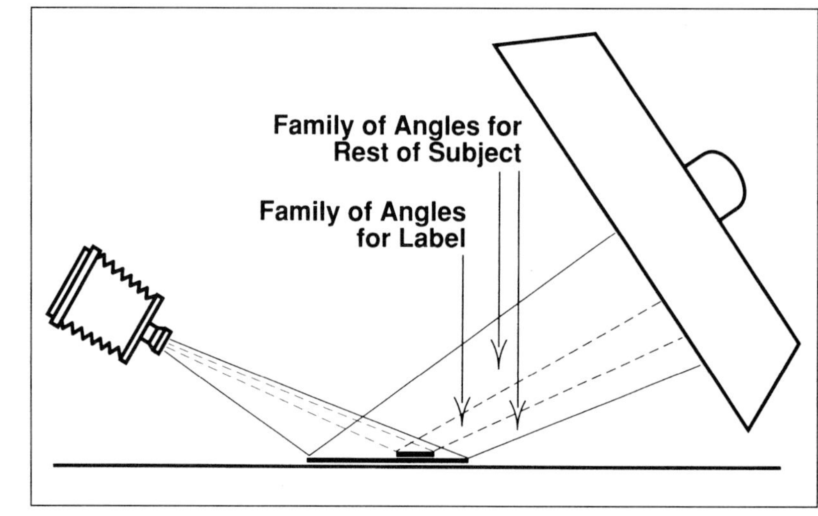

4.22

The light coming from the family of angles causing direct reflection lights the black plastic well. The rest of the rays from this source strike the surface from angles that can only produce diffuse reflection and, therefore, light the label well.

This solution is especially effective using a light, plus an independently supported diffusion sheet, rather than a soft box. Then we can light one part of the diffusion sheet more brightly than another to place slightly more direct reflection on the black plastic than on the label.

Unfortunately, this approach is a compromise, not a complete solution. The type will not be quite as black as it was in the first photograph of this scene, and the plastics will not have as much detail as they did in the second picture. Both types of surface might be lit adequately, but not as well as possible.

Use More than One Light

We could also combine the lighting used in Figure 4.20 with that in Figure 4.21. Such a two-light arrangement is shown in Figure 4.23. In principle, this solution is the same as using a single very large light: Some of the rays come from angles that cause direct reflection, while others come from angles that can only cause diffuse reflection.

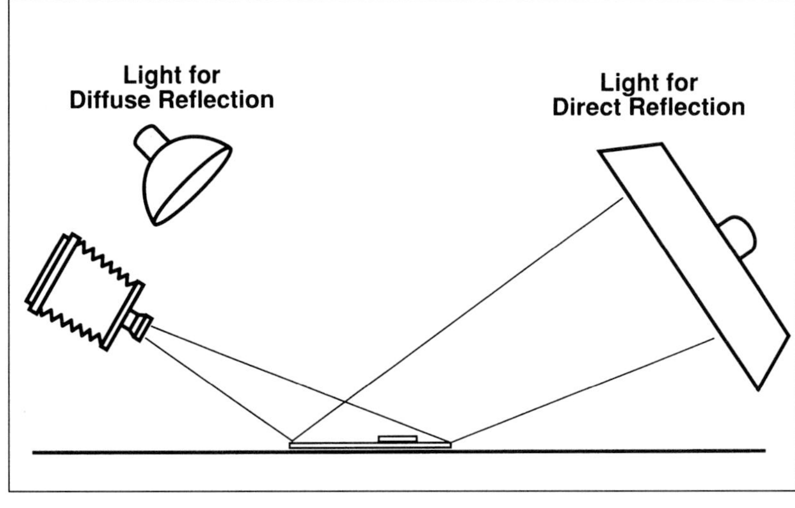

4.23

◀ *The large light produces direct reflection, while the small one near the camera produces only diffuse reflection. The result is a compromise.*

In practice, however, using multiple sources offers the opportunity to regulate their brightness independently, thereby allowing finer control over the relative brightness of the direct and the diffuse reflection.

Like a single very large source, the multiple light solution is also a compromise see Figure 4.23. The independent control of the two light sources sometimes makes it a better compromise, but neither the diffuse reflection nor the direct reflection will look as good as it might if we had to light for only one of the two.

The size of the subject often determines whether to use multiple lights or a single very large one. All other things being equal, smart photographers do whatever requires the least work. In this case, it is easy to come up with a single source that is very large compared with the disk and the film holder. If the subject were larger, it might be easier to use two lights.

Use a Gobo

We have been careful to point out that the preceding techniques are compromises. They work for many competing surfaces, but not all.

If the label on the software is not very glossy, and if the advertising photograph is going to be well reproduced, the compromise is usually adequate. But if the label is glossy, none of the lighting we have seen so far will be adequate. If there is enough direct reflection for the black surfaces, there will be too much direct reflection on the label. Furthermore, if the advertisement is to be used in a newspaper or printed on other inferior paper, the defect is magnified.

The only remedy for this problem is a small gobo that fills the family of angles that cause direct reflection on the label, but that is not large enough to extend into the family of angles that produce direct reflection on the rest of the subject. Figure 4.24 shows the position and size of a gobo that could accomplish this.

▶ *The small gobo blocks the family of angles that causes a direct reflection on the label, but not that which causes direct reflection on the rest of the subject.*

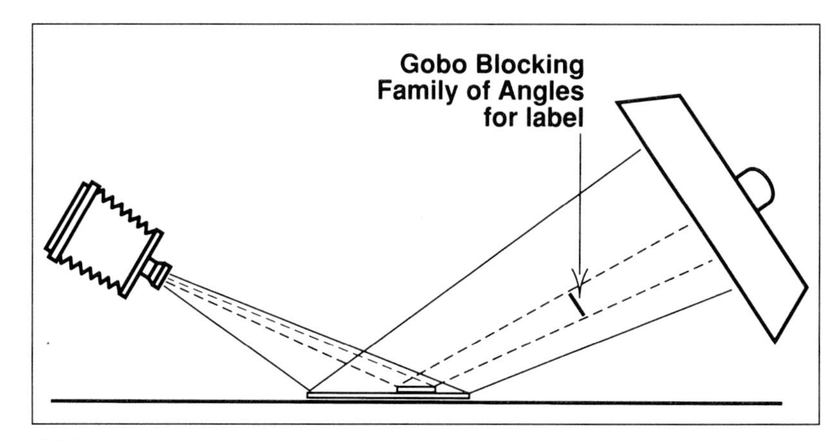

4.24

Although the gobo is large enough to block all direct reflection on the label, notice in the diagram that it does not block much of the total surface of the light source. We still obtain a lot of light from those angles that cause diffuse reflection on the label. Therefore, the total exposure is not significantly affected.

Getting the gobo to be the right size and at the right distance is not always easy. Notice that the *closer* the gobo is to the light source, the *larger* it needs to be to fill the same family of angles; and the larger the gobo is, the more it blocks the total illumination and the more likely it is to affect exposure. This seems to suggest that we might want the gobo as close to the subject as possible so that a smaller one will do the job.

But a gobo closer to the subject is more likely to cast a visible shadow on the table top. This is because moving the gobo farther from the light makes the light effectively smaller *compared with the gobo.* Since smaller light sources produce harder shadows, we are more likely to be able to see the shadow.

So the gobo needs to be far enough from the subject to avoid casting a visible shadow, yet far enough from the light to be small enough to block as little total illumination as possible. It also needs to be exactly large enough to block the direct reflection on the label, but not on the rest of the subject. This is why we saved the gobo for the last solution to the competing-surfaces exercise. It is the most effective solution, but it requires the most work and the most time. On the first occasion you attempt it, you may find positioning the gobo with precision to be a bit tedious. Fortunately, it soon gets easier with a little practice.

We can usually support the gobo on a wooden dowel clamped to a nearby light stand. This arrangement provides plenty of freedom to move the gobo in any direction until we get it right. However, if anything in the scene is mirror-like, then the wooden support becomes a visible reflection in the picture. In those cases, we tape the gobo directly to the diffusion material above the subject. Then we can move the light itself until the gobo is properly positioned.

Figure 4.25 is the result of this arrangement. The direct reflection is gone from the label, but not from the disk or the film holder.

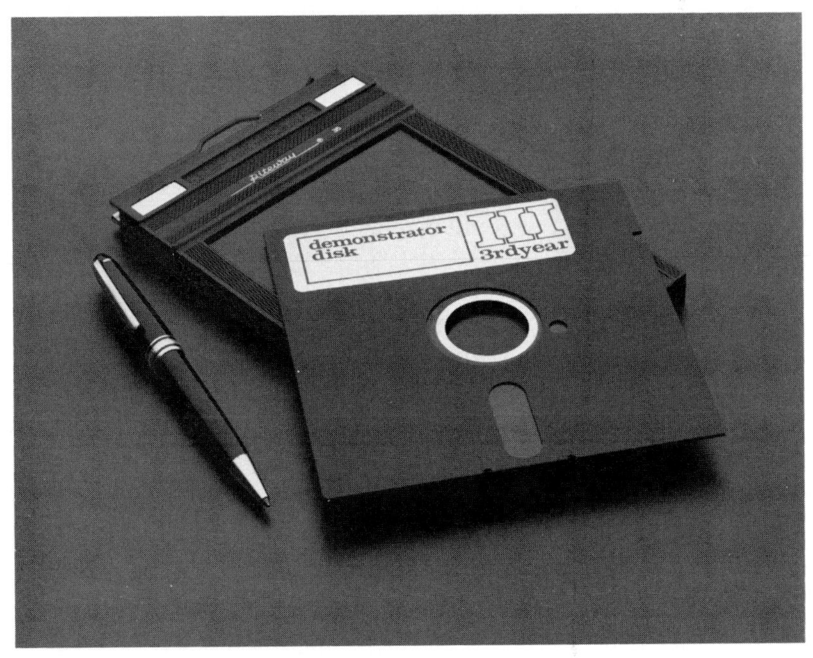

4.25

◀ *The result of the technique illustrated in Figure 4.24: detail in the disk and film holder, plus legible type on the label.*

COMPLEX SURFACES

In this book we will use the term *complex surface* to mean a *single* surface that requires both diffuse and direct reflection to define it properly. Glossy wood is a good example. Only direct reflection can tell the viewer that the wood is glossy, but diffuse reflection is essential to reveal the color and the grain of the wood beneath the gloss.

Figure 4.26 is a piece of highly polished wood lit to produce both direct and diffuse reflection. A medium-sized light source has been positioned to reflect in the lower portion of the wooden surface to show the glossy finish. Notice that the slight physical texture in the surface is also revealed by the direct reflection.

► Direct reflections in the bottom of the scene show the gloss, while diffuse reflection in the top reveals the wood grain.

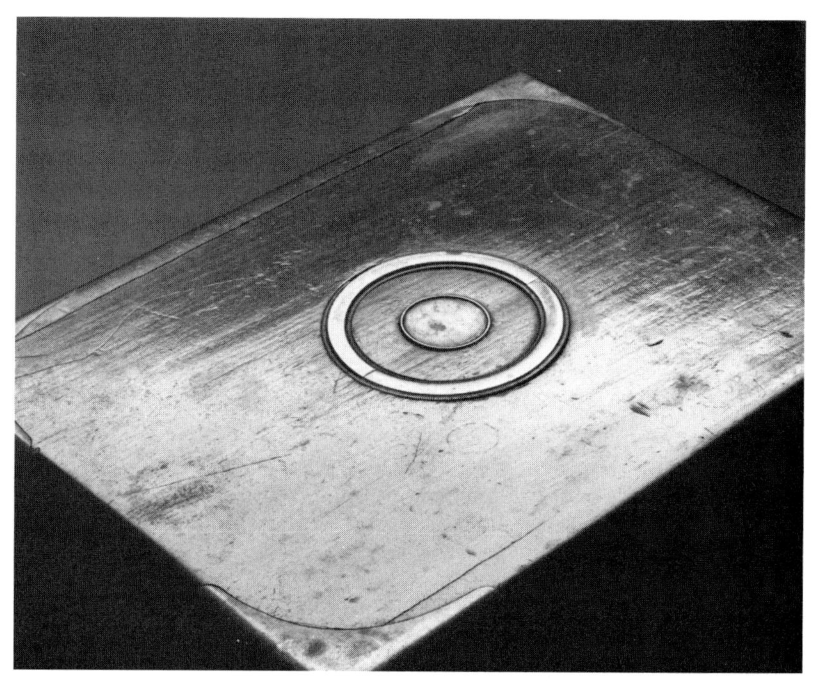

4.26

The light has been kept small enough that it cannot fill the entire family of angles required to produce direct reflection over the whole surface. So the upper part of the surface produces only diffuse reflection, which allows us to see the fine-grain structure in the wood. In a color photograph, this would also be the only area in which the true color of the wood would be clearly apparent. Figure 4.27 diagrams the lighting.

► Lighting to produce both the direct and the diffuse reflections, used to illuminate the wood box in Figure 4.26.

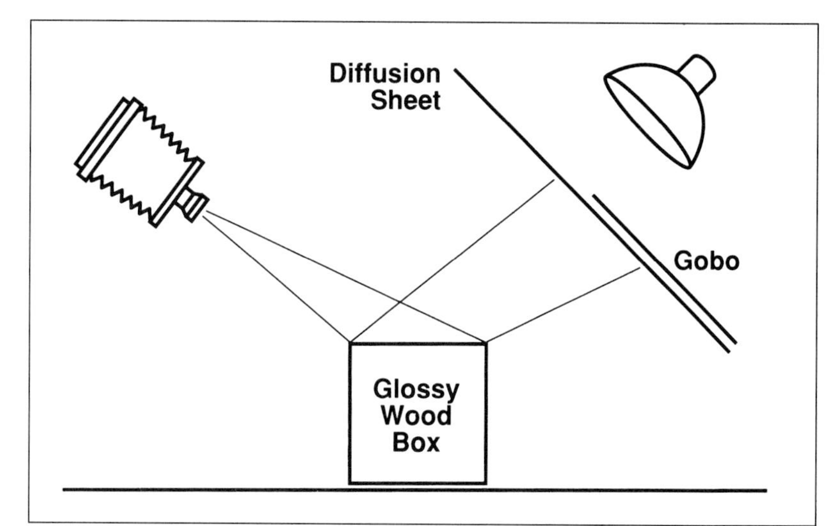

4.27

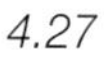

Notice especially the transition zone between the areas of diffuse and direct reflection. This area has some of each type of reflection, which often reveals the surface better than either diffuse or direct reflection alone. If you want to capitalize on this effect, you can enlarge the transition zone to fill more of the surface. Just move the camera farther from the subject and use a longer lens to keep the subject a similar size.

Finally, see how much easier this exercise becomes if we do not restrict ourselves to a two-dimensional surface. Look at what happens in Figure 4.28 if we put a three-dimensional object on the wood surface. The reflection of the glasses in the wood tells the viewer that the wood is glossy. Adding a secondary subject reveals the wood better than we are likely to be able to render the wood alone.

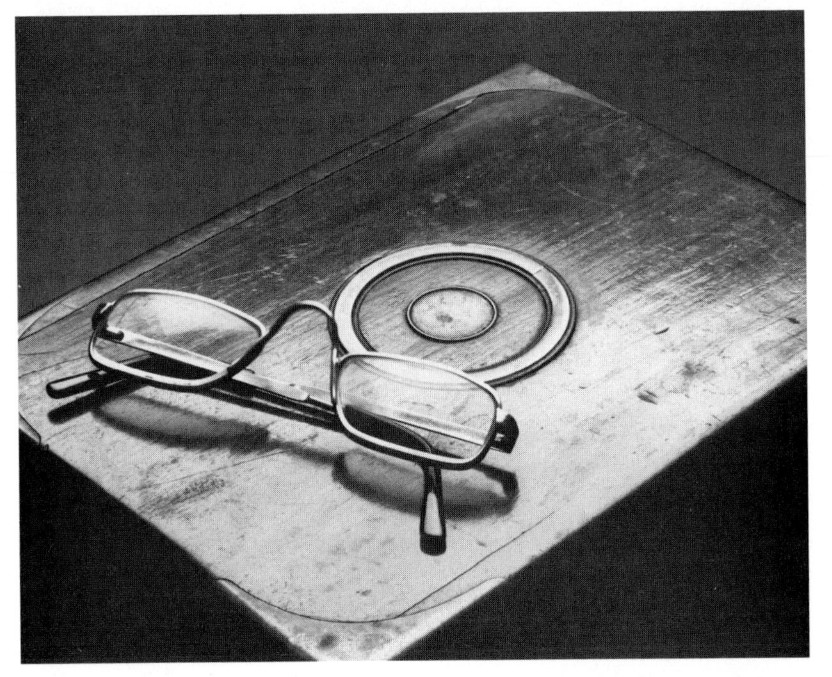

4.28

◀ *The glasses add a three-dimensional element, which provides additional visual clues (the reflection of the glasses) to prove the surface is glossy.*

Adding a three-dimensional subject to this kind of scene often makes the lighting easier. We cannot pursue this approach very far, however, because we promised that this chapter would be about two-dimensional and nearly two-dimensional subjects. In the next chapter we will see what happens when those surfaces face three different directions at once.

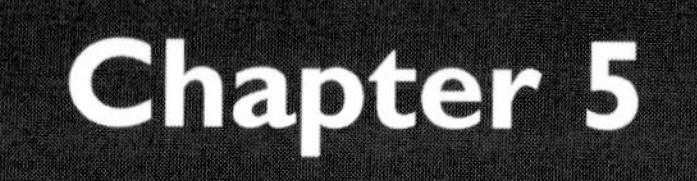

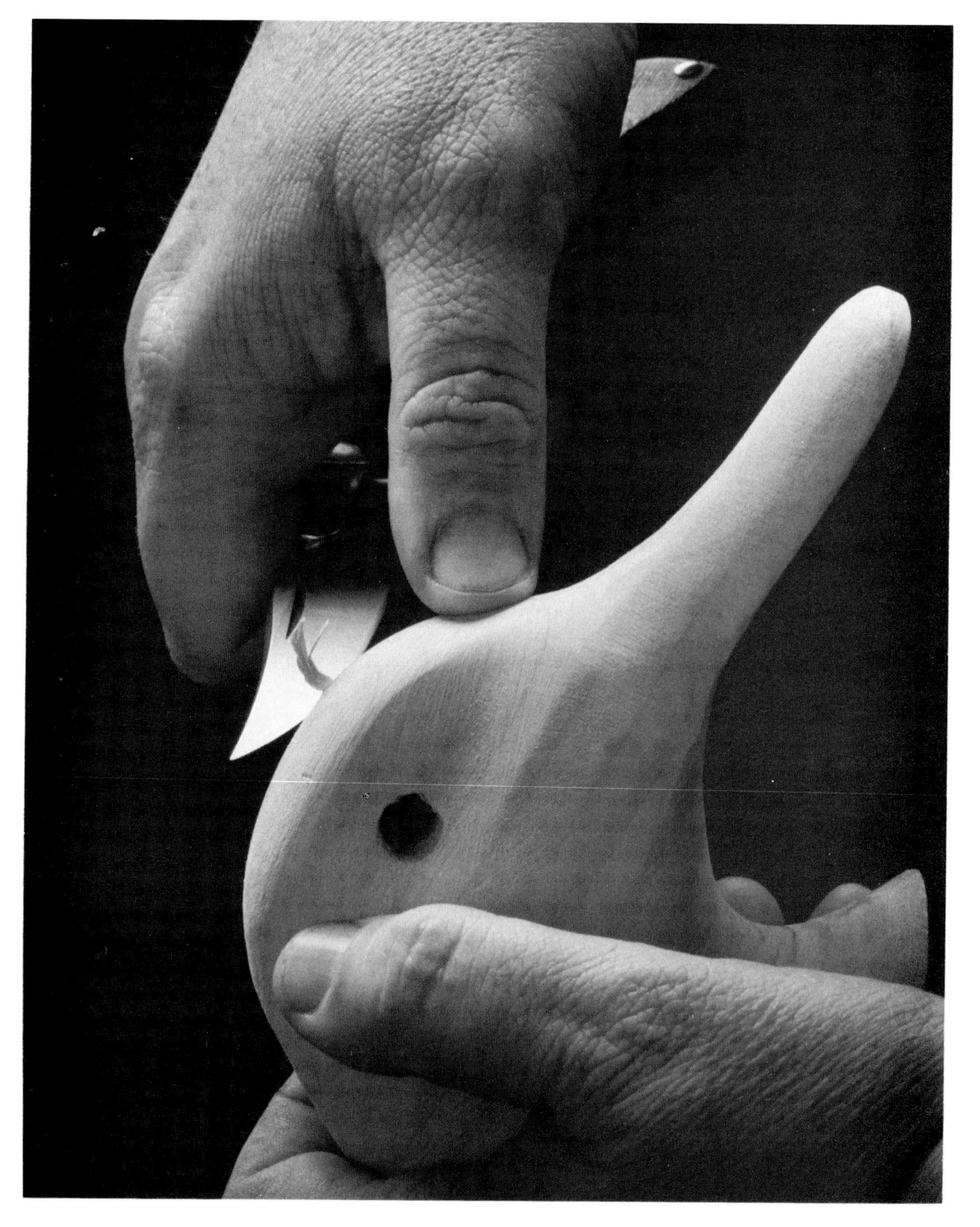

Revealing Shape and Contour

In the last chapter, we dealt with the problems and opportunities for lighting objects that are flat, or nearly so—things that are visually defined only in terms of length and width. In this chapter we add the third dimension—*depth*.

A box, for example, is a group of only three visible surfaces. Since we know how to light *any* of the surfaces well, we can also light all of them well. Does this mean we can light any of these surfaces using *only* the principles in the previous chapter? Usually not. Lighting each visible surface well is not usually enough. We also have to think about how those surfaces *relate* to one another. Then we have to light and compose to add depth, or at least the illusion of depth, to the picture.

Three-dimensional subjects require their own lighting techniques. The lighting techniques that we are going to demonstrate are designed to produce the visual clues that our brains need to interpret depth.

Visual clues is the key concept on which this whole chapter hangs, so we will begin by describing what some of these visual clues are. It is difficult to make a photograph with absolutely no visual clues to represent depth. However, it is easy to draw such a picture. Figure 5.1 is an example. No one can say for sure what this drawing is intended to represent We say that it is a cube, but you could just as reasonably insist that it is a hexagon with a "Y" drawn in the center.

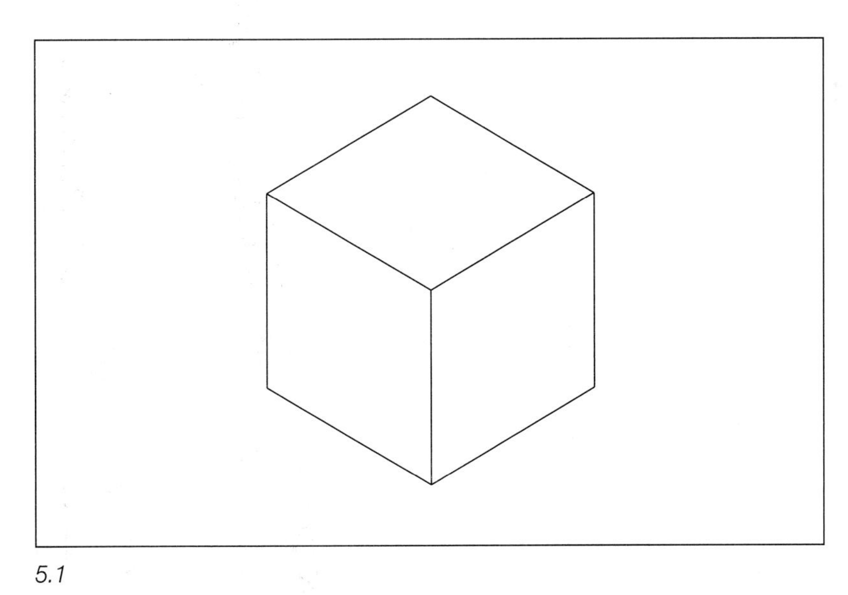

5.1

◀ *This diagram fails to provide any visual clues that would make us perceive it as a three-dimensional object.*

Figure 5.1 fails to supply our eyes with the essential visual clues that our brains need to process the information coming from our optic nerves and to decide, "This is a three-dimensional scene."

The only way we can be sure that a viewer can understand that an object is a cube is to add these visual clues. Figure 5.2 has exactly the visual clues the brain is looking for. Compare it with Figure 5.1.

► *Here we have added those visual clues that the brain needs to see depth.*

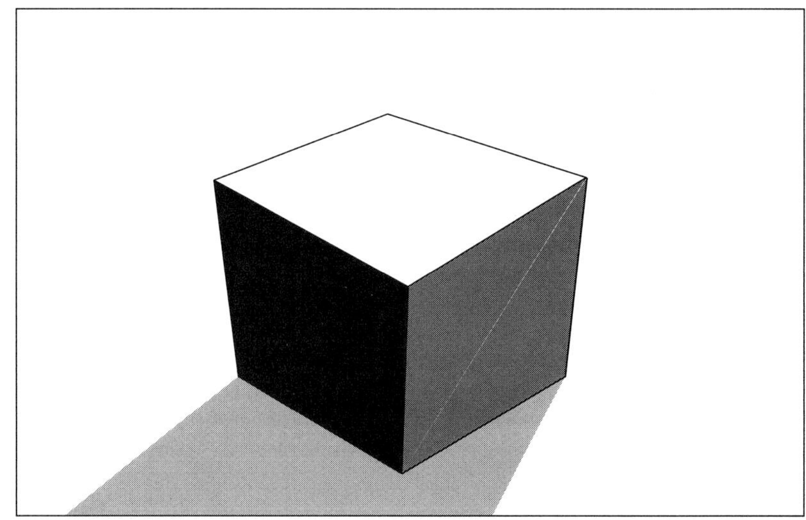

5.2

DEPTH CLUES

What is it that makes such a difference between the two images? What is it in the second picture that makes it look "three dimensional"? A look at the drawings gives us two immediate answers. The first is *tonal variation*. The tonal differences in the second picture, the dark shadow against highlight, provides our brains with visual clues that the scene is three dimensional.

Besides tonal variation, there is a second clue that our brain uses to perceive depth. *Perspective distortion* also provides our brains with important information.

Notice that these visual clues are so powerful that the brain perceives depth that does not and never did exist! This is not really a cube; it is only a bit of ink on paper. Photographers record real subjects with real depth, but that depth is lost in the picture. A photographic print is as two dimensional as these drawings. Therefore, photographers who want to maintain a sense of depth need to use the same techniques that illustrators do.

Both tonal variation and perspective distortion influence lighting decisions. Lighting *produces* highlights and shadows, so its effect on tonal variation is obvious. The relationship between lighting and perspective distortion is less obvious, but still important. Viewpoint determines both perspective distortion *and* the family of angles that cause direct reflection. Changing viewpoint to control that family of angles also alters perspective distortion, and vice versa.

PERSPECTIVE DISTORTION

Subjects appear smaller when they are farther away. Furthermore, if the subject is three dimensional, the part of the subject that is farther away appears to be smaller than the closer part of the same subject. Similarly, the closer part of the same subject appears to be larger. We call this effect *perspective distortion*.

Some psychologists believe that infants perceive more distant subjects to be actually smaller. No one is sure about this, because by the time we are old enough to talk about the matter, our brains have learned to interpret perspective distortion as depth.

Distortion as a Clue to Depth

Our eyes deceive us when we look down railway tracks, but our brains do not. The rails appear to converge in the distance, but we know very well that the rails are parallel. We know that they are the same distance apart a mile down the track as they are where we are standing, so the brain says, "The tracks only *appear* to converge because they are distant." But how does the brain know that the tracks are distant? The brain answers, "They *must* be distant, because they appear to converge." (The flow of this logic must shock computer programmers, but they are accustomed to the limitations of inferior hardware.)

We assume the brain actually uses a more complex process, but the effect is the same: Perspective distortion is one of the major visual clues that our brains use to perceive depth. This is why the ability to handle perspective distortion is such an important tool. Understanding the principles enables us to control the perspective distortion in the picture. This allows us to manipulate the illusion of depth in the picture.

Conventional photography is two dimensional. Viewers notice the length and width of a photographic print, but not the thickness of its paper. We perceive depth in the photograph despite the fact that it does not really exist. Figure 5.3 proves it. The foreground chess pieces clearly appear to be in front of those in the background. But the "foreground" and "background" existed only in the scene, not in this print. Here the chess pieces are all on the same paper surface. Perspective distortion is critical to this sense of depth that photography conveys.

► *Although this photograph (like all others) is a flat, two-dimensional representation of the scene, we perceive depth in it.*

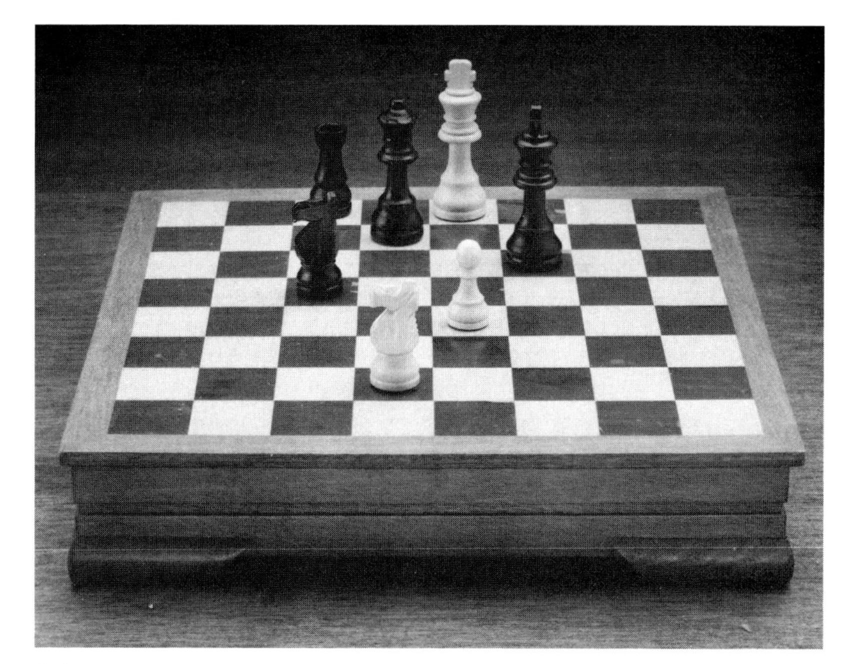

5.3

One of the main reasons that we know this scene has depth is that the lines that delineate the edges and the squares of the chess board and the squares on it look distorted. Those lines are parallel to each other in reality, but not in the picture. Like the railroad tracks we discussed earlier, these lines converge at a point on an imaginary horizon. This distortion gives the brain a strong visual clue that it is seeing length, width, *and* depth.

Manipulating Distortion

Within limits, we can increase and decrease the amount of perspective distortion in a photograph. This means that we can control the sense of depth our pictures give to viewers.

Controlling the degree of perspective distortion in a picture is simplicity itself. The *closer* we move the camera toward the subject, the *greater* the distortion will be. Conversely, the *farther* the camera is from the subject, the *less* it will be distorted. It is that easy.

In Figure 5.4, we see the effect of the first half of the rule. It is the same chessboard, but the camera has been moved much closer to it. (Of course, changing the camera distance also changes the size of the subject on film. But we made the prints the same size to make the perspective distortion more apparent.)

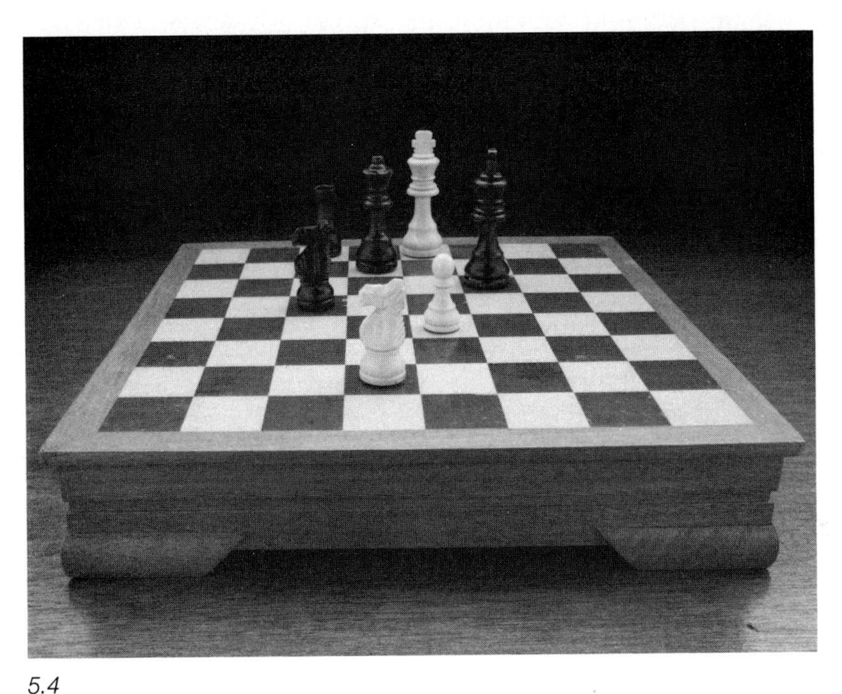

5.4

◀ *Moving the camera closer increased perspective distortion and made the parallel lines that run toward the horizon appear to converge. This is one of the visual clues that the brain uses to perceive depth.*

See that the closer viewpoint increases the distortion. The lines that define the chessboard appear to converge much more radically than they did in the first photograph.

Exactly the reverse takes place in Figure 5.5. This time we moved the camera back. Notice how there is less distortion in this picture. The lines in it converge far less obviously than they do in either of the two previous illustrations.

► *With the camera farther away, parallel lines appear to converge less.*

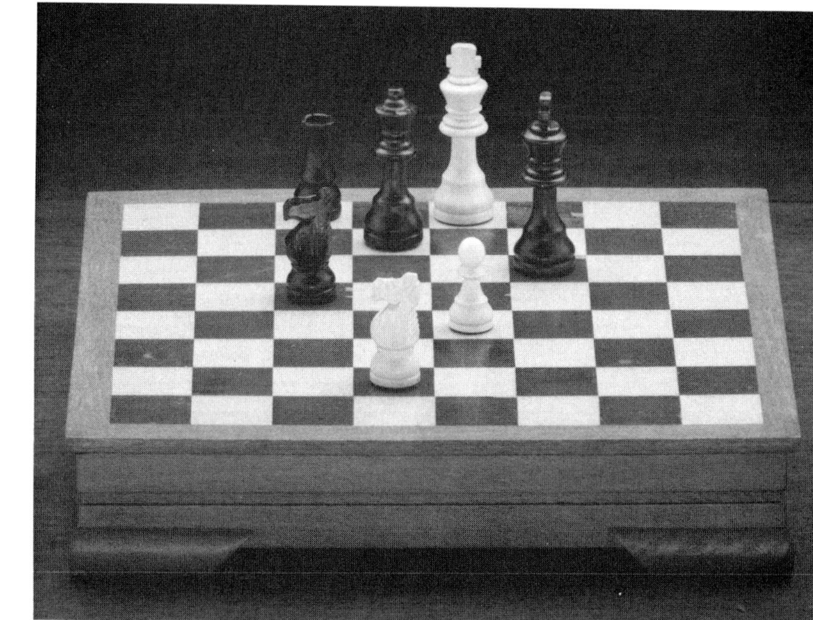

5.5

Do Lenses Affect Perspective Distortion?

When most photographers first use a wide-angle lens, they decide that the lens introduces a great deal of distortion. This is almost never accurate. Camera position determines perspective distortion, not the lens.

To prove this, we made every picture of the chessboard with *the same* wide-angle lens. This means that we had to enlarge the image made at an intermediate distance somewhat, and we had to greatly enlarge the image made at a greater distance. Those enlargements produced images whose sizes match the one made with the camera closer. Had we used longer focal length lenses, we would not have had to enlarge those two images so much, but the shape of the chess board would have been the same as the shapes in the three pictures we show.

Choosing a lens of the appropriate focal length *does* allow us to control image size to make it fit the film size. Assuming we want the usable image to exactly fill the film, a short focal-length lens *allows* us a viewpoint that produces perspective distortion. A longer lens *allows* us to get far enough from the subject to minimize perspective distortion without having to greatly enlarge the image later. In each case, the viewpoint determines the distortion, not the lens.

Extremely wide-angle lenses and inferior lenses may produce their own other types of distortion, but not perspective distortion.

TONAL VARIATION

The second major depth clue is tonal variation. Tonal variation means that there are light areas and dark areas in the subject. If the subject is a cube, ideal tonal variation means that the viewer sees a highlighted side, a shadowed side, and a side that is partly shadowed. (We use "side" for convenience. One of these sides could be the top of the cube, or even the bottom, if the cube is suspended above us.) Good lighting does not always require this ideal, but the ideal is still the standard we use to evaluate whatever lighting exists.

These highlights and shadows are determined by the *size* and *position* of the light used. We treat size and position as two different concepts, but they are not mutually exclusive. One can greatly influence the other. A large light, for example, illuminates the subject from many different "positions" at the same time. In the rest of this chapter we will see how these two variables relate.

THE SIZE OF THE LIGHT

Selecting the size of the light is one of the most important steps in studio lighting. Time of day and weather determine the size of the light outdoors. This is why those factors are critical to architectural and landscape photographers.

The previous chapter discussed how adjusting the size of the light makes the edges of the shadows harder or softer. If two shadows record on film as the same gray, a hard shadow will be more visible than a soft one. For this reason, a hard shadow often increases the illusion of depth more than a soft one. When we understand this we have another way to manipulate the tonal values, and thus control the sense of depth, in our pictures.

This seems to say that hard lights are better lights, but depth alone does not make a good picture. A shadow that is too hard can be so visible that it competes with the primary subject. Since we cannot offer firm rules about what size light is always best, we will explore the general principles in more detail.

Large Lights versus Small Lights

We have already discussed the basic principles involved in Chapter 2: A *small* light source produces *hard*-edged shadows, and a *large* one produces *soft*-edged shadows. Most of our lights are small. Portability and cost require it. Therefore, photographers more often need to enlarge a small light than the reverse.

Diffusing screens, umbrellas, and bounce cards all increase the effective size of any light. The effect of any of these is about the same as that of another. Since all of these devices can produce identical pictures, we pick the one that is most convenient. Thus, if the subject is small, we are more likely to use a framed sheet of diffusion material because we can place it close to the subject for brighter illumination. It is more difficult to construct a very large diffuser, so we are more likely to bounce the light from a white ceiling to light a large subject.

Outdoors we can achieve the same effect by waiting for an overcast day. Clouds make excellent diffusion material, effectively increasing the size of the sunlight source. Depending on the available time and the accessibility of the site, some photographers even wait for a day with just the right amount of cloud cover.

Lacking the time to wait for the best day, the same framed diffusion material we use in the studio is also good for small outdoor subjects. Alternatively, we can keep the subject in the shade. Then the large open sky, instead of the small direct sun, serves as the primary light source. (Remember to use color-compensating [CC] filters to compensate for the blue color of the sky!)

Distance from the Subject

You may have been surprised that in the preceding section we referred to the clouds and the sky as larger light sources than the sun. A corollary to the effect of the size of the light relates to the distance between a light and the subject it illuminates. The *closer* a light is to the subject, the *softer* the shadows are. Conversely, the *farther* a light is from the subject, the *harder* the shadows become. The sun behaves as a small light source to people on earth because it is so far away.

Remember that low-contrast lights produce soft shadows because they illuminate the subject from more different directions. Figure 5.6 shows this, but look at what happens in Figure 5.7 when we move the same light source farther away. The light still emits rays in many directions, but only a narrow range of these rays strikes the subject.

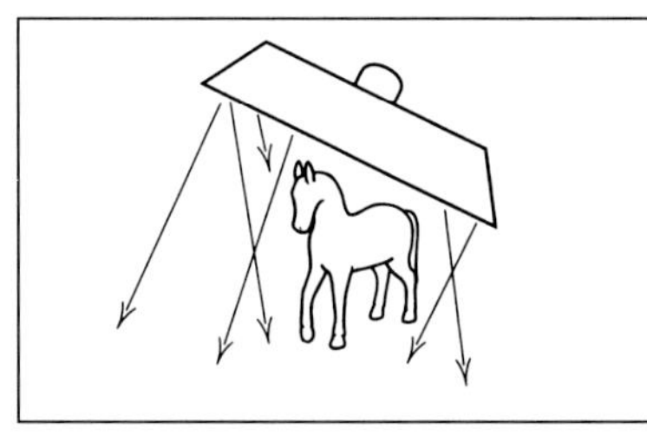

5.6

◀ *Close to the subject, the light rays from a large light source strike the subject from many angles. The closer the light is, the softer its shadows are.*

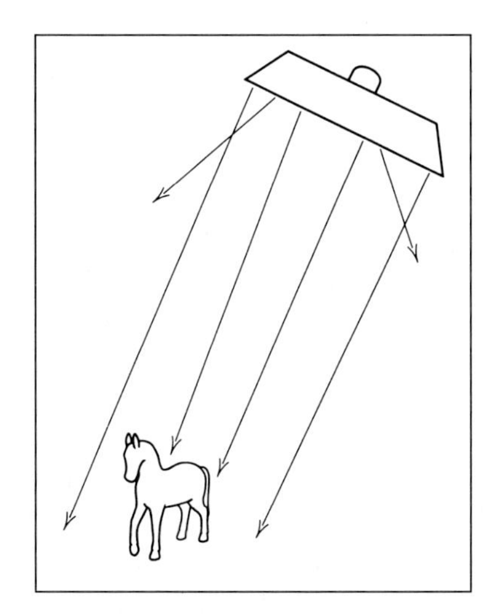

5.7

◀ *Moving the light farther away causes the rays striking the subject to be more parallel. This produces harder edged shadows.*

Moving a light farther from the subject increases its contrast by reducing the range of angles from which the rays can strike the subject. This is just another way of saying that large lights produce soft shadows and small lights produce hard ones. The *closer* we move a light to a subject, the *larger* that light source becomes in relation to it.

Photographers using portable strobes in small rooms sometimes insist that the opposite is true. They know that moving the light farther from the subject softens the shadows, rather than making them harder. This is because moving the light farther away reflects more of the rays from the surrounding walls. The room itself becomes a more important component of the lighting. The room is larger than the strobe, so the principle is not contradicted.

THE DIRECTION OF THE LIGHT

The direction of the light relative to the subject determines what part of the subject is highlighted and where the shadows fall. Light from any direction may be good in any particular case, but only a few of them are good for emphasizing dimension.

Light coming from the direction of the camera is called *front lighting* because primarily the front of the subject is illuminated. Front lighting shows the least possible depth because the visible part of the subject is entirely highlighted. The shadow falls behind the subject where the camera cannot see it. The camera sees no tonal variation and, therefore, no depth. For this reason, front lighting is often called *flat lighting*. Front lighting is good for smoothing skin texture in a portrait or fashion picture, but not for emphasizing depth.

Back lighting also fails to reveal the depth of an object. Coming from behind the subject, back lighting puts the visible part of the subject in shadow. This can add drama, but without other lights, not dimension.

Since the perception of depth requires both highlight *and* shadow, a lighting direction between front and back lighting maximizes that perception. Such lighting is called *side lighting*. Most good lighting is, at least to some extent, side lighting.

Still life photographers usually use *top lighting* for tabletop subjects. Top lighting represents depth to the same extent as side lighting because it gives the subject the same proportion of highlight and shadow. We base our choice between them entirely on taste. This is a question of where we want the highlight and shadow, not of how much of each.

Light directly from the side or the top often conceals too much of the subject detail in shadow. So photographers may pull the light toward the camera to a position between those of side lighting and front lighting. This compromise is called *three-quarter lighting*.

You may justifiably decide to use any of these lighting directions for any subject. The thinking process you use is more important than whatever rules we offer. Your decision will almost always be good, as long as you consider what each direction accomplishes and how well it fulfills your objective for a particular subject.

Now we will look at a real subject and decide on one good way to light it. The subject will be a wooden box, and our objective will be to light it to emphasize depth.

Light on Side

One way of producing the shadows that we need as depth clues is to position the main light on one side of the subject. We tried this in Figure 5.8, using a small, high-contrast light so that you could see the shadow easily.

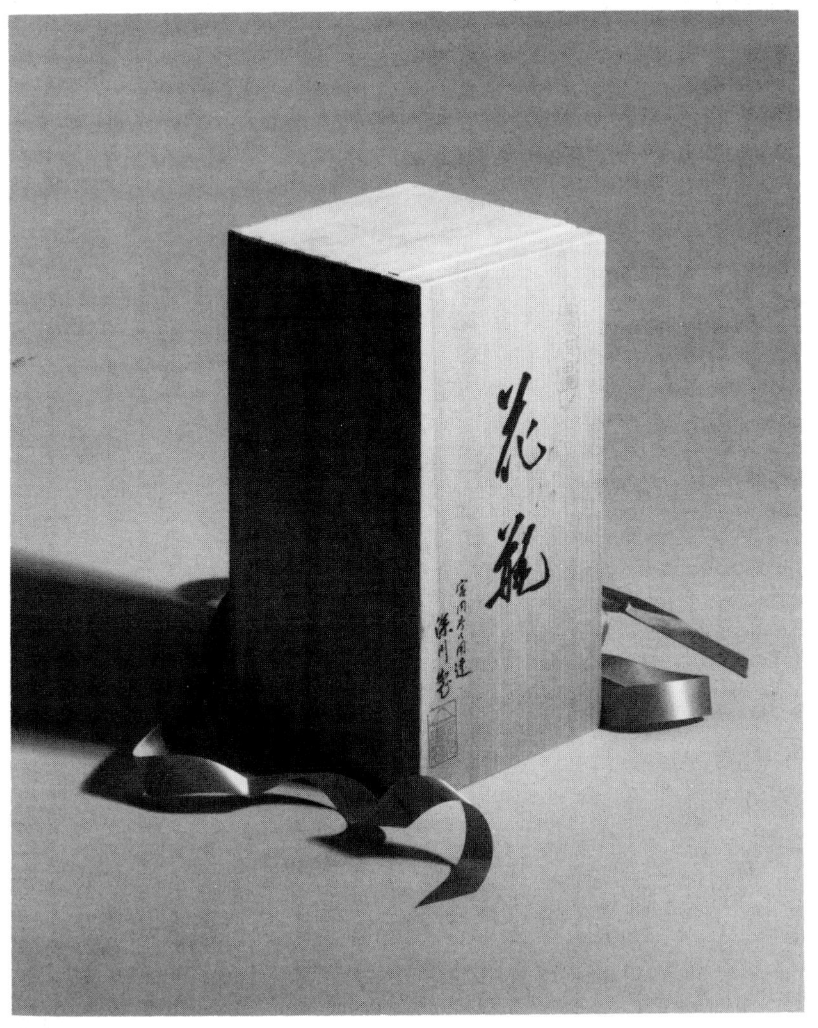

5.8

◀ *The shadow helps the brain to perceive depth, but in this case the shadow is obtrusive.*

This is a potentially good approach, but it is usually not the best one for tabletop subjects. The combination of highlight and shadow does show dimension. The hard shadow, located where it is, distracts from the primary subject. We could improve this photograph with a larger light. That would soften the shadow, making it less noticeable. But the position of the shadow would still cause it to compete. (Remember that we have decided that *the box* is the subject, not the shadow. On any other day we might decide the shadow is the subject, or at least an important secondary subject. Then we would light and compose the picture to capitalize on that shadow.)

The only way to keep this shadow from drawing the eye away from the subject would be to soften it so much that it would not exist at all. But notice that the shadow also proves that the subject is sitting on a table. Without the shadow, the brain would have no way of knowing whether the subject is on the table or floating above it.

The relationship of the subject to the background tells the viewer an essential message about the depth in the scene. Conveying that message requires keeping the shadow. Since we must not get rid of the shadow, then we need to put it somewhere else.

Light Above the Subject

The least distracting place for the shadow in most compositions is directly under and in front of the subject. This means placing the light above and slightly behind the subject. Figure 5.9 was shot with such an arrangement. Notice that the shadow gives the subject a "ground" on which to sit.

► *With a small light above the subject, the shadow is small enough to be less obtrusive, and it gives the box a "ground" upon which to sit. However, the shadow is still too hard.*

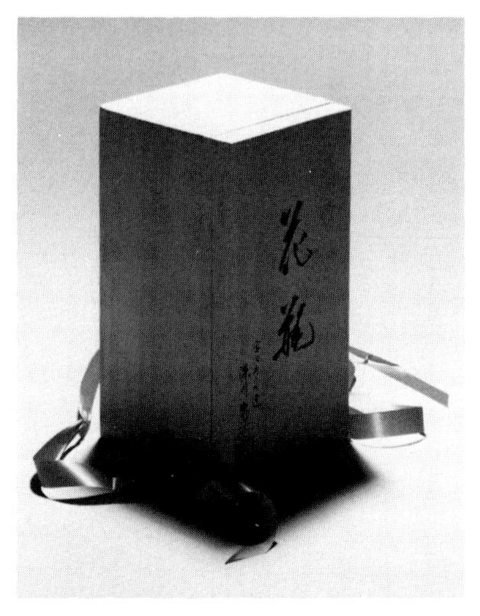

5.9

Although the placement of the shadow is improved, the picture still has two problems. The first is that the subject still does not have as much depth as it needs. The top of the subject is highlighted, but either side is about the same gray as the other. The lack of tonal distinction between the left and right sides detracts from the illusion of depth. The second problem, to many photographers, is that the shadow under the box is too hard. Being so hard makes it obtrusive, too much of an element in the picture.

We will first deal with the hard shadow. We used a small light in this example to make it easier to see where the shadow falls. Now that you have seen the shadow clearly, we will soften it. In Figure 5.10, we substituted a large soft box for the small light used earlier. Figure 5.11 is a diagram of the lighting.

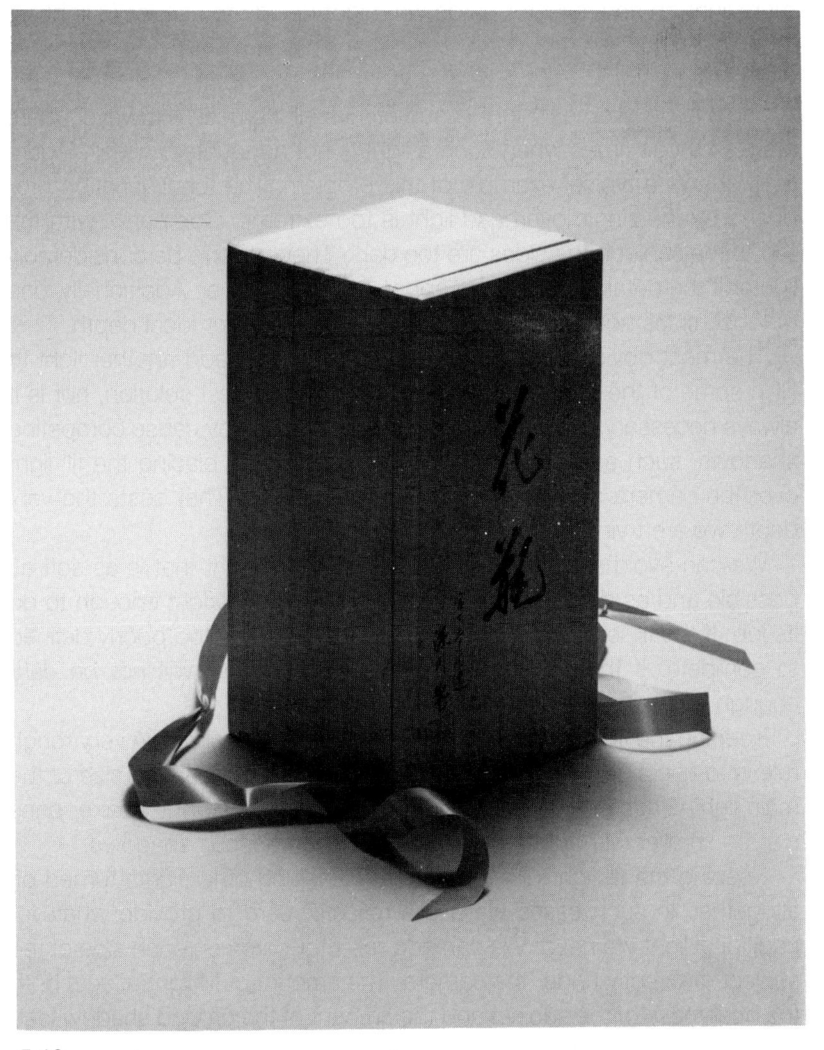

5.10

◀ *Lighting with a soft box makes the shadow much softer and unobtrusive.*

▶ *The lighting diagram for Figure 5.10.*

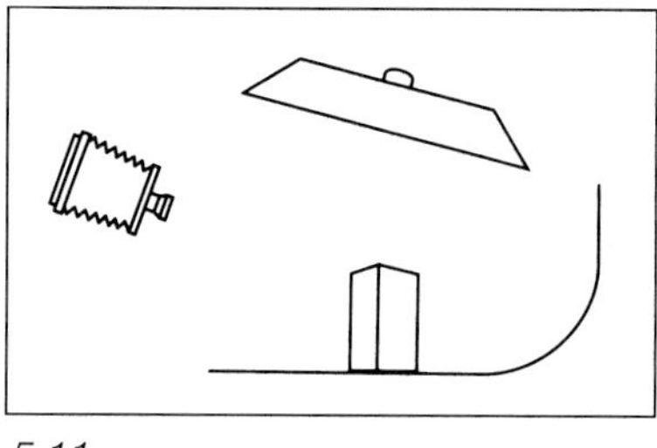

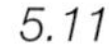

5.11

Notice in the lighting diagram that the soft box is angled slightly toward the camera. This tilt is not essential, but it is common. The tilt keeps the seamless background evenly illuminated. Notice that the light is closer to the top part of the background and that keeping the light level could light that area too brightly. The other reason for tilting the light is to cast more light on any reflector cards we might decide to use for fill light.

Fill Light

A single large overhead light is sometimes all we need. However, there are also those times when such a light is not adequate by itself. Figure 5.10 shows a typical example of this problem. The tonal variation produced by the single overhead light is too extreme. Compared with the top of the subject, the sides are too dark. They need to be considerably lighter if the detail on it is to be apparent to the viewer. Additionally, one of those sides needs to be brighter than the other for ideal depth.

The most obvious solution to this problem is to add another light to fill in some of the shadow. This is not always the best solution, nor is it always necessary. Placing the fill light to one side may cause competing shadows, such as those shown in Figure 5.8. But placing the fill light over the camera may light the subject too evenly. That costs the very depth we are trying to achieve.

We can avoid adding problems by using a fill light that is as soft as possible and as dim as possible, provided it is still bright enough to do its job. If the fill is soft, the additional shadow will be too poorly defined to compete. If the fill is dim, a competing shadow will not be dark enough to be visible.

Keeping the fill soft means using a large enough source. A *very* rough rule is to use a fill light near the subject that is about half the size of the main light. Brighter fill lights usually need to be larger, but weaker ones can be smaller without creating noticeable extraneous shadows.

Keeping the fill light dim often means keeping other lights turned off altogether. In such cases we use a reflector card to provide whatever additional light we need. We can add reflector cards on each side of the subject or directly under the camera. The amount of fill light affects both the brightness of the subject and the amount of the ground shadow lost. Our choice of fill card will vary with both the subject and the background.

Figure 5.12 was made with a silver reflector card to the right of the box. The light gray background reflected enough light to eliminate any need for a fill card to the left of the subject. A white background might have reflected so much light that we would have needed no reflector cards at all. A black background would have reflected so little light that we would have needed stronger fill.

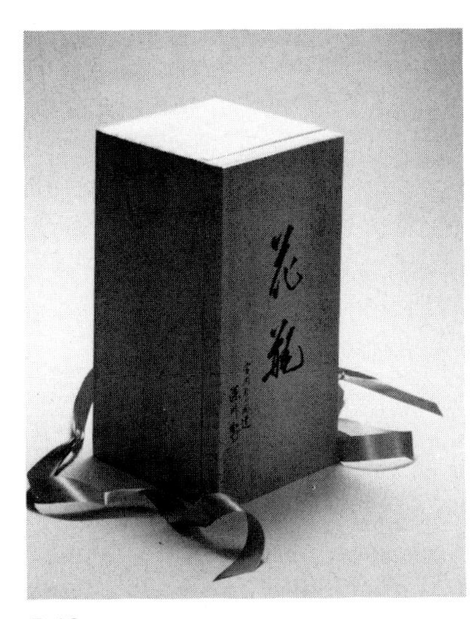

◀ *A fill card lightens the front of the box by reflecting some of the light from the overhead soft box.*

5.12

We can use any combination of reflector cards and additional lights, depending on how much fill the specific subject needs. The least amount of fill we are likely to use is the light reflected from a light background surface on which the subject sits. In those cases we may also decide to put a black card on one side of the subject so that both sides do not get equal fill. The most fill we are likely to need is a light behind a large sheet of diffusion material on one side of the subject, plus a smaller silver card or a white one on the other side.

The physical arrangement of the apparatus used in the photograph influences how much freedom we have in positioning the reflector card. Sometimes we can put the card wherever we please, but on other occasions there is only one possible position that is close enough to the subject but still out of the image area. This may require using a white card when we might otherwise prefer a silver one.

A silver card usually reflects more light onto the subject than a white one, but not always. Remember that a silver card produces direct reflections. For this reason, the silver card has its own limited family of angles from which reflection can occur. In a crowded arrangement, the only possible position of a silver card may be at an angle from which it can reflect no light to the subject. In contrast, most reflection from a white card is diffuse. Because the angle of a white card is less critical, from some positions it will reflect more light to the subject than a silver one.

Notice that the size of the main light also influences our choice of reflector cards. A bright, smooth silver card produces a mirror image of the main light. Therefore, if the main light is large, then a large silver card will serve as a soft fill light. A small silver card will behave as a hard fill for the same reason any other small source is hard. On the other hand, if the main light is small, a silver card reflecting that light will always be a hard fill, regardless of its size. A white reflector card is the only reflector that can provide soft fill light from a small main light.

Finally, even though the background surface can often provide adequate reflected fill, beware of colored backgrounds, especially if the subject itself is white or pastel. Fill reflected from a colored background can color the subject. Sometimes we have to add more fill from a white light source to overcome the color cast caused by the background surface. We may also need to cover part of the background surface with black cards to get rid of off-color reflected fill.

Stopping Flare

While the lighting in Figure 5.14 is useful, it does have one potentially serious drawback. Unless you are careful, the main light can produce flare. Fortunately, flare is easy to avoid - if you understand and anticipate it.

Flare is the scattering of light so that it goes where the basic laws of optics say it ought not. For this reason flare is sometimes called *nonimaging light.* There are two different kinds of flare: lens flare and camera flare. The effect of these two can look the same. The difference between them is where the light gets scattered. *Lens flare*, thanks to modern optics, is rarely a problem if the lens is kept clean. *Camera flare*, on the other hand, is relatively unimproved by optical advances, and it remains a serious problem.

Figure 5.A shows what causes camera flare. Light from just outside the field of view enters the lens. It then reflects from inside the camera to the film. This then fogs the film and degrades the image.

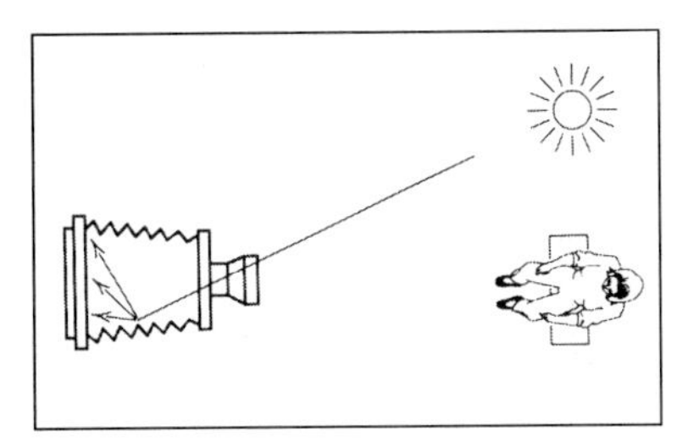

◀ *Camera flare is caused by light outside the field of view passing through the lens and reflecting from the inside of the camera. Blocking the light before it reaches the lens is the only way to prevent it.*

5.A

The whole purpose of a lens hood is to block light coming from outside the scene before it enters the lens. Lens hoods, unfortunately, sometimes do not extend far enough forward to be of any help in preventing camera flare. This is particularly true of view cameras, because a lens hood deep enough to be effective can block part of the scene when the lens is tilted or shifted. The solution is to use opaque cards as gobos, as in Figure 5.14.

If the light source is hard, we can position the gobo so that its shadow just barely covers the lens. However, placing the gobo is more difficult if the light source is soft. The shadow of the gobo may be so soft that we cannot tell when it adequately blocks the light falling on the lens.

Since we normally compose and focus with the lens opened to its maximum aperture, there is little depth of field in the image we see in the camera. This lack of depth of field may make the image of the gobo so unsharp that it is impossible to see it even when it is intruding into the picture area. It can be a tricky business to place the card close enough to the field of view to be useful without getting it in the picture.

Just remember that, because the lens is made of glass, it reflects like a mirror. If the light source is too soft to cast a definite shadow of the gobo, then instead look into the front of the lens at the reflection of the light source. Move the gobo in front of the lens just far enough that you can no longer see the light source reflected in the lens. Then pull the gobo back slightly for safety. A gobo in that position eliminates almost all flare without extending into the image.

Adding Depth to the Background

If you refer to Figure 5.11, you will see that we have used a curved paper background called a *sweep*. Hung in this manner, the background covers the table on which the subject sits and also conceals whatever might be behind the table. The camera sees no horizon. Nor is the gentle curve of the paper visible as long as we do not let the shadow of the subject fall on that part of the background. The brain thinks the entire surface is horizontal and extends, possibly, an infinite distance behind the subject.

Up to now we have used simple, single-tone backgrounds for the sake of simplicity in our examples. Not only can this produce boring pictures, but such lighting also fails to capitalize on the illusion of infinite depth in the background. We can greatly enhance this illusion by illuminating the background unevenly.

We call this uneven illumination *falloff.* As we are using the term, it means a transition in the scene from light to dark. Falloff can occur in any area of the picture. Photographers more commonly use falloff at the top of the picture because that is the easiest place to put it without interfering with the lighting of the primary subject.

Look at Figure 5.13. Notice how the background tone falls off from light gray in the foreground to black in the background. The difference in the tonal value of the foreground and background tones provides another visual clue to suggest depth.

► *The uneven illumination of the background, called falloff, adds depth to a picture and helps to separate the subject from the background.*

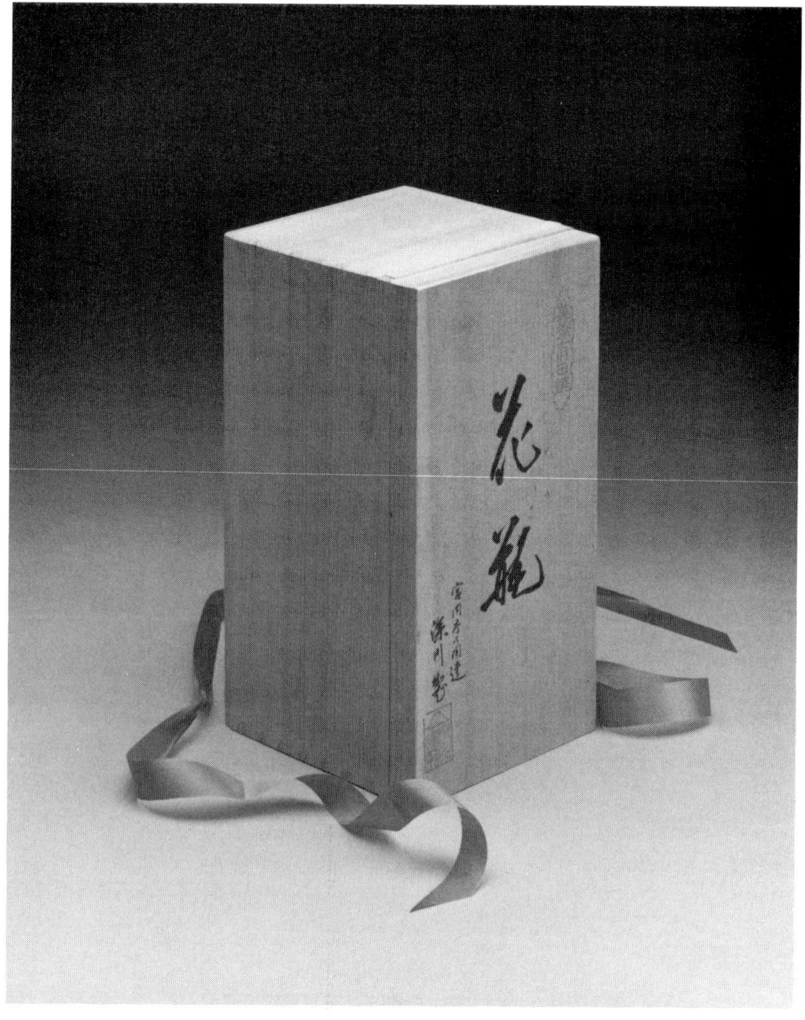

5.13

Figure 5.14 shows how we produced the falloff. All we had to do was to aim the light more toward the camera. This simple change in our set allowed less of it to fall on the seamless paper at the back of the set.

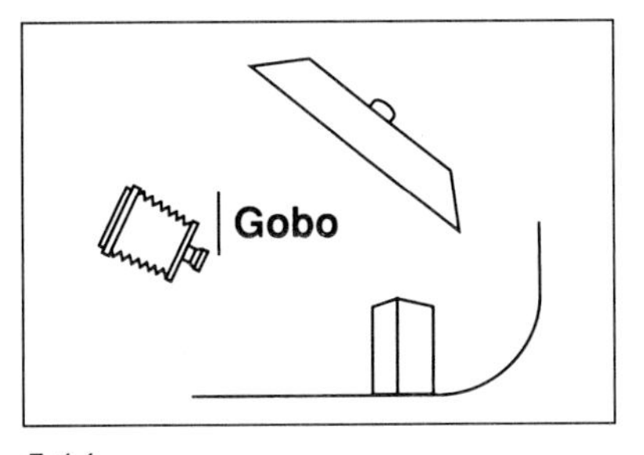

◀ *Aiming the light toward the camera produced the background falloff. The gobo is often essential to prevent flare.*

5.14

Notice that we added a gobo over the lens. It was important because the more we aimed the light toward the camera, the greater was the possibility that we would produce serious camera flare.

HOW MUCH TONAL VARIATION IS IDEAL?

We have told you that a box with three visible sides needs to have a highlight side, a shadow side, and a side whose tone is between those two. Nowhere have we said how bright the highlight must be or how dark the shadow should be. We have not told you this because we cannot. This decision ought to be based on the specific subject.

If, for example, the subject is a simple cube with no important detail on any of its sides, we may choose to make the shadow black and the highlight white. However, if the subject is the package for a product we want to sell, there may be important detail on all sides. This requires keeping the highlight only slightly brighter, and the shadow only slightly darker, than the third side.

Nevertheless, we do not want to simply leave you with the vague reminder to base the amount of tonal variation on the subject. Instead, we will amplify the principle with two more general three-dimensional examples: architecture and cylinders. These present a case in which photographers are very likely to want less tonal variation, and another in which we tend to prefer more variation.

Photographing Buildings: Decreasing Tonal Variation

Most of the examples that we have included in this chapter are of relatively small objects. Figure 5.15 is quite a departure from this trend. It is a building. However, even though it is huge in comparison with the other subjects that we have shown in this chapter, it shares many problems with them.

► *This building is the same basic shape as the other boxes shown in this chapter. The sun was in a position to produce relatively even illumination. (Copyright 1990 by Dan Cunningham.)*

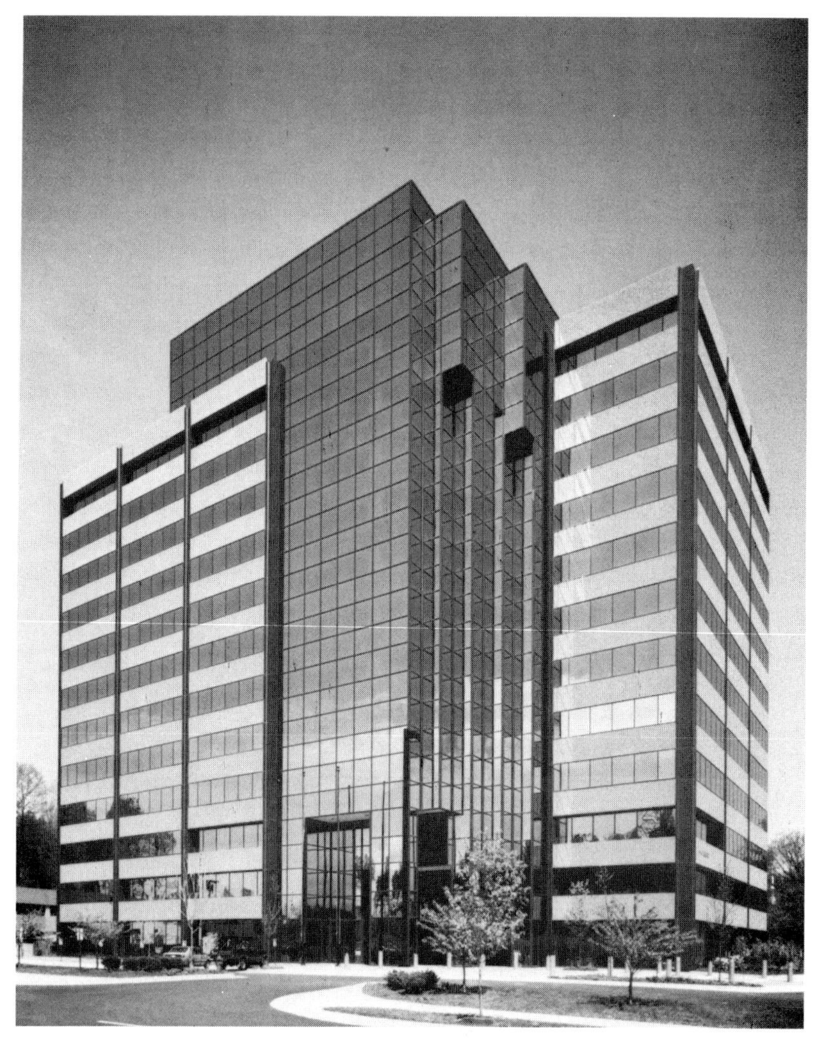

5.15

The building in this picture is the same basic shape as the earlier subjects. They are all three-dimensional objects. They are all boxes. With this in mind, the same techniques apply as well to photographing a building as to making a picture of a brick. Both cases need those visual clues that add the illusion of depth.

However, we have to add some special considerations. The first of these is that we are likely to prefer a smaller light source. This does not suggest that buildings do not photograph beautifully on an overcast day. The opposite is true. But architectural photography almost always includes the sky. Furthermore, clean blue skies usually make more pleasing architectural backgrounds than dingy gray ones, and such a sky probably has a hard, undiffused sun in it.

Choosing a day with harder light has further implications about where we "position" that light. The harder shadow is more visible and, hence, more likely to compete with other detail. The undiffused sunlight also causes brighter highlights and darker shadows. Unfortunately, such highlight and shadow is more likely to obscure details.

Because of the need to minimize shadows to increase the legibility of the architectural detail, many photographers prefer to take pictures that are lit much like that shown in Figure 5.15. They like to work with the sun behind them, slightly to the side that the building faces, and low in the sky. Not only does such lighting produce a less distracting shadow, but because it occurs just after sunrise or just before sunset, such sunlight often warms the color pleasingly.

We know that less tonal variation produces less sense of depth. But remember also that more perspective distortion increases the depth illusion. So as we opt for more even illumination, we are also likely to locate the camera relatively closer to the subject. (Architectural photographers tend to use shorter focal-length lenses to make this possible.) The consequent increase in perspective distortion regains some of the lost depth.

Photographing Cylinders: Increasing Tonal Variation

So far in this chapter, all the examples that we have shown have been rectangular. We did this to make the three-dimensional considerations more apparent. It is easy to see length, width, and depth in the three visible faces of a box. Now we are going to look at a cylinder and the special problems that it presents.

Figure 5.16 is a cylindrical object, but the tonal variation does not reveal the shape very well. Because the lighting is so even across the entire surface of the wooden doll, it is difficult to tell whether the object is three dimensional or not. There are not enough visual clues in the photograph for our brains to make an informed decision.

► *This subject is basically cylindrical, but the flat lighting does not give enough visual clues to show it.*

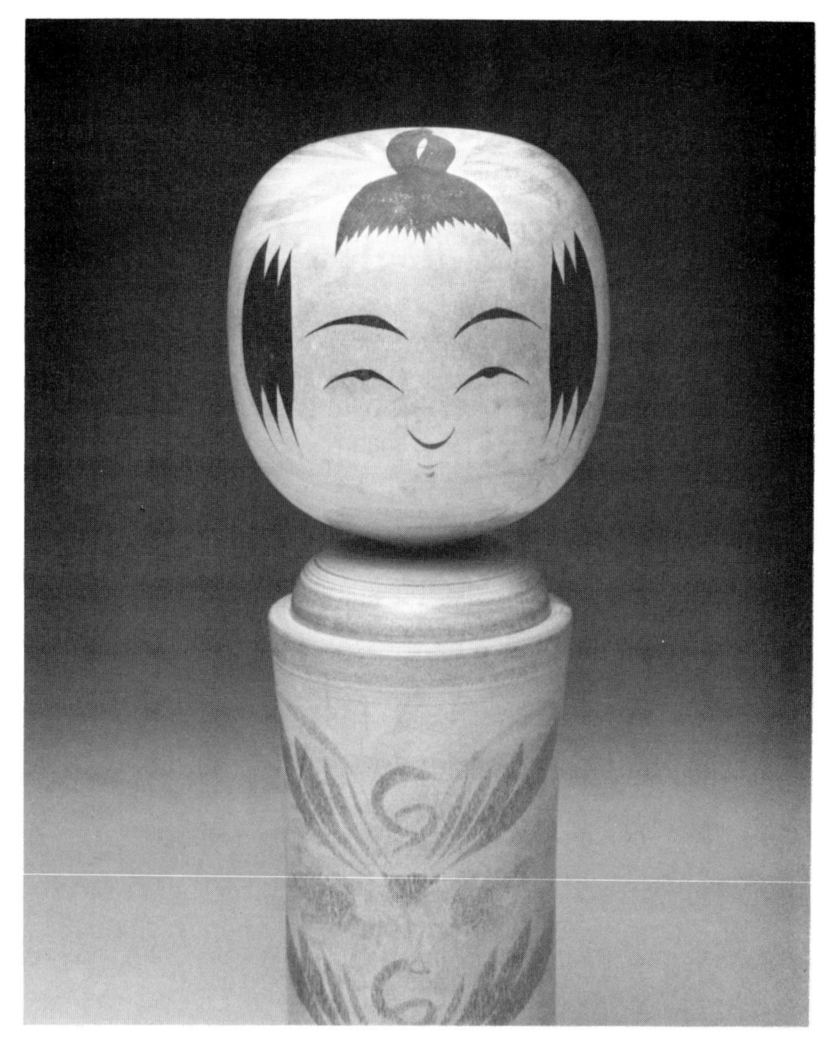

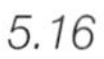

5.16

The problem is caused by the fact that the "sides" of the cylinder are not separated by any clearly defined edge. The shadow blends so gradually into the highlight that some of the dimensional distinction is lost. The solution to this problem is to build more tonal variation into the scene. Cylinders usually need a brighter highlight side or a darker shadow side than boxes do. Figure 5.17 shows what happens when we modify the lighting to achieve this.

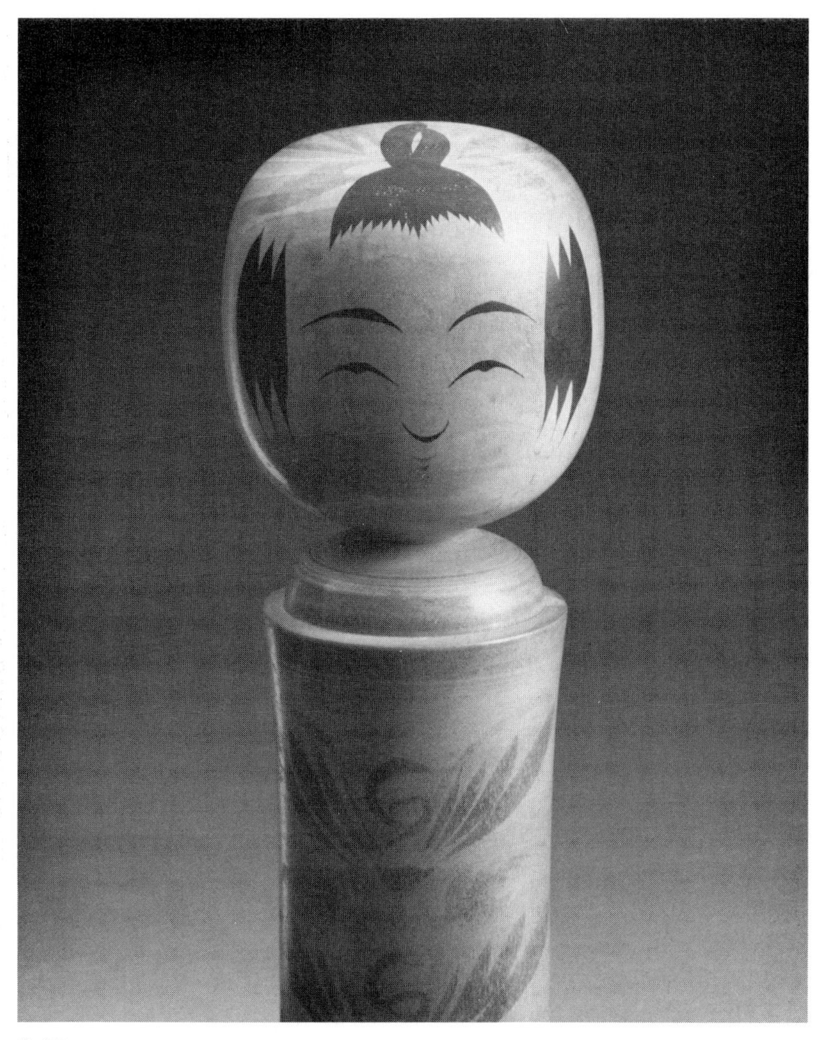

◀ *Lighting the doll from the side gives pronounced tonal variation - just the clue that the brain needs to perceive depth.*

5.17

There are two good ways to obtain this increased tonal distinction. One is to keep the basic lighting similar to that in our box examples but to use a brighter reflector on one side. Then we use no reflector or, if necessary, a black card on the other side.

We could also produce Figure 5.17 by putting our main light beside instead of above the subject. By lighting one side of the cylinder more than the other, enough variation from highlight to shadow supplies the illusion of depth.

Unfortunately, placing the light to one side of the subject creates a potential problem. The shadow of the subject falls on the table surface beside it. As we saw earlier, the shadow is least likely to become a strong compositional element if it falls at the bottom of the picture, under the subject.

If we do place our main light to the side of a cylindrical subject, we usually use an even larger light source. This further softens the shadow and makes it less likely to compete for attention.

THE GLOSSY BOX

In Chapter 4 we saw that good lighting requires distinguishing between diffuse and direct reflection and making an informed decision about which we are going to use. Everything we said about lighting a simple, flat surface applies equally to the group of surfaces that make a three-dimensional object.

In this chapter we have discussed perspective distortion, light direction, and light size. These all determine whether the camera can see a light source within the family of angles that produces direct reflection. Now we are going to talk about some of the special techniques that are helpful when photographing a glossy box.

Look at Figure 5.18, a diagram showing a glossy box. Notice that it shows the family of angles that produce direct reflection from two of its sides. We know that each visible side of a box has a similar family of angles. (Most camera viewpoints require photographers to deal with three families of angles, but it is easier to see these families of angles if we diagram them for only the top and front.)

► *Here are two of the families of angles with which we must contend when shooting a box. A light source in either of them will produce direct reflection.*

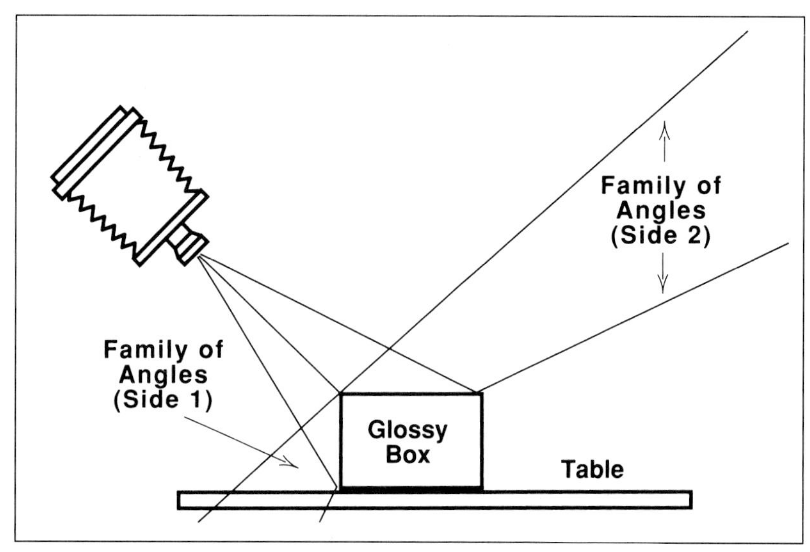

5.18

To light a glossy box, our first decision must be whether to produce direct reflection or to avoid it. Remember that any light source within the indicated families of angles will cause a direct reflection, but a source outside those families cannot.

Figure 5.19 is a glossy box whose detail is all but completely obscured by direct reflection. We should be able to remedy the loss of detail by keeping light sources out of the family of angles that produces such reflection. The following is a series of steps that can accomplish this.

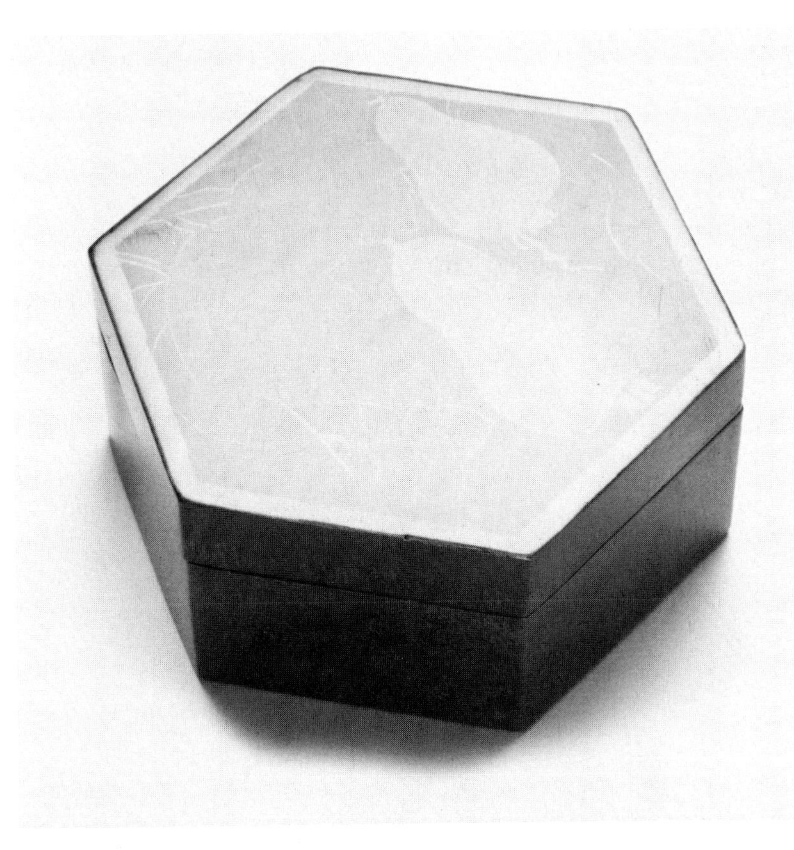

5.19

◀ *Details on the top of the box are all but completely obscured by direct reflection. We could remedy this by keeping light sources out of the family of angles producing that reflection.*

1. Use a Dark Background. First, use a dark background if possible. As you can see from Figure 5.18, one of the ways in which glare-producing light gets to the subject is by reflecting from the background. Light from the tabletop can cause direct reflection on the sides of the box. If we are using a sweep, light from its upper part can reflect on the box top. The darker that background is, the less light reflects from it. This step alone may be adequate for some subjects.

Sometimes you may not want a dark background. On other occasions, you will find that light that produces direct reflection comes from some place other than the background. In either case, the next step is the same: Find the light creating the direct reflection and get rid of it.

In the examples that follow we deal with the family of angles defined by the top of the box with one set of techniques. We then use another, slightly different procedure for the families of angles associated with the sides.

2. Eliminate Direct Reflection from the Box Top. There are three effective ways of eliminating direct reflection from the box top. We can use one, or we can use a combination of them, according to the other requirements of the picture.

Move the Light Source Toward the Camera. If the camera is high, then an overhead light can reflect in the top of the box. This is particularly true of a bank light. Such a light is so large that at least a part of it is very likely to be within the family of angles. This causes direct reflection to be brighter and worse than if a light background reflects in the top of the box. One remedy is to move the banklight toward the camera. Doing so in Figure 5.20 clearly reveals the detail on the box top.

► Here are some of the different ways to eliminate direct reflections from the box top. You can use any one or a combination of them.

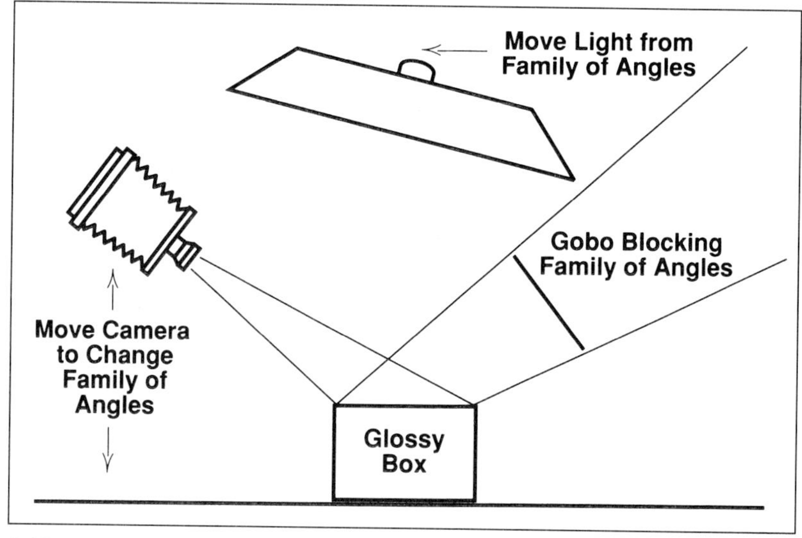

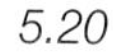

5.20

Raise or Lower the Camera. Moving the camera also changes the family of angles. If an overhead light source reflects in the box top, lowering the camera moves the family of angles so that the light is no longer in it. If the top of a sweep is reflecting in the top of the box, raising the camera causes the studio area above and behind the background to reflect instead. Fortunately, it is usually a simple matter to keep that part of the studio dark.

Use Falloff. If it is not possible to use a dark background, we may at least be able to darken that part of the background that causes direct reflection on the top of the box. Falloff accomplishes this. Keep as much light as you can from the background. The less light hitting the box surface, the less that will reflect from it.

3. Eliminate Direct Reflection from the Box Sides. It is relatively simple to get rid of most of the direct reflection from the top of a glossy box. Things get more difficult when we start trying to eliminate it from the sides. In Figure 5.21 we have turned the box top on edge to show an exaggerated example of the problem that can occur on the sides of the box.

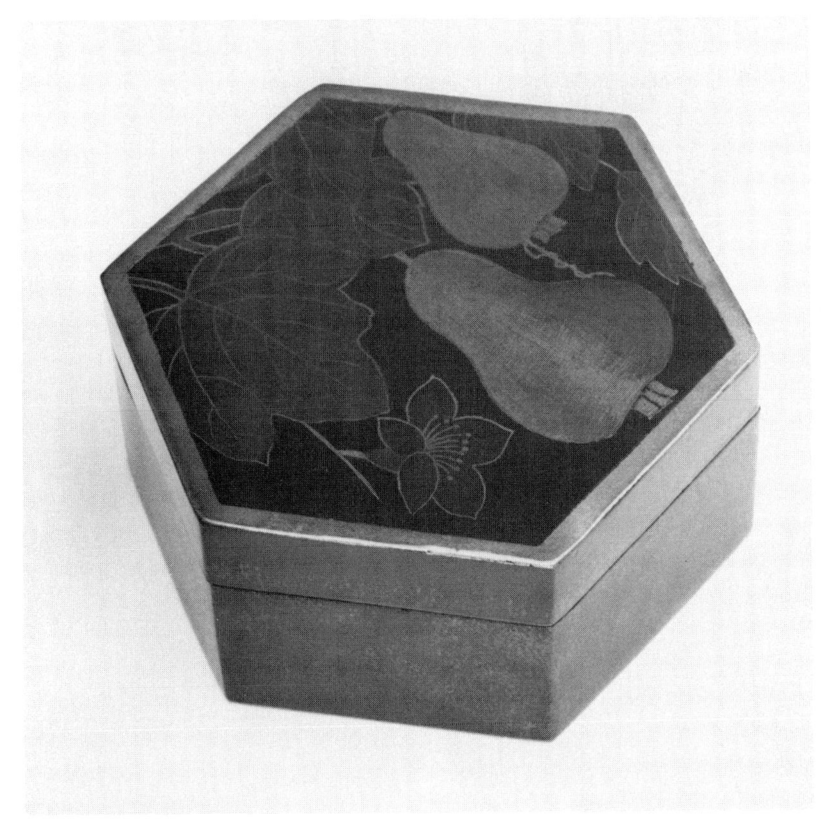

5.21

◀ *Here we see the results of moving the bank light forward. The detail on the box top is now clearly visible.*

From most viewpoints, the box reflects the background on which it sits, and we cannot eliminate that part of the background because it is in the picture. In addition, we usually cannot use falloff because the surface is lit by the same source as the subject. The result of all this is that we usually need the cumulative effect of more than one of the following techniques to produce a satisfactory picture.

Put a Black Card on the Tabletop. This will darken part of the surface and eliminate direct reflection from part of the subject. Figure 5.22 shows how we applied this technique to our earlier subject, and Figure 5.23 shows the result.

► *Here we have turned the box top to the side to show glare coming from another family of angles. It is usually more difficult to get rid of unwanted reflections from those angles.*

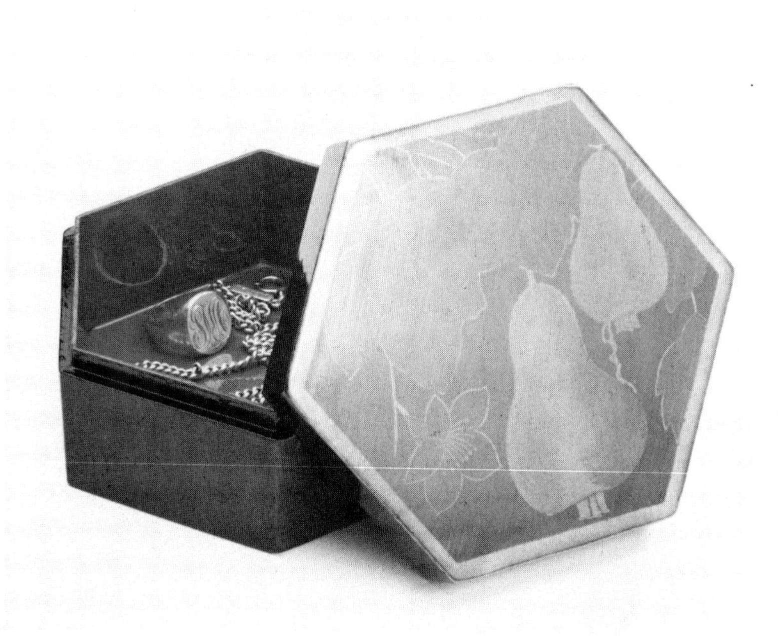

5.22

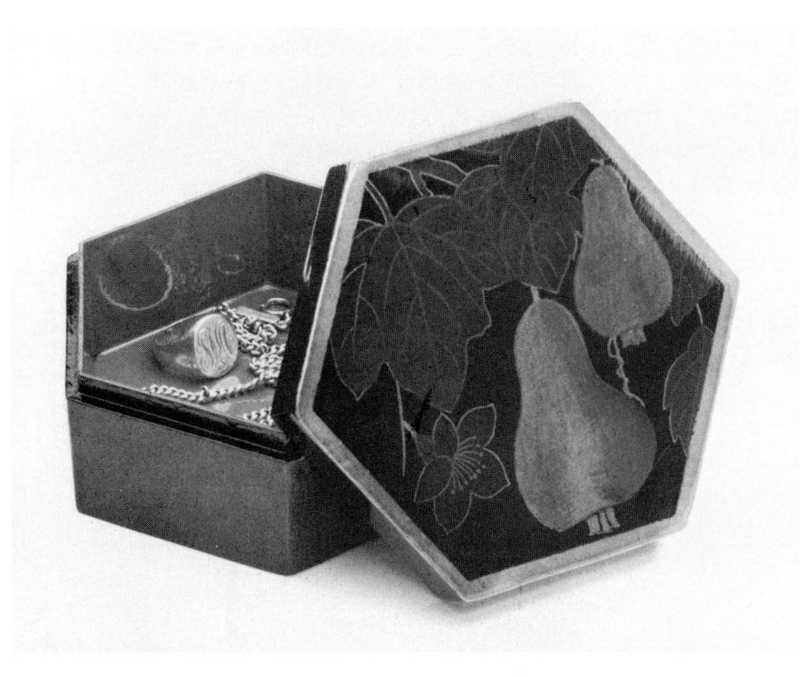

◀ *Using a dark card to the right of the box gets rid of unwanted direct reflections on its side and restores detail.*

5.23

This is a particularly useful technique when we want to eliminate some direct reflections but not others. For example, direct reflection can obscure the plastic dial on a stereo receiver while at the same time making the aluminum face plate look bright and clean. In such cases, cutting the black card to fit just the family of angles that produces direct reflection on the plastic can solve one problem without creating another.

If you look again at Figure 5.18, you will see that if the box side is perfectly vertical, the black card cannot fill all of the family of angles unless it is close enough to touch the bottom of the subject. Nevertheless, getting the card as close as possible without intruding into the image area is often a good start before going on to the next technique.

Tip the Box. Sometimes you can remove a good bit of the offending glare by tipping up the front of the box. The suitability of this tactic depends on the shape of the subject. For example, subjects like computers and kitchen appliances often sit on their own small feet a small height above the table top. Hiding a small support in the shadow under such a subject is simple. Once the camera is tilted to make the subject appear level, the trickery is undetectable.

If the box is supposed to be flush on the tabletop, it is easier for the camera to see that the box is not level. We may be able to tilt the box less, or not at all. Even a slight tilt can be helpful, however, especially along with the following technique.

Use a Longer Lens. There are times when a longer lens can come to the rescue. Figure 5.24 shows how a longer lens allows placing the camera farther from the subject. As we see, the family of angles is smaller than it was in Figure 5.18. This means less of the tabletop reflects in the subject.

▶ *Using a long lens sometimes helps to get rid of unwanted reflections. Comparing the more distant viewpoint in this diagram with that in Figure 5.18 shows that the farther we move the camera, the smaller the family of angles gets.*

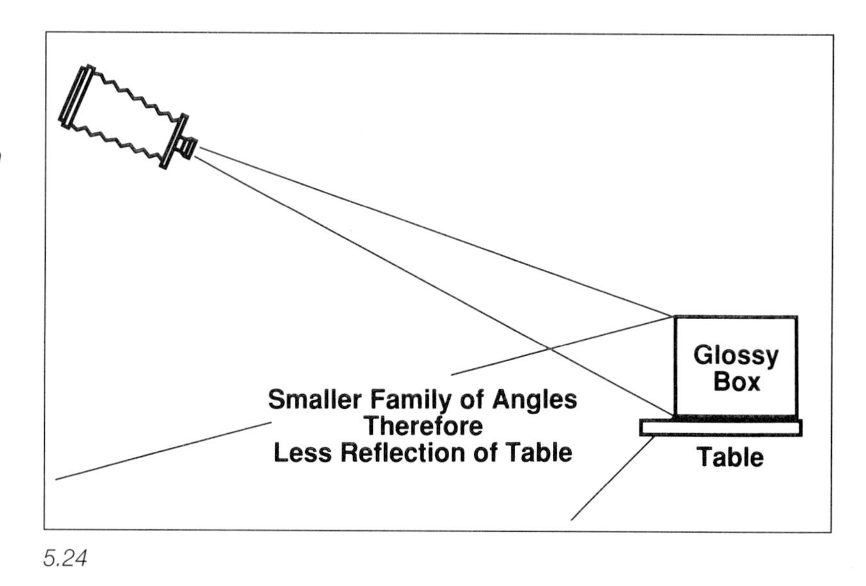

5.24

4. Finish with Other Resources. If there is still some direct reflection obscuring detail, the following techniques can eliminate it completely.

Try a Polarizer. If the direct reflection is polarized, a lens polarizing filter will get rid of it. We suggested this as one of the first remedies to try for the competing surfaces in the last chapter.

If, however, the subject is a glossy box, we more often save the polarizer as a next-to-last resort. The glossy box usually has polarized reflection on more than one side. Unfortunately, the reflection from one side is likely to be polarized in a direction perpendicular to the polarization of the other side. This means that as the polarizing filter eliminates one polarized reflection, it effectively increases another.

Therefore, we first try the preceding steps. Then, whatever direct reflection is left is that which is the most difficult thing to eliminate. Then we use the polarizer to reduce that reflection. If the other remedies have been successful, the slightly increased direct reflection on the other sides will not be any trouble.

Use Dulling Spray. Yes, there are times when the dragon wins! There are times when Mother Nature, physics, and viewpoint produce reflections that cannot be eliminated with any of the techniques we have described. Then we use dulling spray. It may make an otherwise unacceptable picture work.

Be aware, however, that dulling spray can reduce the sharpness of the very detail you are trying to preserve. If that detail happens to be fine type or the like, the loss of sharpness may be more damaging than a loss of contrast caused by direct reflection.

USE DIRECT REFLECTION?

We chose the preceding example to be one in which direct reflection is obviously offensive. But if direct reflection does not obscure detail, we are usually more likely to try to maximize it, rather than to avoid it. After all, if direct reflection is essential to the surface, capitalizing on that reflection produces an image of the subject that looks as much like the real thing as possible. We will discuss the specific technique in the next chapter: Metal.

Chapter 6

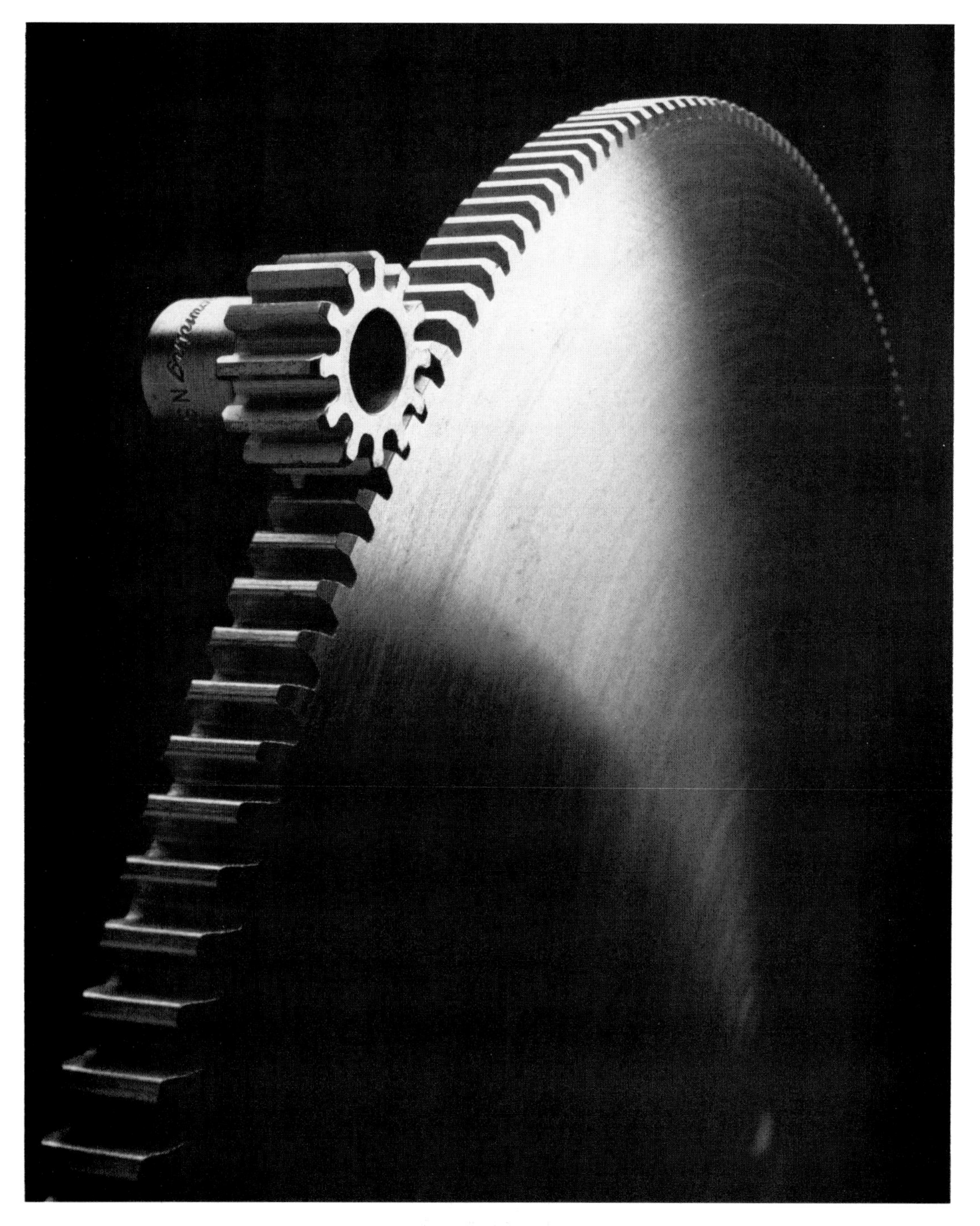

Metal

Many student and apprentice photographers think metal is one of the most difficult photographic subjects and consider such assignments to be nothing less than cruel and unusual punishment. However, when they master the assignment, they discover that nothing could be further from the truth. Metal is not difficult, and teachers have slightly less than sadistic motives when they require such work.

There are about a half-dozen classic subjects that all photographers are supposed to encounter as they learn lighting. These subjects teach basic techniques that enable us to light anything. Metal is one of the classic subjects for good reason. Brightly polished metal produces almost nothing but unpolarized direct reflection. This constancy makes metal a real joy to photograph. It is predictable. It plays by the rules. We can tell before we begin to light the scene where and how big the light needs to be.

On those rare occasions when it is impossible to position the light source where it needs to be to light the picture well, we can also see the problem early in the process. We seldom invest a lot of time, only to find that what we are attempting cannot be done and that we have to start the lighting arrangement over from the beginning.

Additionally, because the direct reflection in metal is largely uncontaminated by other types of reflection, it is easy to see how such reflection behaves. Therefore, learning to photograph polished metal helps to give one the capability to see and to manage direct reflection whenever and wherever it occurs, even when other kinds of reflections compete in the same scene.

We will introduce new concepts and techniques in this chapter. The most important subject matter is the simplest: flat, brightly polished metal. A flat piece of metal, without any other objects in the scene, is easy to light, even without much thought or understanding of the relevant principles. But such simple subject matter can demonstrate the most sophisticated techniques—techniques that can eventually make even the most difficult assignments possible.

Much of what follows is based on the family of angles that causes direct reflection. We introduced this family in Chapter 3. We have used the concept in each succeeding chapter, but in none of them was it as vital as it becomes when dealing with metal.

Brightly polished metal acts like a mirror: It reflects whatever is around it. This mirror-like quality means that when we photograph metal, we do not make a picture of just the metal itself. We *also* make a picture of its surrounding, or environment, as it is reflected in the metal.

The ability of metal to reflect its surroundings means that we have to prepare a suitable environment before we photograph it. To do this we must analyze the family of angles that produces direct reflection from the particular piece of metal with which we are working.

We know that direct reflection can only be produced by a light source that is within a limited family of angles, relative to the subject and to the camera. Since the metal reflects its environment, it makes sense that the smaller that family of angles is, the less of the environment we have to worry about. A small piece of flat metal has only a small family of angles from which direct reflection can be produced. This makes such a piece of metal the simplest example we can use to talk about the general principles of lighting any metal.

FLAT METAL

We have talked about the basic principles of direct reflection in earlier chapters. Since almost all reflection from bright metal is direct reflection, we will reexamine the same principles in more detail.

Figure 6.1 is a diagram of a piece of flat metal and a camera. Note that the camera position is essential in any lighting diagram involving metal. This is because the family of angles depends on the position of the camera relative to the subject. Therefore, the relationship between the camera and the subject is at least as important as the subject itself. We know that direct reflection can only be produced by a light located within the limited family of angles shown here.

► *The family of angles that produces direct reflection depends on the position of the camera relative to the subject.*

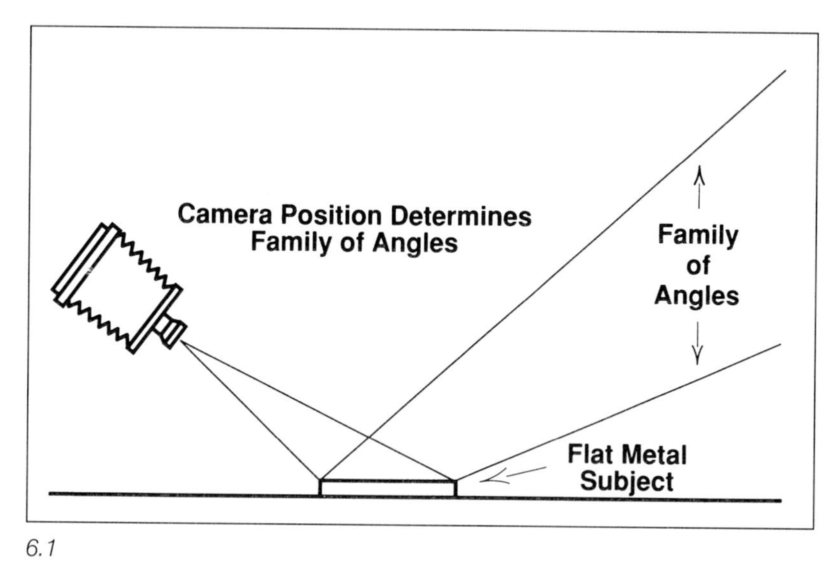

6.1

Bright or Dark?

One of the first decisions that we have to make when we photograph a piece of metal is how bright we want it to be. Do we want it to be bright, dark, or something in between? The answer to this question determines the lighting.

If we want the metal to appear *bright* in the photograph, we make sure our light source *fills* that family of angles that produces direct reflection on the metal. If, on the other hand, we want the metal to be dark in the picture, we put the light anywhere else. The first step in lighting metal is to find that family of angles. After that, the task is straightforward.

Finding the Family of Angles

Practice makes it easy to anticipate where the family of angles will be. Experienced photographers usually get the light so close to the ideal position on the first try that only minor adjustment needs to be made after the first look in the camera. However, if you are new at this type of work, or if you are a veteran photographer photographing the metal from an unusual angle, it can be a bit difficult to visualize where the family of angles exists in space.

We are going to show you a technique that always finds exactly where the family of angles is. You may decide to use it often or you may decide to use it only for more difficult setups, depending on your need. Either way, an abbreviated version of this routine is adequate for most photographs. But if this is the first time you have tried to light metal expertly, it is probably worth trying the entire following sequence of steps at least once as an exercise.

1. Position a White Target where you think the family of angles will be. This white target can be any convenient large surface. The easiest will be whatever large piece of diffusion material you might eventually use to light the metal. Figure 6.2 shows two possible positions where we might suspend a large diffusion sheet over the metal.

► *The possible positions for the test surface in this exercise are also where we might suspend diffusion material if we wished to light the metal brightly.*

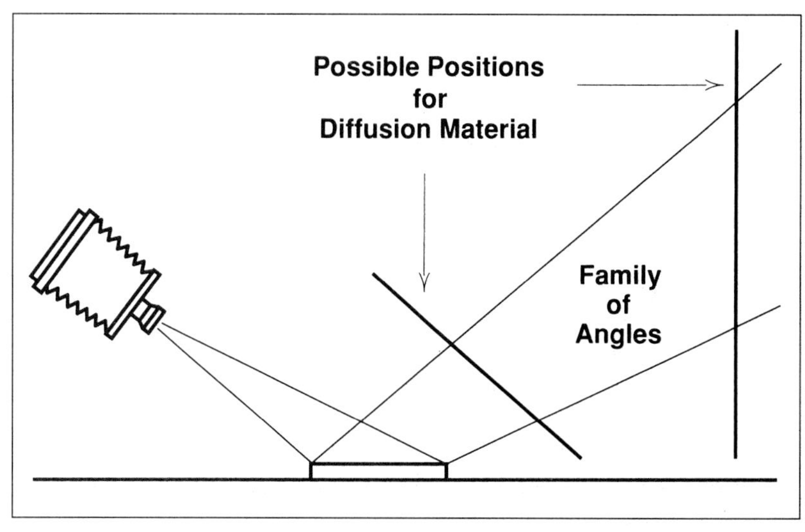

6.2

You do not know exactly where the family of angles is at this point. Use a larger white surface than you think you need to fill those angles. The less sure you are of where the angles are, the bigger the surface needs to be.

2. Place a Test Light at the Camera Lens. We call this a "test" light to distinguish it from whatever light we eventually use to make the picture. The test light needs to have a small enough beam to light the metal without illuminating the surrounding area. A small spotlight is ideal, but a flashlight is adequate if you can keep the room dark.

If you are photographing a small piece of metal from a close working distance, the test light needs to be exactly at the lens position. This may require temporarily removing the camera from the tripod. Alternatively, if the camera is a view camera, you may be able to temporarily remove both the lens and the camera back and aim the test light through the camera. But be careful of this tactic! A photographic light too close to a black camera can quickly heat up the camera enough to cause very expensive damage.

When the camera has a long lens and the distance to the subject is great, it is usually not necessary to place the test light at exactly the lens position. Positioning the light as close to the lens as possible approximates the ideal well enough for more practical purposes.

3. Aim the Test Light at the point on the metal surface that is nearest to the camera. The light will reflect off the metal and onto the test surface. As we see in Figure 6.3, the point at which the beam strikes the test surface marks the near limit of the family of angles. Use a piece of removable tape to mark the spot.

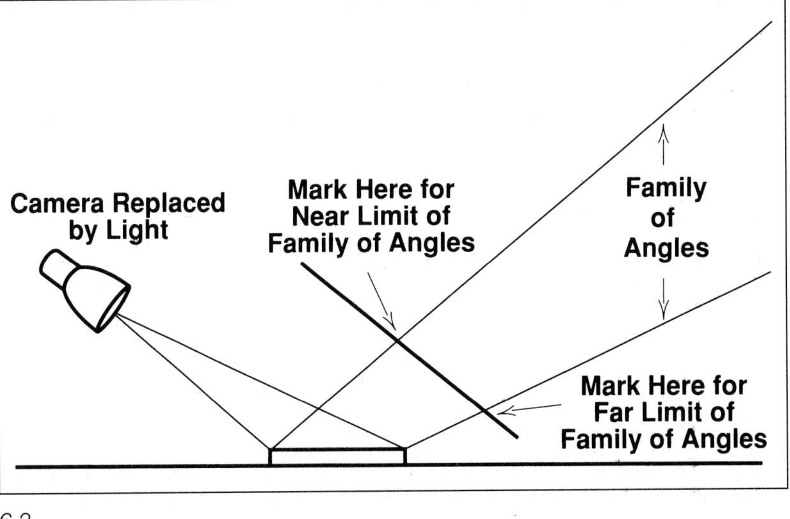

◀ A test light in place of the camera reflects from the metal to show where the family of angles is located.

6.3

If the beam of light is broad enough to cover the entire metal surface, you can leave it in position without moving it for the rest of this exercise.

If, however, the test light illuminates only part of the surface, aim it now at the farthest point on the metal. The light reflected from that point on the metal will strike the test surface at the far limit of the family of angles. Once again, mark the test surface with tape.

Similarly, mark as many points as you need to see where the family of angles lies. The shape of the metal subject determines the necessary number of points. At the least, you will probably decide to mark the left and right limits of the family of angles. If the metal is rectangular, you may decide to mark the points at which the corners reflect light onto the test surface, instead of the edges.

4. Study the Position and Shape of the Area marked on the test surface. You will almost never need either a light source or a gobo that *exactly* fits the family of angles. Nevertheless, this is good practice, so use this opportunity to examine exactly where those angles are. A little extra time invested now will pay back dividends later. Precisely locating the family of angles now will make it quicker to guess its position in a future project without going through this whole measurement procedure again.

Note especially that the point reflecting in the metal edge at the *bottom* of the image corresponds to the limit marked at the *top* of the test surface, and vice versa. Remembering this will make it easy to find the source of glare or hot spots on any type of subject from now on.

The relationships you prove in this exercise apply to other camera and subject orientations. The diagram here represents a side view of a camera photographing a small piece of metal on a table. Of course, it could just as easily be a bird's-eye view of a camera photographing a building with a mirrored glass front. Then the area marked on the test surface might correspond to the portion of the sky reflected in such a building.

Lighting the Metal

Using the foregoing test, experienced judgment, or a combination of the two, we find the family of angles from which a light can produce direct reflection in the metal. Next, we have to decide whether we want the metal to be bright or dark in the picture. This is a critical step because it leads to two exactly opposite lighting setups.

In some photographs, the metal needs to be absolutely white while the rest of the scene is as dark as possible. On other occasions, it might be preferable to render the metal black in an otherwise high-key scene. More often we like to see something between these extremes, but learning to produce the extremes makes the compromise easier to obtain.

Keeping the Metal Bright

Since photographers usually choose to make the metal in their pictures look bright, we will deal with that case first. If we assume that we want the entire surface of the metal to photograph brightly, we then need a light source that *at least* fills the family of angles that produces direct reflection. When we use a light this size, it will produce direct reflections over the entire surface of the subject. These reflections make the subject bright in the picture.

It is worth noting that because polished metal produces almost no diffuse reflection, light coming from any other angle will have practically no effect on the metal, regardless of how bright it is or how long the exposure.

It is also important to realize that a light that just fills the family of angles is the *minimum* light size we can use. Later, we will show you why we routinely use a light larger than the minimum. For now, we will assume that the minimum size is adequate.

Figure 6.4 shows one possible lighting arrangement. We have used a light on a boom above a diffusion sheet and have adjusted the distance from the light head to the diffusion material so that the beam approximately fills the family of angles that we marked earlier.

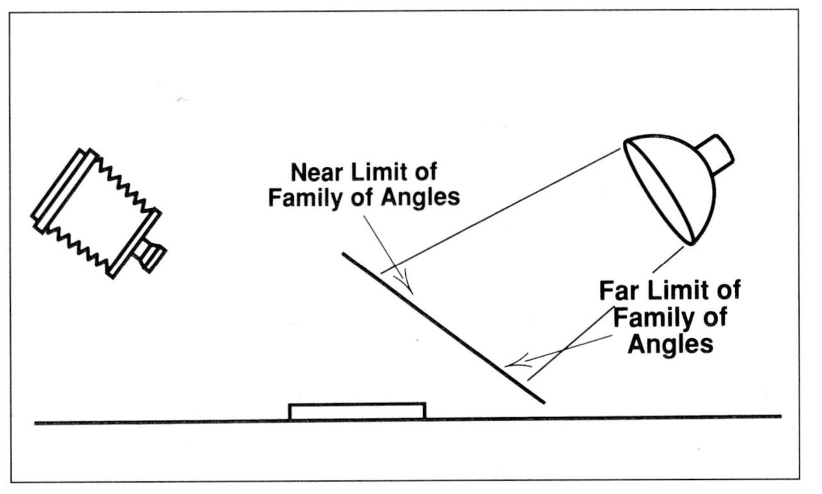

6.4

◀ *The main light positioned so that it fills the family of angles we marked in Figure 6.3.*

We could use an opaque white reflector card instead of the diffusion sheet. Then we would use the alternative lighting shown in Figure 6.5. A spotlight near the camera, with the beam of the light focused to approximately fill the family of angles, would light the subject identically to the light through the diffusion sheet.

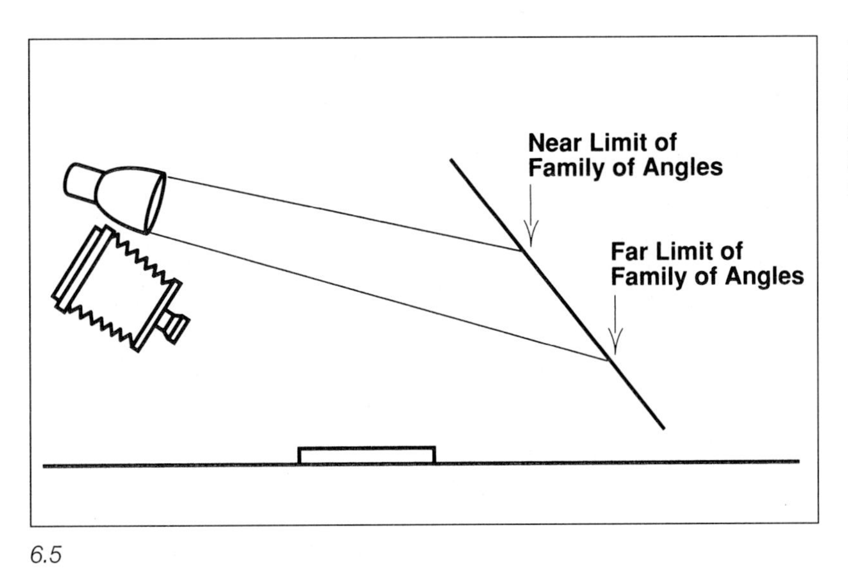

6.5

◀ *An alternative to the lighting shown in Figure 6.4 uses an opaque white reflector card and a spotlight focused to fill the family of angles.*

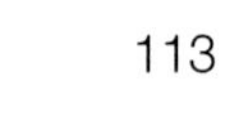

Most soft box arrangements do not allow adjustment of distance of the head to the diffusion material on the front. The light is fixed inside the box to illuminate the entire front of the box as evenly as possible. However, we can achieve a similar effect by attaching black cards to the front of the soft box to regulate its effective size, as shown in Figure 6.6.

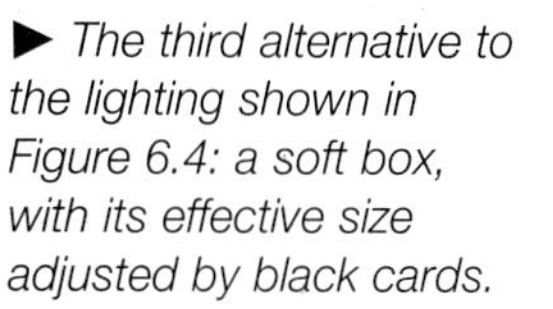

► *The third alternative to the lighting shown in Figure 6.4: a soft box, with its effective size adjusted by black cards.*

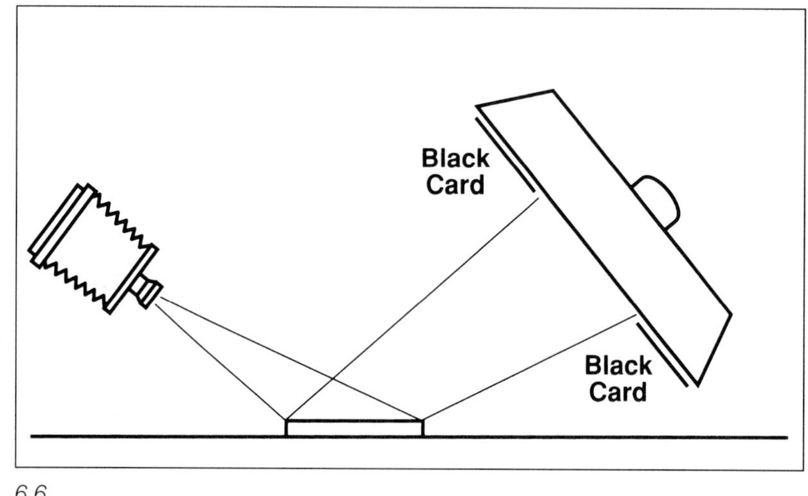

6.6

We used the first of these three alternatives to photograph a brightly polished metal spatula on a white paper background. Figure 6.7 is the result.

► *The bright metal spatula blade is placed against a white background. Do you know why the background is so dark?*

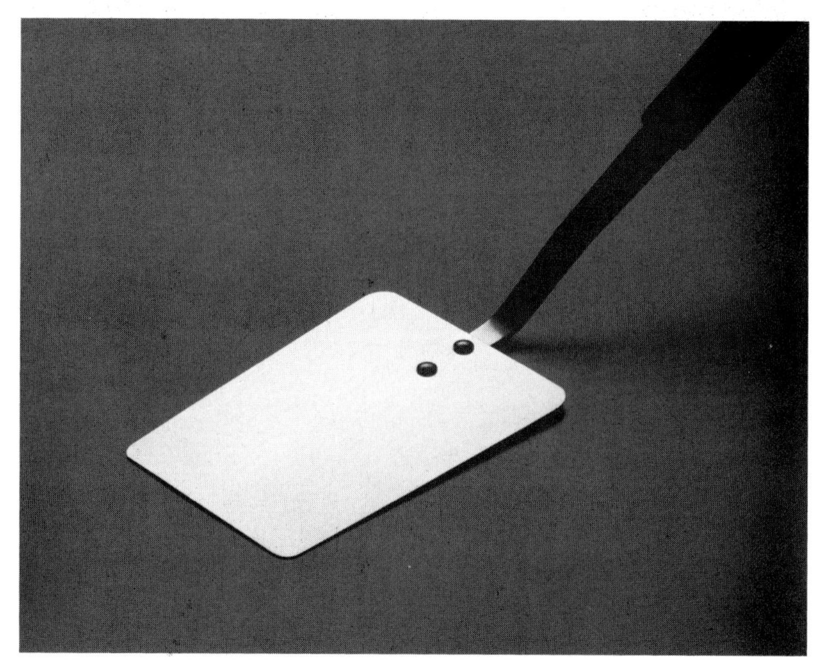

6.7

As we expected, the metal is a pleasing light gray. If you have never lit a scene this way, you might not have expected the photograph to render the "white" background so dark! This is a necessary consequence of the lighting. The exposure is "normal" for this scene.

What Is a "Normal" Exposure for Metal?

Since the metal was the important subject matter in Figure 6.7, we exposed to get it right and ignored the background. How might we expose the metal to "get it right"? One good way is a spot meter reading on the metal, remembering to expose two to three stops more than the meter indicates. The meter tells us how to expose the metal to be an eighteen-percent gray. However, we want it brighter than that. Just *how much* brighter is a creative decision, not a purely technical one. Two to three stops is a reasonable range.

Keep in mind that in the last example, we lit the metal to be as bright as possible without bothering with any other considerations. Since the metal produces almost nothing but direct reflection, its brightness in the image approximates that of the light source. A gray card reading of the scene cannot produce an acceptable exposure *if the metal is the important subject*. The rule of thumb that tells us to place the middle grays accurately, letting the extremes fall where they may, fails when the important subject happens to be very much brighter than an eighteen-percent gray card. Thus, the "proper" exposure for this scene renders the white background as a dark gray.

Suppose, however, that the metal is not the only important subject. This could happen even in this simple scene. There are no other important objects here, but the white background could be critical in an advertisement requiring legible black type in the image area.

In that case, a gray card reading would give an excellent exposure of the white background, but at the expense of hopelessly overexposed metal. There is, unfortunately, no "normal" exposure that works for both. If the metal and the white paper are both important, we have to relight the scene. We will soon see several ways to do so.

Keeping the Metal Dark

In the previous section we talked about how to photograph metal to appear bright. Now we will relight the scene to keep the metal as dark as we can. In principle, nothing could be easier. All we have to do is to light the metal from any direction we please, *other* than from within that limited family of angles that produces direct reflection. One simple way to do this is to put the light near the camera. We will start by showing what happens when we do.

The light position shown in Figure 6.8 is one of many that would work. Note that the same family of angles we determined earlier now marks the positions where we must not place the light if we want to keep the metal dark.

► *This light position is one of the many that would work, if we want to keep the metal dark. The important point is to keep the light outside the family of angles.*

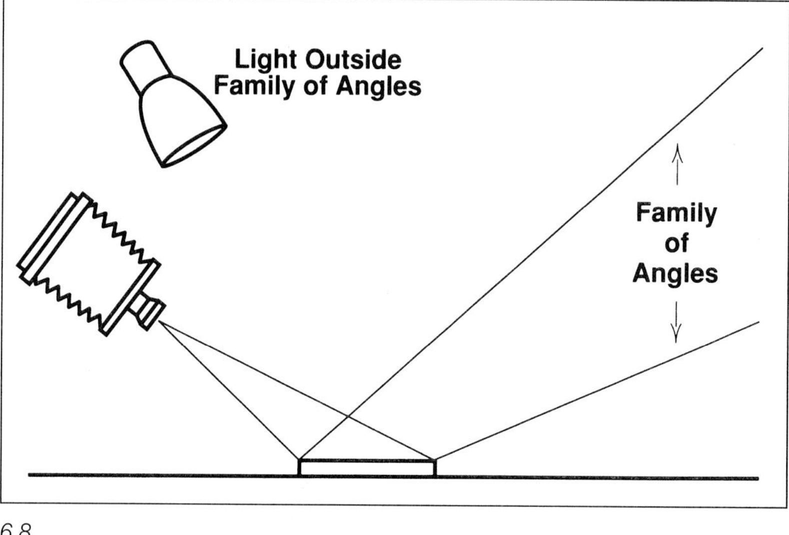

6.8

Although the family of angles is still in the diagram, notice that the white test surface on which it was marked is gone. Had we left it in place, it would have reflected some of the general illumination, behaving as an additional light source.

Figure 6.9 proves the theory. It shows graphically what happens when we place the light source outside the family of angles that produces direct reflections on the metal spatula. The lighting setup in Figure 6.8 can cause only diffuse reflection. Since the metal cannot produce much diffuse reflection, it is black. The paper can produce diffuse reflection from a light from any direction, so it is rendered white.

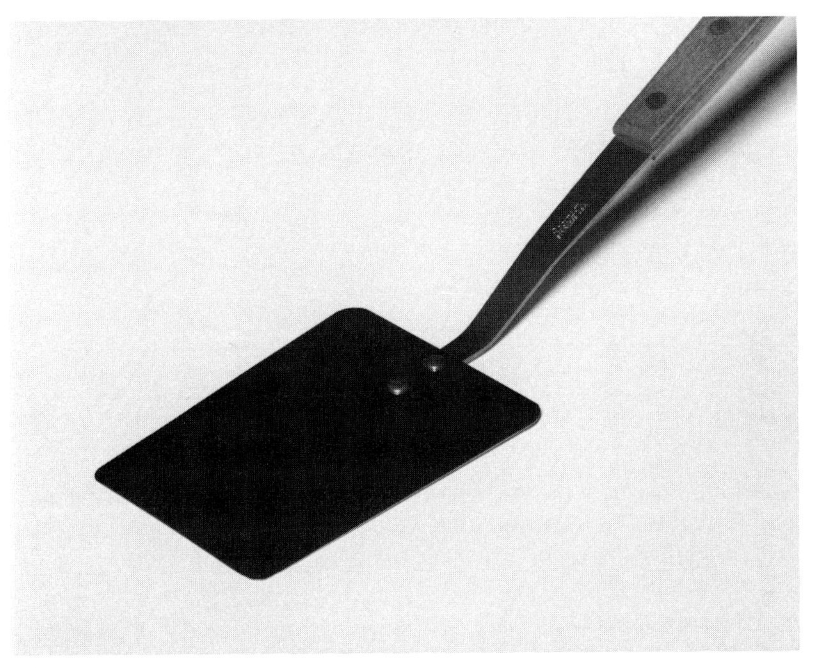

◀ *The light is outside the family of angles reflected by the spatula. With no direct reflections on the metal surface, it is black in our picture.*

6.9

An incident reading, a gray card reading, or a reading of the white paper (with the appropriate compensation) would all be good exposure indicators. This is true of almost any scene with reasonably even illumination and little or no direct reflection. With neither direct reflection nor important dark subjects in shadow, we do not have to think about the extremes. Getting the middle grays exposed properly is all we need to worry about.

We are unlikely to use the lighting in Figure 6.8 as the principal lighting of a scene except to demonstrate the principle. The position and the hardness of the shadow are too displeasing. With that in mind, we will move to a slightly more difficult variation on the same theme. We will keep the metal surface black but remedy the objectionable shadow.

The test target we used to find the family of angles was much larger than the minimum needed to fill those angles. If we light the subject with every point on the surface *except* the marked family of angles, we will have a large, soft source that still keeps the metal black. Figure 6.10 shows how we can accomplish that.

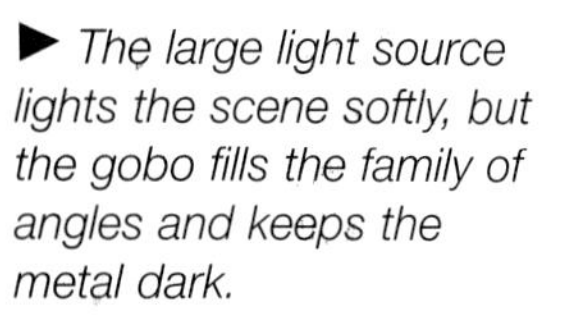

► *The large light source lights the scene softly, but the gobo fills the family of angles and keeps the metal dark.*

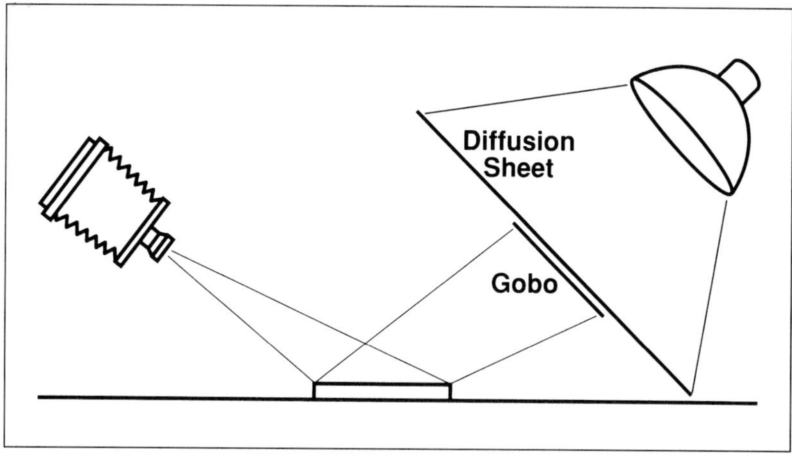

6.10

Notice that we have backed up our light to illuminate the entire diffusion sheet as evenly as possible. Then we have attached a gobo cut to a size and shape that barely fills the family of angles. Figure 6.11 is the result.

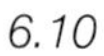

► *We used a gobo to block the family of angles reflected by the metal when we took this shot. This darkened the spatula.*

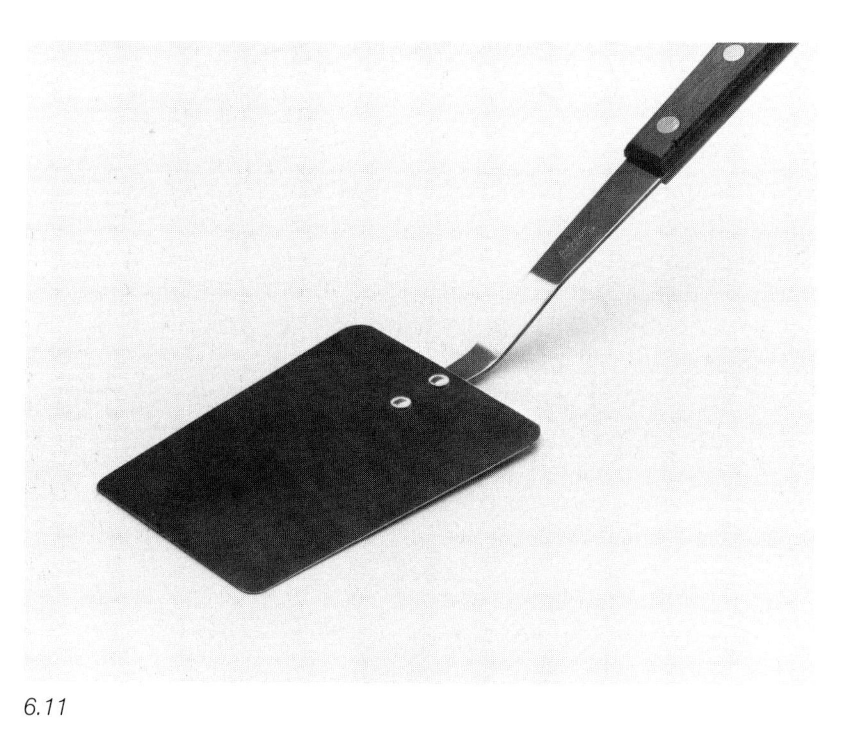

6.11

This technique would also work very well using a soft box instead of a framed diffusion and a light on a boom, but it would be less effective using an opaque white reflector card. The light illuminating the reflector card would also illuminate the gobo brightly. The gobo would behave more like a reflector than a light-blocking device, even though it might be black. Since that black gobo would absorb some photons and reflect others, it would not be a very good way to demonstrate either bright-metal or dark-metal lighting. However, it might be the most pleasing compromise of all.

The Elegant Compromise

We almost never use the bright-metal or the dark-metal lighting techniques by themselves. More often we prefer a combination of the two, a compromise between the extremes.

Figure 6.12 is a compromise. It was made with light filling the family of angles that produces direct reflection from the metal *plus* illumination from other angles to produce diffuse reflection from the background.

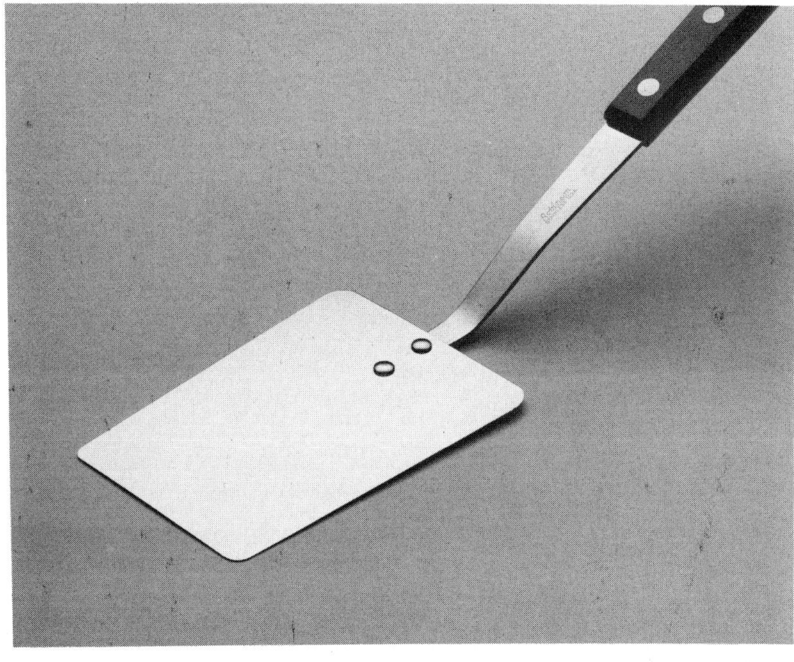

6.12

◀ *An elegant compromise between Figures 6.7 and 6.9. Light fills the family of angles that produces direct reflection from the metal, and light from other angles produces diffuse reflection from the background.*

Figures 6.13, 6.14, and 6.15 show some possible lighting arrangements that could have produced the photograph. Every arrangement uses light from within the family of angles *and* from other directions. We used the lighting in Figure 6.15, but any of them could produce equivalent results. The best way is whatever suits the equipment you have on hand.

► *One way to light the spatula is shown in Figure 6.12. The main light is positioned within the family of angles to produce the large, bright direct reflection on the spatula. The fill light brightens the background.*

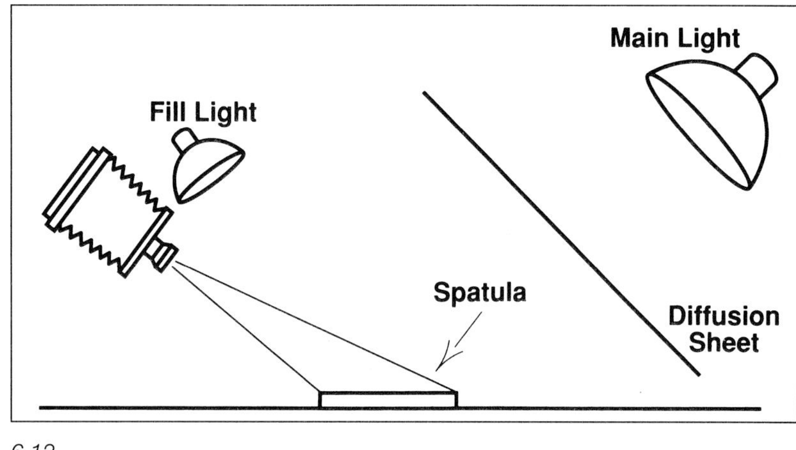

6.13

► *Another way to light the spatula is shown in Figure 6.12. The gobo partly blocks the light from the part of the reflector within the family of angles, marked* **A,** *but not from the rest of the reflector card, marked* **B**.

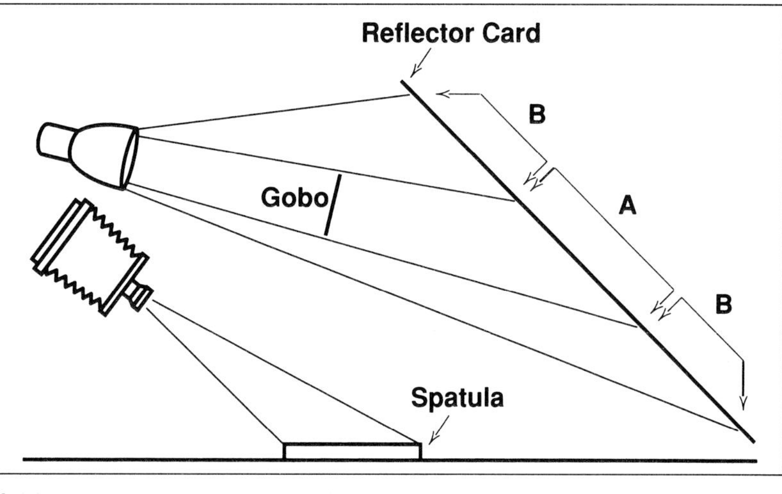

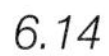
6.14

► *The part of the soft box,* **B,** *outside the family of angles,* **A,** *lights only the background, not the metal.*

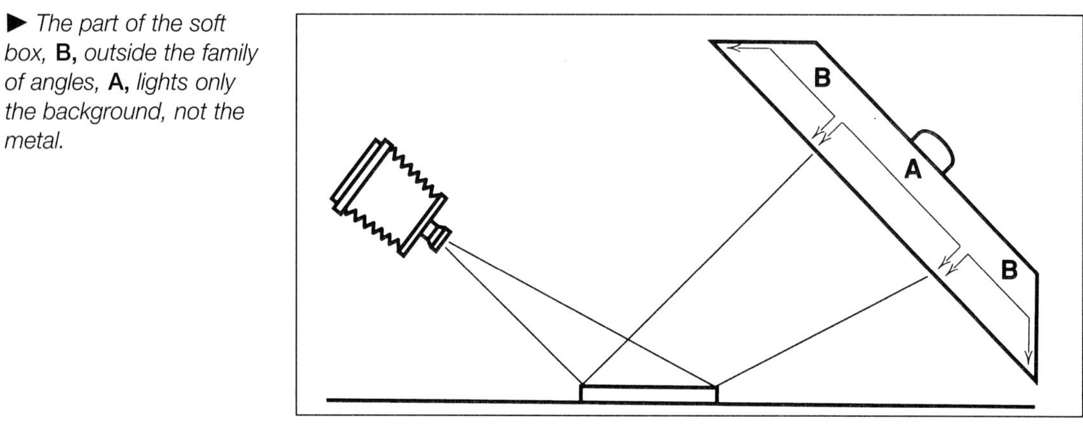

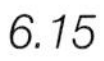
6.15

The most important point behind this demonstration is not that the compromise lighting makes the best picture, but the *thinking* that leads up to the compromise.

We can *decide* exactly where we want to place the metal on the gray scale. The precise tone of the metal is fully controllable, independently of the rest of the scene, and it can be any step between black and white that the photographer's creative judgment determines.

If we had used the lighting in Figure 6.13, for example, we could have made the metal brighter by increasing the power of the light above the diffusion material, or we could have made the paper background brighter with a more powerful fill light near the camera. Using two lights in this manner gives infinite control of the relative brightness of the metal and the background.

Even a single light provides excellent control if it is large enough. Look again at the single soft box in Figure 6.15. Notice that the entire light source produces diffuse reflection from the paper, but only that portion that covers the family of angles produces direct reflection on the metal. Having more of the surface of the soft box within the family of angles makes the metal brighter. However, if the soft box is large enough to have very little of its surface within the family, then the background will be brighter.

The distance between the light source and the subject determines how much of that source will be within the family of angles.

Controlling the Effective Size of the Light

In previous chapters, we have seen that control over the size of the light source is one of the most powerful manipulative tools a photographer has. We have also seen that the physical size does not necessarily determine the effective size. Moving a light closer to the subject makes it behave like a larger one, softening the shadows and, for some subjects, enlarging the highlights. Moving the light farther away does the opposite. This principle is even more significant if the subject is bright metal.

In Figure 6.16 we see the same camera and subject relationships used earlier. Now there are two possible positions for the same soft box. One position is much closer to the subject than that used in the previous example, while the other is much farther away.

► *Two possible positions for a soft box. Either position lights the metal identically. However, the closer we move the light to the subject, the brighter the background becomes.*

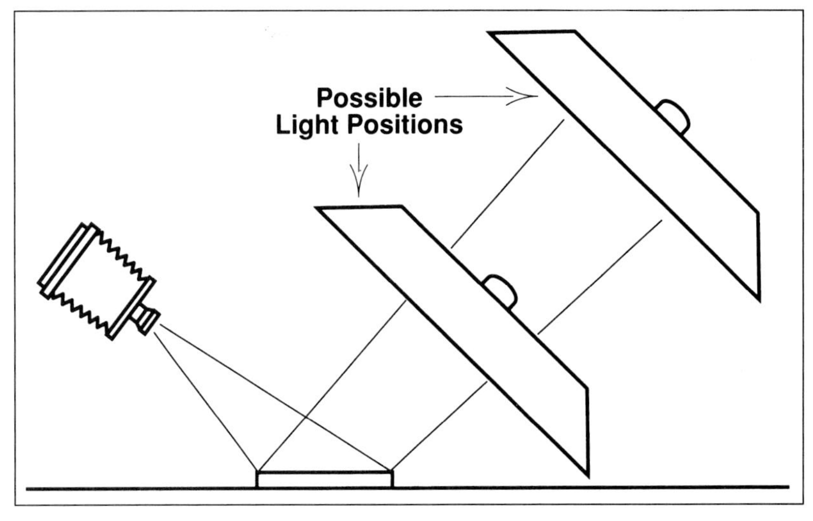

6.16

We expect the closer light to illuminate the background more brightly, but the brightness of the metal should not change because the brightness of the image of direct reflection is not affected by the distance to the source. Figure 6.17 confirms that expectation. Moving the light closer has greatly lightened the background without affecting the brightness of the metal. Compare it with Figure 6.12, made with the same soft box farther away.

► *Compare this photograph with Figure 6.12. Moving the soft box closer has brightened the background, but not the spatula.*

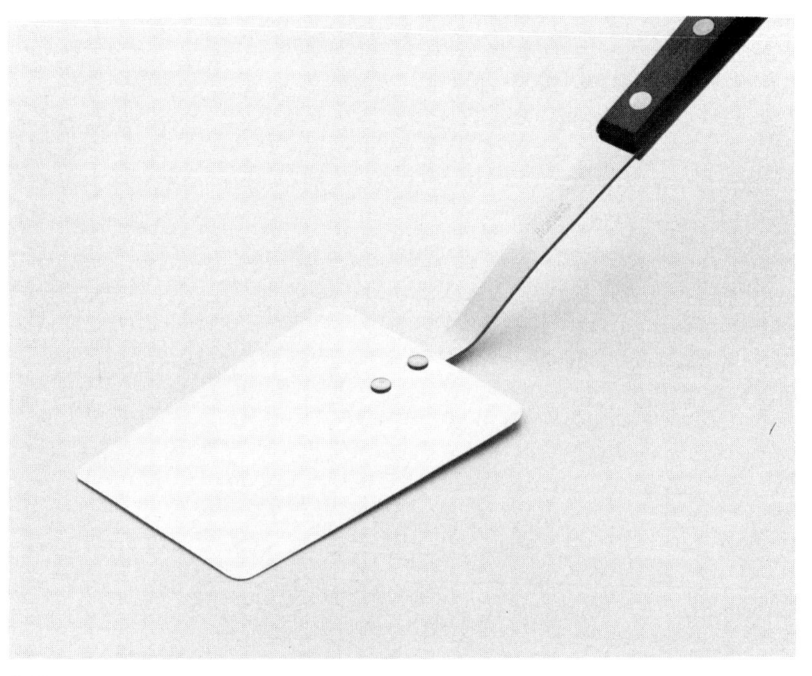

6.17

Similarly, moving the light farther from the subject would darken the background, still without affecting the brightness of the image of the metal.

Changing the distance of the light source changes the brightness of the background, but not of the metal. This seems to give us nearly infinite control of the relative brightness of the two. Sometimes it does, but not always. This is because the focal length of the lens can also indirectly influence the effective size of the light. This is often surprising, even to highly experienced photographers, but the diagrams in Figure 6.18 show how it can happen.

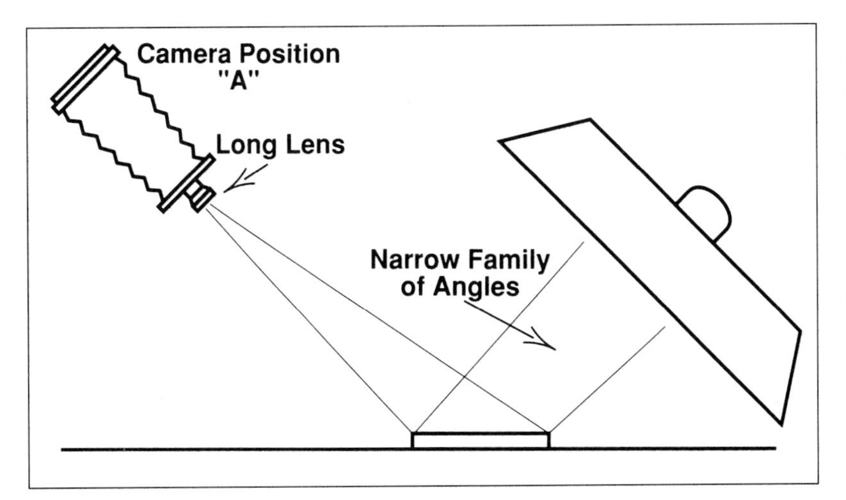

6.18 A

◀ The distance from the subject to the camera affects the effective size of the light. Camera **B** *is close, and the resulting family of angles is large. Camera* **A** *is farther from the subject than* **B,** *and the resulting family of angles is much narrower.*

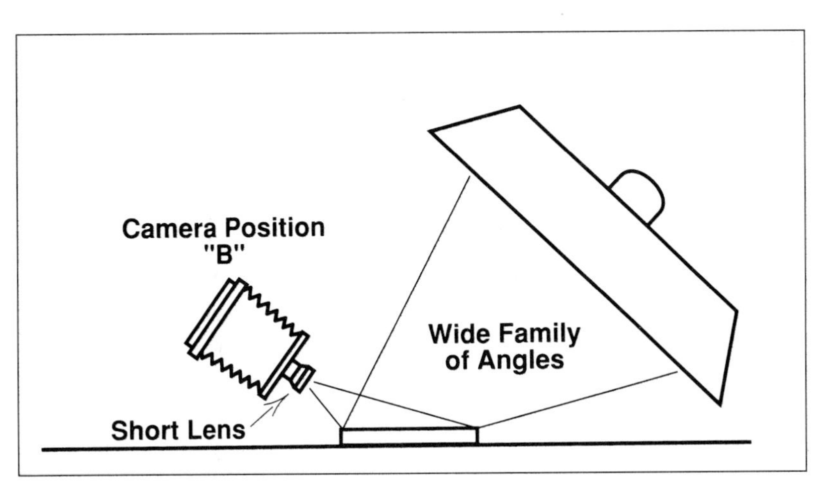

6.18 B

In Figure 6.18 the camera closer to the subject (A) has a short focal-length lens, and the camera farther away (B) has a long lens. Therefore, the image will be the same size in either photograph.

To camera A, farther from the subject, the soft box is much larger than the family of angles that produces direct reflection. We could move the light much closer or much farther away without affecting the lighting of the metal. The longer lens, by allowing a more distant viewpoint, offers a more flexible choice of places to put the light. Thus, it maximizes the control over the relative brightness of the subject and the background.

But look at the difference in the effective size of the light seen by camera B. The soft box just fills the family of angles defined by the close viewpoint. We cannot move the light farther away without the edges of the metal becoming black.

In Chapter 5 we saw that camera viewpoint also determines perspective distortion. Sometimes this is of great creative importance and there is not much choice about where to put the camera. In other scenes, there is a wide range of satisfactory camera positions. In those cases, if the subject is bright metal, we recommend using a longer lens and getting the camera farther away to allow more freedom in lighting.

Keeping the Metal Square

In none of the preceding examples was the camera perpendicular to the metal surface. Sometimes we need a photograph in which the camera viewpoint appears to be perpendicular to the metal and centered directly in front of it. Since the metal is a mirror, the camera is likely to reflect in the subject. Now we will see several ways of dealing with this problem. You will probably use each of them at one time or another, depending on the specific subject and the available equipment.

1. Use a View Camera. This is the best solution. (If everyone used view cameras, we might not even mention any other techniques.) As long as the camera back is parallel to the reflective metal, the metal will appear to be centered in front of the camera to most viewers.

In Figure 6.19, we positioned the camera off center so that it does not reflect in the metal. The film is still parallel to the subject so the viewpoint does not introduce perspective distortion. We then shifted the lens to center the subject in the image area, just as it would be if the camera were directly in front of the subject. Notice that this places the family of angles to one side of the camera.

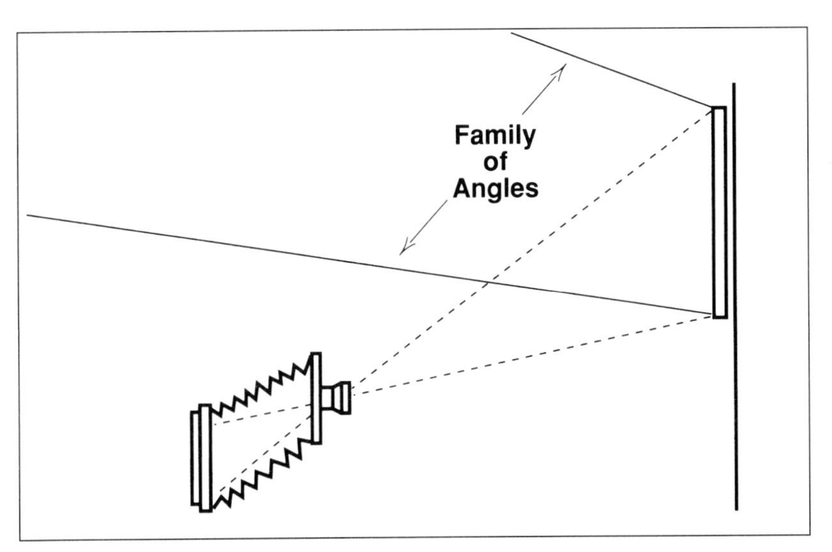

◀ *The camera will not reflect in the metal because it is outside the family of angles. The metal will not be distorted because it is parallel with the film.*

6.19

All lighting tactics discussed earlier are applicable: We use a light large enough to fill the family of angles, keep the light out of the family of angles, or use a combination of the two, depending on how bright we want the metal to appear.

If the camera position requires shifting the lens a great distance off center, we may encounter two special problems. First, the lens may begin to vignette the image. This creates black corners at the edge of the picture. Second, viewing the subject too far off center can produce geometric distortion or reveal the slight distortion that can be present even in good lenses. Keeping the camera as far from the subject as possible, and using a correspondingly longer lens, minimizes both of these problems.

2. Aim the Camera through a Hole in the Light Source. Assuming we want to keep the metal bright, we sometimes position either a diffusion sheet or a reflector card to light the metal. We then cut a hole in that light source that is just large enough for the lens to see through it.

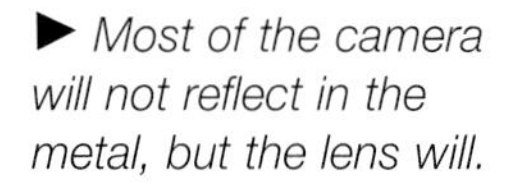
► *Most of the camera will not reflect in the metal, but the lens will.*

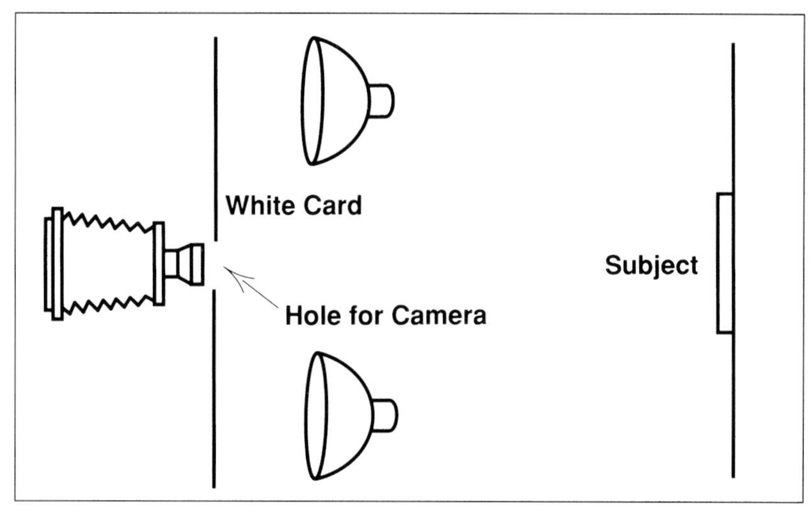

6.20

This solution minimizes the problem of camera reflection, but it does not get rid of it. Although the camera is not visible in the subject, the hole in the light source is. This technique works fine if there is enough irregularity in the metal subject to camouflage the offending reflection. If, for example, the subject is a machine with a complex control panel, reflection may be invisible among the knobs and meters.

Whether the light source is a reflector card or a diffusion sheet, we have to be especially careful in lighting the area near the camera. A light aimed at a reflector card can cause flare if the rays fall directly into the lens. Lights projecting through a diffusion sheet can cause a shadow of the camera on the diffusion sheet that reflects visibly in the subject.

3. Photograph the Metal at an Angle. Keep the camera as far from the subject as possible to minimize perspective distortion. Then correct the distortion in post production.

In theory, we can achieve view camera perspective control by tilting the easel under the enlarger when we make the print. However, most enlargers do not allow tilting the lens to compensate for the print not being parallel with the negative. Keeping the image sharp may not be possible. Furthermore, the extra step makes it impossible to send an original transparency to a color separator.

Digitally removing the distortion may be a better solution, but not an ideal one. Your image editing software may allow no numeric control—only a clumsy "slider"—for this purpose. Furthermore, this is one of the slowest kinds of manipulations for the system process.

Keep these solutions in mind as an available option if circumstances force it upon you. A bad remedy may be better than no remedy. If you use this alternative, be sure to compose your picture with a generous amount of extra space around the subject. You will have to crop the trapezoidal projected image to fit the rectangular print.

4. Retouch the Reflection. Shoot the metal straight on, let the camera reflect, then remove the reflection digitally. This is not a lighting solution, so we will not discuss it in detail. Nevertheless, for some subjects, especially large ones, retouching is so much easier than any of the lighting solutions that we should not forget the option. Spending a half-day lighting instead of an hour at a computer makes no sense.

METAL BOXES

A metal box presents the viewer with up to three visible sides. Each side needs a treatment similar to that of any other flat piece of metal. Each surface has its own family of angles to consider. The difference is that each family of angles faces a different direction and we have to deal with them all at once.

In lighting a metal box, we need to deal with some of the same considerations involved with lighting a glossy box made of any other material. If you are browsing through this book without reading the chapters in sequence, you may want to look at the section on glossy boxes in Chapter 4.

In Figure 6.21 a metal box is positioned so that the camera can see its front and its top. We see that the families of angles are identical to those of the glossy box in Figure 5.18. We may place light within these families of angles, or not, depending on whether we want the surfaces to be bright or dark. If the box were turned to show the camera three sides, the same principles would apply but they would be harder to see in a drawing. The family of angles defined by the front of the box would then fall below *and* to the side of the box. The other visible side of the box would produce a similar family of angles on the other side of the scene.

▶ *Two families of angles of a box positioned so that the camera can see both its top and front.*

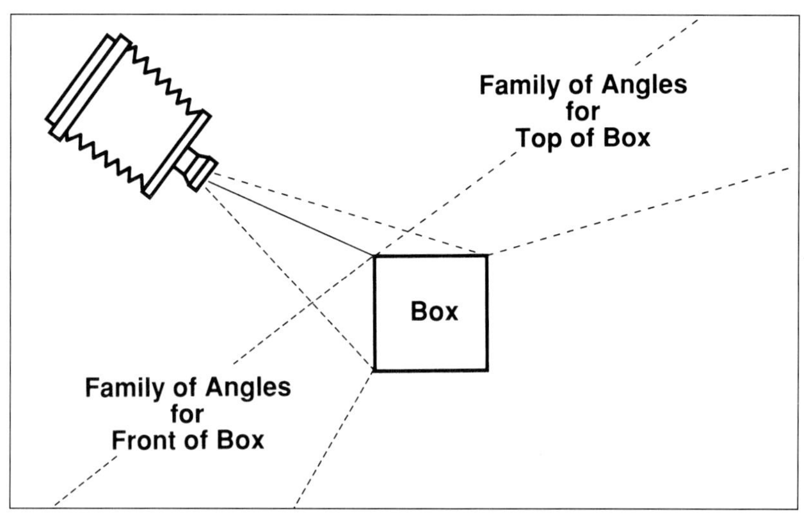

6.21

A glossy nonmetallic box that is not black produces both diffuse and direct reflection. We often avoid direct reflection on a glossy box to avoid obscuring the diffuse reflection. A polished metal box produces only direct reflection. Without direct reflection, we see the metal box as black.

Since we more often like to render metal bright, we usually want to *create* direct reflection rather than to avoid it. This means that we need to fill each family of angles with a light source.

The family of angles defined by the top of the box is easy to light. We treat it just as we did the flat metal in our earlier examples.

The sides of a metal box are more difficult. If we position the camera and subject like Figure 6.21, then at least one of the light sources *must* be in the picture! The family of angles defined by the front of the box falls on the table where the box sits. That means the table surface *is* the light source for the front of the box, whether we like it or not.

We cannot use a reflector card, or any other light source, for the sides of the box without it showing in the scene. The closer to the box we can crop the picture, the closer we can put the reflector. Even so, some of the bottom of the box will still reflect the table.

If we do not want to crop the bottom of the box out of the image, and if the box is truly mirror-like, the line where the reflector meets the table will be visible and objectionable. Figure 6.22 shows the problem. We have left the picture uncropped so that you can see the reflector card.

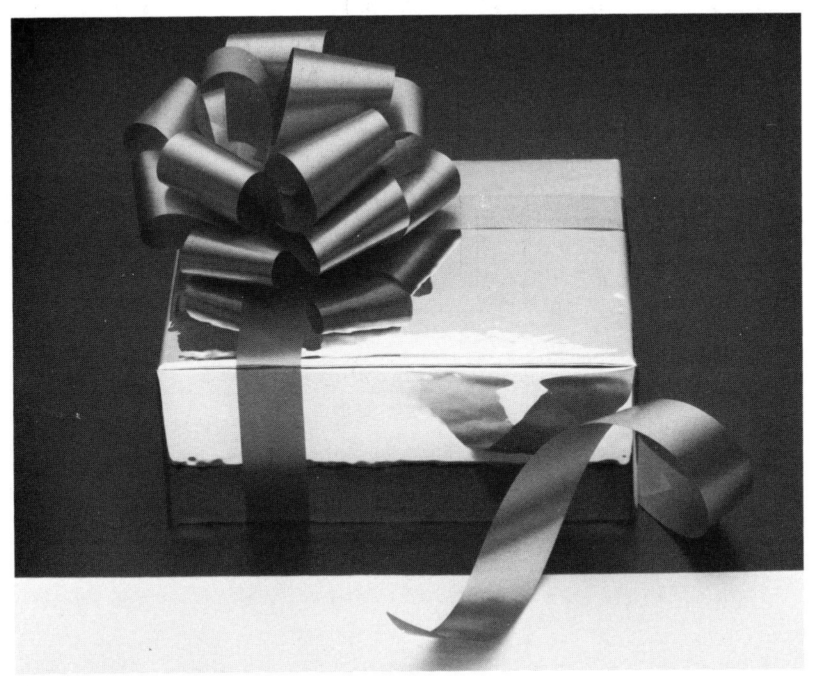

◀ *The bottom of the box "disappears" into the dark table. The only way to prevent this would be to place the reflector so that it touches the front of the box.*

6.22

Brightly polished metal boxes almost always present this problem. Fortunately, it is usually the only major problem; the remainder of this section is a collection of techniques for dealing with it. Pick the one you need according to the circumstance.

A Light-Toned Background

By far the easiest way to photograph a three-dimensional metal subject is to use a light-gray background. The background itself is the light source for much of the visible metal. As soon as we place the subject on such a surface, much of the work is done and we need only a few adjustments to perfect the lighting.

To produce Figure 6.23, we began with a background surface larger than we needed to fill the image area. Remember that the background needs to fill the family of angles reflected by the metal, not just the area the camera sees. Then we lit the top of the metal box with a soft box, just as if it were any other piece of flat metal.

► *The light-gray surface on which we photographed this box acted as a light source for the front of it.*

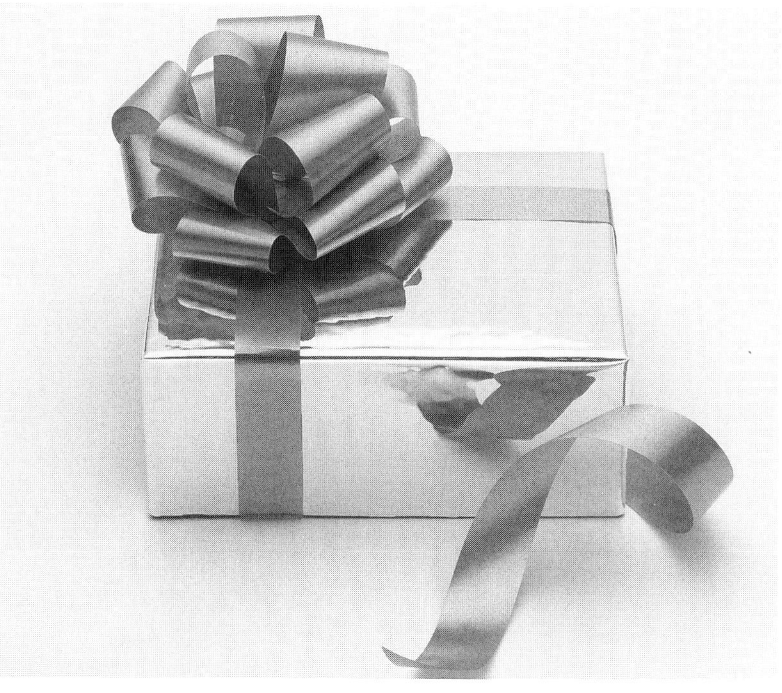

6.23

That was almost all we had to do. The setup was completed by silver reflectors on each side of the scene to fill the shadow in the ribbon.

If good lighting for the metal box were the only objective, we would *always* use a light-toned background. But art and emotion often impose other requirements, so we will look at some other techniques.

A Transparent Background

The only way in which we can orient a metal box as we did in the previous examples *without* having a light source in the scene is to put the box on a transparent surface. When we do that, the camera sees the reflection of a light source (in this case, a white card) in the metal without having that light source in direct view of the camera. Figure 6.24 shows how.

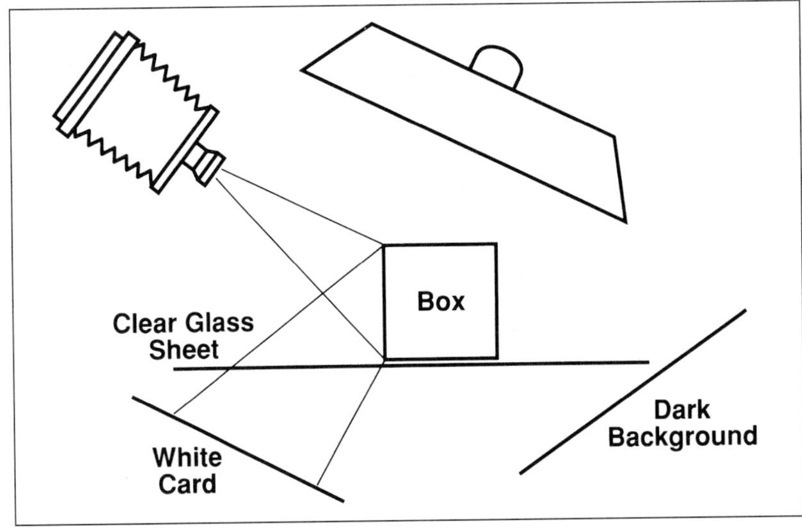

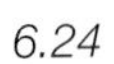
6.24

◀ One way of lighting the front of a metal box without having a light source in the scene. Placing the box on a sheet of clear glass allows reflecting light through the glass to the box.

This arrangement allows us to position a dark card large enough to fill the background, but small enough that it stays out of the family of angles that lights the front and the side of the metal box.

The photograph in Figure 6.25 was made this way. Notice that the background is dark, but not black, and that the table surface has a reflection in it. From this viewpoint, any light source producing direct reflection on top of the metal will also create direct reflection on the glass surface supporting it.

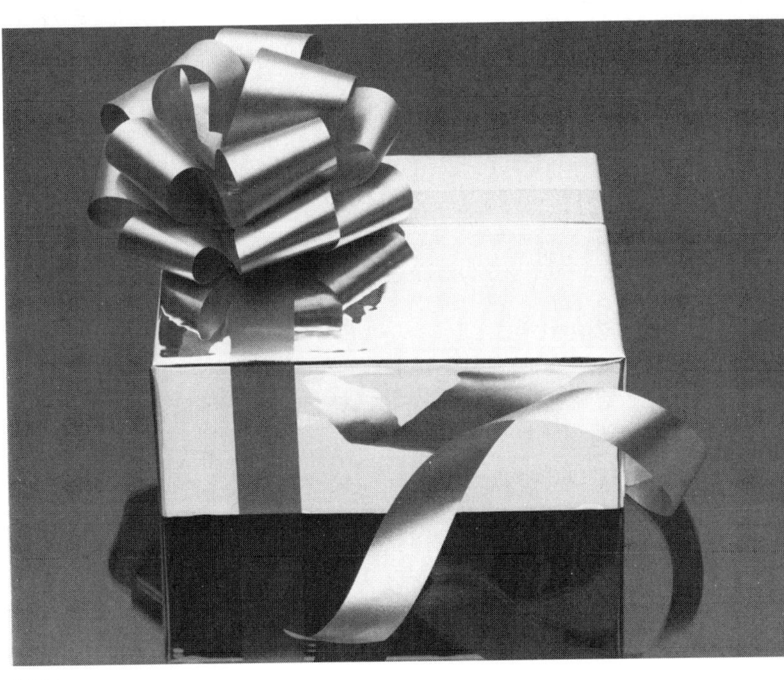

6.25

◀ This is the same scene drawn in Figure 6.24. However, this time we used a polarizing filter over the lens to eliminate the reflection from the glass, making the background dark.

The picture is good. But suppose we disliked the reflection in the glass and wanted the background to be absolutely black. We could eliminate the reflection of the box by using frosted glass, but that would make the background lighter instead of darker.

Fortunately, most of the direct reflection from glass viewed at this angle is polarized, so we were able to eliminate that reflection in Figure 6.26 by putting a polarizing filter on the lens. The glass is now black. Remember, too, that direct reflection from metal is never polarized unless the light source itself is polarized. So the polarizing filter did not block the direct reflection from the metal.

► *The same scene as in Figure 6.24, but with a lens polarizer removing reflection from the glass. The polarizer does not affect the metal.*

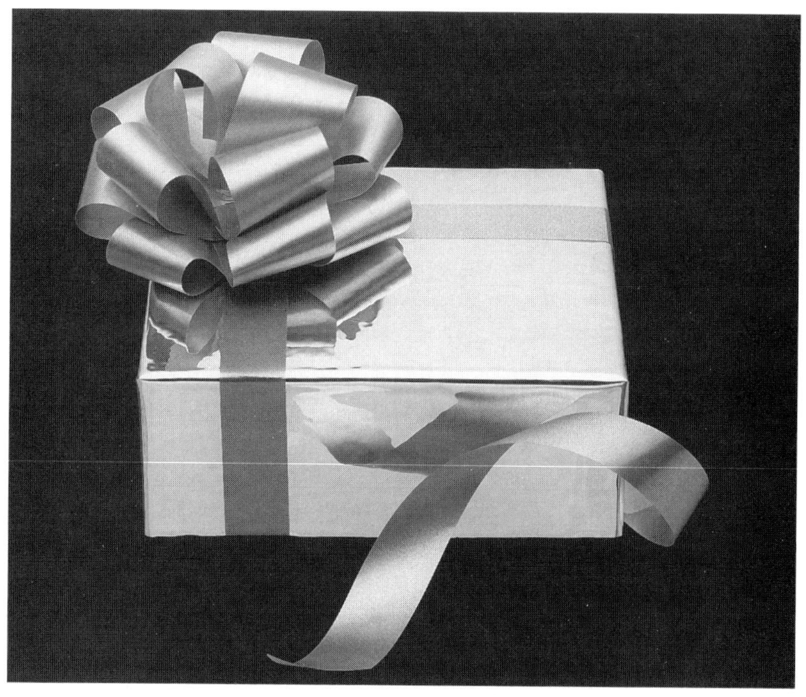

6.26

A Glossy Background

If the metal is on a glossy surface, it is possible to have the light source *in* the image area *without* the camera seeing it! We call this technique *invisible light*. Here is how it works: Look back at Figure 6.21, but this time assume the subject is sitting on a glossy black acrylic sheet. The family of angles defined by the front surface tells us that the *only* possible place from which the metal could get light would be from the black plastic surface; but "black" is a short way of saying that the plastic reflects no light. Together, these facts suggest that the front of the metal cannot be lit.

However, we have also said that the black plastic is glossy. And we know that glossy things *do* produce direct reflection, even if they are too black to produce diffuse reflection. This means that we can light the metal by bouncing light off the plastic surface as in Figure 6.27.

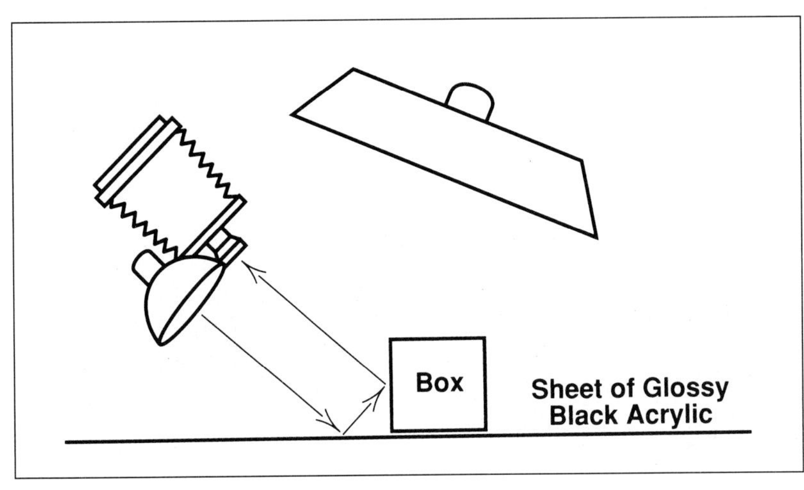

◀ *"Invisible" light reflected from the glossy black plastic lights the metal. No light reflects directly from the plastic to the camera, so the camera cannot see the light source for the metal.*

6.27

If you examine the angles, you see that a light under the camera can bounce light from the glossy plastic to the metal. That light strikes the metal at such an angle that it then reflects back to the camera to record on film. The metal is lit, and the bright metal in Figure 6.28 proves it. As far as the metal can tell, it is being lit by the plastic surface in the scene. However, the camera cannot see that light is reflecting from the black plastic; the family of angles defined by the plastic makes it impossible.

► *The result of "invisible" light. The light source for the box is in the scene—the black plastic directly in front of it.*

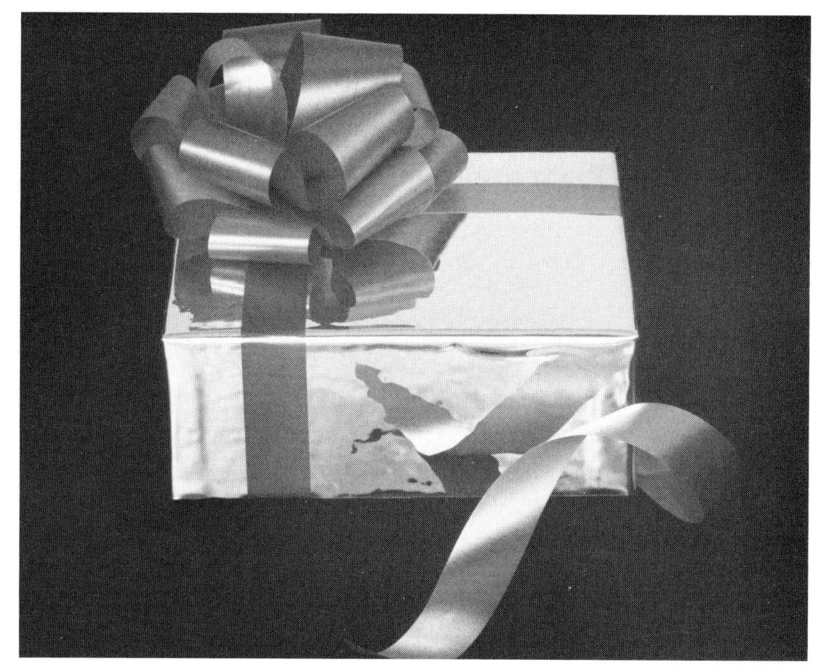

6.28

Like the earlier glass surface, the acrylic surface will reflect the overhead light source. Once again, we used a polarizing filter on the lens to eliminate the glare.

Finally, notice that the front of the box now shows a texture not seen in the earlier examples. This is because invisible light is only effective in a small area on the tabletop. When metal is not absolutely flat, the family of angles required to light it becomes larger. We will next examine an extreme example of that circumstance.

ROUND METAL

Lighting a round piece of metal begins, like any other metal shape, with an analysis of the family of angles that produces direct reflection. Unlike any other metal shape, the family of angles defined by a piece of round metal includes practically the whole world!

Figure 6.29 shows the relevant family of angles for a camera photographing a round metal object at a typical viewing distance. Remember, lighting metal requires the preparation of a suitable environment. Round metal requires a lot more work to light because it reflects so much more of that environment.

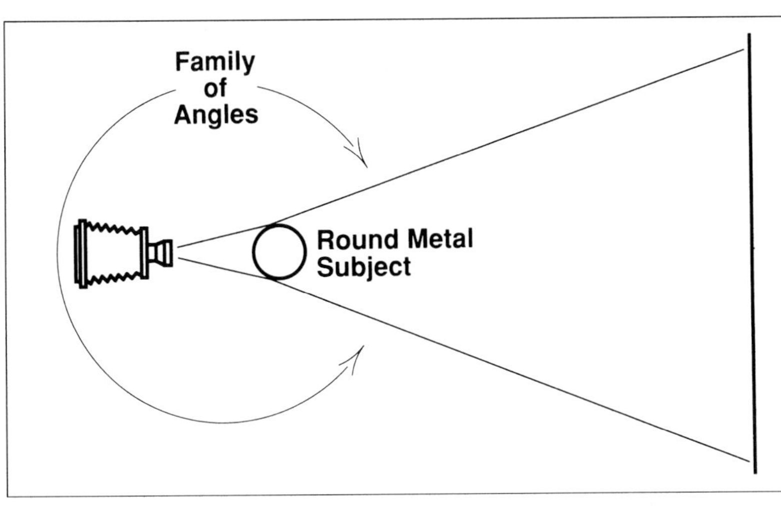

◀ *The family of angles for a round metal subject includes the whole environment, including the camera.*

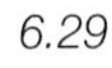

6.29

Notice that the camera will always be in that environment seen by the metal. There are no view-camera tricks to remove the camera from the family of angles reflected by round metal. Furthermore, the reflection of the camera will always fall exactly in the center of the metal subject, where it is most noticeable to the viewer.

For this exercise we will use the most difficult example possible: a perfectly smooth sphere. Figure 6.30 shows the problem.

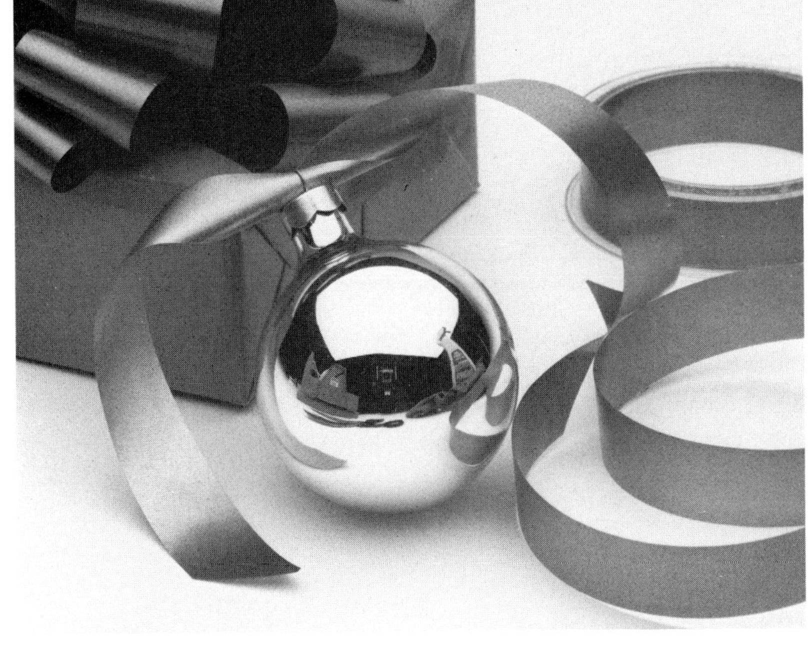

◀ *The common problem presented by round metal.*

6.30

The first step in fixing this problem would be to get rid of unnecessary objects. However, the camera is the one offending object that no cleanup effort can remove. There are three ways of eliminating the camera reflection. We can camouflage the reflection, keep the camera in the dark, or put the subject in a *tent*.

Camouflage

For our purposes, camouflage is any desirable clutter that helps make unwanted reflections less obvious. Sometimes the subject provides its own camouflage. If the surface is irregular, the camera reflection may fall between the cracks.

Additional subjects in the scene can also provide camouflage. The reflection of surrounding subjects in the metal can break up other reflections that we do not want the viewer to see. If the surrounding objects in Figure 6.30 were items appropriate to the scene, instead of studio tools, they could make good camouflage. Small subjects can be put directly on top of a reflection of a larger one.

Keeping the Light off the Camera

If the camera is kept in the dark, then it cannot see itself reflected in the subject. Whenever possible, confine the lighting to the subject. Long lenses help. A camera farther from the subject is less likely to have extraneous light falling on it.

If it is impossible to keep the light off the camera, covering it with black material can work as well. A few pieces of black tape could have covered the bright parts of the camera in Figure 6.30. Black cloth or a black card with a hole in it can conceal the camera entirely.

However, this works only in a studio large enough that the surrounding walls do not reflect. In a smaller room, building a tent may be the only solution.

Using a Tent

A tent is a white enclosure that serves as both the environment and the light source for the subject. The subject goes inside the tent and the camera is almost always outside, looking in through a small opening. Tents are usually used for subjects such as metal, which produce a great deal of direct reflection, but they are sometimes used simply to produce very soft light for such subjects as scientific specimens and for fashion and beauty.

A tent can be made of opaque white material such as a collection of reflector cards. Then we can put the lights in the tent and bounce them off the inside walls. This produces a very soft light, but the lights themselves reflect visibly in any mirror-like subject. More often we use translucent material such as frosted plastic and project the lights through the tent wall.

An ideal tent would be a translucent white dome with no visible seams. Most photographers approximate this ideal as closely as possible with translucent paper or plastic. Figure 6.31 shows one way to do this.

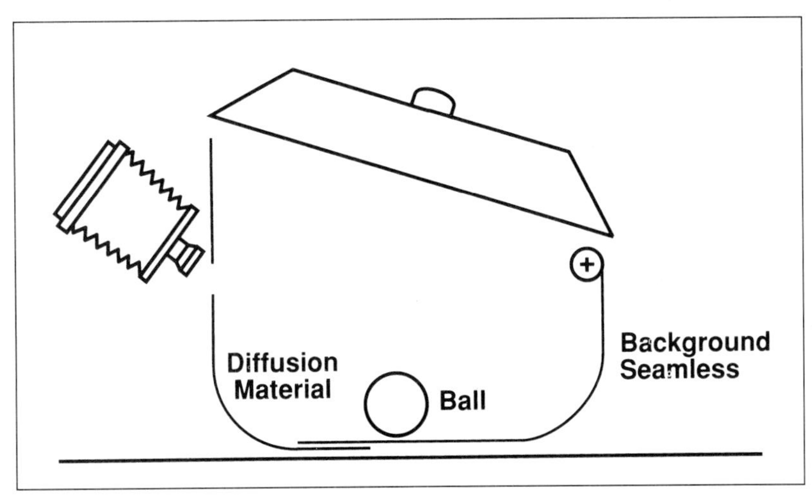

6.31

◀ Building a tent around the subject and shooting through a hole in it is one way of cutting down on unwanted reflections on shiny round subjects.

We do not show any lights other than the soft box that is a structural part of this tent. Additional lights are almost always useful, but their exact positions and sizes are highly optional. Some photographers like to light the whole tent uniformly, while others tend to light only a few small areas.

First 6.32 was shot in such a tent. This photograph is a good example of the principle, but a bad picture. The lighting on the ball is acceptable, except for the dark spot in the middle. That is the hole through which the camera is seeing.

► *A photograph of a shiny round subject shot with the help of a tent such as the one diagrammed in the previous figure. By itself, the tent does not solve the problem, but it is a start. Camouflage would complete the setup.*

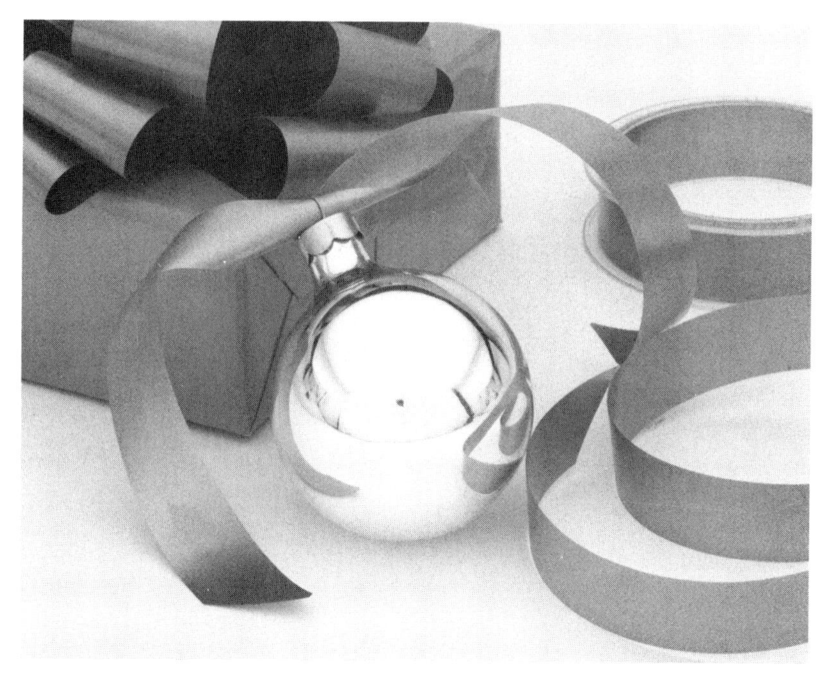

6.32

One of the authors once made a picture similar to this for the cover of a department store Christmas catalog. But the peripheral areas also included bits of ribbon and greenery to camouflage the seams in the tent. Looping a piece of the ribbon "accidentally" across the front of the ball hid the camera. If the intent of the image had precluded additional subject matter to use for camouflage, the only remedy to the problem would have been retouching.

It is tempting to build a very large tent to keep the camera as far from the subject as possible. Intuitively we know that if the camera is farther from a metal subject, then the reflection of the camera will be smaller. However, the image of the subject also becomes smaller. We can enlarge the subject back to usable size in the dark room, or we can shoot with a longer lens. Either technique also enlarges the reflection of the camera back to its original size. The camera itself is the *only* reflection whose size cannot be reduced by moving it farther away. It always remains constant, relative to the subject. Resist the temptation. Such extra work would be wasted.

OTHER RESOURCES

The basic approach to lighting metal is determined by the family of angles and, therefore, by the shape of the metal. Beyond the basic lighting, there are a few more techniques you may want to try at any time with any piece of metal.

Any of these additional options can be purely creative decisions, but they can serve technical purposes too. For example, you may find that the edge of a piece of metal is disappearing into the background. Keep in mind, the closer the metal comes to producing *pure* direct reflection, the closer that reflection comes to photographing at the same brightness as the light source. As we have seen, the surface on which the metal is sitting is often the light source. If they are of identical brightness, the camera cannot see where one surface ends and the other begins.

This is a case where polarizing filters, "black magic," or dulling spray can add the finishing touches to the lighting.

Polarizing Filters

Metal does not produce polarized direct reflections. Therefore, we cannot usually use a lens polarizer to block the direct reflections coming from metal. Remember, however, that the light source may have some polarized rays. If so, they remain polarized as they reflect from the metal. This is frequently the case if the metal is reflecting blue sky. In the studio, the light reflected from the surface on which the metal rests is often partly polarized. In either case, a polarizer on the lens gives additional control over the brightness of the metal. Even if there is no polarized light in the scene, we can put it there by using a polarizing filter over the light.

Black Magic

Black magic is anything added to the basic lighting setup solely to place a black "reflection" in the metal surface. Black reflected in an edge can help to differentiate it from the background. Reflected across the center of a slightly irregular surface, black magic can also add dimension.

Black magic usually involves the use of a gobo. This works especially well with a diffusion sheet. Placing the gobo between the diffusion sheet and the subject makes a hard black reflection. Putting it on the other side of the diffusion sheet from the subject creates a softly graduated reflection. The farther behind the diffusion sheet you place the gobo, the softer it becomes.

Occasionally you may decide to use an opaque reflector (reflecting another light somewhere else in the set) as a light source for the metal. In this case, a gobo cannot produce softly graduated black magic, but a soft-edged stripe of black spray paint across the reflector will create the same effect.

Beware of Blue Highlights

Polarizing both the lights and the lens may create special problems if the film is color and the subject is metal.

Polarizing filters allow more light from the blue end of the spectrum to pass through than from the red. This makes such a filter behave like a very light blue filter. The effect is so slight that we do not notice the color imbalance in a color photograph unless extremely accurate color rendition is necessary.

Even when there are polarizing filters on both the lens and the lights, the increased blue shift is rarely a problem if the subject is one that produces mostly diffuse reflection. However, if the subject produces much direct reflection, some of the highlights may be offensively blue!

It is easy to overlook these blue highlights if you do not anticipate them. Light lost through the combined polarizers makes the image too dark to examine carefully on a view-camera ground glass. Depending on black-and-white Polaroid tests to shoot color film can conceal the problem until after the final film is processed.

Dulling Spray

Dulling spray creates a matte surface that increases the diffuse reflection and decreases the direct reflection from a piece of metal. This allows a little more freedom to light the metal without strictly obeying the limitations imposed by the family of angles. Unfortunately, metal with dulling spray on it no longer looks brightly polished and may not even look like metal any longer!

Heavy-handed use of dulling spray is a habit to avoid. To an educated eye, it reveals, rather than conceals, a photographer's inability to light metal well. With that said, we should also admit that both of the authors keep dulling spray handy in their studios.

Try to light the metal as well as possible. Then, if necessary, add a little dulling spray just to an overly bright highlight or a disappearing edge. Keep as much of the gleam of the metal as you can, and avoid thickly coating the entire surface.

WHERE ELSE DO THESE TECHNIQUES APPLY?

The techniques we use for metal are good to remember any time direct reflection is important. We will see more of them in the rest of this book. Some of these applications may not be obvious yet. For example, we will see in Chapter 9 why much of the technique for lighting metal is useful for almost any black-on-black subject, regardless of the material of which it is made.

Other subjects that produce direct reflection are readily apparent. One of them is glass. Glass, however, offers some additional opportunities and challenges of its own. We will see why in the next chapter.

Chapter 7

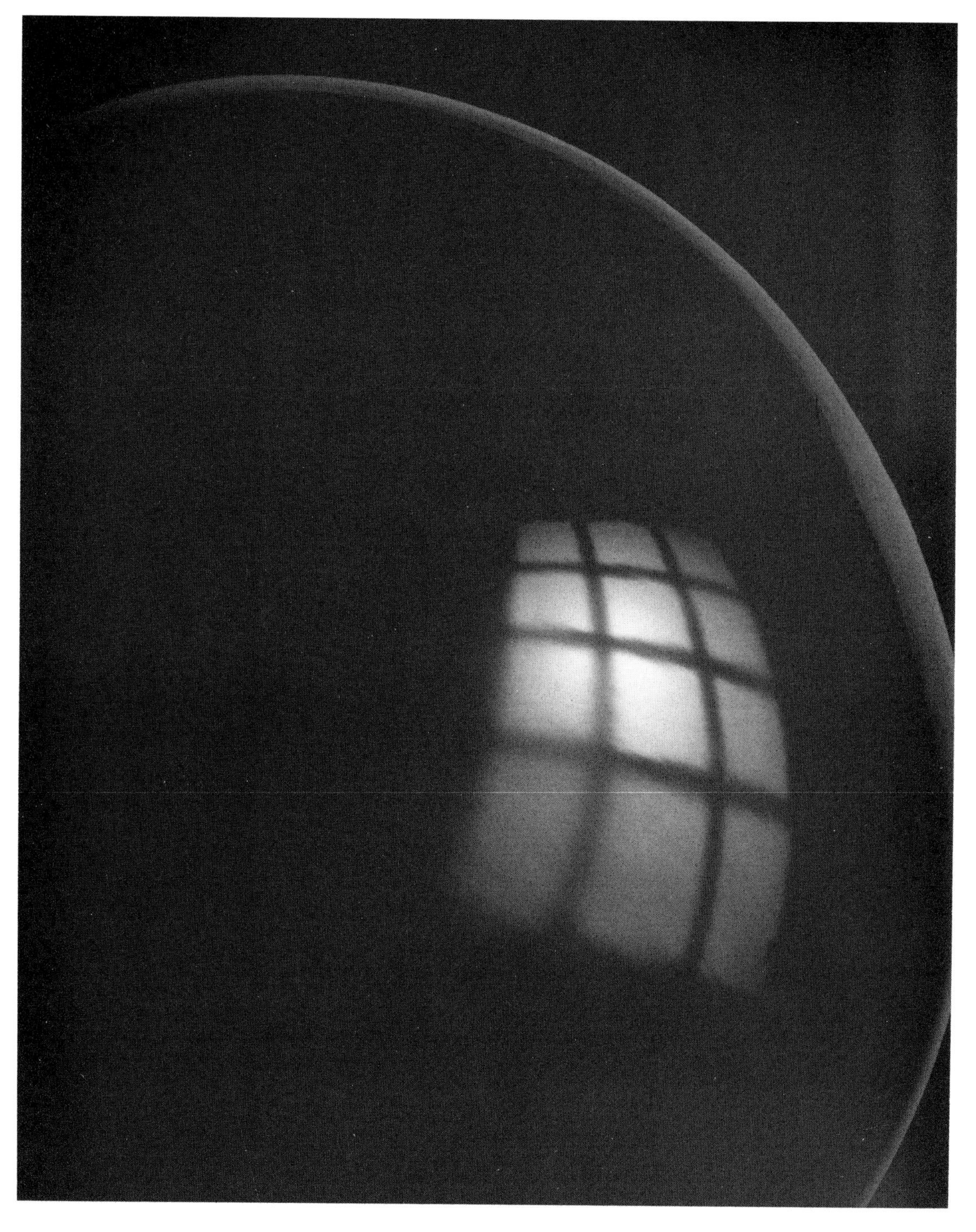

The Case of the Disappearing Glass

The handiwork of the distant genius who first fused sand into glass has tricked the eyes and delighted the brains of every generation of humans to follow. It has perhaps also grayed the hair and wasted the film of more photographers than any other substance.

However, an attempt to reproduce the appearance of glass on film need not lead to the photographic disasters we so often see. This chapter will discuss the principles, the problems, and some very straightforward solutions to the basic challenges that glass offers.

THE PRINCIPLES

The appearance of glass is determined by many of the same principles we discussed in the preceding chapter on metal. Like metal, almost all reflection produced by glass is direct reflection. Unlike metal, however, this direct reflection is often polarized.

Since polarization does not make much difference to the appearance of direct reflection, we might expect the techniques used for lighting glass to be similar to those used for metal. We might find a polarizing filter useful more often, but otherwise apply the same methods.

However, this is not so. When we light metal, we are primarily interested in the surfaces facing the camera. If they look right, then minor adjustments can usually take care of the details. Lighting glass, on the other hand, requires attention to the edges. If the edges are clearly defined, we can often ignore the front surface altogether.

THE PROBLEMS

The problems caused by glassware are a result of the very nature of the material. It is transparent! From most angles, light striking the visible edge of a piece of glassware does not reflect in the direction of the viewer. Such an edge is invisible. An invisible glass has no shape or form.

To make matters worse, the few tiny reflections we *do* see are often as bright as the light source itself! They are too small and too bright to tell the viewer of a photograph anything about surface detail or texture.

Figure 7.1 shows both problems. The direct reflections of the lights illuminating the scene do nothing but distract from the composition. They are not adequate to define the surface of the glass.

► The problems with this picture are caused by the nature of the glass from which the subjects are made. The glass is both transparent and highly reflective.

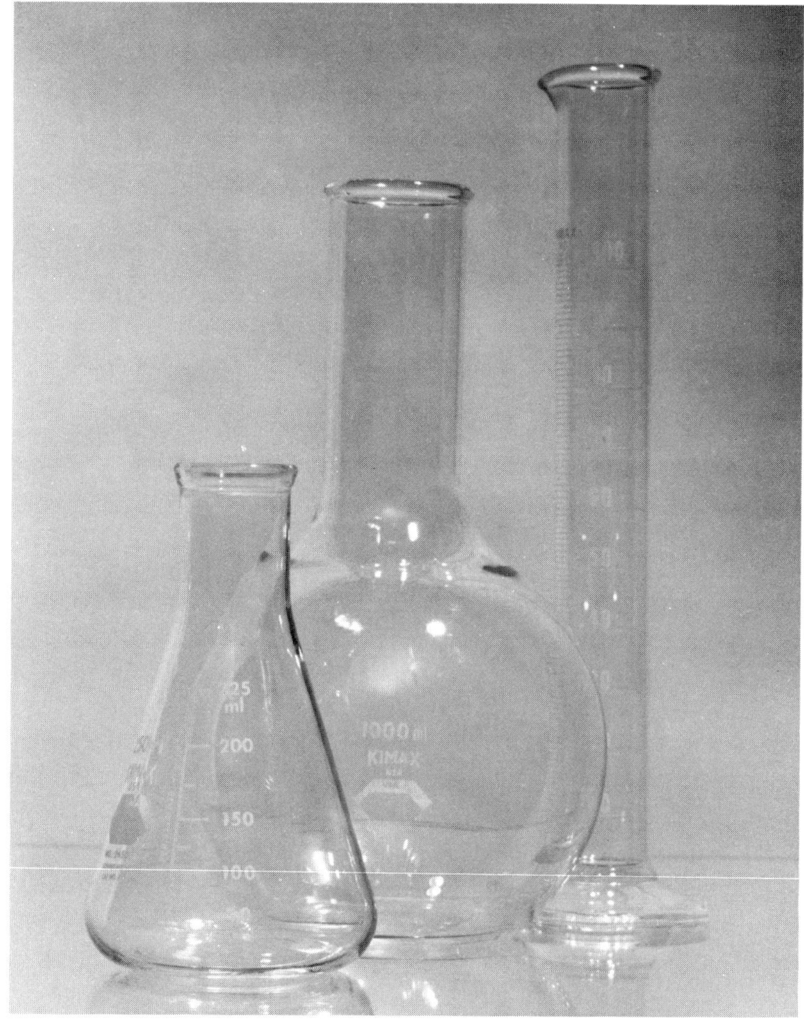

7.1

The lack of a clearly defined form is an even more serious problem. With no clear outlines and no marked differences in edge tonality, the glass merges with the background.

THE SOLUTIONS

Having seen what does not work, look now at Figure 7.2. Compare the visibility of the glass shown in it with that shown in the earlier photograph. Both photographs show the same glassware and the same background, and both are made from the same viewpoint with the same lens. But, as you can see, the difference is dramatic.

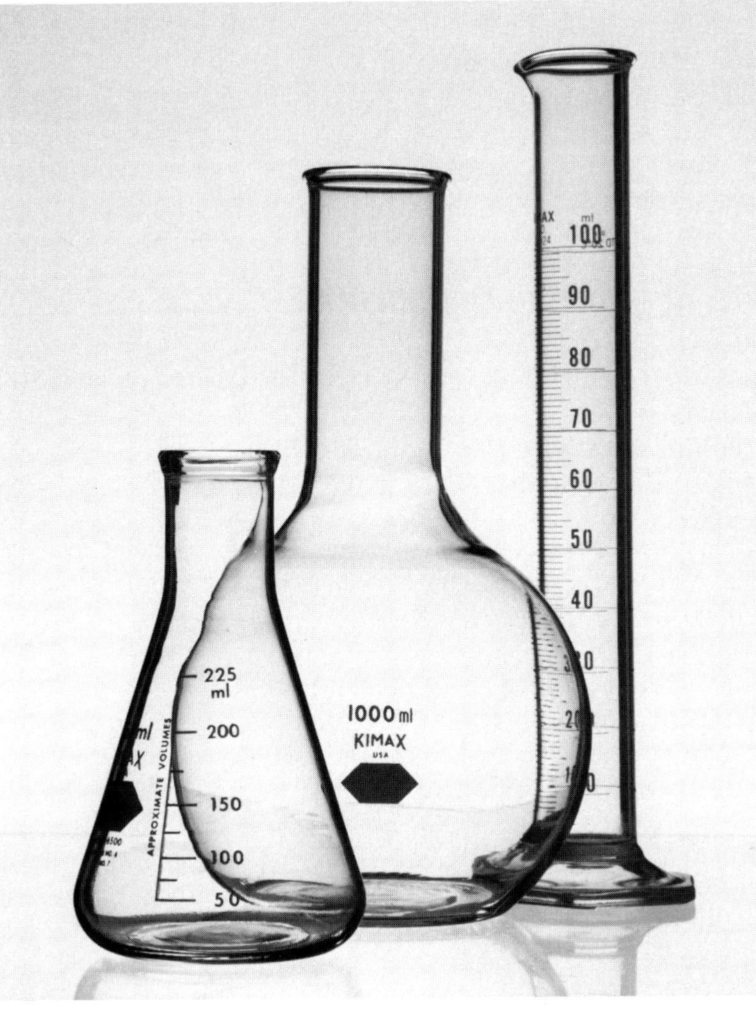

◀ Good edge definition is essential to lighting glass.

7.2

In the second photograph, the form leaps out from the background. Strong black lines delineate the shape of the glass. No distracting reflections mar the surface. By comparing these two photographs, we can list our objectives in glassware photography. If we want to produce a picture that clearly and pleasingly reproduces the glassware, we must

1. Produce strong lines along the edges of the subject. These lines delineate its shape and set it apart from the background.
2. Eliminate distracting reflections of the lights and other equipment we are using.

It is time to look at some of the specific ways we can accomplish these objectives. We will begin by looking at some "ideal" shooting situations. These will help us to demonstrate the basic techniques. Later, we will have to go beyond those basics to overcome problems that arise whenever nonglass objects are in the same scene. We will begin by talking about our first objective, edge definition.

TWO ATTRACTIVE OPPOSITES

We can avoid almost all the problems associated with edge definition by using one of two basic lighting arrangements. We will call these the *bright-field* and the *dark-field* methods. We could also call them "dark-on-light" and "light-on-dark" approaches. The results of these two are as opposite as the terms imply, but we will see that the principles guiding them are identical. Both methods produce the strong tonal differences between the subject and the background that delineate edges to define the shape of glassware.

Bright-Field Lighting

Figure 7.2 is an example of the bright-field approach to lighting glass. The background dictates how we must treat any glass subject. On a bright background, we have to keep the glass dark if it is to remain visible.

If you have read Chapter 2 and the chapters following it, you have already guessed that the bright-field method requires eliminating all direct reflection from the edge of the glass surface. Then you also see why we need to begin this discussion by examining the family of angles that determines direct reflection from this particular subject.

Look at Figure 7.3, a bird's-eye view of the family of angles that can produce direct reflection on a single round glass. We could draw a similar diagram for each piece of glassware in our example photograph.

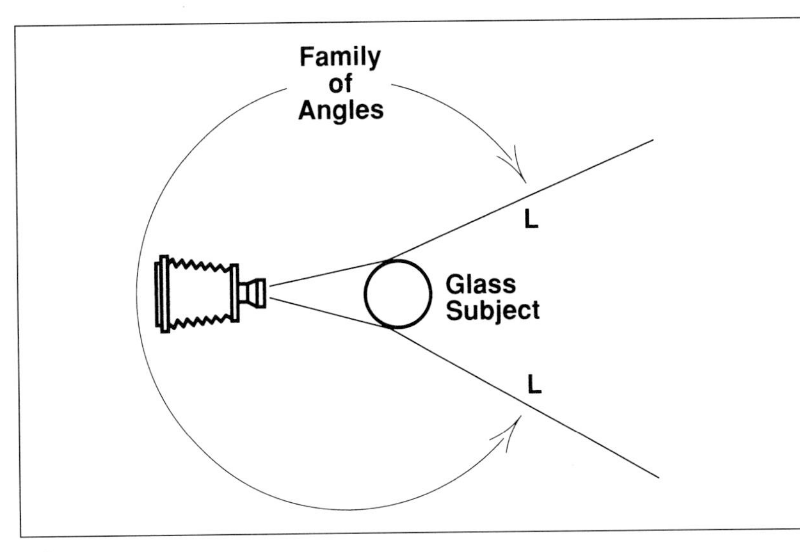

7.3

◀ *The limits of the family of angles in this diagram are marked by* **L.** *Light from these two points determines the appearance of the edge of the glass.*

The family of angles in this diagram is similar to that defined by round metal in the last chapter. This time, however, we are not interested in most of that family. For now, we only care about the extreme *limits* of the family of angles, labeled *L* in the diagram. Light from these two angles determines the appearance of the edge of the glass. These limits tell us where the light must be if the edges of the glass are to be bright in the pictures or, conversely, where it must *not* be if the edges are to remain dark.

Since, in the bright-field approach we do not want the edge of the glass to be bright in the photograph, then there must be *no* light along the lines marked *L* in the diagram.

Figure 7.4 illustrates one good way to produce a bright-field glass photograph. It is not the only way, but it is a good exercise that we suggest you try if you have not done it before. Look at the way the light behaves in each step. This will make it easy to predict what will work and what will not in any variation on this arrangement you decide to try in the future.

► *This is one way to produce the bright-field illumination used in Figure 7.2. We would rarely use both lights shown. Either lighting position works, depending on the background.*

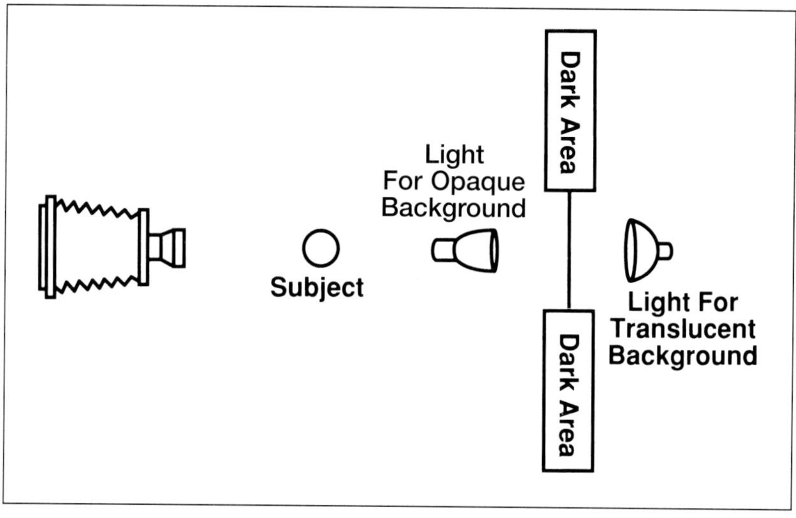

7.4

These steps work best in the listed sequence. Notice that we do not bother to put the subject into the scene until near the end of the process.

1. Choose the Background. Begin by setting up a light-toned background. We can use any convenient material. Translucent materials such as tracing paper, cloth, and plastic shower curtains are a few good materials to try. We might also use opaque surfaces, such as light-toned walls, cardboard, or foamcore.

2. Position the Light. Now, place a light so that it illuminates the background evenly. The diagram shows two possible ways to accomplish this; both can produce identical results.

Figure 7.2 was shot using a light behind translucent paper. This is a particularly convenient setup because it keeps the work space around both the camera and the subject free and uncluttered.

We can also use an opaque surface such as a wall for the background. If we do, we need to find a place to position the light so that it will light the background without reflecting in the glass or appearing in the image area. Putting the light on a short stand behind and below the glass is one good way.

3. Position the Camera. Now, place the camera so that the background exactly fills its field of view. This step is critical because the distance from the camera to the background controls the effective size of the background. Moving the camera closer makes the size of the background larger and moving the camera farther away makes it smaller.

The effective size of the background is the single most important consideration when using this technique! For this exercise to be most effective, the background must *exactly* fill the field of view of the camera, no more and no less.

A background that is too small is an obvious problem: It simply will not fill the picture! A larger background causes a more subtle problem. A background too large will extend into the family of angles that produces direct reflection on the edge of the glass. Light from those points eliminates the dark outline that we need to define the edge of the glass.

If the background surface is so large that we cannot keep it from extending beyond the limits of the viewfinder (e.g., the wall of a room), we can also reduce its effective size by lighting only a small portion of its total surface or by covering part of it with dark cards.

4. Position the Subject and Focus the Camera. Next, move the subject back and forth between the camera and the background until it is the desired size in the viewfinder.

As we move the subject, we notice that the closer it is to the camera, the more clearly the edges are defined. This increase in edge definition is not brought about by the simple principle that larger detail is easier to see. Rather, it is caused by the fact that as the subject moves farther from the lighted background, less light reflects off its edges. The closer the subject is to the background, the more the bright background falls within the family of angles that produces direct reflection to obscure those edges.

Now, focus the camera on the subject. Refocusing will slightly increase the size of the background, but that increase will usually not be enough to cause any practical problems.

5. Expose the Film. Finally, use a reflection meter (the one built into most 35mm cameras is fine) to read the light on an area on the background directly behind the subject.

Bright-field illumination does not require a pure white background. As long as the background is any tone significantly brighter than the edges of the glass, then that glass will be adequately visible. If the glass is the only subject to worry about, we can control the brightness of the background by the way we interpret the meter reading:

- If we want the background to appear as a medium (eighteen-percent) gray, we use the exposure that the meter indicates.
- If we want the background to photograph as a light gray that approaches white, we increase the exposure up to two stops more than the meter indicates.
- If we want the background to be dark, then we expose the film as much as two stops less than indicated. This will produce a very dark-gray background.

In this scene there is no such thing as "correct" exposure. The only correct exposure is the one that we like. We can place the tone of the background anywhere we like on the gray scale *except* black. (If the edge of the glass is black and the background is black, there is nothing left to record on film!) In practice, the lighter the background, the more graphically the glass is defined.

If we do expose to keep the background very light, we do not have to worry about extraneous reflection in the front surface of the glass. Whatever reflections exist are almost always too dim to be visible against the background. However, if we decide to expose to produce a medium- or dark-gray background, the brightest metal parts of the camera may reflect visibly in the glass. We will offer some ways to eliminate these reflections later in this chapter.

In principle, there is nothing particularly complicated about the bright-field approach to photographing glassware. Of course, we have used an "ideal" example in order to demonstrate the principle as clearly as possible. In practice, complications may occur whenever we decide to deviate from this ideal. For example, many compositions will force us to keep the glass much smaller, compared with the background, than in our exercise. That will reduce edge definition. Whether the sacrifice will be significant depends on what else is in the photograph.

Of course, understanding the principle and becoming familiar with *why* the ideal works gives us the understanding that provides the best solution in less than ideal situations. If a composition produces bad lighting, the ideal explains the problem and suggests a remedy. If a particular composition prevents any remedy, then the ideal tells us that, too. We need not waste time trying to accomplish what physics says is impossible.

Dark-Field Lighting

In the preceding section, we showed how to produce a photograph in which *dark* edges around the subject separate it from a lighter background. The dark-field method produces the opposite result, as illustrated in Figure 7.5.

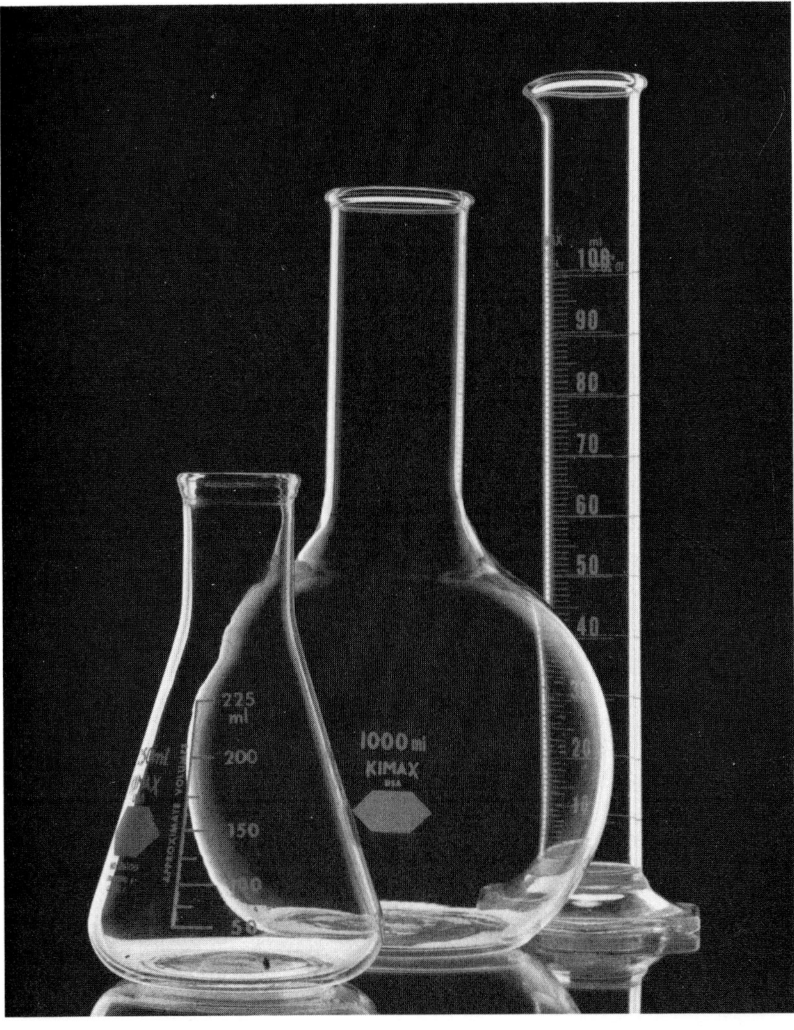

7.5

◀ *In dark-field illumination, shape and form are delineated by light lines against a dark background.*

Review the family of angles that produces direct reflection in Figure 7.3. We saw that in the previous arrangement there must be no light at the limits of the family of angles, L, if the edge of the glass is to remain dark. It makes sense to suppose, then, that the light *must* come from L if the edge of the glass is to be bright.

Since we now want the edge of the glass to be *bright* in the photograph, then there *must* be light at the far limits of the family of angles. Furthermore, if we do not want other bright distractions in the glass, then the glass must not see light at any other point.

Figure 7.6 shows the specifics to put the theory to work. Once again, we will present the technique in five steps. Some of them are identical to those used in the earlier bright-field approach.

► *This is one good way to produce dark-field lighting.*

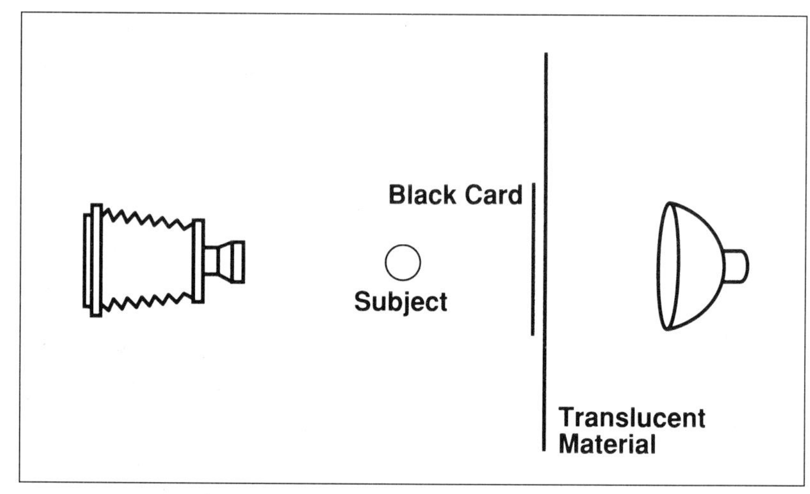

7.6

1. Set Up a Large Light Source. Upon first examination, the bird's-eye view in Figure 7.3 seems to indicate the need for light at two points. This, however, is a representational defect caused by having to draw in only two dimensions. In actuality, such an arrangement would light only a point on each side of the glass.

To keep the rim bright, a similar light source must be placed above and behind the glass. Furthermore, if the glass is a stemmed glass with a bowl, then yet another light source must be added to illuminate the bottom of that bowl.

So we need four large sources to light just the edges of a single tiny glass! This arrangement would be unwieldy at best. So we usually avoid such a complex clutter by replacing all of these lights with a single source large enough to illuminate the top and bottom of the glass, as well as the sides. The exact size of this light source is not critical. Any size between ten and twenty-five times the diameter of the subject will work well.

Figures 7.6 and 7.7 show two good ways to create an appropriately large light source. One is translucent and the other is opaque.

2. Set Up a Dark Background Smaller than the Light Source. There are several ways to do this. The easiest way, shown in Figure 7.6, is to attach a dark card directly to the translucent light source.

An opaque surface such as a wall can also make an excellent light source. We simply need to illuminate it with reflected light. However, such an arrangement usually precludes putting the dark background directly on the bright light source.

Instead, we like the setup used in Figure 7.7, which allows lighting the opaque reflective surface as brightly as we like without allowing significant light to fall on the background that the camera sees. Attaching the dark background to a light stand or suspending it from above with string works fine.

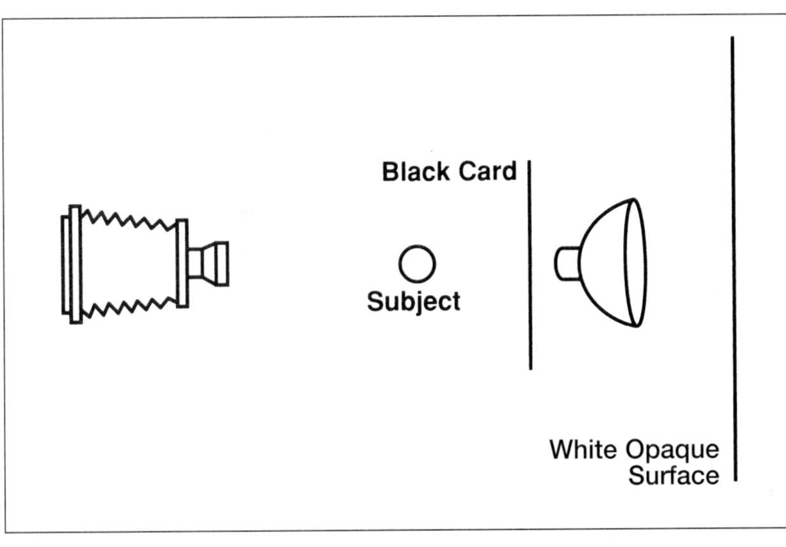

◀ *This setup allows you to light the opaque reflective surface brightly without lighting the background that the camera sees.*

7.7

The result of both of these arrangements is the same: A dark background is surrounded by bright light.

Like the light source, the exact size of the background is not critical. As with the bright-field approach, we can adjust the effective background size by the camera distance. The only size limitation is that the dark background be small enough to leave plenty of the light source visible around it.

3. Position the Camera. The background should exactly fill the field of view of the camera; no more and no less. This is important for reasons similar to those in the bright-field approach. If the dark background is too large, it will extend into the family of angles that produces direct reflection. That blocks light needed to brightly define the edge of the glass and to keep it from disappearing into the dark background.

4. Position the Subject and Focus the Camera. Next, move the subject between the camera and the background until it is the size we want. Once again, edge definition improves as the subject moves closer to the camera. Finally, focus the camera on the subject. As in the bright-field method, the change in background size caused by refocusing will be too minimal to cause problems.

5. Expose the Film. Accurate exposure determination with this setup requires the use of a very narrow-angle spot meter to read the highlights on the edges of the glass. In most compositions of this sort, "very narrow angle" means much less than one degree. Almost no photographers have such a meter.

Do not despair. Fortunately, any conventional reflection meter (including those in many cameras) can give an acceptably close approximation of the desired exposure with the help of bracketing.

To see why the following method works, we must remember that pure direct reflections from a subject are as bright as the light source that produces them. Those reflections may be too small to read, but the large source is not.

First, place the meter close enough to the light source to read it alone. Read the edge of the light source, since that is the part illuminating the glass.

Next, to photograph the glass as near white, expose the film two stops more than the meter indicates. (This is because the meter thinks it is seeing eighteen-percent gray instead of white.) This is a good exposure if the highlight on the glass is *perfect* unpolarized direct reflection. Such an exposure is theoretically important because it determines the starting point for the bracket. In practice, there is no practical chance that the direct reflection is perfect and unpolarized, so we may want simply to note this exposure and to move on to the next one.

Since perfect direct reflections rarely occur, bracket with additional film giving still one, two, and then three stops more exposure.

All of this assumes the background remains black, since little or no light is falling on it. If, however, we desire it to be a lighter value, it will then be necessary to use additional light just for the background. Omitting this additional light and attempting to lighten the background by increasing exposure (according to the metering procedure recommended in the discussion of the bright-field method) will usually overexpose the subject.

Once again, we have used an ideal example that avoids complexities for the sake of simplicity. Deviate from this ideal as much as the composition requires, but no more.

THE BEST OF BOTH WORLDS

Bright-field and dark-field methods are easy to learn, but they can be difficult to combine. Most failures in photographing glass result from deliberately or naively using both simultaneously.

For example, we have known some photographers who tried to light glass in a tent like the one described in the previous chapter. They successfully eliminated extraneous reflections, but they equally successfully eliminated the edge of the glass. The part of the tent visible to the camera provided a light background. The rest of the tent lit the glass. The result was the light-on-light approach!

Using the two methods together requires that we keep them separate, even in a single picture. We make a mental division of the scene and decide that one part of the picture is to be bright field while the other is to be dark field.

We have done this in Figure 7.8, in which the frosted white plastic is illuminated from below. A gobo behind the light keeps the background plastic dark.

► *A classic lighting arrangement in which part of the scene is bright field and the other part is dark field.*

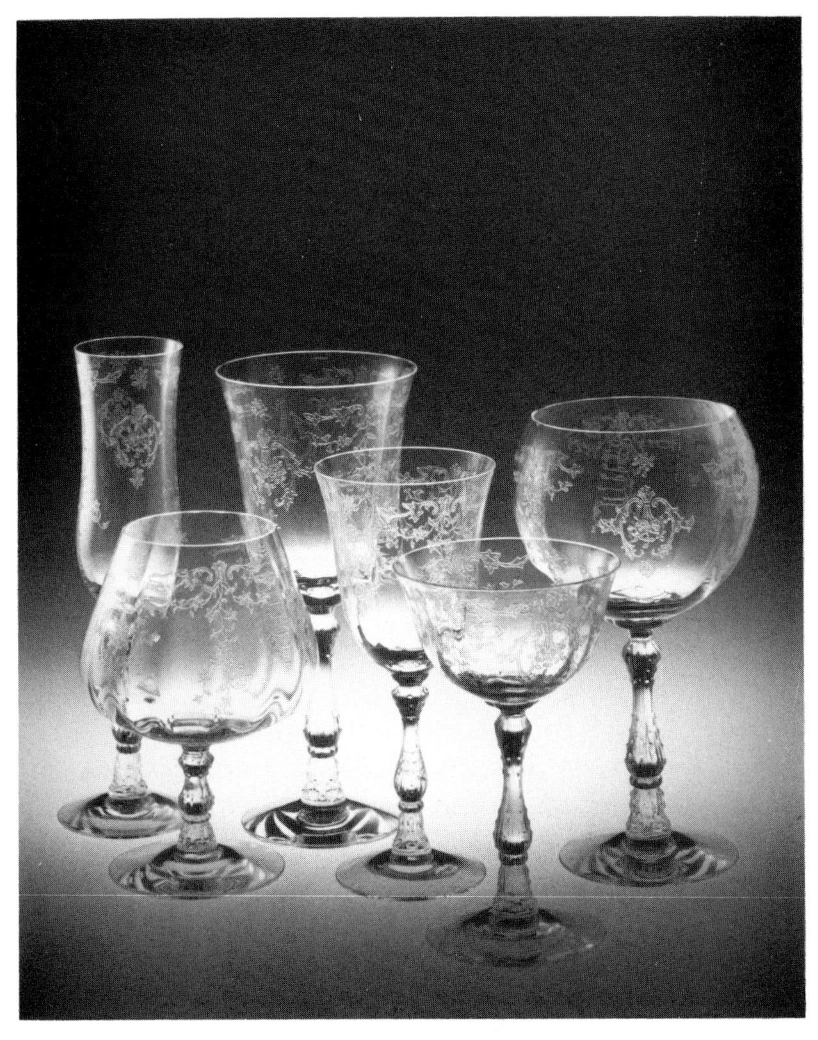

7.8

Notice that we have not truly combined the two basic methods. The top of the picture is dark field and the bottom is bright field. Wherever the two methods remain distinct, the glass is well defined. Only in the transition area between do the two methods mix. Predictably, there is a loss of definition in that transition. But lighting to ensure that the transition area is small keeps the defect from becoming objectionable.

SOME FINISHING TOUCHES

Up to this point we have discussed techniques that define the shape of glassware. As you have seen, we can define the subject shape by using either *dark lines against a light background* or by using *light lines against a dark background.* These two techniques are the foundation for lighting glass. However, we often need additional techniques to produce a satisfactory photograph. In the remainder of this chapter, we will discuss some finishing touches. Specifically, we will examine how to accomplish the following:

1. Define the surface of glassware
2. Illuminate the background
3. Minimize the horizon
4. Stop flare
5. Eliminate extraneous reflections

Since these techniques are primarily useful in dark-field situations, we will demonstrate them using that approach.

Defining the Surface of Glassware

In many situations, it is not enough merely to define the edges of a subject. It is not enough just to show its shape, no matter how beautifully we do it. Frequently, the photograph must also clearly show the glass surface. To accomplish this, we must carefully manage the highlights that reflect from the surface of the subject.

Large highlights are essential to glass surface definition. To see proof of this, compare the highlights on Figure 7.9 with those seen earlier in Figure 7.1.

► *Large highlights add surface definition to the glassware in this picture.*

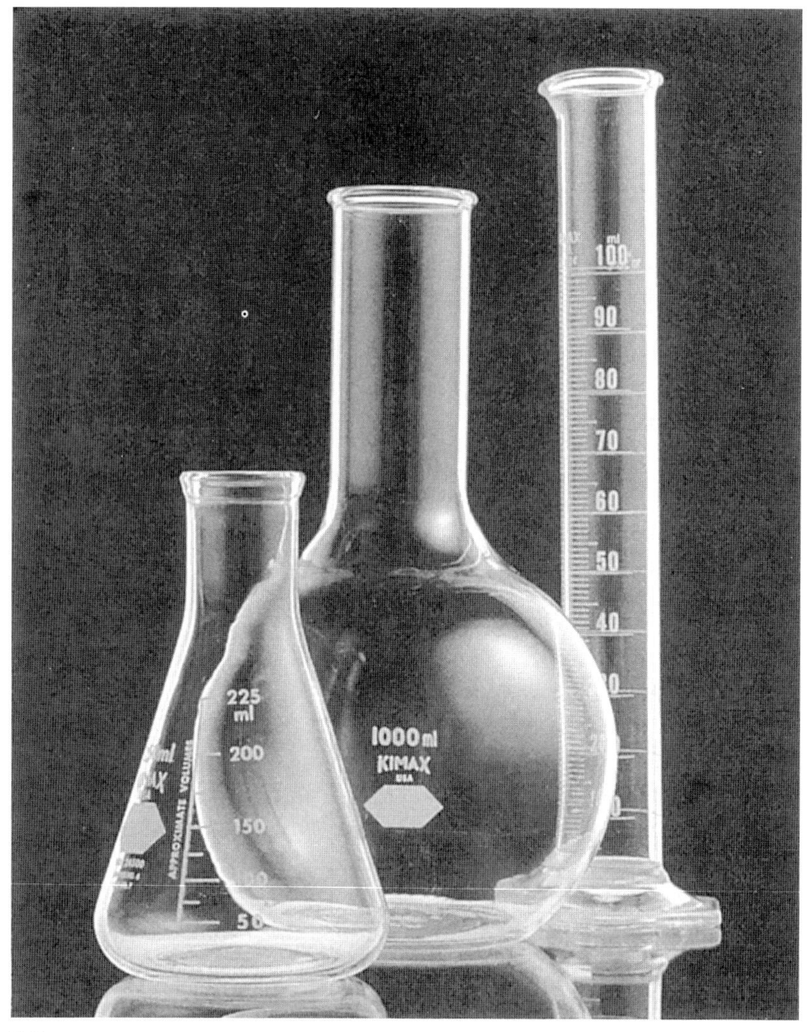

7.9

The tiny bright spots in Figure 7.1 are harshly distracting at the least and meaningless at best. The opposite is true in Figure 7.9. Instead of competing, the larger highlights provide the viewer with information. Rather than cluttering the other elements of the photograph for the attention of the viewer, it serves the constructive purpose of saying, "This is how this glass surface looks and feels."

Defining a glass surface requires a highlight of the right size in the right place on the surface of the subject. Fortunately, that is not too difficult. Doing it successfully simply requires remembering what the theory of reflection tells us about how direct reflection behaves.

We have seen that almost all reflections from a glass surface are direct reflections, and that direct reflections always obey strict rules that predict the angles at which they occur. Now, look at Figure 7.10.

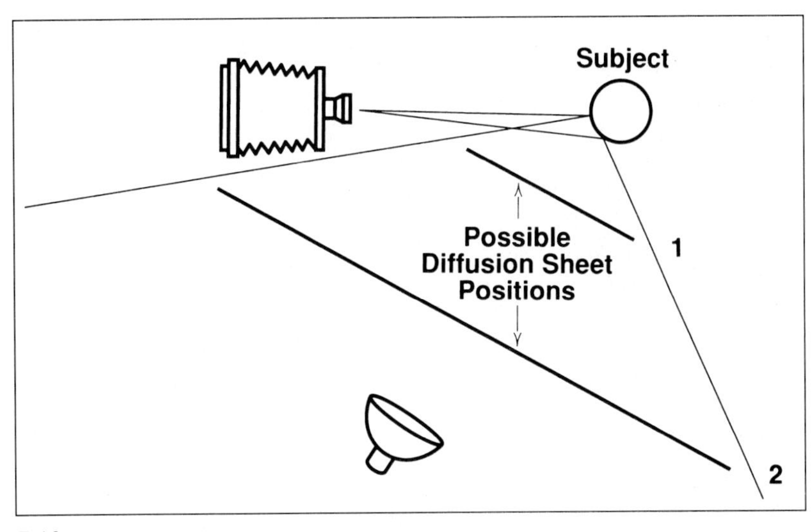

7.10

◀ *Creating a highlight on the indicated surface requires filling its family of angles with light. In this diagram, a lighted diffusion sheet reflects on the glass surface to produce the highlight.*

Assuming we want to create a highlight on the area shown on the glass surface, we need to fill the indicated family of angles with light. These are all of the directions and the only directions from which light can produce direct reflection on that part of the glass.

Notice that the rounded glass causes this small subject to reflect much of the studio in its surface! For this reason, lighting for surface definition can sometimes require surprisingly large light sources.

Light sources at positions *1* and *2* would light the glass equally well. However, the one at position *2* needs to be *twice* as large as the other if it is to cover the required family of angles.

Figure 7.10 shows one way to provide such a light source. In this example, we have placed the diffusion sheet (still more tracing paper in this particular example) close enough to the glass that it does not have to be inconveniently large. Lit by a small light head, the diffusion sheet reflects in the surface of the glass, giving us the desired surface highlight.

Determining the distance between the photographic light and the diffusion sheet can be an important decision. Notice that in the first photograph in this series the light was close enough to light brightly only the center of the diffusion material. Figure 7.11 shows an alternative method. Here we have pulled the light head farther back. This allows the full rectangle of the diffusion sheet to be lit and to be reflected in the glass surface.

► *Compare the large highlight in this picture with that in Figure 7.9. This time we positioned the light far enough away from the diffusion sheet that the entire sheet was lit and reflected in the glass.*

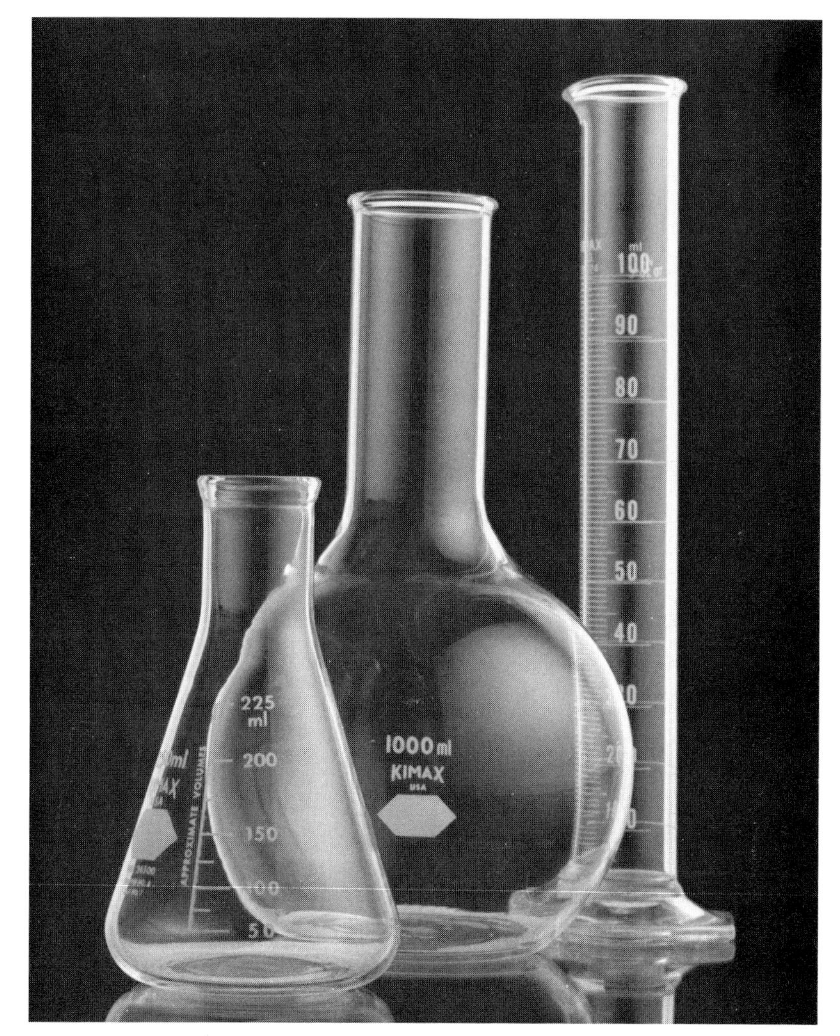

7.11

Lighting the whole diffusion sheet more evenly produces a larger highlight, but we usually want to keep that larger highlight dimmer. Had we lit the whole diffusion sheet brightly, it would have reflected in the glass as an obvious hard-edged rectangle. This reflection would have advertised the presence of a studio light and detracted from the reality of the scene.

Regardless of where we put the light, we sometimes minimize the studio look with strips of black tape on the diffusion sheet. Then the reflection of the light appears to be that of a window, as shown in Figure 7.12.

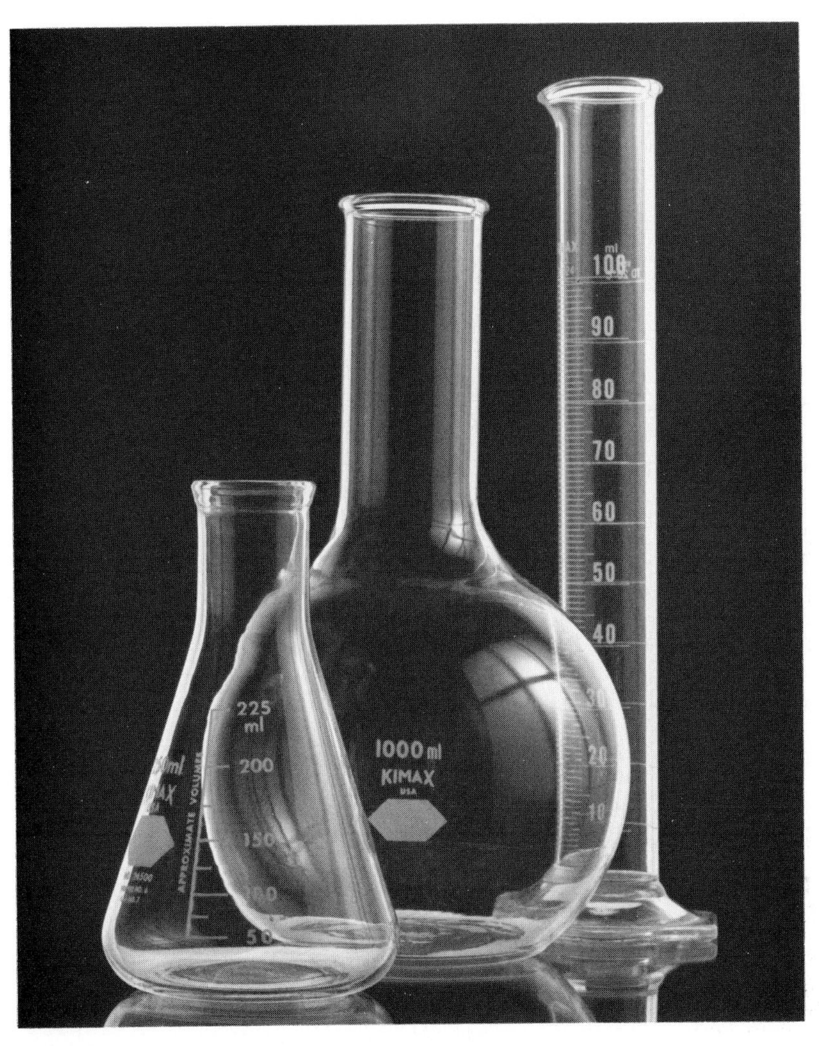

7.12

◀ *We used tape to reduce the "studio look" of this shot and to give the illusion of a window being reflected on the glass surface.*

Before we move on, notice that these are the first examples in this chapter in which the light does not come from behind the glass. This makes it a form of lighting that is useful when there are additional subjects in the scene that, unlike the glass, are not transparent. Later in this chapter we will see more of this kind of lighting.

Illuminating the Background

The basic dark-field approach produces a picture in which the background appears dark regardless of the actual tone of the background material. Brightening that background material requires an additional light source.

To brighten a dark-field background, we simply aim an additional light at the dark background. We position this light similarly to one used to produce bright-field illumination on a white opaque background. Usually, we can even use a light of similar intensity because the darker background material will keep the result from becoming a bright-field photograph.

Figure 7.13 was made this way. Notice that the tone of the background has been lightened to a medium gray and that the glass is free from any extraneous reflections.

► *A light on the background significantly brightened areas of the background in this dark-field shot.*

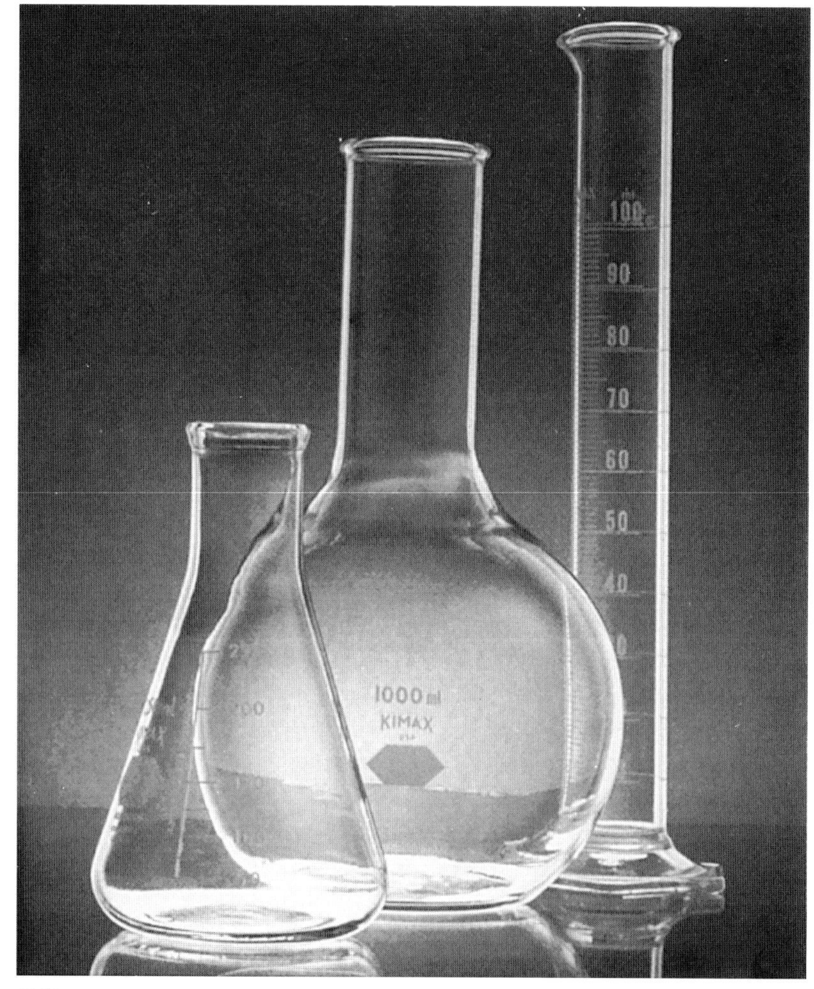

7.13

Minimizing the Horizon

Glass things need to be put on tables. Tables cause horizon lines in photographs. What can we do if we decide that the horizon is an undesirable distraction?

Eliminating the horizon is easier in photographs of subjects other than glass. Nonglass photographic subjects allow us to use a large enough table to keep the table edge out of the image area. Alternatively, we can use a sweep of seamless paper, raising its top edge high enough to prevent the camera from seeing it. These methods will work for glass subjects, too, but not as well.

Remember that the best lighting of the glass requires a background that barely fills the image area. Large tables and paper surfaces interfere with this requirement. We can overcome the problem by putting black gobos on a light-toned table, just outside the field of view. This produces reasonably good bright-field illumination.

We can also use white or silver reflectors to cover part of a dark table for dark-field illumination. This tends to be somewhat less effective, because the light on the reflectors is the same source illuminating the table. The right amount of light on the reflectors may be too much for the table. Therefore, if the table is not an essential element in the composition, we would prefer to get rid of it altogether. We cannot do that, but there are several ways to approximate the effect.

A table surface of transparent glass resembles a nonexistent table more closely than anything else. In all preceding photographs, we used a glass table. The background was visible through the table, so the distracting horizon line was minimized. The transparency of the table allowed the background light to pass through and illuminate the scene as if the table did not exist (Figure 7.14).

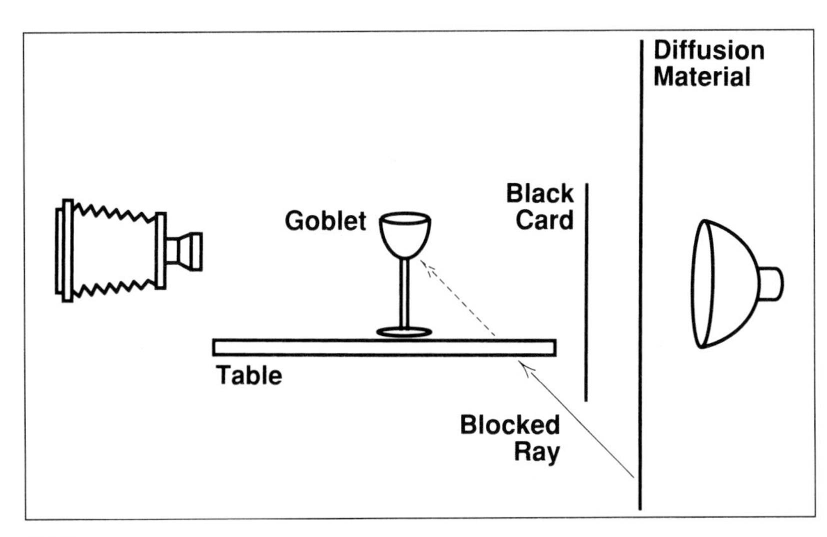

7.14

◀ *This large table could block light from the bottom of the glass, causing us to lose the delineation of the shape of the glass.*

Another approach would have been to place the subject on a mirror. The reflection of the background in the mirror would show a less abrupt tonal difference between the background and the foreground. The horizon would still have been visible, but less obtrusive.

An interesting variation on both of these approaches is to mist the glass table with water, thus disrupting and camouflaging any potentially disturbing reflections of the subject.

However, even a transparent table or a mirror can produce a slight horizon line, and there are situations when reducing the visibility of the horizon is not good enough. Some pictures require that the horizon be eliminated altogether. In these instances, we can use a paper wedge like the one shown in Figure 7.15.

► *A paper wedge such as this will eliminate the horizon but maintain edge definition.*

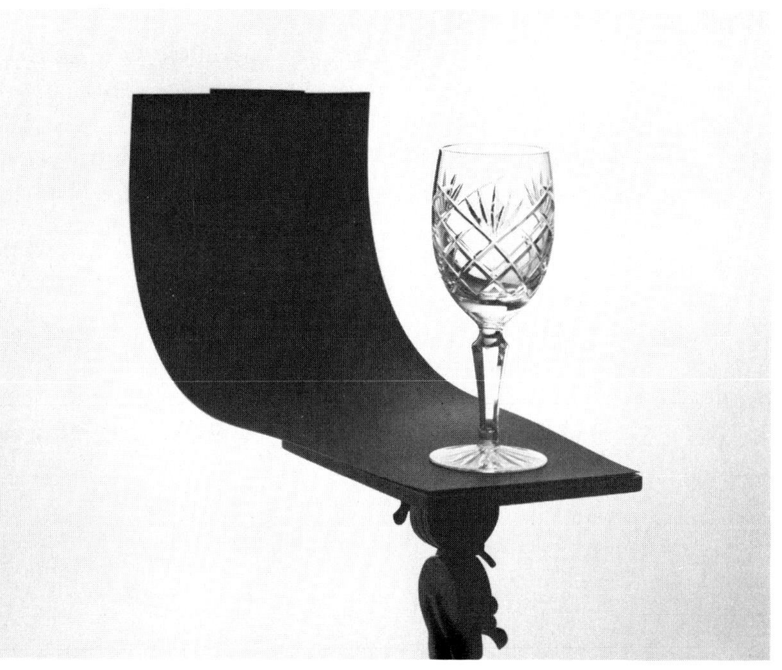

7.15

In this example, the paper wedge is taped directly to a large sheet of diffusion material. A light behind the diffusion material provides illumination. If we cut the paper wedge carefully so that it fits the field of view of the camera exactly, there will be no sacrifice of the lighting quality. Figure 7.16 shows the result of such an arrangement.

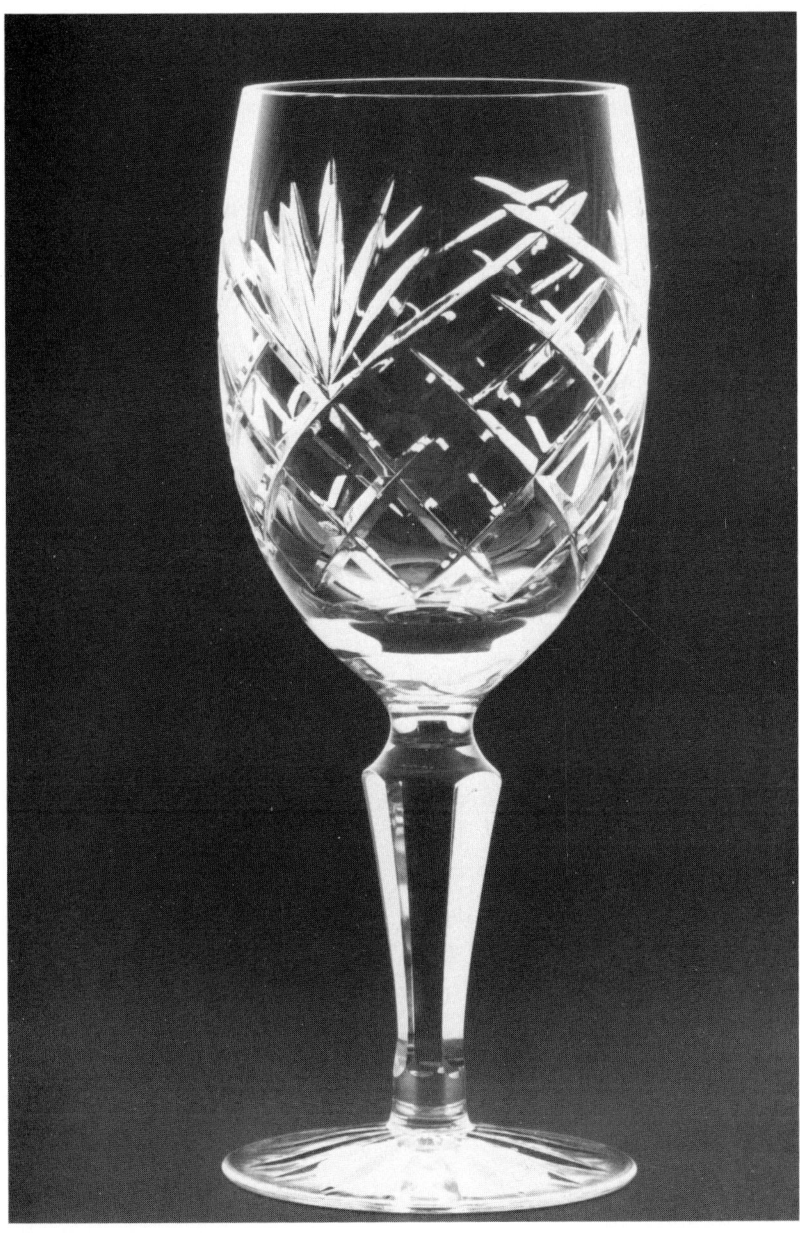

◀ *A photograph using the wedge illustrated in Figure 7.15. Notice the good edge definition and complete lack of horizon.*

7.16

Stopping Flare

The basic dark-field approach to photographing glassware is probably the worst flare-producing arrangement that we could encounter. We have discussed the principles of camera flare in earlier chapters. Dark-field lighting exaggerates the problem by giving camera flare the opportunity to occur on all four sides of the image. Figure 7.17 is an extreme example.

► *Because camera flare can occur on all four sides of the image, it is essential to use gobos to prevent it when using dark-field lighting.*

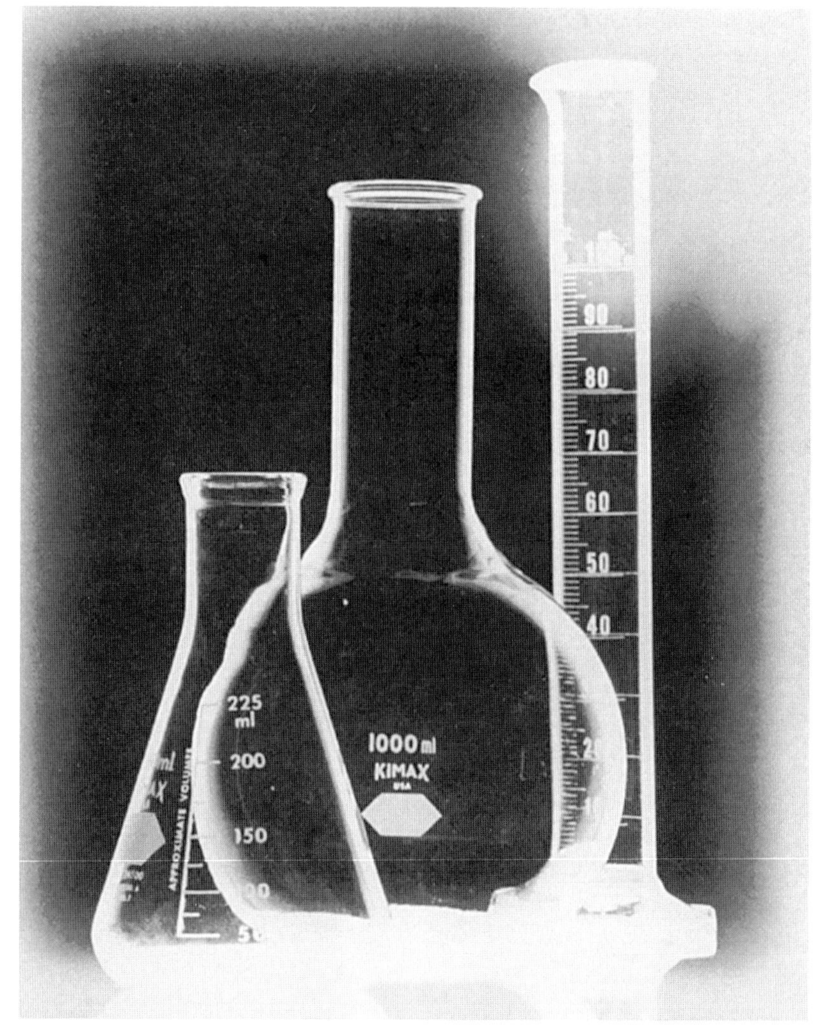

7.17

Even if the flare is not bad enough to produce a visible fogging of the edge of the film, the general degradation of the image from all sides accumulates. At best, we get a picture with low contrast.

Fortunately, this problem is easy to correct if we understand and anticipate it. We use gobos just as we did earlier in this book, *but* we have to remember to block the nonimaging light striking the lens from *all four* sides of the field of view.

We make such a gobo of four cardboard blades or of a single board with a rectangular hole. Then we clamp it to a light stand in front of the camera.

Eliminating Extraneous Reflections

Since glass reflects in a mirror-like manner, anything in the room may reflect in the subject. Therefore, after satisfactorily lighting a piece of glassware, we must finish the job by removing any extraneous reflections caused while putting together the setup. This is especially true of dark-field lighting, because the dark background visible through the glass makes the brighter extraneous reflections particularly visible.

The first step in getting rid of these unwanted reflections is to find which objects in the surrounding area are being mirrored in the glass surface. Once we have done this, there are three basic strategies from which to choose. Often we use a combination of them.

1. Eliminate Objects that Create Offending Reflections. The easiest way to deal with highly reflective objects such as extra light stands and unused reflector cards is simply to get them out of the room.

2. Block the Light Falling on the Offending Objects. Notice that in Figure 7.18, the light that is supposed to light the diffusion sheet next to the camera is also falling on the camera itself.

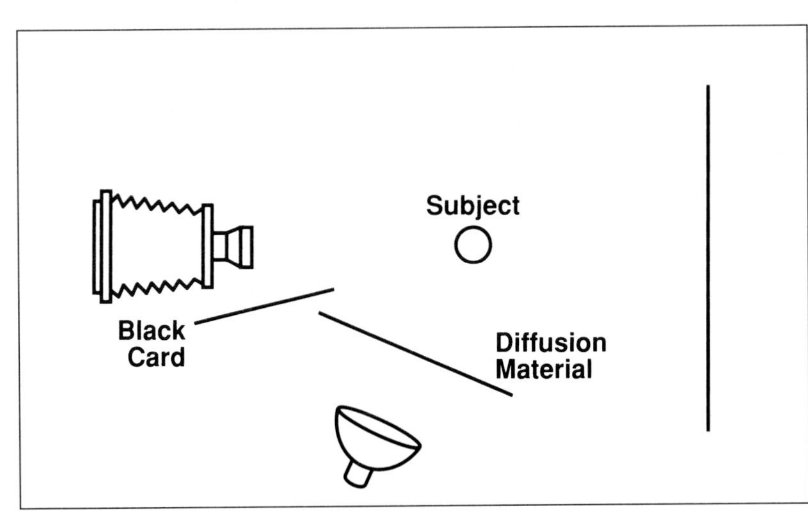

7.18

◀ *Light aimed at the diffusion sheet could fall on the camera, causing a reflection of the camera in the subject. In this setup we have used a black card as a gobo to prevent the problem.*

A gobo between the light on the camera darkens the reflection of the camera sufficiently that it is no longer visible in the surface of the glass.

3. Darken the Object. Finally, if the light cannot be blocked from the offending object, we may be able to sufficiently darken the object by covering it with black cards or cloth.

COMPLICATIONS FROM NONGLASS SUBJECTS

The information that we have presented so far in this chapter is all we need to light glass subjects. However, in many cases we need to include nonglass objects in the same picture. The best lighting for the glass may be the worst lighting for the rest of the objects in the picture.

As examples, we will look at the two subjects most likely to accompany glass: a liquid in a glass and a label on a bottle. The remedies we propose will be useful for other subjects as well.

Liquids in Glass

We are often called on to photograph glassware filled with liquid. Bottles full of beer, glasses full of wine, vials full of perfume, and bowls full of fish all produce an interesting challenge.

Liquid as a Lens. Optical laws dictate that a round, transparent container filled with a liquid act as a lens. The troublesome result of this is that a liquid-filled subject may reveal surroundings that we would prefer the viewer not see.

Figure 7.19 is a good example of what can happen. It was made from the same "normal" viewpoint used earlier for the glass without liquid.

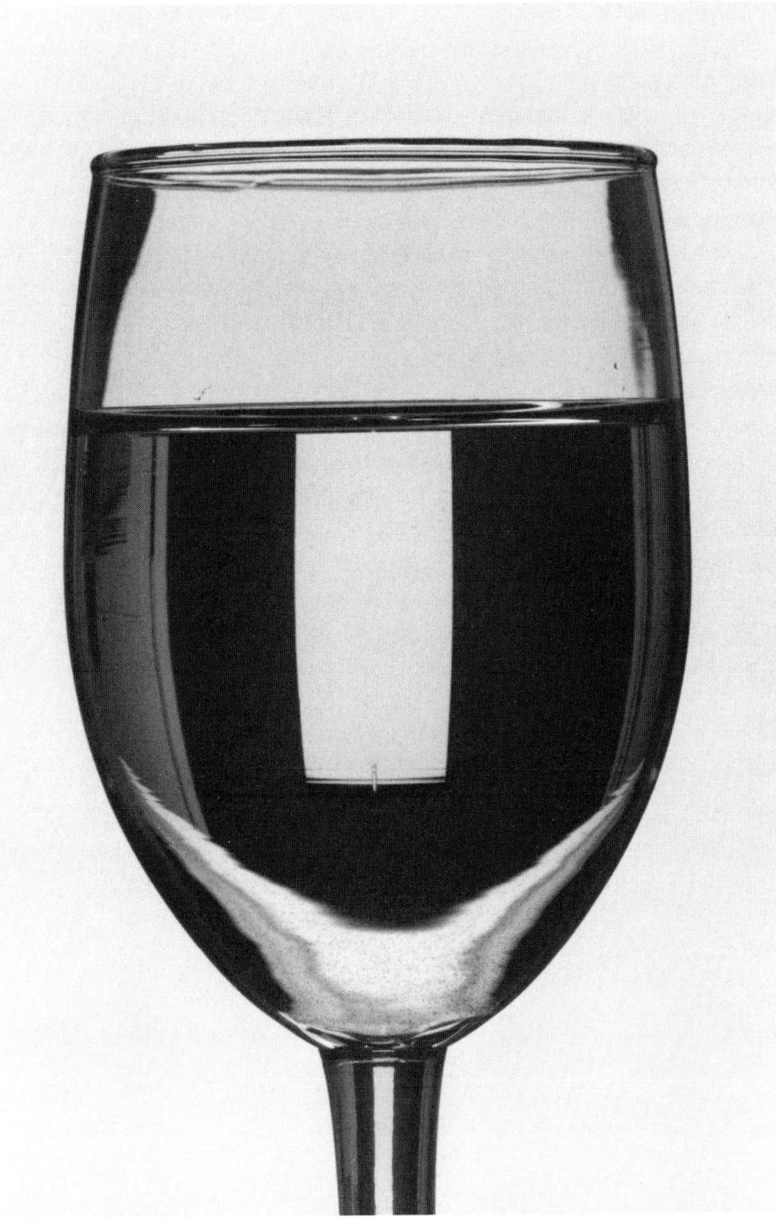

◀ *Notice how the "liquid lens" in this wine glass reveals the edge of the background and darkens the apparent color of the liquid.*

7.19

We see that a background large enough to fill the field of view of the camera is not large enough to fill the field of view that is seen through the liquid. The white rectangle in the center of the glass is the background. The dark area around it is the rest of the studio.

Our first inclination might be to use a larger background (or to increase the effective size of the background by moving it closer). However, we have seen that using a background larger than the field of view sacrifices the best delineation of the glass. Such a solution is sometimes practical, but not in a chapter devoted specifically to well-defined glass! For the present need, we will have to think of another technique.

The solution to this problem requires simply moving the camera closer to the subject. Then, if necessary, substitute a shorter focal-length lens to obtain a similar image size. This enables the existing background to fill the area seen through the liquid.

Remember, though, that a closer viewpoint always increases perspective distortion. The increased distortion is apparent in the deeper ellipse of the rim of the glass, as shown in Figure 7.20. Most people would not consider this a defect in this particular photograph, but the distortion could be offensive in another scene with other important subjects or from a higher or lower viewpoint.

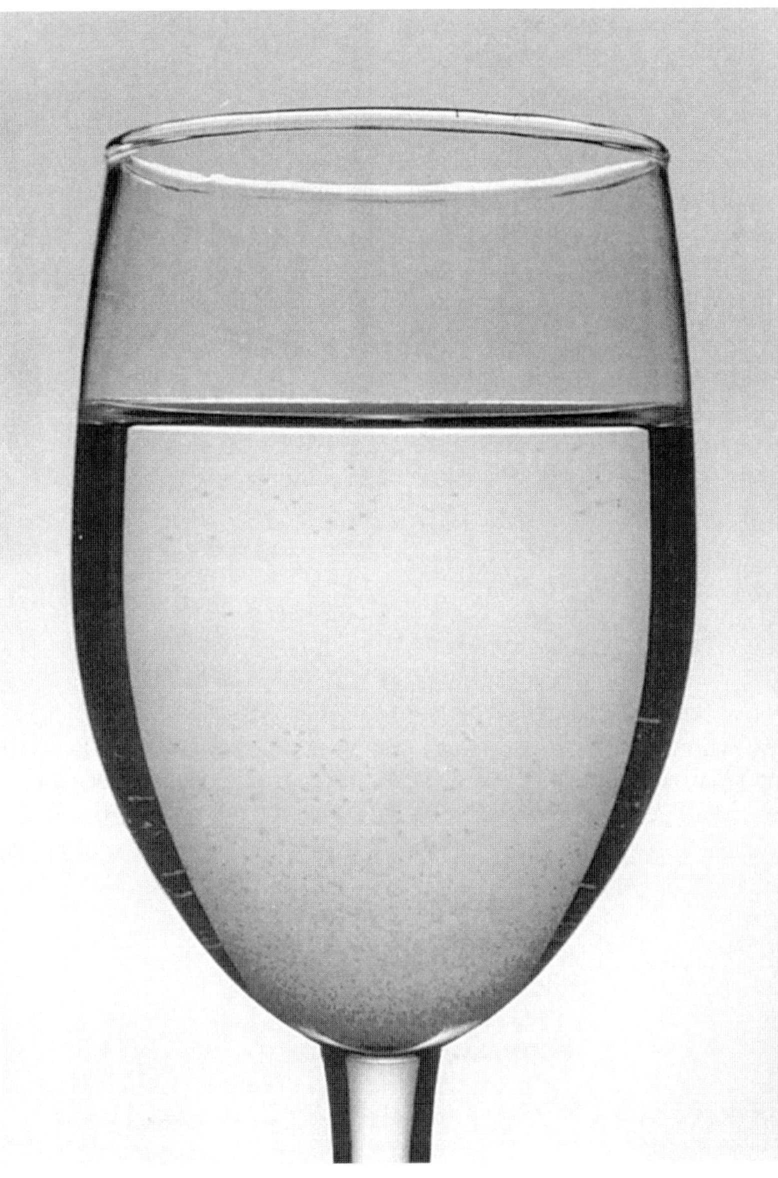

◀ *Moving the camera closer to the subject allowed the background to fill the entire area seen through the liquid-filled glass.*

7.20

Keeping True Color. Suppose a client needs a picture of a glass of light beer in front of a dark background. A liquid in a transparent container always takes on the color of its background. If we are not careful, we will turn the light beer into a dark one! The problem is shown in Figure 7.21.

► *In this shot, a dark background has turned a light beer into a dark one.*

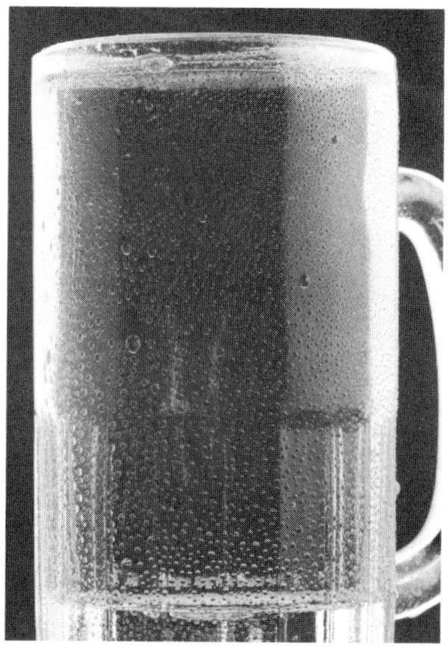

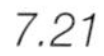
7.21

The solution to this problem is to set up a secondary background of a light, neutral tone. This secondary background must be the same shape as the subject, even if the glass is stemmed or has an irregular shape. The secondary background must also be large enough to fill as much of the area behind the liquid as possible, without extending far enough to be visible beyond the edges of the glass. All this sounds tedious, but in practice it is not. Figure 7.22 shows one easy way to construct the setup. Here are the steps:

► *One setup that uses a secondary background with a light, neutral tone.*

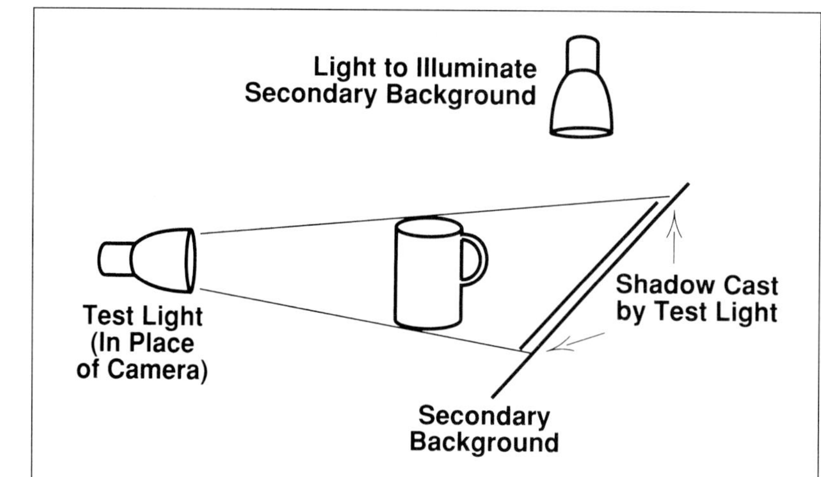

7.22

1. Place a Light-Toned, Thin Card Behind the Subject. White or silver cards are good. Some photographers prefer a foil with a color similar to the liquid, such as gold for beer. A flexible wire taped to the table surface can make an invisible support for the card, but do not attach the card firmly yet.

2. Remove the Camera. Replace It with a Test Light Aimed at the Subject. This will cast a shadow of the subject on the material from which we cut the background.

3. Outline the Shadow of the Subject on the Background. A felt-tip marker is handy for this. After outlining the shadow, remove the card and cut it out.

4. Reposition the Cutout Behind the Subject. At this point, we can also remove the test light and replace it with the camera. Look at the subject through the camera and make sure that the card and the camera are accurately positioned and that the edges of the card cannot be seen.

5. Place an Additional Light so that It Illuminates only the Cutout. Use barndoors to keep the light off the lens and the subject. Figure 7.23 shows the result.

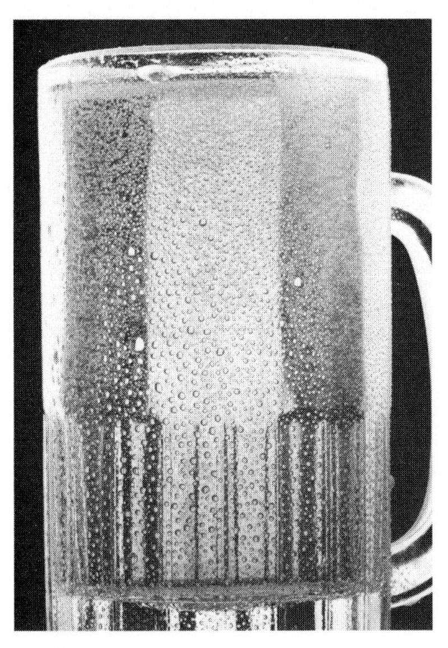

7.23

◀ *The beer has the right color this time, thanks to a light-colored secondary background.*

Secondary Opaque Subjects

A liquid is likely to be the only transparent secondary subject in a photograph of glass. Other secondary subjects are more often opaque and, therefore, more likely to need lighting techniques beyond those adequate for the transparent glass.

The usual lighting for such a scene begins with the lighting arrangement used earlier in Figure 7.10. The same light that produces a highlight on the front surface of the glass can also give good illumination for an opaque secondary subject. In many cases, this is enough. The next step is to expose the film.

Unfortunately, other subjects require more work. A paper label is one of the most common examples. Remember that we see neither perfect direct nor perfect diffuse reflection in nature. Although most of the reflection produced by most paper is diffuse reflection, some of it is direct. The lighting that produces direct reflection on the glass surface is also likely to obscure the paper label. Figure 7.24 is an extreme example.

► *The same lighting that produces direct reflection on glass can also cause it on a paper label. The result is reduced legibility.*

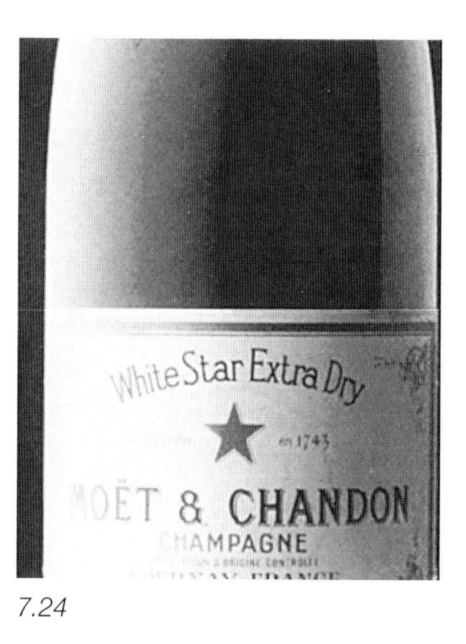

7.24

This particular camera position allows two remedies to this problem. One is to move the offending light higher; then any direct reflection from the paper goes downward instead of toward the lens.

If good highlight placement on the glass prevents moving the light, use a small opaque card to block the light from just those angles that produce direct reflections on the label. The position and size of this gobo are critical. If it extends beyond the family of angles defined by the label, it will reflect in the glass. We see the resulting photograph in Figure 7.25.

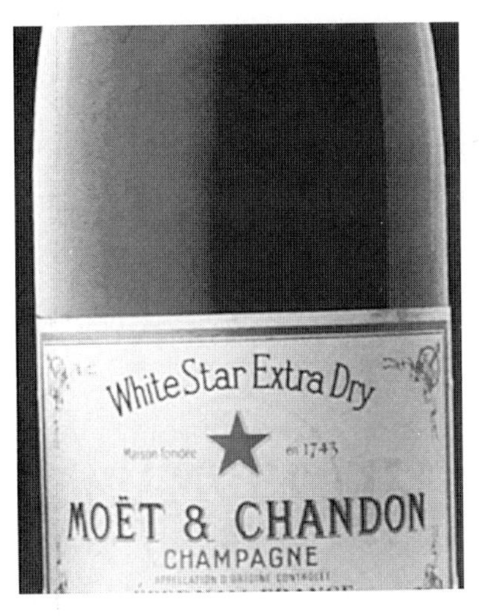

7.25

◀ *Using a gobo to block light from those angles that produce direct reflections on the label produced this picture.*

Changing the position of the light or adding a gobo will almost always remove the direct reflection from a secondary subject without harming the lighting of the glass. We may also consider a polarizing filter as a third remedy. However, this solution is rarely effective because much of the desirable highlight on the glass is usually already polarized. If the polarizer eliminates the offending reflection from a label, it is also likely to interfere with the light the glass needs.

RECOGNIZING THE PRINCIPAL SUBJECT

In this chapter we have talked about using bright-field and dark-field methods for lighting glass. We have also discussed some remedies to manage complications caused by competing nonglass subjects. However, we have not said very much about when to use which of these techniques.

The nature of the subject determines the best lighting. Deciding which subject is more important is the first step in lighting a scene that includes both glass and nonglass. Should we light the glass as well as possible, then make adjustments to accommodate the rest of the composition? Should we first establish the general lighting, and then add any secondary lights, reflectors, or gobos needed to enhance the glass a bit?

We cannot make these editorial and artistic decisions on a purely technical basis. We might light two identical scenes differently, depending on what is the intended picture caption or on who is paying our bill or on personal whim.

Seeing how light behaves matters more than the mere ability to make a routine glassware shot look professional. We devote a whole chapter to lighting glass because generations of photographers have found glass to be one of those classic subjects that teaches us that ability to see.

Chapter 8

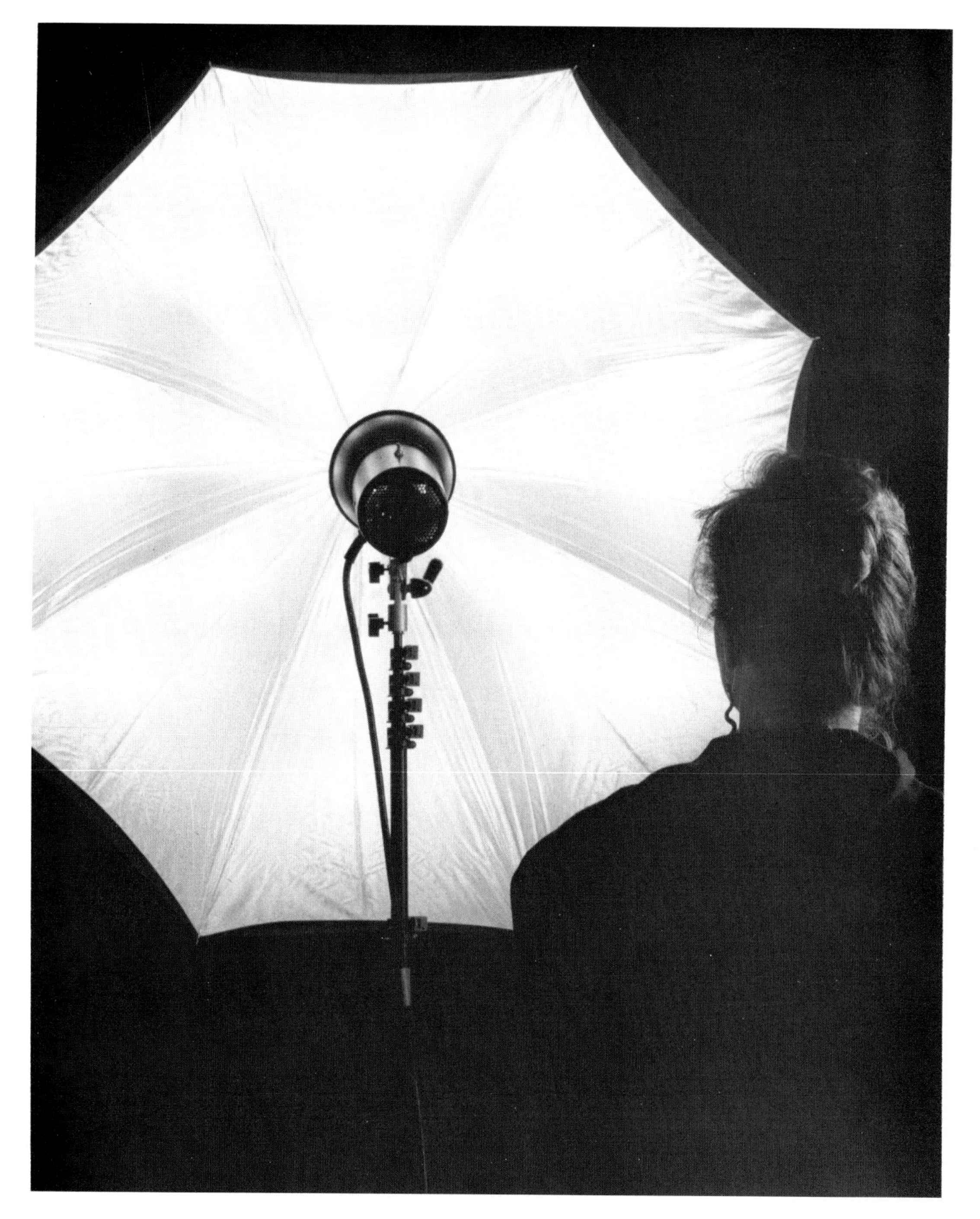

An Arsenal of Lights

Good lighting is the key to good portraiture. Posing, location, rapport, camera angle (the list can go on) are all important. However, that said, the lighting matters even more. We can do everything else beautifully, but if our lighting is bad, our portrait will be bad. It is that simple. And now, with the above sermon in mind, let us look at what it takes to light a portrait properly.

In this chapter we will start by explaining the simplest of all portrait setups—that which uses a single light source. The light that provides most of the illumination for the picture is the *main* or *key* light. We handle this light in the same manner, whether we use it alone or with many additional lights.

Aside from the main light, this chapter will introduce a more complex lighting arrangement than any we have discussed earlier. Classic portrait lighting usually requires several lights. Whether you do it this way is your own choice. Either way, we hope you will think about the purpose of every light we use here. Most of these lights could serve similar needs for *any* subject. If you decide not to use all of them for portraiture, you probably will use them for something else later. Therefore, we say more about the fill light than we have before. From there we will move on to explain the use of other lights, such as kickers and hair lights.

THE SINGLE-LIGHT SETUP

Simple, yes. Simplistic, no. A single light is adequate for most portraits; the rest are optional. However, even one light needs to be used well. Otherwise, no amount of additional lighting will salvage the picture.

The Basic Setup

Now look at Figure 8.1. It is a diagram of the simplest possible setup. In it the subject is lit by a single bare bulb placed to one side.

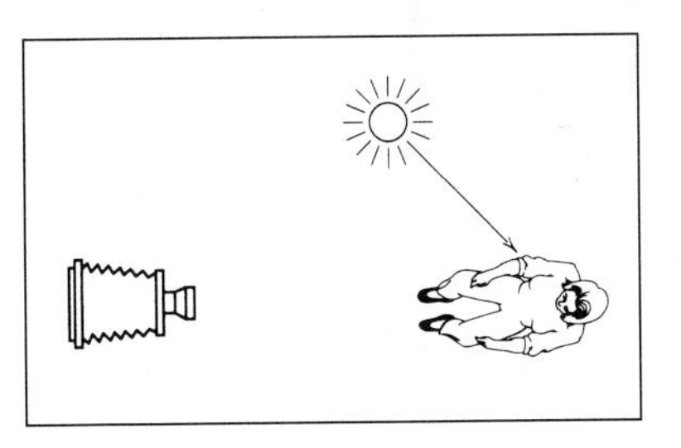

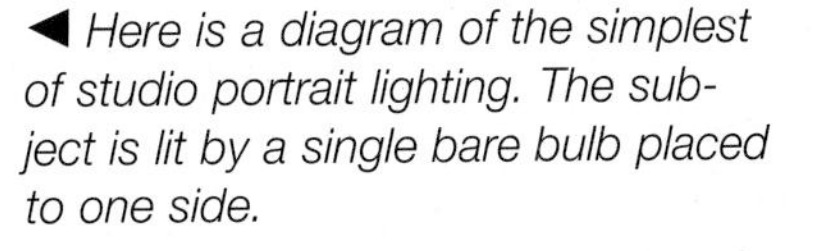

◀ *Here is a diagram of the simplest of studio portrait lighting. The subject is lit by a single bare bulb placed to one side.*

8.1

Notice that we positioned the model several feet in front of a plain wall that serves as a backdrop. This positioning is important. Had we placed the subject closer to the wall, her body would have cast a potentially distracting shadow on it.

Figure 8.2 is a portrait made with the lighting setup we have just described. In many ways, it is a satisfactory picture. It is sharp, properly exposed, and acceptably composed. However, it suffers from one very serious fault. Harsh, distracting, and very uncomplimentary shadows clutter the model's face.

► *The result of the lighting diagrammed in Figure 8.1. The harsh, uncomplimentary shadows in the portrait distract from the features.*

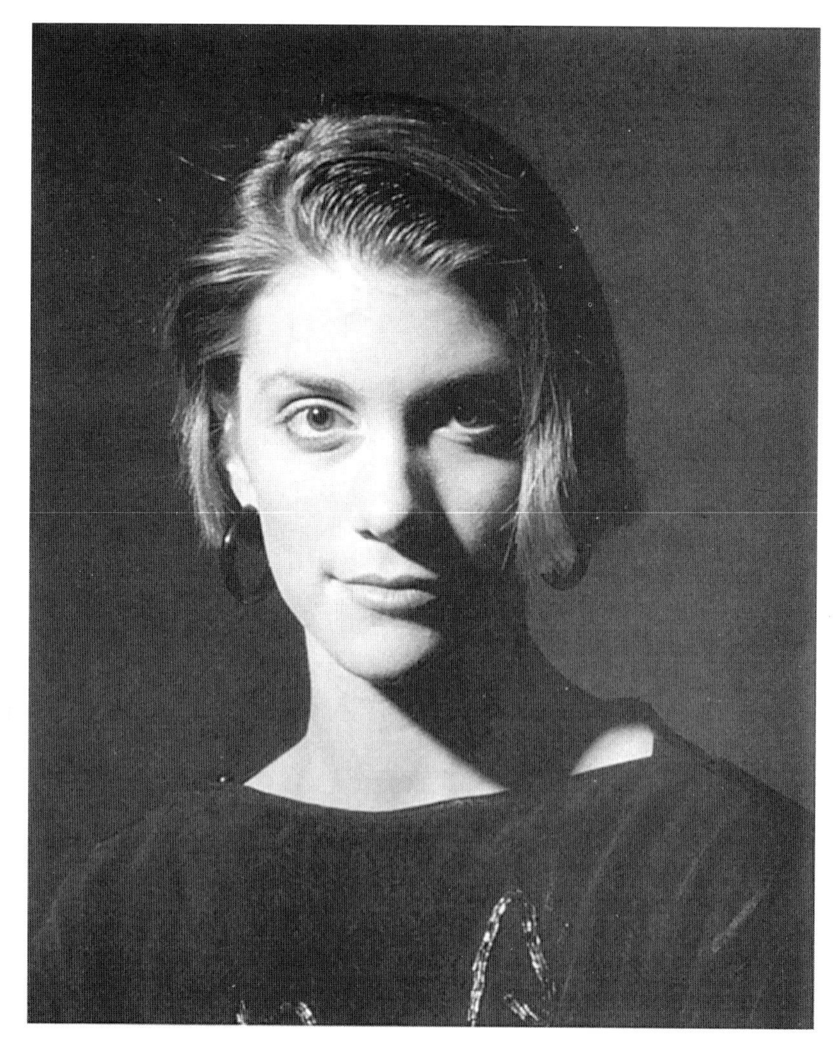

8.2

Now look at Figure 8.3. It shows the same girl in the same basic pose, and it was made with a single bulb in the same place as before. But look at the difference between the pictures. The hard-edged, unattractive shadows that produced such an unpleasant picture before have vanished.

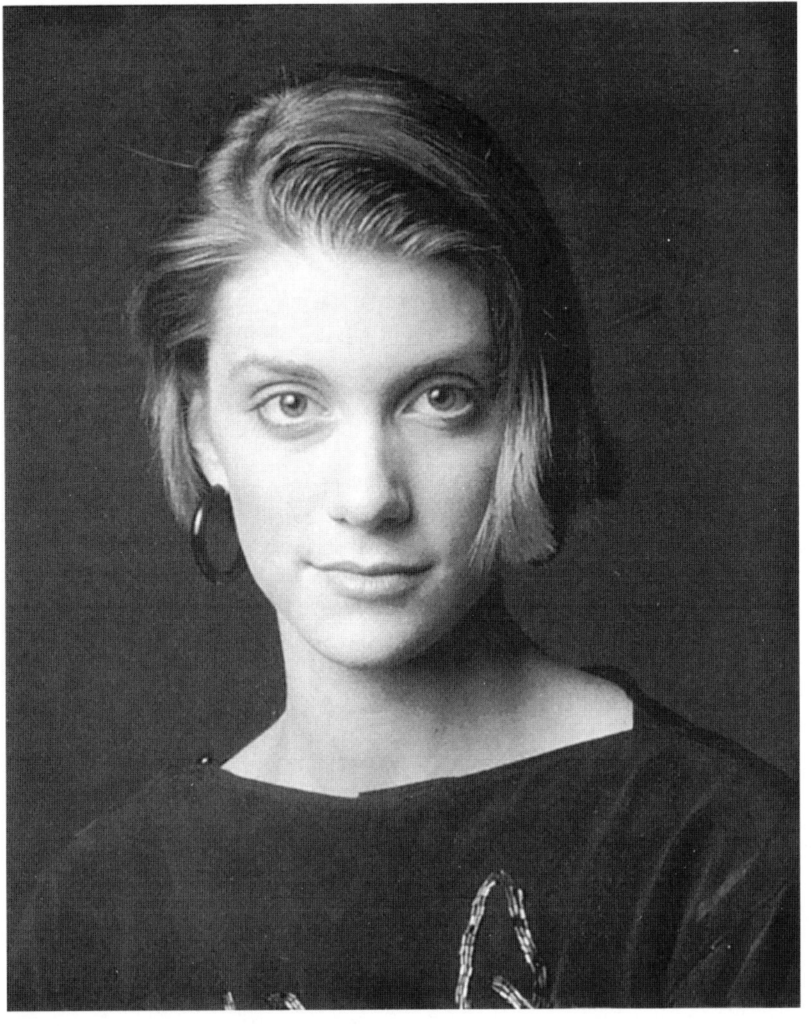

◀ *The softer shadows in this picture are the result of a larger light source. These shadows define the features of the subject and add depth.*

8.3

The softer shadows of this lighting help, rather than detract from, the picture. They help to define the features and add an element of depth and interest to the picture. The result is more likely to please most people, especially the subject!

Light Size

What made the difference between the two portraits? Why were the shadows hard and unpleasant in one, and soft and flattering in the other? The answer is simple and familiar: light size. The first portrait was made with a single small, bare bulb. As we have seen, such small sources of light produce hard, sharply defined shadows. The second picture was made with a large light source. The results prove the principle that large light sources produce soft shadows.

In this particular example we enlarged the light size in the easiest manner possible. We put a translucent lamp shade over the lamp. This increased its effective size tenfold.

The lamp shade was a quick and easy solution to the problem of hard shadows, but it was far from the only one available to us. For example, we also could have increased the effective size of our light source by hanging a sheet of tracing paper or plastic diffusion material between the light and the subject. We could have accomplished the same thing by bouncing a light from an umbrella. These approaches all do the same thing. They make the light size larger and thus the shadows softer.

Skin Texture

The size of the lights also influences the amount of texture we can see in the skin. Skin texture appears as microscopic shadows in the photograph. Such shadows may be either hard or soft, just as the shadows of the general features may be. We can see this clearly in the enlargements in Figure 8.4.

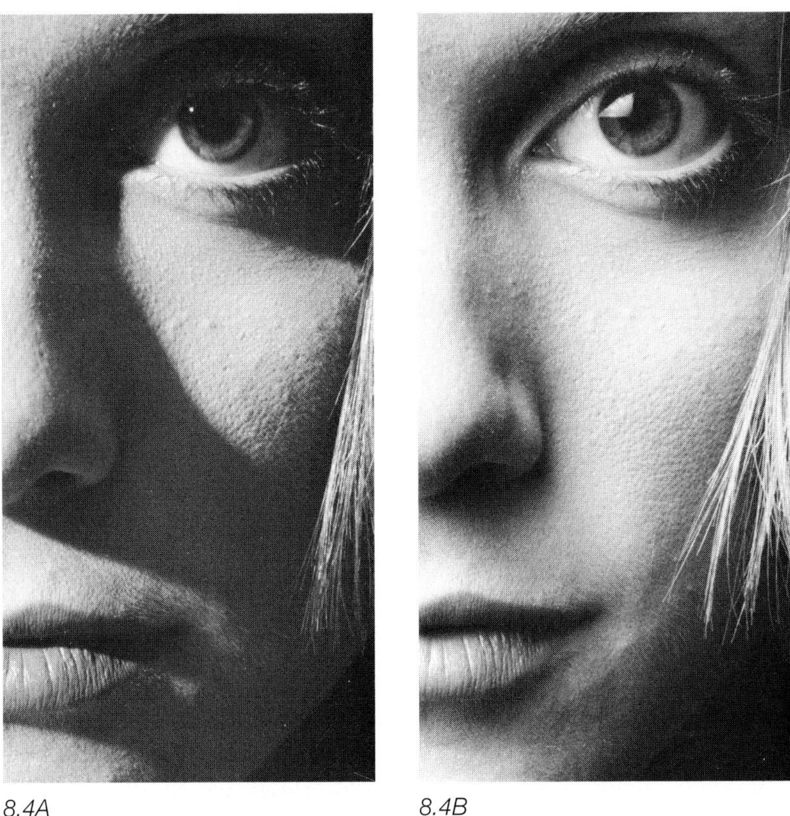

8.4A 8.4B

◀ *Compare the skin texture in these enlargements. Picture* **A** *was made with a small light. Notice how pronounced the skin texture is. Picture* **B** *was made with a soft light and looks smoother.*

This difference in texture may not matter if the image is reproduced at a small size in a book or magazine, especially if the subject is young. However, people often hang very large portraits on the wall. (Many photographers who do consumer portraiture usually try to sell prints as large as possible to increase their income.) Age and weather add enough skin texture to be visible in even small pictures of many people.

Where to Put the Main Light

Turning briefly from people portraits to egg portraits, look at Figure 8.5. It is an ostrich egg that we lit like Figure 8.3. That is to say, we placed a large, soft main light in front of and to one side of it.

► *Notice the transitions from light tones to dark ones in this ostrich egg. Such tonal transitions model and show the contours of the face of a portrait subject.*

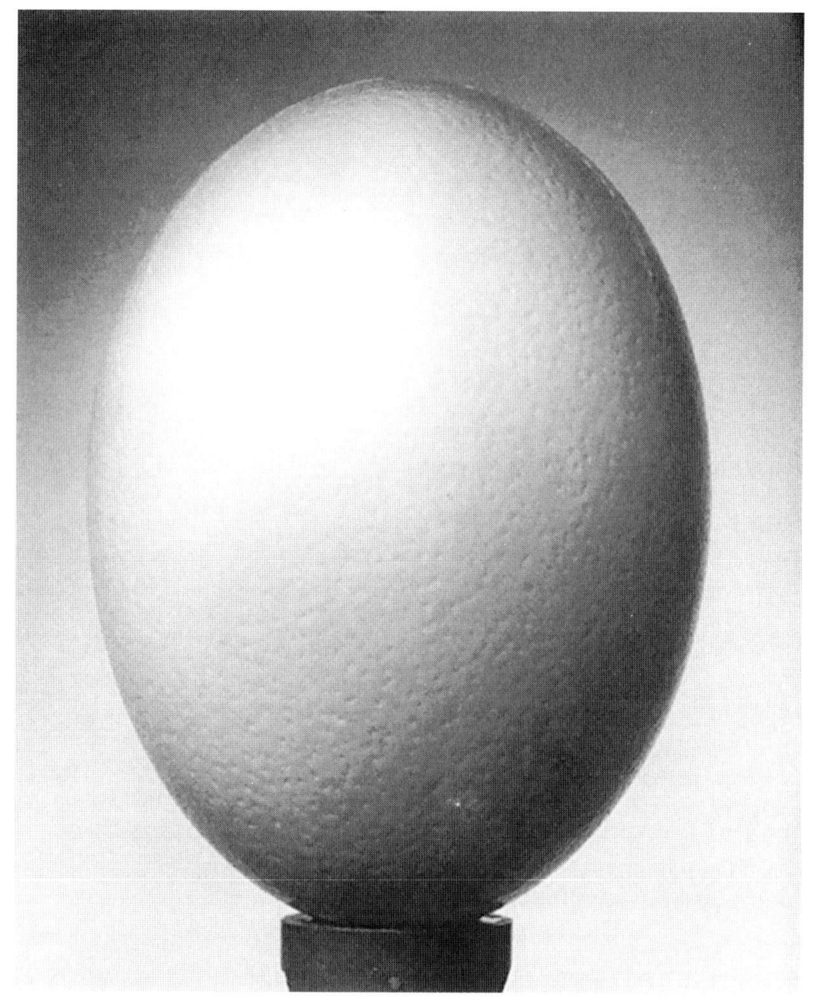

8.5

Notice that this lighting setup produces a transition from highlight on one side to shadow on the other. In addition, because the light source is high in relation to the egg, there is a similar light-to-dark tonal transition from the top to the bottom of the egg.

These transitions from light to dark, from highlight to shadow, are all important in portrait photography. They show the shape and contours of the face of the subject, just as they show the shape and contours of the egg.

Eggs are simpler to light than faces. Eggs have simple shapes and smooth surfaces. Faces are more complex. They have noses, eye sockets, mouths, wrinkles, creases, and all the other irregularities that come as part of the human form. These all cause complications by casting shadows and otherwise affecting the behavior of the light. Fortunately, we can handle these complications quite simply. All we have to do is move the light around a bit.

Generally speaking, we prefer to position the light so that there is a shadow on one side of the face. This, as we have seen, is accomplished by keeping the light to one side. In addition, we want to keep it high enough so that there are similar shadows under the eyebrows, nose, and chin. Look back at Figure 8.3. See how these discrete areas of highlight and shadow give contour and depth to the facial features.

Having read this, however, you may well ask just *how far* to keep the light "to one side" and *how high* is "high enough." These are valid questions. We begin to answer them with a look at the *key triangle.*

The Key Triangle. The proper placement of this triangular highlight is the basis of much good portrait lighting. Using the key triangle as a guide to good lighting is simplicity itself. All we have to do is to move the light around until we see a triangular-shaped highlight on our subject's face like the one shown in Figure 8.6. The base of the key triangle should run through the eye, and its point should extend down the cheek approximately to the lip line.

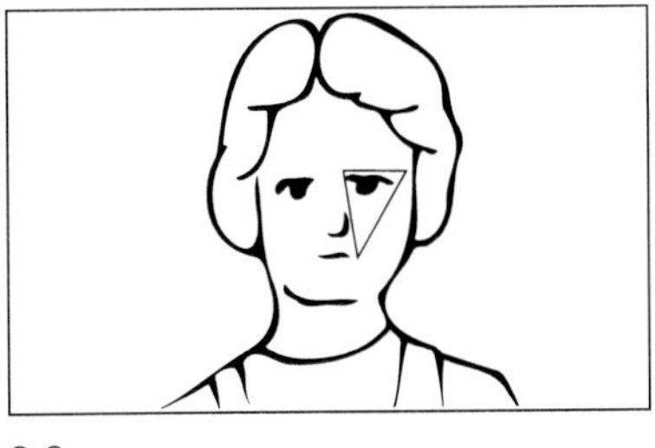

8.6

◀ *The key triangle extending from the eye, through the cheek, to the lip line is the starting point for good portrait lighting.*

The importance of the key triangle is its ability to let us see lighting defects before exposing the film. Some of the subtleties of good lighting become easy to see when we look at the boundaries of where the key triangle falls.

We will look at the three most common potential problems now and see how the key triangle reveals each of them. None of these potential problems is an inevitably fatal sin in every picture. They are, however, deviations from "standard" portrait lighting, which we should commit only if we have good reason and full awareness that we are doing so.

Key Triangle Too Large: Main Light Too Near the Camera. As Figure 8.7 illustrates, placing the light too near to the camera lights the subject too uniformly to show good contour in the face. (The extreme example of such "flat" lighting comes from mounting a strobe directly on top of the camera.)

► *Flat lighting, far too uniform to show contour, is the result of placing the main light too near to the camera.*

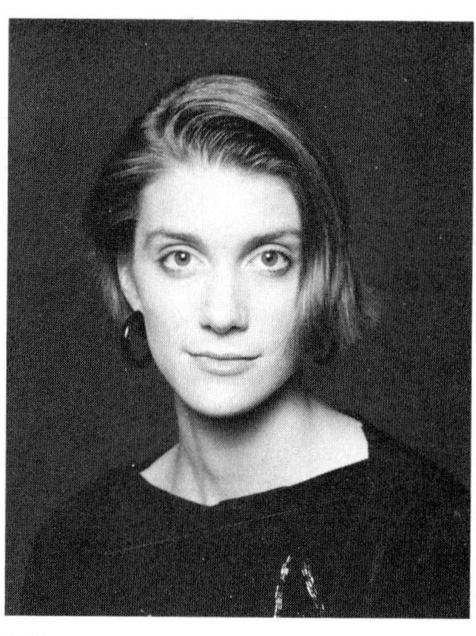

8.7

Evaluating whether the lighting is too flat can be difficult for photographers who are just beginning to learn portrait lighting. Anticipating how film will see shades of gray takes practice. But the decision becomes simple when we see that such lighting also makes the key triangle so large that it is no longer a triangle.

We can usually improve such lighting by moving the light farther to the side and higher to reduce the size of the key triangle. To maximize contour, we move the light far enough to get the key triangle as small as possible, but stop just short of moving it far enough to create either of the following two problems.

Key Triangle Too Low: Main Light Too High. Regardless of whether the eyes are the window of the soul, they are certainly essential to almost any portrait. Keeping the eyes of the subject in shadow can be unsettling to anyone looking at the portrait. Figure 8.8 illustrates this problem. Notice how the strong eye shadow eliminates the top of the key triangle and produces an unnatural and ghoulish picture.

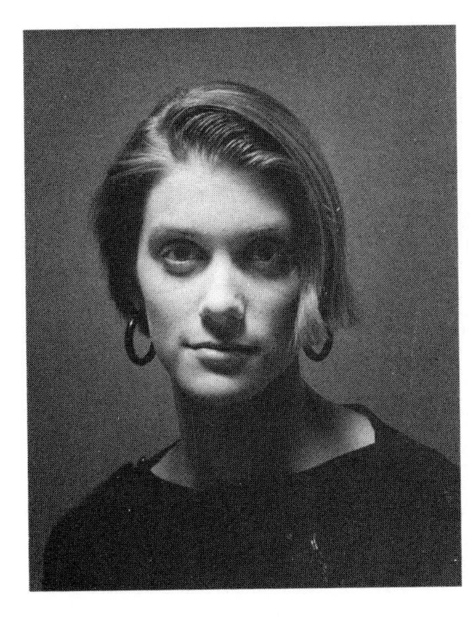

◀ *The unsettling "raccoon eyes" that we see here come from lifting the main light too high above the model's face.*

8.8

This shadow is there because we positioned our light too high above the head of the subject. Happily, it is an easy matter to remedy. All we have to do is to lower the light a bit.

Key Triangle Too Narrow: Main Light Too Far to Side. Figure 8.9 illustrates still another potential problem. We positioned the light so that the nose casts a dark shadow across her cheek. This shadow blocks the key triangle. Once more the cure is simple. To avoid a shadow such as this one, all we have to do is move the light a bit more to the front. When we do this, the key triangle will reappear.

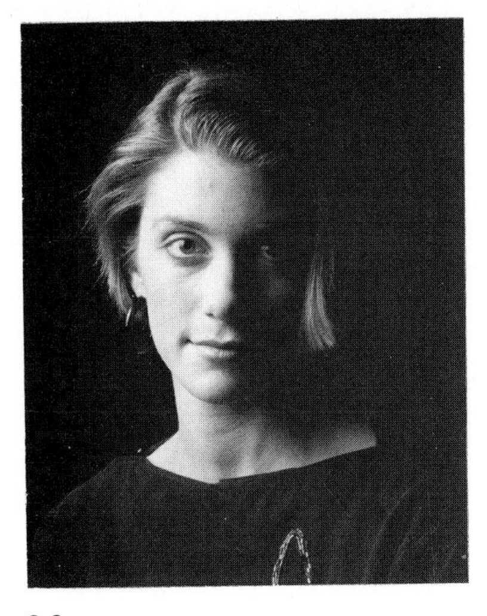

◀ *The result of positioning the main light too far to one side. The nose of the model casts a shadow across her cheek, blocking the key highlight.*

8.9

Left Side? Right Side?

Photographers generally prefer to put the main light on the same side as the subject's *dominant eye,* or the eye that appears to be more open than the other. The greater the visible dominance of the eye, the more important it is that we light that side. Of course, there are those subjects who do not appear to have a dominant eye; then it makes no difference on which side we put the main light.

The other influence on our decision is where the person's hair is parted. Lighting on the same side as the part prevents extraneous shadows, especially if the hair is long.

Some people absolutely insist that we photograph them from one side or the other. Very often we should listen to such opinions because they are based on that individual's dominant eye or hair style, whether the person knows it or not. Just be sure that the subject has not confused his "good" side from his "bad" side when looking in a mirror!

Broad Lighting or Short Lighting

So far we have made all pictures with the model approximately facing the camera. Whether the light was on the right or the left would have made only a minor difference. However, the difference is major if the subject turns his or her head to either side. Where do we main light then? Figures 8.10 and 8.11 show the options. We either put the light on the same side as the subject's visible ear or on the other side.

► *Putting the main light on the side opposite the visible (were it not covered by her hair) ear produces short lighting.*

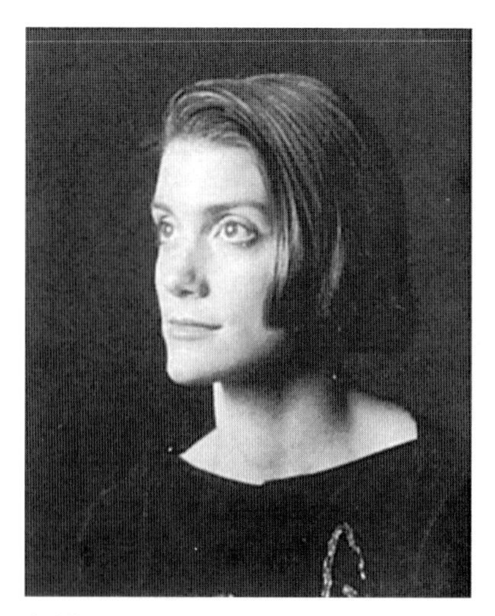

8.10

◀ *Broad lighting means putting the main light on the same side as the visible ear.*

8.11

A main light on the *same* side as the visible ear is called *broad lighting.* Positioning the main light on the side *opposite* from your subject's visible ear produces *short lighting*. (Whether the hair covers the "visible" ear has nothing to do with which side of the face we are talking about!)

If you look at Figures 8.10 and 8.11 again, the reason behind these two somewhat confusing names becomes apparent. First, look at the picture that we made with broad lighting. Notice that a broad, or wide, highlight runs from the back of the model's hair, across her cheek, all the way to the bridge of her nose. Now, look at the portrait that we made with short lighting. This time the highlight is quite short, or narrow. The brightest part of it only extends from the side of the model's cheek to her nose.

There are no firm rules to dictate when to use broad and when to use short lighting. Our own personal preference, however, leans decidedly to short lighting. It puts the light where it will do the most good, on the front of the face. This, we feel, produces by far the most interesting portraits.

Other photographers have a completely different bias. They feel strongly that the short or broad light decision should be based on the subject's body build. They prefer to use short lighting if their subject has a broad face. Such lighting, they argue, helps to make the subject look thinner by concealing their heavy cheeks and throats in the shadows. If, on the other hand, the subject is very thin, the proponents of this approach feel that broad lighting is the way to go. This increases the amount of the image that is highlighted and makes the subject appear more substantial.

Eyeglasses

Eyeglasses sometimes dictate the position of the main light, regardless of the other preferences of the photographer. Figure 8.12 was shot with short lighting. Look at the resulting direct reflection from the glasses.

▶ *Short lighting produces an objectionable glare on the eyeglasses.*

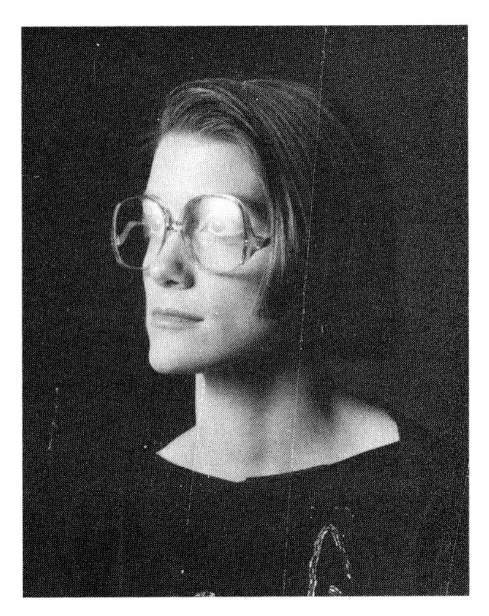

8.12

It impossible to eliminate the glare with the light positioned as it was for this portrait. We could, of course, raise it, but that would cause another equally serious problem. It would fill the eye with a very unattractive shadow.

Figure 8.13 shows the only solution that always works. It is the same subject shot with broad lighting. Changing from short to broad lighting positions the main light outside the family of angles that produces direct reflection.

▶ *Broad lighting eliminates the glare problem.*

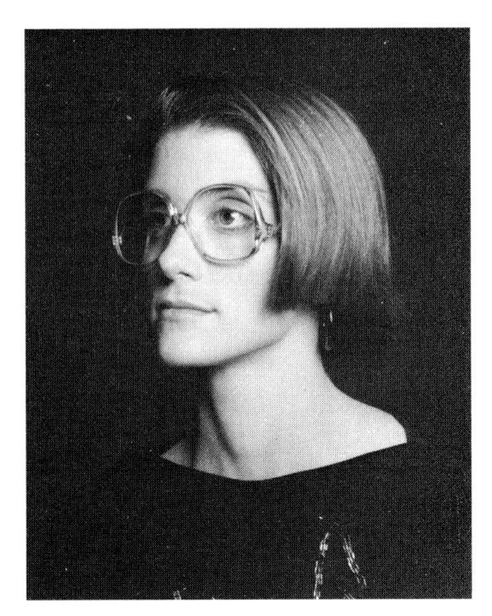

8.13

Problems with eyeglasses increase with the diameter of the eyeglass lenses. From any particular camera position, the family of angles that produces direct reflection is greater if the glasses have big lenses. If the subject has small eyeglass lenses, we can sometimes keep a short lighting arrangement by using a smaller main light. It is easier to position the smaller light so that no part of the light is within that family of angles.

Still life photographers exploring portraiture are sometimes tempted to use polarizing filters on the main light and on the camera lens to eliminate reflection from glasses. However, this can cause problems. Human skin also produces a small amount of direct reflection. Consequently, eliminating all direct reflection in the highlights of a portrait may give the skin a lifeless appearance.

ADDITIONAL LIGHTS

Up to this point, we have shown some of the different ways to position and manipulate highlights and shadows using a single light source. These techniques are powerful because they produce fine work even if we have only one light at our disposal. Depending on taste, we may be satisfied with the results of a single light and proceed no further with the lighting, even if we have a whole studio full of strobes available.

Again, depending on taste, there are many times in portraiture when we do want to do things that simply are not possible with a single light. For the rest of this chapter we will point out how to use additional lights to their best advantage.

Fill Lights

As we have seen, shadows are an important part of any portrait. They help to model and give contour to the features and to give depth to a portrait. There are many times, however, when we prefer to lighten a shadow or even eliminate it altogether. We can do this with a single light source only if we place it near the camera lens. But if we want to keep the main light farther from the camera, we need some kind of fill light.

Photographers commonly use a fill light that gives the subject about half as much illumination as the main light, but this guideline is by no means absolute. Some photographers like to use a lot of fill in portraits, while other equally talented ones prefer to use none. The important thing is not to try to memorize any set of rules, but rather, to adjust your lighting until it is satisfactory to you.

Some photographers use additional lamps for fill, while others prefer flat reflecting surfaces. Both methods have their advantages.

Additional Lamps as Fill Lights. The most basic multiple light arrangement consists of a main light plus a fill light. An additional lamp allows good flexibility in fill light placement. We can put the fill light far enough from the subject to be out of the way and still expect it to be bright enough.

Figure 8.14 was made with a single fill light. We turned off the main light so that you could see exactly what effect a fill light has by itself.

► *The fill light was all that was used to make this exposure. Notice that it is much dimmer than the main light.*

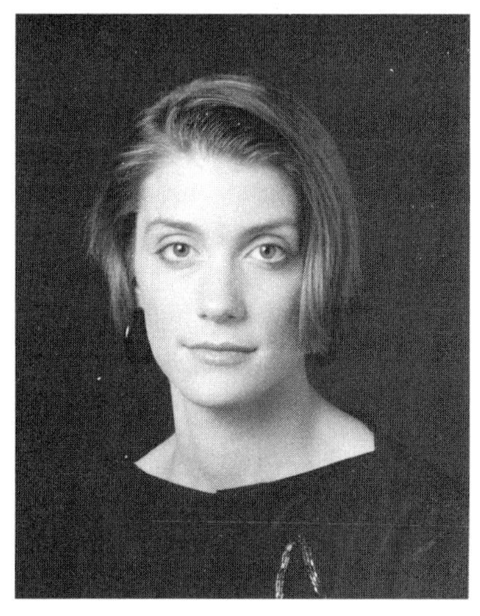

8.14

Now look at Figure 8.15, in which we turned the main light back on. This is a typical example of the combination of fill light and a main light.

► *We used a main and a fill light together to make this exposure.*

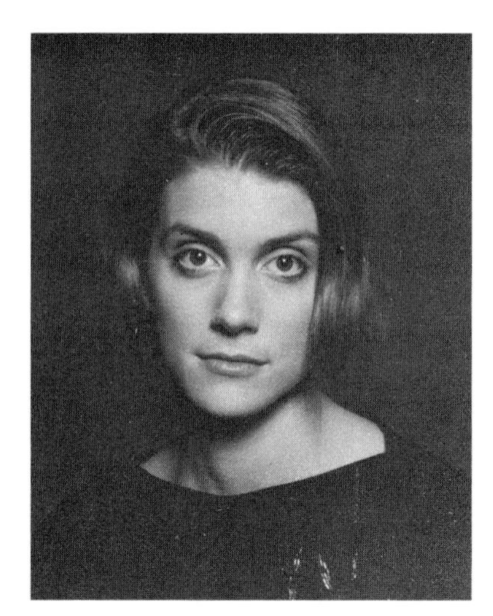

8.15

Notice that the shadow under the chin is darker than the other shadows in the scene. This area receives little illumination from either the main light or the fill. The shadow is not offensive, but it would be if it were a bit darker or harder. We will talk about how to keep that from happening.

Size is important when you are using fill lights. Generally speaking, the rule is, "the bigger, the better." As you will remember, the larger a light source is, the softer the shadows it produces. The soft-edged shadows produced by a large fill light are less visible and less likely to compete with shadows produced by the main light.

The use of a large fill light allows greater freedom in deciding where to place the light. Because the shadow of a large fill light is not clearly defined, the position of the light is, within a wide range, of no importance. That means we can put it nearly anywhere that we will not knock it over and the lighting differences will be too minor to matter.

Figure 8.16 shows a two-light portrait arrangement including a main light and two possible fill lights, labeled *A* and *B*. (Photographers are not likely to use *both* alternatives.) We could successfully use either *A* or *B*, depending on our preference and available equipment.

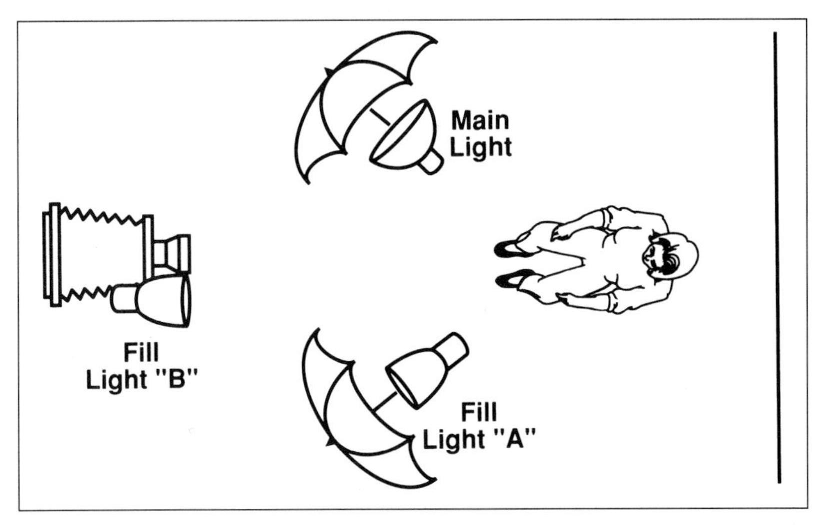

8.16

◀ *Two fill light alternatives. Bouncing the light* ***A*** *into an umbrella produces softer lighting. Small light* ***B****, placed near the camera, produces hard shadows. However, they fall behind the subject, where the camera cannot see them.*

Fill light *A*, like the main light, uses an umbrella. This increases its effective size and softens the shadows it produces. Because it is large, we could move the fill light around a good bit without a major effect on its shadow pattern. Such an arrangement makes it easy to vary the fill light intensity by moving it closer to or farther from the subject.

Alternatively, the fill light can be small if we position it like light *B*. Notice that the fill light is as close to the camera lens as we can put it. Such a fill light still casts hard shadows, but most of these shadows fall behind the subject, where the camera cannot see them.

Reflector Cards as Fill Lights. One of the simplest and least expensive ways of brightening dark shadows is to use reflector cards to bounce light coming from the main light onto the face of the subject. Figure 8.17 uses a main light position similar to that in previous photographs, but now a white reflector card has been added to provide fill light.

► *In this photograph, light from the main light bounced off a reflector to the face of the subject to fill some of the shadows.*

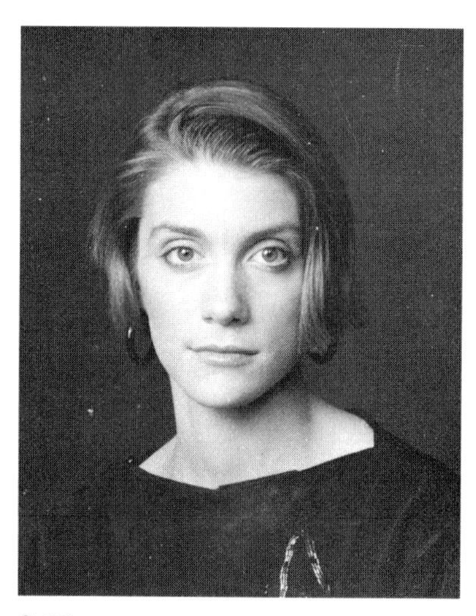

8.17

We would like to show you the effect of the reflector fill card alone, but this is impossible. Since the reflector is illuminated by the main light, it has no effect by itself. However, it is useful to compare its effect with that of the additional lamp in Figure 8.15.

Notice that the dark shadow we saw under the chin in Figure 8.15 has been greatly reduced by the reflector card. The shadow is still present, but is softer. This is because the reflector card is much larger than the fill light used earlier. We could, of course, have used a fill light as large as the reflector card to produce the same result.

The only common problem with a reflector fill is that it may not be bright enough to suit some photographers' preferences. This is especially likely when we move the camera back to include more than the head and shoulders. The reflector has to be moved back, also, to get it out of camera range.

The amount of fill light a reflector provides is determined by numerous factors, including the following:

- **The Reflector Distance from the Subject**. The closer the reflector is to the subjects, the brighter the fill light becomes.

- **The Reflector Angle.** A reflector card illuminates the subject most when it faces an angle *between* the subject and the main light. Turning it more to the subject reduces the intensity of the light falling on it. Turning it more to the main light reflects more light in a direction away from the subject.
- **The Reflector Surface.** Different reflector surfaces reflect different amounts of light. In our example, we used a white reflector card. If we had wanted to bounce more light onto the subject, we could have used a silver reflector.

  Remember, however, that the choice of reflector surface also depends on the size of the main light. A large silver reflector fill can be a soft source *only* if the main light is also soft.
- **Colored Reflectors.** When shooting in color, you may also want to experiment with colored reflector cards. At times they are useful for either adding or subtracting shadow color.

In a daylight portrait, for example, the sun is usually the main light and, without reflectors, the open sky is the fill. The blue sky adds blue to the shadow. Using a gold reflector warms the shadow, thus eliminating the blue and producing a more neutral color.

Using exactly the opposite approach can make a studio portrait resemble daylight. A pale-blue reflector cools the shadow color enough to look more like that in an outdoor photograph.

Since we personally prefer the reflector to the earlier strobe fill, we will keep it in place for all of the subsequent photographs. Figure 8.18 shows where we placed the reflector in a more complex portrait lighting arrangement. Now we will talk about the other lights in that arrangement.

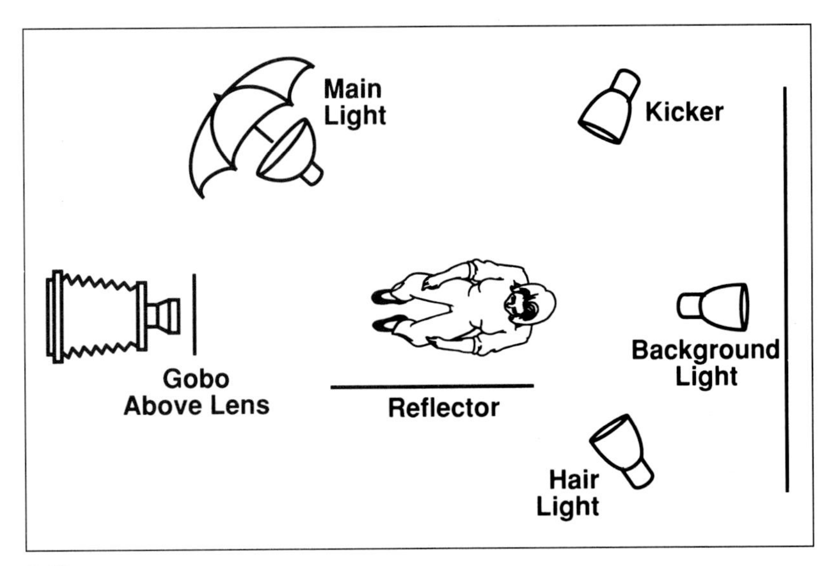

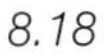
8.18

◀ *A main light, reflector fill, plus other common portrait lights. While some photographers use fewer lights, and others use more, this arrangement is typical.*

Background Lights

So far we have talked about lights aimed at the subject. *Background lights* illuminate, as the name implies, the background rather than the person being photographed. Figure 8.19 shows the effect of the background light by itself.

► *In making this picture, we used a background light to separate the subject's head and shoulders from the background. Notice how this adds depth.*

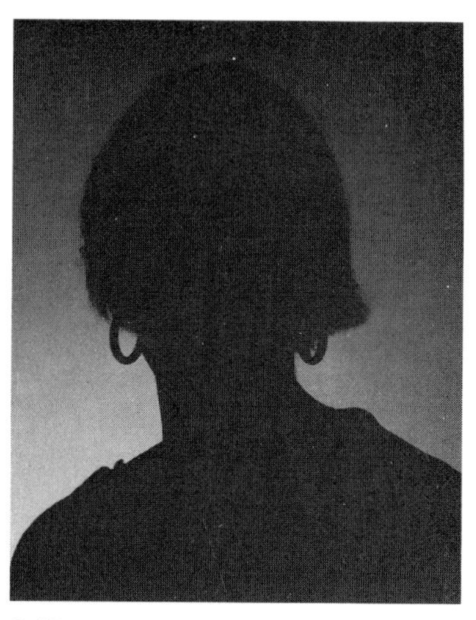

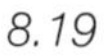

8.19

Figure 8.20 was made with a three-light setup. Besides the main and fill lights that we used before, we added a background light. Compare it with Figure 8.17, which was made with just a main light and a fill.

► *Adding the background light to the fill and main lights surrounds the subject with a pleasing glow.*

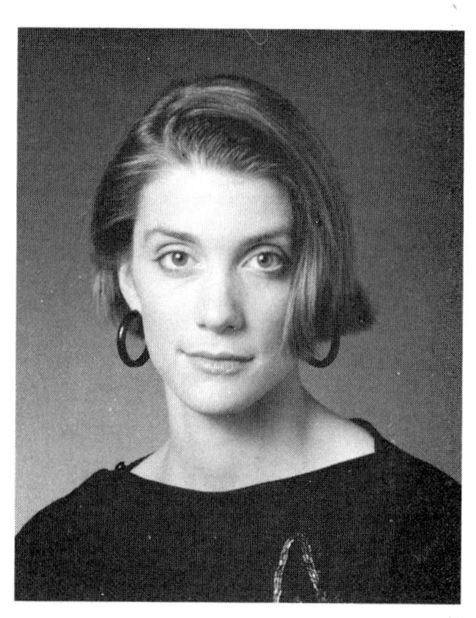

8.20

As you can readily see, the two pictures are very similar, but look at how nicely the back of the model's head and her shoulders are separated from the background in Figure 8.20. That is exactly what background lights do. They provide a degree of tonal separation between the subject and the background. This separation helps to give a feeling of added depth to a portrait and surrounds the subject with what is often a very visually pleasing "glow."

Background lights can also add color to portraits. We do this by attaching colored gels, or filters, to the light. Gels are not expensive and they come in a wide range of colors. By using them and a white background, photographers can reduce the number of different colored backgrounds that they need to keep around the studio. Several background lights with filters of different colors can create color combinations impossible with colored seamless paper and white lights.

Figure 8.18 shows one common background light position. The light is placed on the floor and aimed up to lighten the background. This arrangement works well for a head-and-shoulders portrait.

Hiding the background light behind the subject is more difficult in a full-length portrait. Furthermore, lighting the background uniformly, instead of a bright center spot, is almost impossible with the background light in such a position. To photograph the whole body or to illuminate the background evenly, we prefer using two or more background lights on each side of the subject.

Background lights may be very bright or very dim. Experiment until you come up with the lighting you like.

Hair Lights

The next light that we are going to discuss is the *hair light*. This light is often used for highlights that separate dark hair from a dark background. However, even if the hair is blonde, brightening it with additional light can make the photograph less somber. Figure 8.21 was made with a hair light alone to show the effect.

▶ *We made this exposure using nothing but a hair light. Notice the highlights that it puts on the subject's hair.*

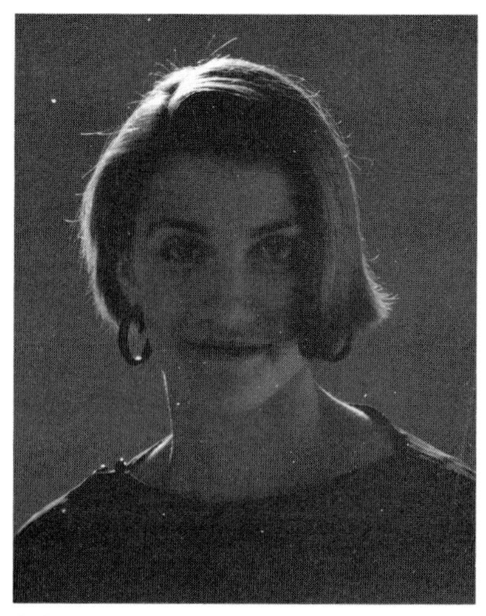

8.21

Now look at Figure 8.22. It was made with a main light, a fill light, and a hair light. This combination has the hair light set at a typical brightness. Some photographers might prefer to keep it dimmer, providing separation in the dark areas, but attracting less attention to it. Others prefer a brighter hair light for a more theatrical look.

▶ *A hair light used along with the main and fill lights. This one is of typical brightness. Some photographers like brighter highlights, others prefer them dimmer.*

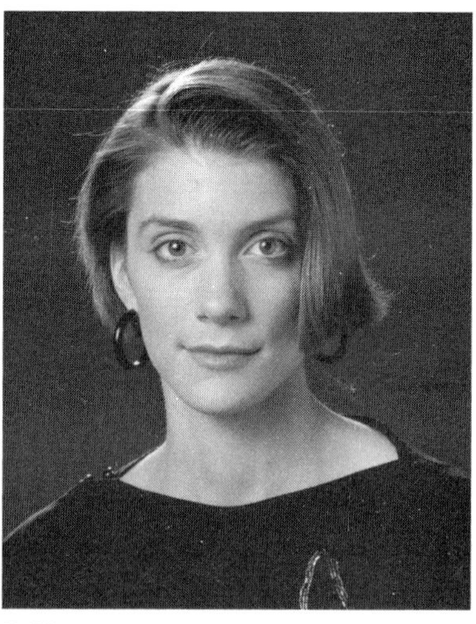

8.22

The diagram in Figure 8.18 shows one common position for the hair light, on the side opposite the main light and behind the subject. Alternatively, a boom can suspend the hair light above and to the rear of the subject. The boom allows better freedom to position the hair light without getting the light stand in the picture.

The hair light, like any other light coming from behind the subject, reveals loose strands of hair. Whether or not this is a problem depends on personal taste and current style. (Some people prefer to look meticulously tidy, while others are happy to be absolutely shabby. Either way, their children are probably the opposite!) If we do not want the loose hair, we have to use hair spray, anticipate retouching, or forego the hair light entirely.

It is important to position the hair light so that light coming from it does not produce flare. Remember to look at the lens as you position the hair light to see if the light is falling directly into the lens. If it is, you may be able to move the light a bit. If you do not want to change the light position, block the offending light from the lens with a barndoor or a gobo. The gobo above the lens in Figure 8.18 serves this purpose.

Kickers

Along with the different lights that we have talked about so far, some photographers also like to use a kicker as a part of their setup. Figure 8.23 was lit by a kicker alone.

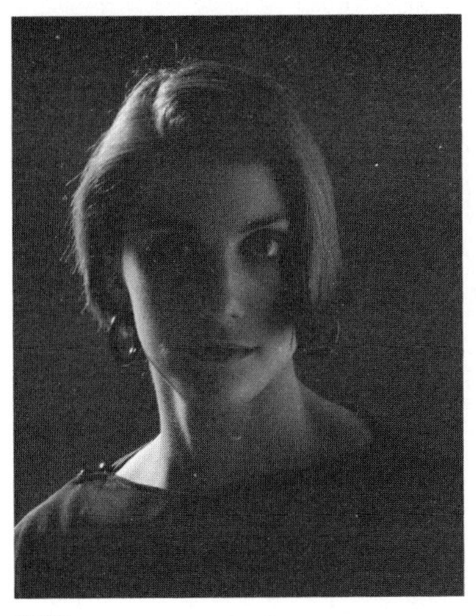

8.23

◀ *A kicker by itself. Kickers are lights that are sometimes used to brighten (or "kick up") a small extra highlight.*

As you can see, a kicker adds extra illumination to, or "kicks up," the brightness on part of the face by providing an extra highlight. Kickers are usually about half the brightness of the main light.

Figure 8.24 shows what happens when you use a kicker with a main light and a fill light. Notice how the kicker added an appealing highlight on one side of the model's face.

► *The kicker added an appealing highlight down the side of the model's face.*

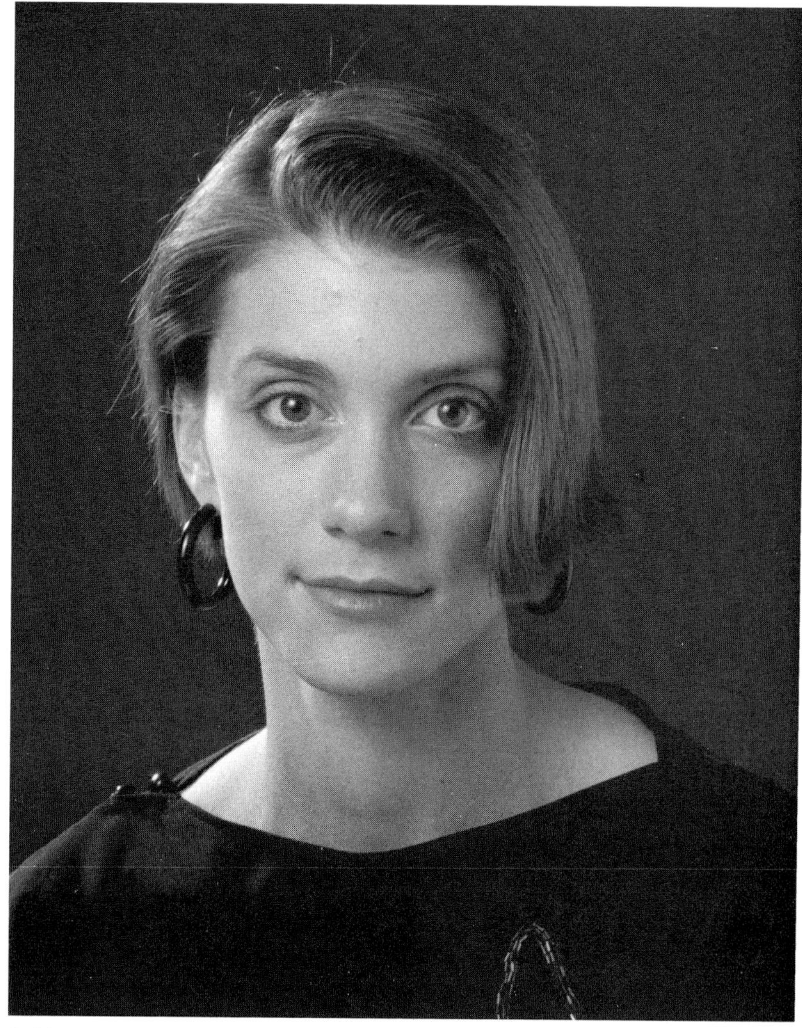

8.24

The position of the kicker is the least standardized of any portrait light. Figure 8.18 shows one possible way. We placed it to the rear of the subject and on the same side as the main light.

As was the case with hair lights, whenever you are using a kicker you have to be careful that light from it does not spill into the lens. If it does, it will cause flare. The gobo we used over the lens to prevent flare from the hair light in Figure 8.18 will do the same for the kicker.

Rim Lights

Some photographers use *rim lights* to illuminate the edges of the subject. Rim lighting is often a combination of hair lights and kickers so similar to the arrangements described in the preceding sections that it makes no difference which terms we use to describe the lights.

However, one variation on rim lighting is quite different from anything we have seen. This technique places the light directly behind the subject in a position similar to that of a background light but aims the light at the subject rather than the background.

Figure 8.25 shows such a rim light used alone. Figure 8.26 is a combination of the rim light plus other lights, and Figure 8.27 diagrams the setup.

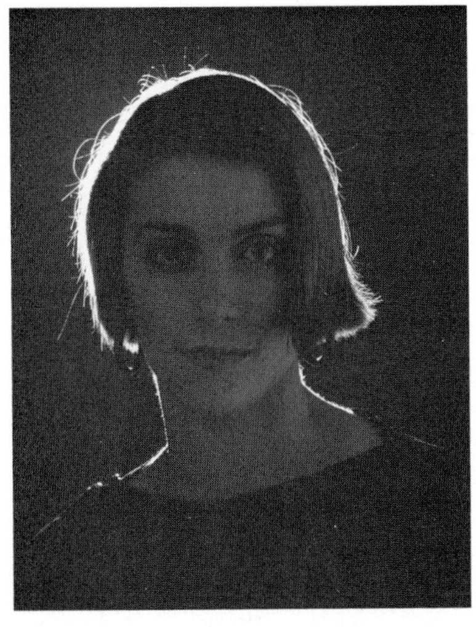

8.25

◀ *Rim lighting by itself places a bright "halo," or rim of light, around the head.*

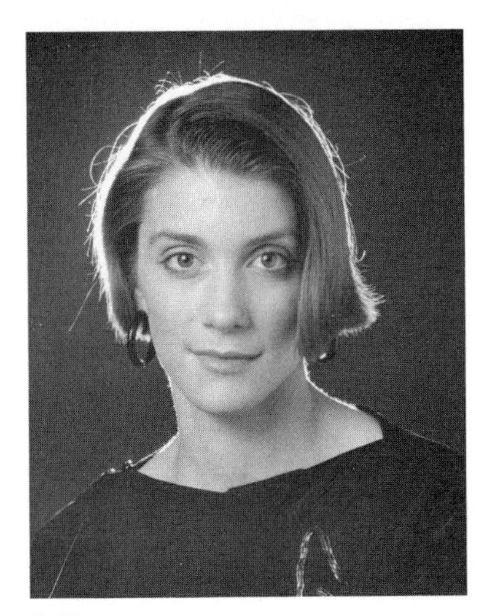

8.26

◀ *A rim light along with a main and a fill light. Notice how the rim of light around the model's head separates it from the background.*

► *Notice how we placed the rim light in much the same position as we might have placed a background light. Only in this case we pointed the light at the back of the head.*

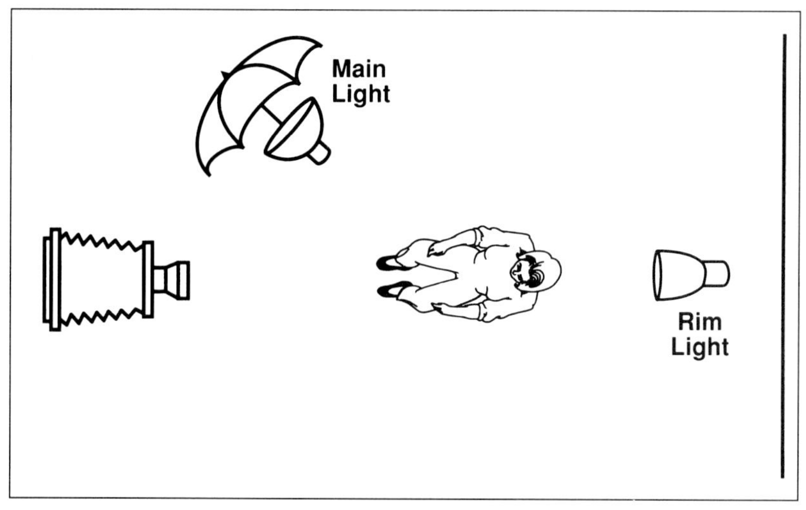

8.27

MOOD AND KEY

Mood is one of those subjective ideas hard to discuss and still harder to quantify. It is one of those terms that often has different meanings to different people. That withstanding, we are, however, still safe in saying that lighting greatly affects the mood of a picture. In addition, at the very simplest level, we will all agree that pictures that have a dark and somber lighting evoke a different response than those that are light and brilliant.

To keep from confusing each other with different personal perceptions, photographers talk about the *key* or *brightness key* instead of mood. No one factor determines key. Lighting may be the most essential factor, but subject matter and exposure also greatly influence key.

Low-Key Lighting

Large, prominent areas of dark are characteristic of *low-key lighting*. Pictures made with this kind of lighting tend to be somber. They tend to be serious, formal, and dignified in mood.

Low-key lighting requires more side and back lighting. Front lighting does not produce enough shadow area to keep the key low. Most of the examples that you have seen so far in this chapter were made with fairly low-key lighting. We did this because it is easier to see the effect of each light in a multiple-light setup using low-key lighting.

High-Key Lighting

High-key lighting is quite the reverse of the above. Pictures made with high-key lighting are light and bright. They convey a youthful, open, and happy mood. They have many white and light gray tones in them. This tends to give them their characteristic "upbeat" look.

Figure 8.28 is of the same model that we have used so far in this chapter. Look at how different her portrait looks when done with a high-key approach. Its mood is completely different from those presented so far. Notice that in this treatment, we have changed more than just the lighting. We have also changed the costume and the background, making them far brighter than in the previous pictures.

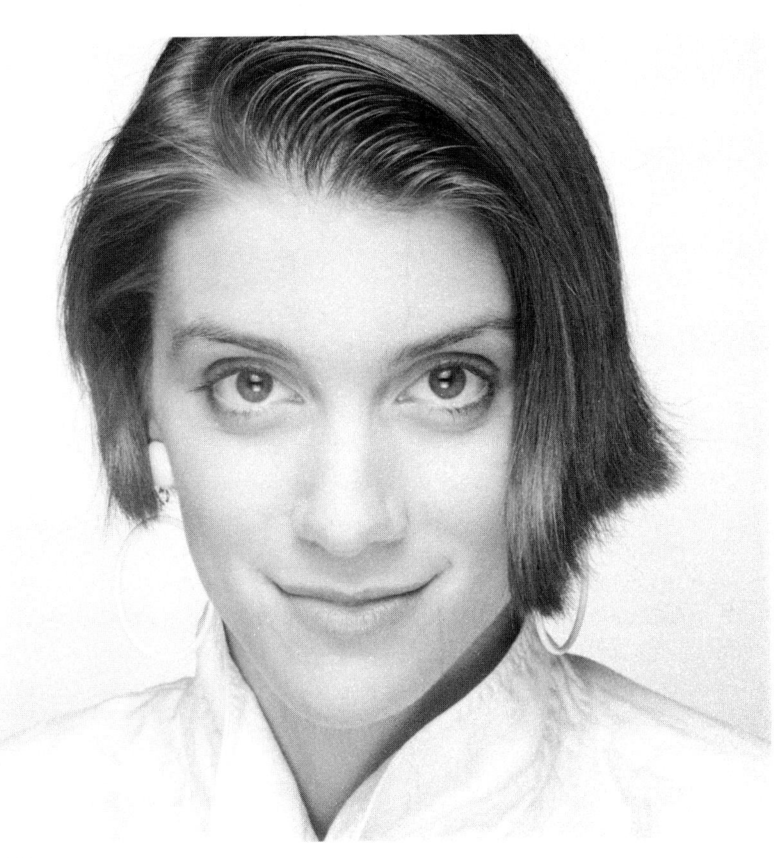

◀ *The preponderance of light tones gives a high-key picture a decidedly young, happy, and open mood or look.*

8.28

Many of the lower key portraits you have seen in this chapter used lighting that produced highlights of one kind or the other along the edges of the subject. We needed these highlights to delineate the subject's features and to separate them tonally from the background. Without them, the features of the subject would have melted into the background.

High-key portrait lighting always uses a great deal of front light. Edge highlighting is less beneficial in high-key lighting because the edge of the subject threatens to disappear against the light background. Thus, we tend to omit many of the lights that are important in low-key work. It is usually easier to light high-key pictures than it is to light low-key ones.

Figure 8.29 shows how we arranged the lights for the high-key example you have just seen.

► *A diagram of the lighting used for the previous high-key picture. Both the lights and reflectors bathed the model in soft, almost shadowless, light. Other lights turned the background into a large, evenly lit highlight.*

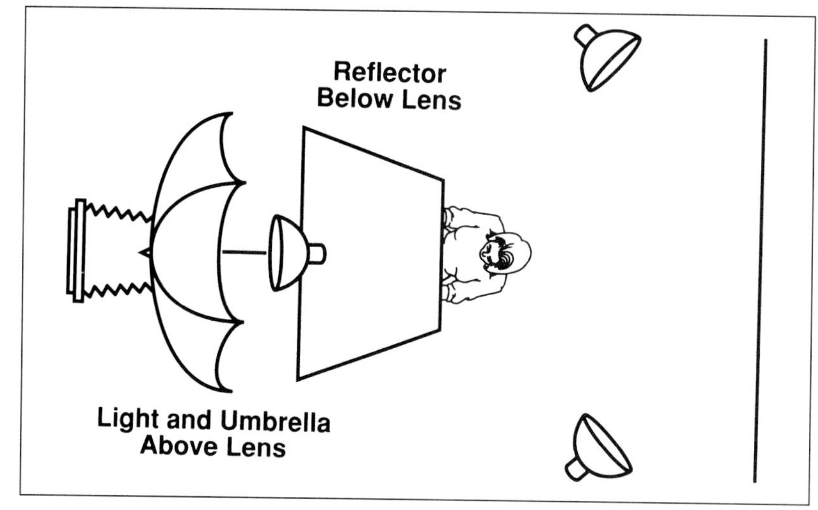

8.29

Notice that all we needed was one large main light, a reflector, and a pair of background lights. We put the main light above the camera, but as close to the lens as possible. In this position, it bathed the model in soft and almost shadowless illumination. We placed the reflector under the camera and close to the model. So positioned, it bounced some of the main light illumination back onto her. The two background lights turned the background into one large and evenly lit highlight.

This setup produced a very flat lighting with few shadows to help delineate the features. This lack of shadow is both the advantage and the disadvantage of such lighting.

Because such lighting reduces contrast, it helps to make blemishes and other skin imperfections less noticeable. Most photographers consider this to be flattering and appropriate to young women and children. If you have any doubts about this, just look at the covers of fashion and beauty magazines. Many of the images are made with lighting similar to this.

However, you should use “beauty” lighting with care. The lack of shadows can also produce pictures that appear flat and formless and seem to be wholly without character.

Staying in Key

Many photographers consider it a good idea to keep a portrait definitely low key or definitely high key whenever possible. They do not mix low- and high-key subject matter and lighting techniques unless there is a definite reason for doing so.

Everyone knows that this rule cannot always be followed. Exceptions include a fair-skinned blonde in dark clothing or a dark-skinned, dark-haired person in light clothing. Unless you crop to include only the face, either one forces you to mix high- and low-key elements in the portrait. On other occasions, you may decide to move the main light more to the side to increase the shadow area in a high-key portrait to emphasize facial contour, or you may decide to minimize shadow in an otherwise low-key portrait to make the skin appear smoother.

Nevertheless, staying in key has some merit. If most of the composition is in the same tonal range, the picture has less clutter to compete with the face. This is especially useful for photographers beginning to learn portraiture who have not yet learned to fully combine lighting, posing, and cropping to unify the composition.

DARK SKIN

We know that photography is most likely to lose detail in the highlights and in the shadows. Few light-skinned people are light enough to cast highlight detail, and we rarely encounter such problems. However, a few dark-skinned people are dark enough to present potential shadow detail problems.

Some photographers improve the exposure by using a wider aperture to let more light reach the film. Sometimes, and we must emphasize only sometimes, this strategy works well. If, for example, the subject is dark skinned and wearing a dark shirt and coat, it is safe to open the lens considerably to compensate for the light lost by skin absorption.

However, if the subject is a very dark-skinned bride in a white wedding dress, the preceding strategy could lead to disaster! The face would still be properly exposed and have nice shadow detail, but imagine her dress! It would be one huge highlight. The dress would be hopelessly overexposed by the exposure increase.

Fortunately, there is a better way to approach this problem than just opening the aperture and hoping for the best. The key to successfully dealing with dark complexions is to increase the direct reflections from them.

Human skin produces only a small amount of direct reflection, but as you will remember, direct reflection is most visible on a dark surface. Therefore, capitalizing on direct reflection is one way to lighten dark subjects without increasing general exposure.

Another point to keep in mind is that the larger the light source, the greater the group of angles from which its light will strike the subject. This enables a large light to fill more of the family of angles that causes direct reflection. Thus, in a portrait of a dark-skinned person, a larger light produces a larger highlight on the skin without adjusting the exposure at the camera.

Be aware, however, that just a slight increase in the size of the light would offer almost no improvement. Since a human head is roughly spherical, the family of angles that produces a large direct reflection is also quite large. The larger the light we use, the better the result. We may still have to open the aperture a bit, but not very much, and both the bride's face and her dress turn out well. (If you are not reading these chapters in order, we suggest you look back at Figure 6.29, round metal, or Figure 7.10, glass, to see the family of angles of direct reflection on a round object.)

AVAILABLE-LIGHT PORTRAITURE

Undoubtedly, from time to time you, or your client, will decide that a portrait needs to be made away from the studio. Location portraiture can be completely frustrating if you are used to the command that the studio gives you. It can also be fascinating and enjoyable. Furthermore, the environment can be an essential part of the person and, therefore, of the portrait.

In Chapter 10 we will talk about using minimal lighting equipment on location. Those techniques apply equally to portraiture and other photographic specialties.

Sometimes logistics make it impractical to use any lighting equipment at all. We will finish this chapter with a few classic available-light portrait techniques. There is no need for a detailed treatment of available-light portraiture because the methods resemble studio portraiture more than they differ.

We will offer just enough examples to illustrate a cardinal rule: Location or studio, the principles are the same! It is that simple. No matter where you are, outside or inside, corn field or studio, light is light. It follows the same immutable laws of physics. We will light our models according to the same principles as we would in the studio. However, this time Mother Nature, rather than our strobes, will be providing the watt-seconds.

A Window as a Main Light

Look at Figure 8.30. It is a typical example of a window-lit portrait. This basic picture has been repeated many times by many photographers, and for good reason. As you can see, soft light streaming in through the window gives good contour and depth, but none of the harshness sometimes seen in portraits that were made with direct daylight.

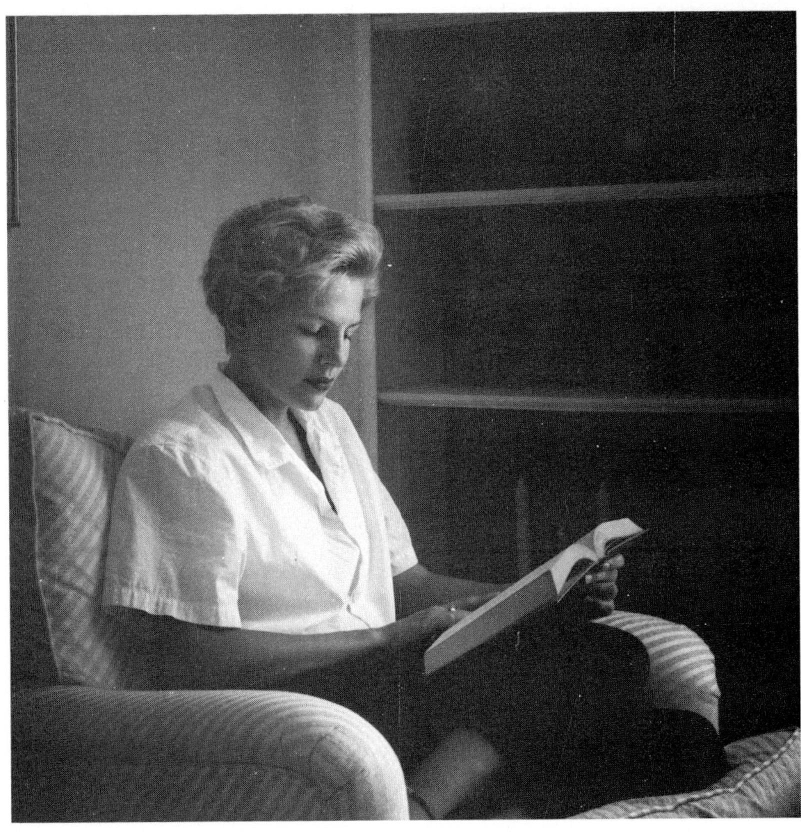

◀ Soft light from the open sky streaming in through a window made this portrait. The soft and pleasing light is well suited for the subject.

8.30

As pleasing as this picture is, the lighting involves nothing new. The key to its success is already familiar. Large light sources produce soft lighting. In the studio, we use a large diffuser or an umbrella for a light source. On location, the sky is our large light source. The tools are different, but the result is the same.

You must remember, however, that the window does not have any magic qualities that inevitably make it a soft-light source. Figure 8.31 proves this. The girl is in the same place, and so is the window, but look at the difference.

► *The sun was lower in the sky. and its direct rays produced the harsh shadows that we see here.*

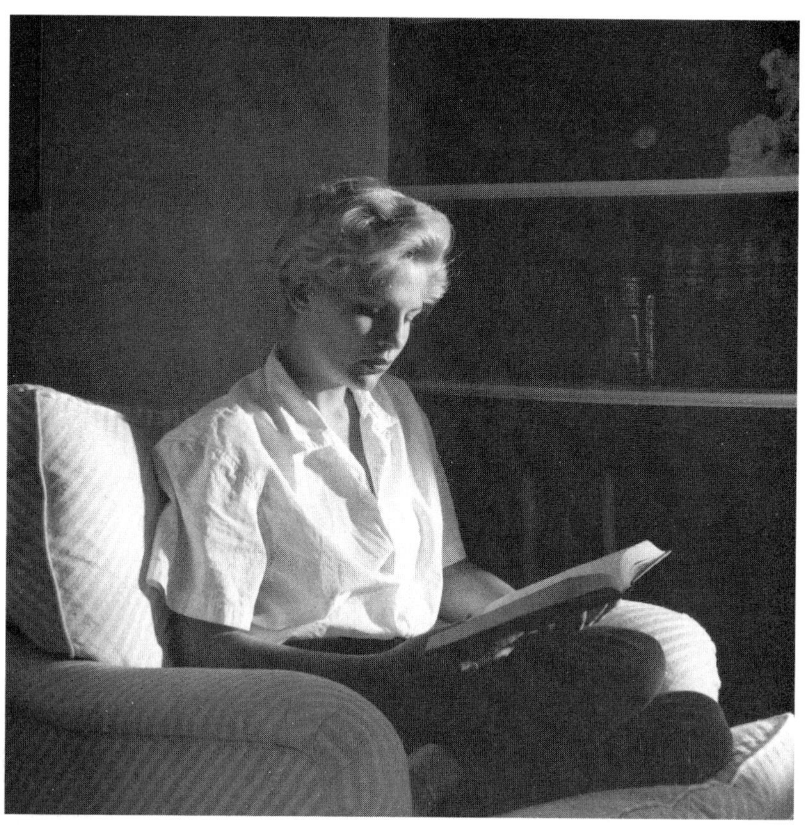

8.31

In the second picture, hard shadows compete with the subject's features. It could still be a good picture, depending on the intent, but it is not a flattering portrait. What caused the difference? Simply put, the answer is light size. The two pictures were made at different times of day, and the sun had moved during the time between them.

In our first picture, the light through the window was from the open sky. The sky is a large light source. The second photograph was made later in the day, when the sun had moved across the sky. It was lit by direct sun, and as you know by now, the sun always behaves like a small light source. Direct sunlight always produces hard shadows. So, once again, we have seen that studio or location, sun or strobe, the results are the same. Light is light. Large lights produce soft shadows, and small lights produce hard ones. The locale may change, but the behavior of light does not.

The Sun as a Hair Light

Figure 8.32 shows another outside setup. We are including it to show how you can duplicate a studio main-light and hair-light setup in the field.

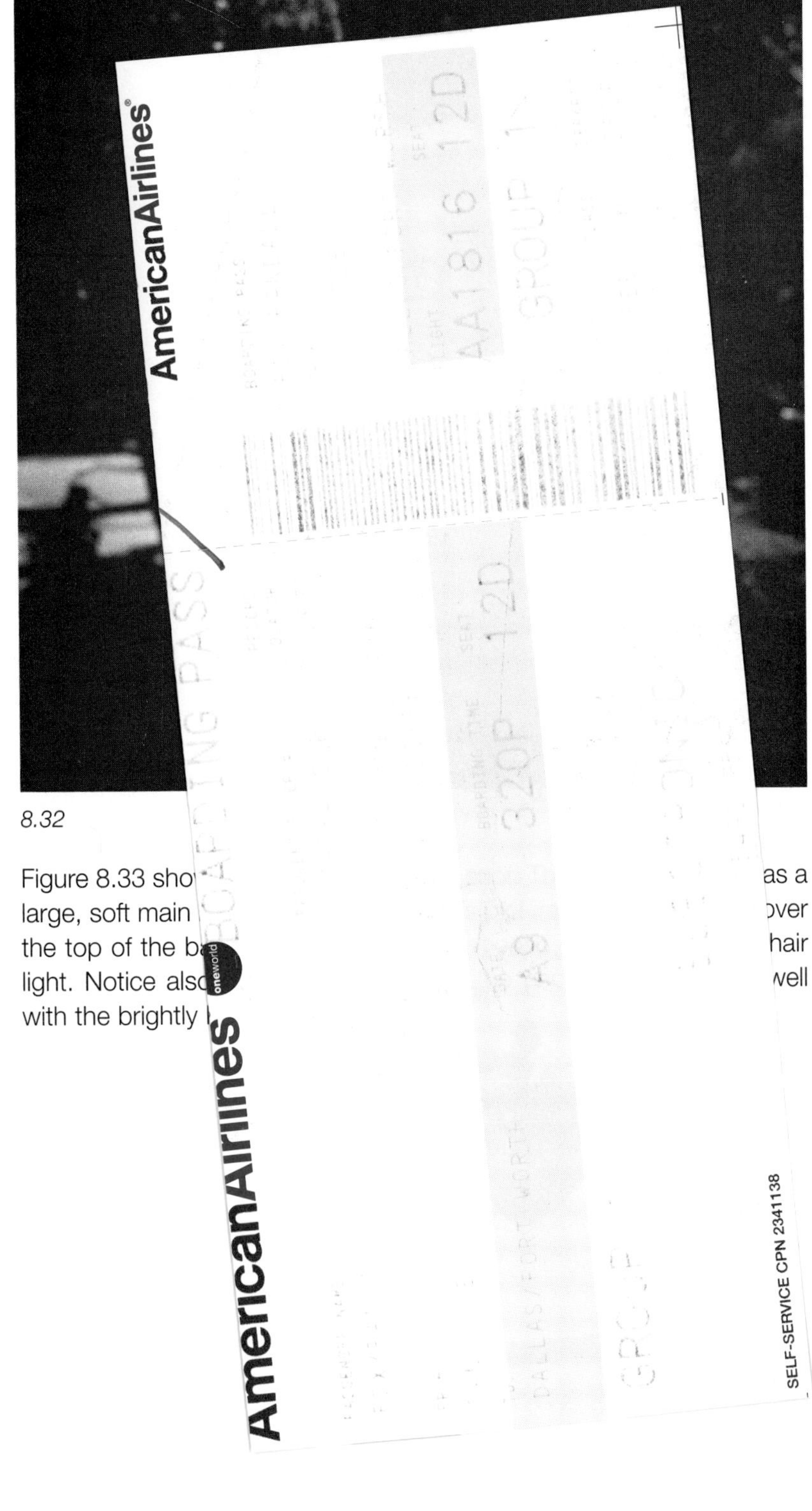

◀ Outside natural light and a reflector produce much the same look as do main and hair lights in the studio.

8.32

Figure 8.33 sho[illegible] as a large, soft main [illegible] over the top of the b[illegible] hair light. Notice als[illegible] well with the brightly [illegible]

► *Here we see how we made the previous shot. Notice that the sky serves as a large, soft main light. The sun was just peeping over the top of a stand of trees in the background, and we positioned the model so that it acted as a hair light.*

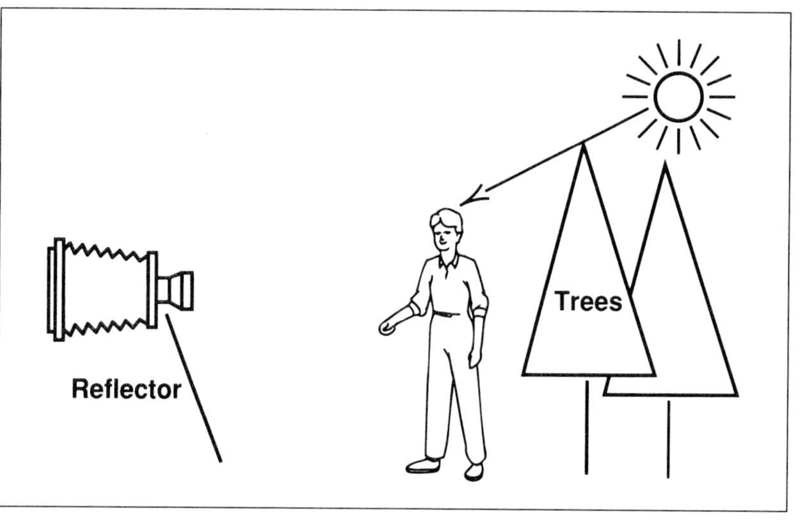

8.33

Once again, the location was different, the light sources were natural rather than artificial, but the principles that we followed were the same. Once again, light behaves like light!

Keeping the Light Appropriate

The only occasions when the principles of location lighting and studio lighting differ are those when a particular lighting is essential to the environment or the event.

A child blowing out birthday candles, a firefighter lit by the harsh red light on the engine, and an orchestra conductor in stage lighting are the worst possible examples of good portrait lighting. However, in none of these cases would we improve the portrait with standard studio lighting. When the light is part of the story, we gain more by capitalizing on it than by tampering with it.

SETTING RULES?

Everything we tell you in this chapter is true, and it all works. Please do things as we say, but not always. There is not a single rule here that has not been successfully and pleasingly violated at one time or another.

For example, we repeatedly recommend a large light source for portraiture. Using a large light to soften shadows tends to make people look prettier, but this does not mean that large light sources inevitably produce the best portraits. Less flattering lighting can give the appearance of dignity, wisdom, or endurance.

If the individual we are photographing happens to be the person paying for the portrait, we usually want the person to look as attractive as possible. But we are more likely to please a magazine picture editor with a portrait showing character and emphasizing whatever personal qualities relate to the text. Ancient mariners, sainted martyrs, and brutal despots have more interesting traits than their physical beauty.

The size of the light, along with most of the other suggestions we make, is more than a technical decision. Sometimes it is artistic: How does the maker of the image want to represent the subject? Often it is political: Whom is the picture intended to please? Always it is a decision to make rather than a law to obey.

The lighting in this chapter is a basic approach that every photographer ought to learn, not a set of rules that every photographer needs to follow.

Chapter 9

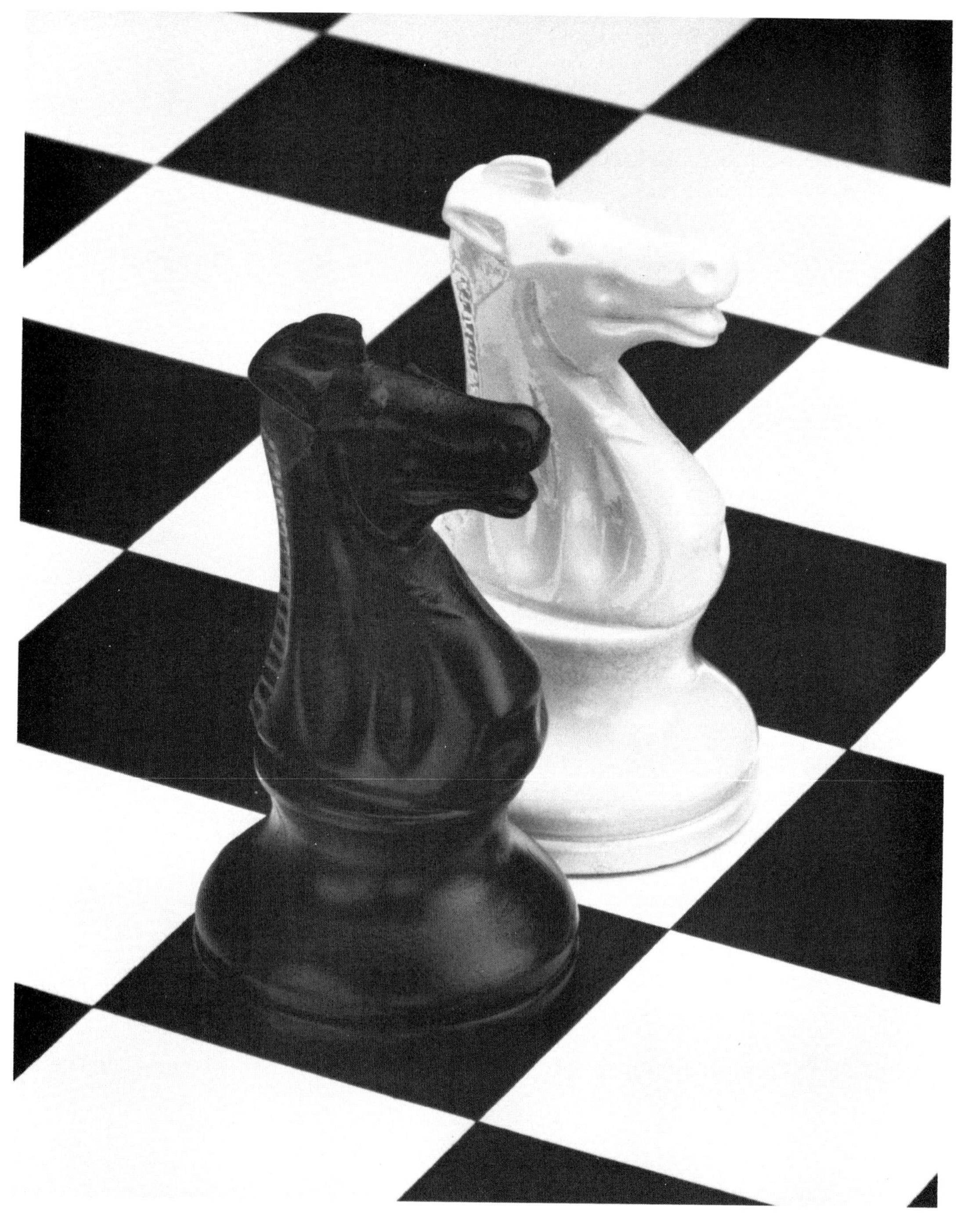

The Extremes

Photographers call the range of tones that can occur in nature or in a photograph the *gray scale*. We divide this scale into a series of steps like the musical scale.

We can imagine an infinite number of grays within this series of steps. (Whether that number is actually infinite is for the physicists to decide. We can imagine them, regardless of their existence!) This is like the continuous range of tones a trombone can play. We prefer to talk about a limited number of steps, like the discrete notes on a piano. This is easier than dealing with infinite numbers.

There are several common ways of mathematically dividing the gray scale, just as the musical scale is divided differently from one culture to another. Many photographers prefer *zone systems* of nine, ten, or eleven steps, such as those devised by Ansel Adams and others. We will not discuss the specifics of any particular gray scale. If you already use such a system, you will find much of what we say familiar. Otherwise, you simply need to realize that the gray scale can be divided into steps.

Several steps in the gray scale can be grouped together as a range of similar steps, just as musical tones can be grouped as low notes and high notes. In this chapter, we are concerned with the groups of grays that make the two extremes of the gray scale: the shadows and the highlights.

When we talk about the gray scale, the terms *highlight* and *shadow* have broader meaning than when we just talk about lighting. Here, we will consider *shadow* to be any dark gray or black in the scene. A dark gray or black subject is a shadow value whether or not the lighting actually places the subject in shadow. Anything that reflects little enough light to record on film as a dark gray is considered to be in the shadow region of the gray scale, even if that subject is fully illuminated in the scene. Similarly, *highlight* is any light gray, including white.

In this chapter, we will talk about *gray* for the sake of simplicity. Everything we say is also true for colors of corresponding brightness. The word *gray*, as photographers use it, is a consequence of the years of photographic history in which colors were largely unavailable. (Painters and illustrators have always had colors, so they lessen the confusion with the term *values*, which means the same thing.)

WHY ARE THE EXTREMES IMPORTANT?

At each phase of the photographic process, photographers evaluate the quality of the image. This often begins with testing a new batch of film before using it for any assignments. As we dodge or burn a print, we think about what we could have done better to eliminate the need for such manipulation. From the first test Polaroid to the brochure or magazine that comes off the offset press, we look at the result to see what we could do with the lighting and exposure of the original to better ensure its survival in later generations.

Achieving photographic quality is not an accomplishment but a process. That process extends through each step needed to make a picture, and beyond. It extends through the duration of a photographer's career.

Novice photographers know *quality* when they see it, but they may know it only as the look of pictures they like. Beyond the obvious basics of adequate sharpness and reasonable exposure, the meaning of the term can be vague. More experienced photographers use the general term to group together several very specific technical judgments; but even if those judgments are specific, any one of them can be an essential consideration for one image and trivial for another. We can be sure of what we mean by *quality* only in terms of a particular photograph.

Having made that disclaimer, we will now go on to list what we think are the most important considerations for achieving and maintaining image quality. We will rank these considerations according to the priority most photographers use to evaluate most pictures:

1. Shadow detail
2. Highlight detail
3. Everything else

The reason for such emphasis on shadow detail and highlight detail is that these are the most defective aspects of the very medium of photography.

The Photographic Defect

Photographers can do a lot of things wrong, more on some days than others; but along with all the mistakes we make, loss of detail in the shadows and highlights is not necessarily our fault. It is inherent in the medium. This is not to suggest that we can do nothing to compound the problem. It does mean, however, that the problem will always exist, even when we do everything right. Photography always suffers a certain amount of loss of detail in the very dark grays and the very light grays.

Very little mastery is needed to record the middle grays acceptably. It is only slightly more difficult to obtain good blacks and good whites; but the near-blacks and near-whites will probably never be quite right as long as we use film. Although film manufacturers do all they can to improve this defect, we cannot expect them to eliminate it altogether.

The error inherent in film is acceptable. This is proven by the existence of millions of high-quality photographs. However, if we do poor work, the film error is likely to magnify it, and these combined problems tend to be most apparent in the shadows and in the highlights.

We do not say all this to depress you, but simply to emphasize where the problems are. The implications are more encouraging. If quality is most defective in shadow and highlight detail, then that is precisely where we ought to turn our attention to get the most improvement.

THE CHARACTERISTIC CURVE

In this book, we generally keep our attention on lighting and stay away from extensive discussion of basic photography. Nevertheless, the *film characteristic curve* dictates some of our technique when we light black-on-black or white-on-white subjects. We have to talk about the characteristic curve to show why this is so. Other writers have explained this material in more detail. You may give this section as much or as little attention as you need, depending on whose books you have already read.

The characteristic curve of a film is a graph of the way the density of a negative varies with different amounts of exposure to light. Each film and development combination has a characteristic curve of a slightly different shape. We, however, are more interested in general principles than in the characteristic curves of specific films.

Because we are not examining differences between specific films, we can also omit discussion of the mathematical definitions of *density* and *exposure*. The appearance of the curve shows the response of film to exposure so clearly that we can see the principles at a glance without any calculation.

We will look at two characteristic curves, one for an ideal film and one for a bad film. They both help to explain how real film behaves.

An Ideal Film

There is no such thing as an ideal film, and there probably never will be. However, if we want to understand the problems with real film, we ought to try to imagine how an ideal film might behave. For simplicity we will theorize about an ideal black-and-white negative. (Color negatives have three curves—one for each emulsion layer. The curves of a reversal film are similar, but slope in the opposite direction.)

The characteristics curve is a way to compare two gray scales: one representing exposure steps produced by the scene and the other representing density steps in the negative.

At this point, it is important to note that when we talk about characteristic curves, *exposure* means something slightly different than when we talk about making a picture. Photographers shooting pictures talk about exposure as if the whole negative received a single uniform exposure, for example, f/22 at 1/60 second. *Exposure* used this way is convenient shorthand for "How I set my camera for this subject under this lighting condition."

However, photographers also know that each shade of gray in the scene exposes the film by a slightly different amount. Thus, assuming we are not photographing a blank wall, the film gets a *group* of exposures that make an image of the grays in the scene.

Therefore, when we talk about exposure steps in the characteristic curve, we mean "the whole scene," and not necessarily a large number of different negatives with a range of different exposures.

Figure 9.1 shows what might happen to an ideal film if we exposed it to a scene containing a gray scale made up of ten steps.

► *An ideal film: Any change in exposure would produce an exactly corresponding change in the density of the film.*

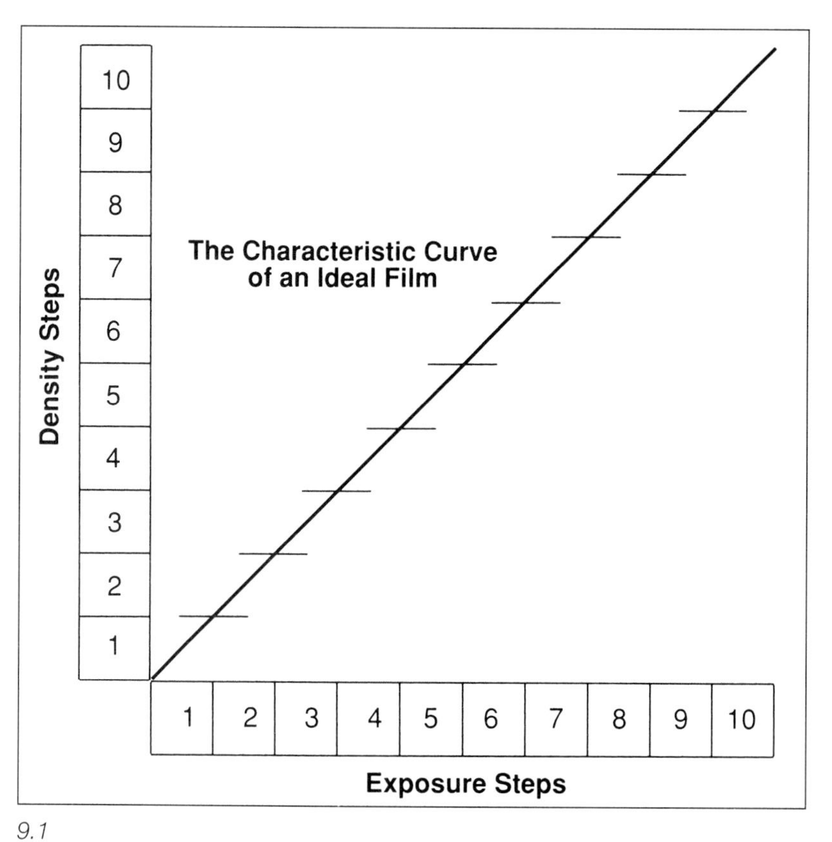

9.1

In this graph, the horizontal line represents exposure steps. Exposure steps are the grays in the original scene. The vertical line represents density steps. A density step is a group of grays in the processed negative that corresponds to an exposure step in the scene.

Each exposure step is the same length on the graph as any other exposure step. This is no accident. Photographers and scientists who invented the scale deliberately decided to divide the range of possible grays into equal steps. However, the size of corresponding density steps in the processed film may not be equal to one another. This difference in the size of the density steps is exactly the film characteristic that the characteristic curve is designed to graph.

The important characteristic of an ideal film is that *each density step is the same size as any other density step.* If you measure the length of the vertical line marked "step 2," for example, you will find it to be the same as the length marked "step 5."

This means that *any change in exposure will produce an exactly corresponding change in the density of an ideal film.* For example, Figure 9.2 is a graph of the same ideal film with the exposure increased three stops.

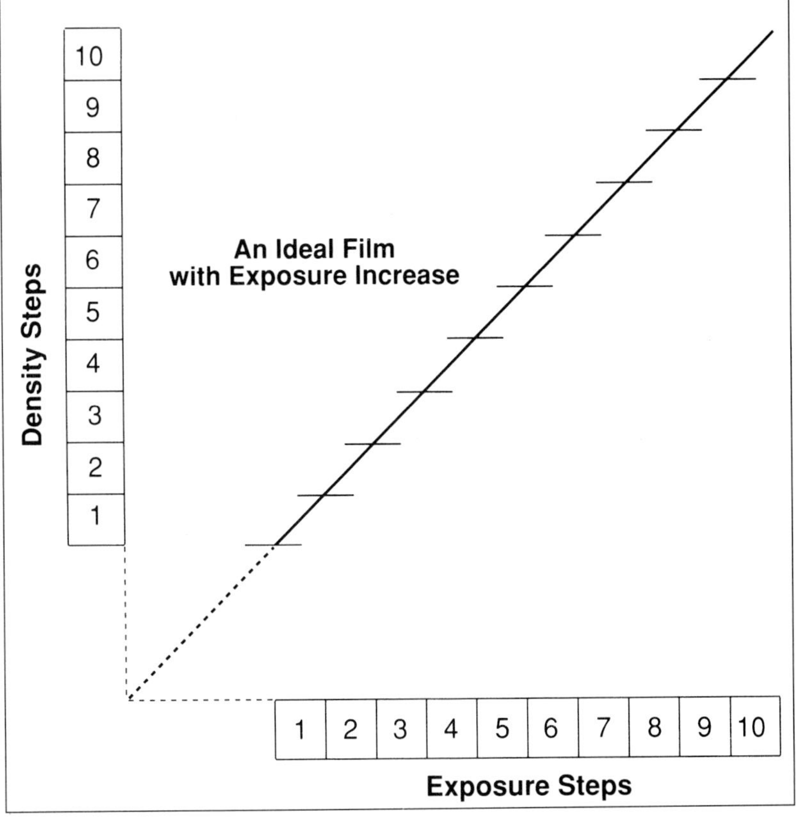

9.2

◀ *An ideal film with exposure increased by three stops. The denser negative would print the same as the previous one because the relationship of the density steps is the same.*

Such a negative would be more dense. The enlarger timer would have to be set eight times as long to make a similar print. However, that similar print would look identical to the first one, because the *relationship* of the density steps is still the same. The segment labeled "step 2" on the vertical line, for example, is the same length in both diagrams.

If an ideal film existed, exposing it would be very easy. Any photographer who had any doubt about the ideal exposure could be safe in simply giving more exposure than necessary. The resulting negative would produce a print with the same gray scale. (Furthermore, as long as we are talking about ideal films, we might as well assume the grain would be fine also.)

Exposing a real film, however, is a more critical decision. This is because the graph of density steps in a negative is not a straight line but a curve.

A Bad Film

Photographers almost never use a diagram of a film characteristic curve in their daily work, but they keep a mental image of the shape of a curve with them always, because it helps them to previsualize how a real scene will appear in the picture. Furthermore, this mental image slightly exaggerates the problems found in a real film. We will call this exaggerated example "bad" film. Figure 9.3 shows how bad film would look if we exposed it like the ideal film in the first example.

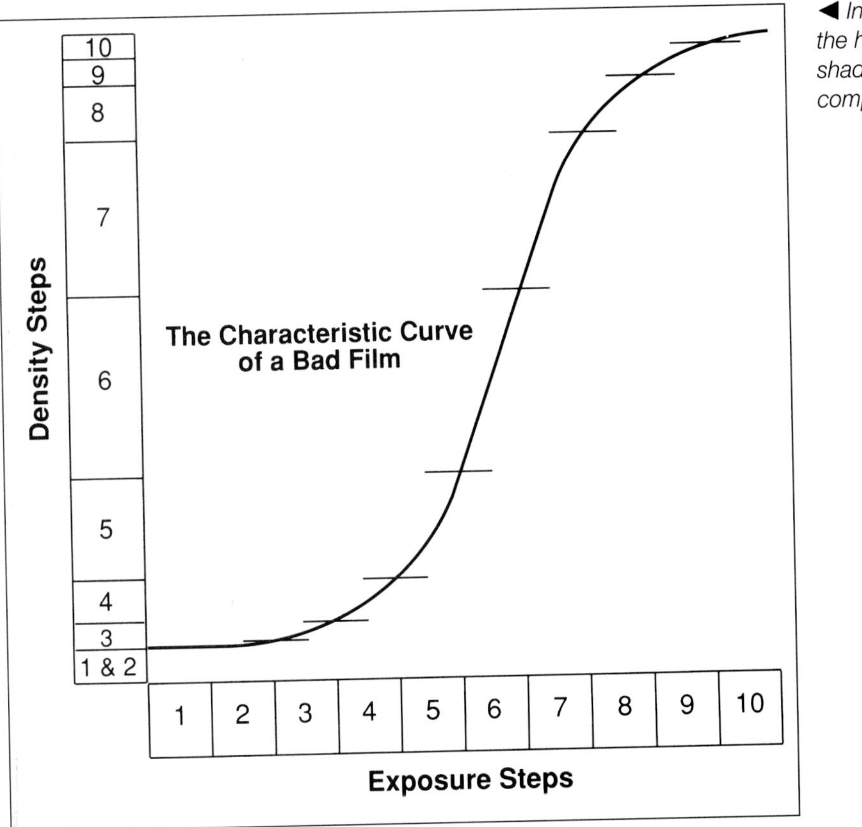

9.3

◀ *In a bad film, both the highlights and the shadows are greatly compressed.*

The exposure steps shown on the horizontal line are identical to those in the first graph, because we are photographing the same scene; but look what has happened to the density steps on the vertical line!

Steps 1 to 3 occupy very little space on the density scale; likewise for steps 8 through 10. Both the shadows and the highlights have been greatly compressed. *Compression* means that tones that were very different and easy to distinguish in the scene are now very similar and difficult to distinguish in the photograph.

Figure 9.4 is a normally exposed scene. The cathedral wall is a nearly uniform gray, but the late afternoon sun gives us a wide range of highlights and shadows to study. Notice that individual stones are faintly visible in both the highlight and shadow areas of the wall. There is some compression in both those highlights and shadows. You cannot see the problems because we had neither bad film nor ideal film to make comparison pictures. You will see these problems, however, in the next section, when they are exaggerated by exposure error.

► *A scene exposed normally on a real film has some compression in both the shadows and the highlights, but the problems are not obvious.*

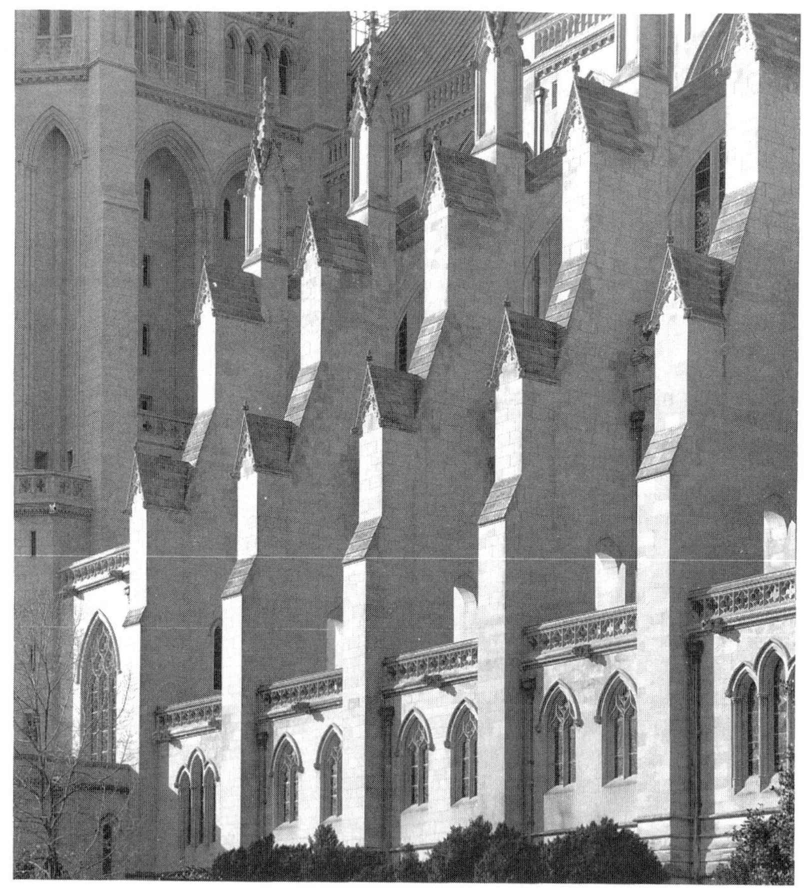

9.4

Overexposure

Keep in mind that in an average scene with a normal exposure, compression occurs at *both* extremes of the density gray scale. Changing the general exposure decreases compression at one end of the gray scale, but it worsens the compression at the other extreme. Figure 9.5 shows the benefits and the sacrifices of overexposure.

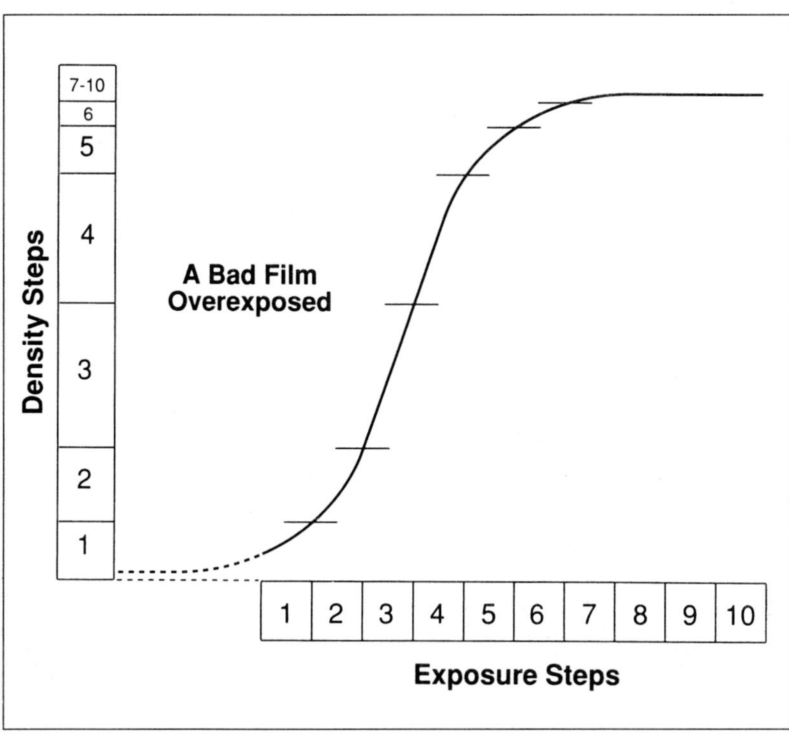

9.5

◀ *Overexposure eliminates some compression in the shadow tones, but at the cost of making the highlight compression much worse.*

As we can see, increased exposure eliminates some of the shadow compression. This is good, but the highlight compression is made much worse. Let us see what might happen if we overexpose the cathedral seen earlier to such a degree.

Figure 9.6 is the result. We see improved shadow detail in the dark foliage at the bottom of the scene. The rest of the picture is much too light. But that is only part of the problem. We can fix that by making a darker print. Let us look at a darker print in Figure 9.7.

► *A real film, greatly overexposed.*

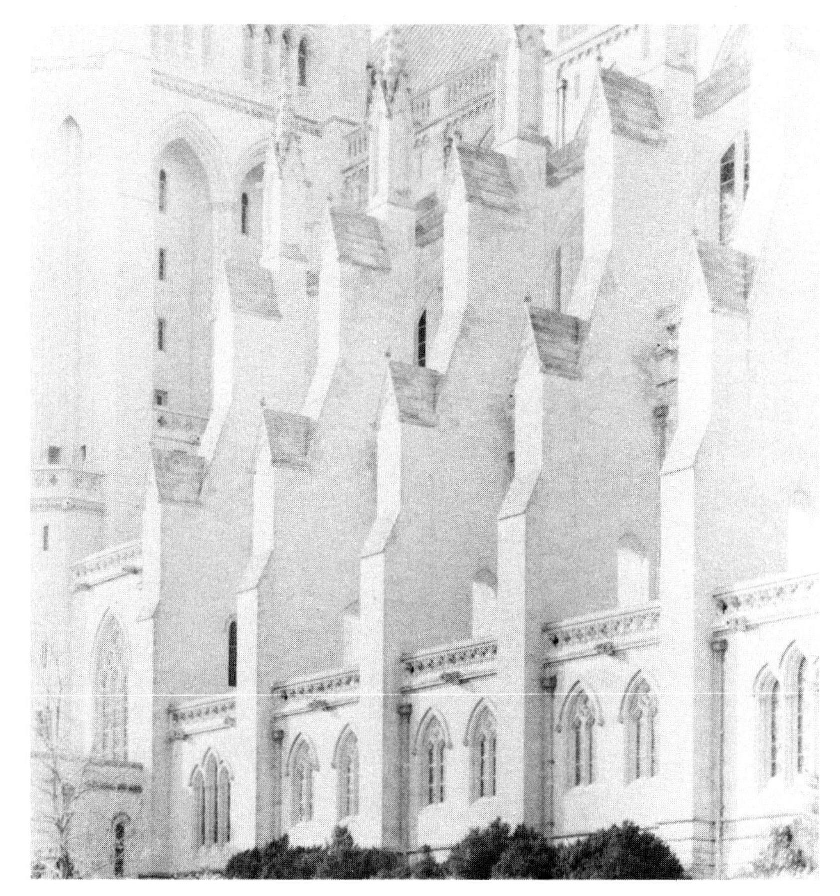

9.6

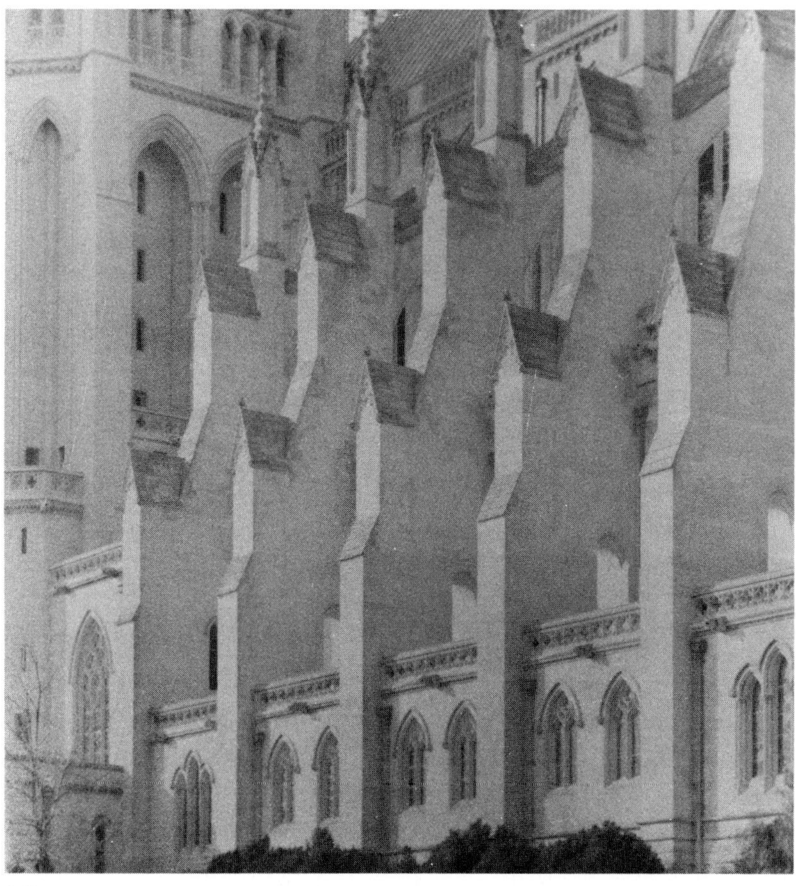

◀ *A darker print from the overexposed negative offers little additional distinction between the highlights. They all printed at nearly the same gray.*

9.7

Now the middle tones are similar to those in the earlier print. However, we cannot remedy the compression caused by overexposing the negative. The distinction between the stones in the highlight area is still not visible. They are all the same muddy light gray. Although the highlights are darker in this print, the detail in them is not improved.

Notice, though, that this terrible picture is not without virtue. Overexposure put detail into the deepest shadows that survived, even in the darker print. The dark foliage still has better distinction in the leaves than it did in the properly exposed photograph.

Underexposure

If the film is underexposed, we see similar problems with the shadow tones. Figure 9.8 is the characteristic curve for an underexposed negative.

► *The characteristic curve that results from underexposure. The shadows are compressed badly.*

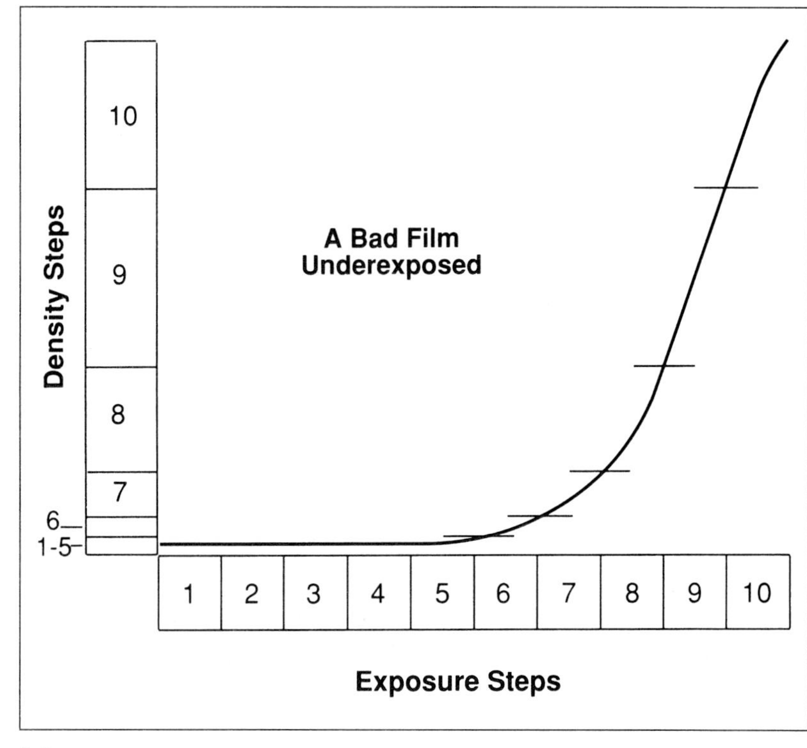

9.8

Figure 9.9 is a print from such a negative. The highlight steps are better separated. In other words, each step appears "more" different from the steps above and below it. Whether this technical improvement is more pleasing depends on the particular scene and the opinion of the viewer. In this scene, a tiny direct reflection on a metal downspout near the top of the wall is now better differentiated from the light-gray stone. Of course, no viewer would consider that gain worth the increased compression of the shadow we see here.

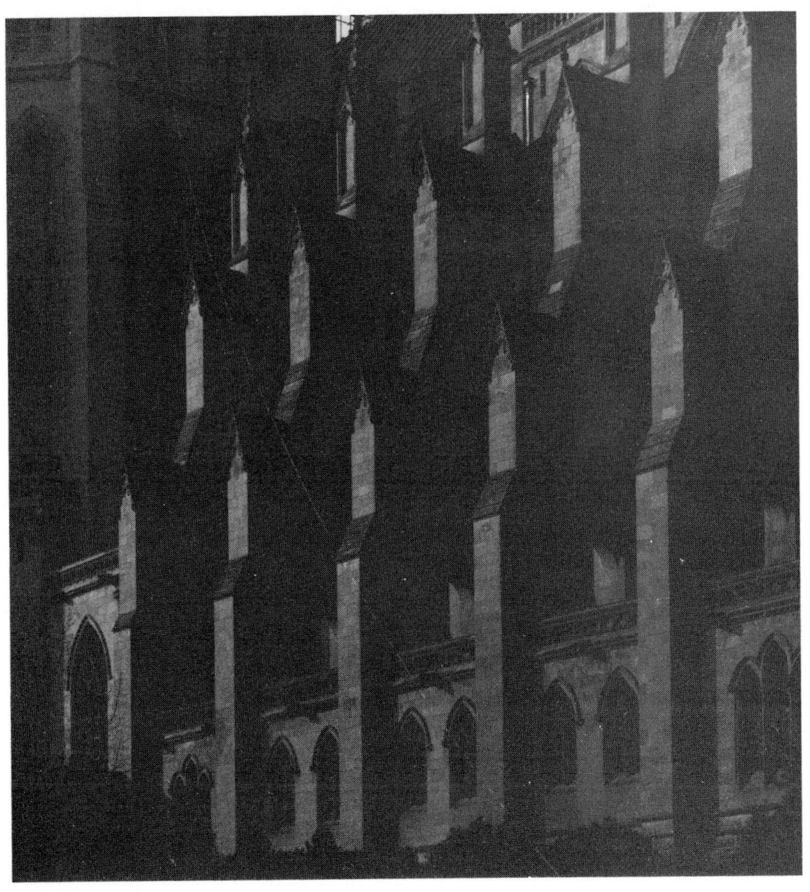

◀ A print from an underexposed negative. The shadow tones are all compressed into one uniform dark gray.

9.9

Once again, we will try to cure the problem in the darkroom. Figure 9.10 is a lighter print from the same negative. As we might have expected by looking at the characteristic curve, the lighter print does not restore the shadow detail. This is because the underexposure has compressed those tones too much for them ever to be salvaged.

► *A lighter print from the underexposed negative. Even though the overall scene is lighter, shadow detail has not been restored.*

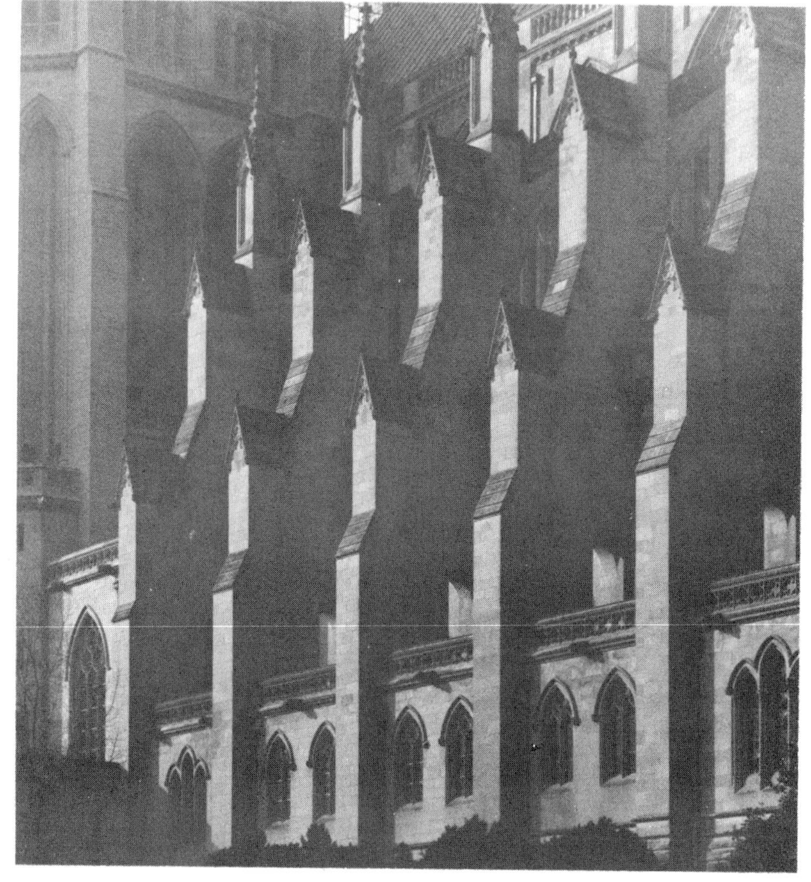

9.10

Real Film

Real film is a compromise between our imaginary ideal film and our imaginary bad film. Unfortunately, the real film may resemble the bad more than the ideal.

The part of the characteristic curve representing the shadow steps is called the *toe* of the curve. The toe of a real characteristic curve is likely to be only slightly straighter than the toe of the bad film curve, so shadow compression is almost as bad in a real film.

The part of the characteristic curve representing the highlight steps is the *shoulder* of the curve. Between the toe and the shoulder is the *straight line*. The straight line of a real characteristic curve is longer than that of bad film. Therefore, the shoulder occurs at higher density ranges than the important highlights in some scenes. Highlight compression is less of a problem in real film than in bad film.

This all seems to suggest that increased exposure improves pictures. Increasing the exposure does, indeed, improve shadow detail more than it hurts highlight detail. This is why photographers who do not precisely control exposure generally prefer the safety of a slightly overexposed negative.

However, the characteristic curve omits an essential consideration. Unfortunately, there is still another influence to further degrade highlight reproduction: grain.

Grain

The two factors that most affect grain size are the sensitivity of the film to light and the density of the image. We usually choose the slowest film that allows an acceptable aperture and shutter speed. After that, we minimize grain by paying attention to density.

The denser the image is, the coarser the grain size is. It makes very little difference whether a density increase is caused by an exposure increase or a development increase. The effect on the grain is similar.

This means that the grain is not uniform throughout the scene. The highlight area has more grain than the shadow area because of the density difference. This fact surprises some photographers, especially those whose negatives are consistent enough to print with very little manipulation.

The denser areas in most negatives produce light gray or white in the print. The grain is coarse in those areas, but it is too light to see. Highlight grain is also concealed in a print by further highlight compression inherent in the characteristic curve of the paper itself.

Suppose, however, the highlight detail is not adequate with a normal printing exposure. Depending on the scene, most photographers remedy the problem by increasing either the general printing exposure or the exposure just in the problem area (a "burn"). This makes some of the highlight steps print as if they were middle steps. Printing the denser gray steps as middle steps reveals the coarsest grain in the negative.

Highlight compression in the negative is not as bad as shadow compression, but the defect is compounded by increased grain. The resulting effect on image quality can be even worse.

USING EVERY RESOURCE

The difficulties of white-on-white and black-on-black subjects are not caused just by the subjects themselves. The problems are related to the very basics of the photographic medium: Scenes get recorded on those portions of the characteristic curve that preserve the least detail. This means that no single technique, or even group of techniques, is adequate to deal with such subjects.

White-on-white and black-on-black require complete command of all types of photographic techniques. The two most essential sets of these techniques are lighting and exposure control. These two work together to produce each picture. The relative importance of each varies from one scene to another. We sometimes think primarily about exposure control and in other situations use lighting techniques as the primary tool. The remainder of this chapter will discuss both and suggest guidelines about when to use which tool.

Zone system practitioners will recognize that we are not giving much attention to one more important tool. This tool is the adjustment of film development to alter the shape of the characteristic curve to fit the grays in the scene. One reason for our lack of emphasis on development control is that we expect photography to continue its gradual evolution into a primarily color medium. Altered development offers minimal contrast control over color transparencies and causes more problems with color negatives than it solves.

A much more significant reason for downplaying the importance of development controls is that we rarely need to apply such controls if we master lighting. The zone system is still essential to establish a basic black-and-white film development suitable to each photographer's equipment and style. After that, using light well makes most day-to-day variations in normal development unnecessary.

WHITE-ON-WHITE

White subjects on a white background can be both practical and appealing. In advertising, such subjects give designers maximum flexibility in the composition of the piece. Type can go anywhere, even over an unimportant part of the subject itself. Black type on a white background is likely to survive even poor reproduction in a newspaper. Furthermore, photographers do not have to worry as much about making the crop fit the available space. If the picture is reproduced to keep the background pure white, readers cannot see in the ad where the edge of the print might have been relative to the subject.

Unfortunately, white-on-white subjects are also among the most difficult of all scenes to photograph. A "normally" exposed white-on-white subject is recorded on the worst portion of the usable film characteristic curve. Lesser contrast in that portion of the curve causes compression of that part of the gray scale. Gray steps that were distinctly different in the scene can become similar or identical grays in the photograph.

Grain is another problem. If we need to use a small camera, the coarser grain of an image composed entirely of highlight gray steps may undo the very mood the picture is most intended to convey. White-on-white subjects need to be clean and airy. Grain can make them appear dirty and foggy.

White subjects on white backgrounds also largely deprive us of the use of one of our favorite lighting ingredients: direct reflection. We have seen in earlier chapters that balancing direct and diffuse reflection can reveal detail that might otherwise disappear. Direct reflection is especially controllable by polarizing filters on light sources or lenses.

White-on-white scenes generally have as much direct reflection as any other scene, but the diffuse reflection is usually bright enough to overpower the direct reflection. With so much competition from diffuse reflection, the film cannot see very much direct reflection, and photographers accomplish little by trying to manipulate it.

However, we will accomplish even less by continuing to complain about the problems. So we will go on to a discussion of how to deal with them.

Good lighting control produces tonal distinctions in white-on-white subjects. Good exposure control preserves those distinctions. Neither control alone is adequate to do the job. We will discuss both.

Exposing White-on-White Scenes

We have told you why it is bad to record the gray scale of the scene near the shoulder of the characteristic curve. Have you, then, assumed that placing those grays on the straight line might be better? Good! Reducing the exposure of a white-on-white scene can dramatically improve image quality. Since you know that, we will discuss *how much* to reduce exposure without getting into other trouble.

Here are some definitions we will be using: We will consider a "normal" exposure to be a reflected light reading from an eighteen-percent gray card or an incident light reading. We will further assume that a "standard" printing exposure will reproduce a negative of that eighteen-percent gray card as exactly eighteen-percent reflectance in the print. Finally, we will consider "reduced" exposure and "increased" exposure to be deliberate deviation from the normal. This differentiates them from accidental underexposure and overexposure.

A typical white diffuse reflection is about 2 1/2 stops brighter than an eighteen-percent gray card seen under the same light. This means that if we meter a white subject, instead of a gray card, we need to increase exposure by 2 1/2 stops more than the meter indicates to get a normal exposure.

Suppose, however, we fail to make that 2 1/2-stop correction and expose exactly as the meter suggests. This means that the same white will reproduce as eighteen-percent gray with a standard printing exposure. This is much too dark. Viewers will almost never accept eighteen-percent gray as "white." However, such an exposure does have its advantages. It places the white subject on the straight-line portion of the characteristic curve. For that reason, exposing in this manner reduces grain and also eliminates compression in the negative.

Looking Good

In theory, similar principles should guide the exposure of both negatives and transparencies. Practicality and politics often dictate otherwise.

Few photographers reproduce the transparencies they shoot. The later steps are usually done by other people. A color separator could obtain better highlight detail by making a denser set of color separation negatives from a darker original, but photographers and color separators communicate with each other too little for this to happen. Almost everyone, including the color separator, fails to appreciate fully the creative potential of color separation. So the color separation all too often approximates the original as closely as possible, for better or worse.

Remember, too, that a transparency is the only form in which a client is likely to see the original film. Clients vary in their technical sophistication. Getting paid sometimes requires presenting a transparency that looks as good as possible. Explaining why a transparency that looks too dark or too light can reproduce better is more likely to confuse than inform an unsophisticated client.

Furthermore, we are under no obligation to print the negative with our standard printing exposure. We can make the print as light as we need so that the resulting image is an appropriately light gray that viewers will call "white." If we do this, any particular light gray in the print may be identical to the same gray printed from a normally exposed negative with a standard printing exposure. Without compression, however, that gray will be better differentiated from other similar grays in the same scene.

Therefore, we recommend that you reduce the exposure of white-on-white subjects by 2 1/2 stops. The way to do this is to use the exposure indicated by a reflection meter and ignore the routine correction.

Photographers who have thoroughly mastered metering techniques may be offended by our suggestion to just point the meter and read, then do what the meter says, without any calculation or compensation. They ought to be! We would be completely irresponsible to make such a recommendation if we did not go on to warn you about secondary black subjects and about transparencies.

Using the uncorrected exposure indicated by the reflection meter works fine if the scene is composed entirely of light grays. If there is an additional black subject in the scene, however, then that part of the scene will lack shadow detail.

Whether this lack of detail is a problem depends entirely on what the subject is in the specific scene. If the black subject is unimportant and if it is too small to advertise the defect, then the lack of shadow detail will not be objectionable.

However, if the significance or the size of the secondary black subject commands the viewer's attention, the defect will also be apparent. In such a case, it would be better to use a normal exposure instead of a reduced one. "Importance" is a psychological judgment not a technical one. It is entirely reasonable to decide to reduce the exposure for one white-on-white scene but to use a normal exposure for another technically identical scene.

A transparency does not simply need to reproduce properly. It also needs to look good in its original form. For this reason, we cannot reduce the exposure of reversal film as much as we can that of a negative. Between one-half and one stop exposure reduction will improve highlight detail and usually will not appear too dark. Bracketing is essential. It is often difficult to decide which exposure looks better until the film is processed.

If we consider the possible errors, and then accept the reflection meter reading of a white-on-white scene without compensation, then that is a deliberate decision to reduce exposure. If we use the exposure that we read on the meter without thinking about the dangers, the result may be accidental underexposure.

We want to end this exposure discussion on a happy note. Because negatives of white-on-white tend to be more grainy, these are also the scenes in which finer grained film is most useful. The only reason photographers do not always use such films is that they are slow films.

Realize that being free to use less exposure in a white-on-white scene also allows using a slower film. Deciding to reduce exposure by 2 1/2 stops means that we can use the same aperture and shutter speed for an ISO 32 film as those of an ISO 180 film exposed normally. Therefore, it is easier to use the slower films for the very scenes in which they are likely to do the most good. There is order in the universe.

Lighting White-on-White Scenes

Lighting a white-on-white scene requires enhancing both texture and depth, like the lighting of any other scene. We can do this with the same techniques we used in Chapters 4 and 5. The other special requirement of white-on-white scenes is to keep all parts of the subject from disappearing!

The easiest way to obtain a true "white-on-white" scene is to simply fix and wash a piece of unexposed photographic paper! Of course, photographers do not really mean "white-on-white" when they use the term. Instead, they mean "very light gray on very light gray, with some whites in the scene."

We have talked about why these very light similar tones tend to become the same tone in a photograph. Good exposure control minimizes this problem. But a light gray still disappears against an identical light gray. The only way to keep such a subject visible is to make one of those grays lighter or darker. This is what lighting does.

Subject and Background. The most important grays to distinguish are those of the subject and its background. Without this separation, the viewer cannot see the shape of the subject. A viewer may never notice the loss of minor detail within the subject, but a lost edge is readily apparent.

We can light either the background or the edge of the subject so that it reproduces as white (or very light gray) in the photograph. Once we decide which of these is to be white, we know that the other must be at least slightly darker. Technically, it does not matter whether the main subject or the background is slightly darker. Either way preserves tonal distinction.

Psychologically, however, it may matter whether the background or the subject is white. This is generally true of those very simple scenes that give the brain fewer clues to decide whether a gray was white in the original scene or was truly gray.

Figure 9.11 shows a white subject against a white background. We have lit the scene to render the background white and the subject light gray. When you look at the picture, your brain interprets the scene as white-on-white.

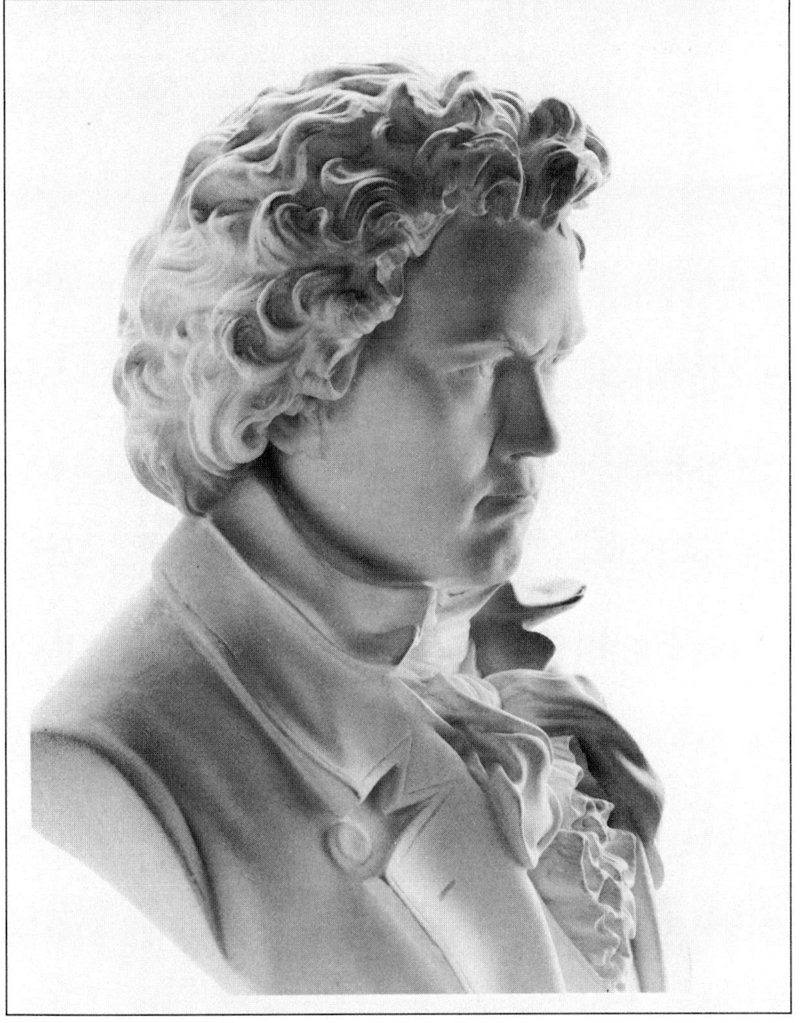

◀ *The background looks white and the Beethoven bust, a light gray. The brain interprets such a scene as "white-on-white."*

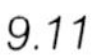

9.11

However, the brain is less willing to accept a gray background as a white one. Look at Figure 9.12. We have relit the scene to render the background light gray and the subject white. You no longer see a white-on-white scene, but a white-on-gray one.

► *The background is now a light gray and the bust, white. The brain now interprets the visual message as white on gray rather than white-on-white.*

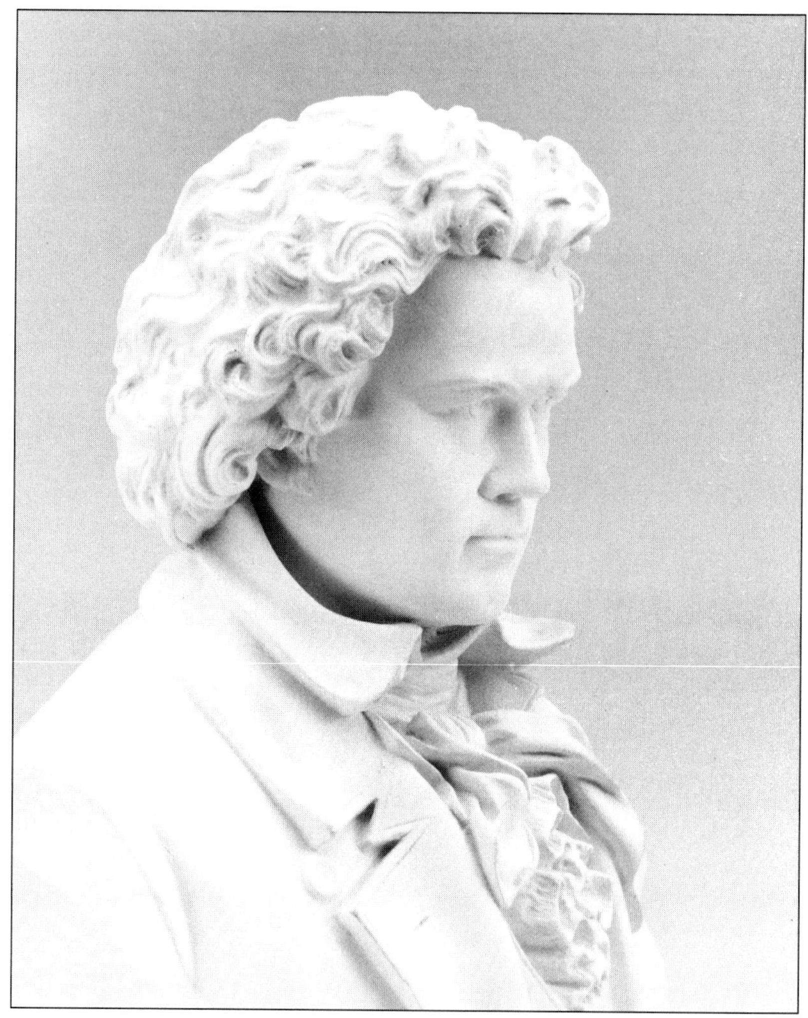

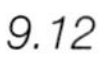

9.12

We are not saying that Figure 9.12 is a bad picture. It still has good tonal distinction between the subject and the background, and it is pleasing in every other way. You may prefer the lighting, and we have no reason to discourage it. We are simply saying that it is not a good white-on-white example.

Since this section is about white-on-white, we will keep the background white, or nearly so, in all remaining examples. In these examples, the background needs to be between one-half stop and one stop brighter than grays in the edges of the primary subject. If it is less than one-half stop brighter, part of the subject may disappear; if it is more than one stop brighter, flare may scatter enough light inside the camera to cost contrast in the subject.

Using an Opaque White Background

The easiest white-on-white subjects are those that allow separate control over the lighting of the primary subject and its background. In those cases, we can slightly increase the light on the background to keep it white. Putting the subject directly on a white opaque background is the most difficult white-on-white arrangement because whatever we do to one also affects the other. This is also the most common arrangement, so we will deal with it first. Figure 9.13 illustrates the process.

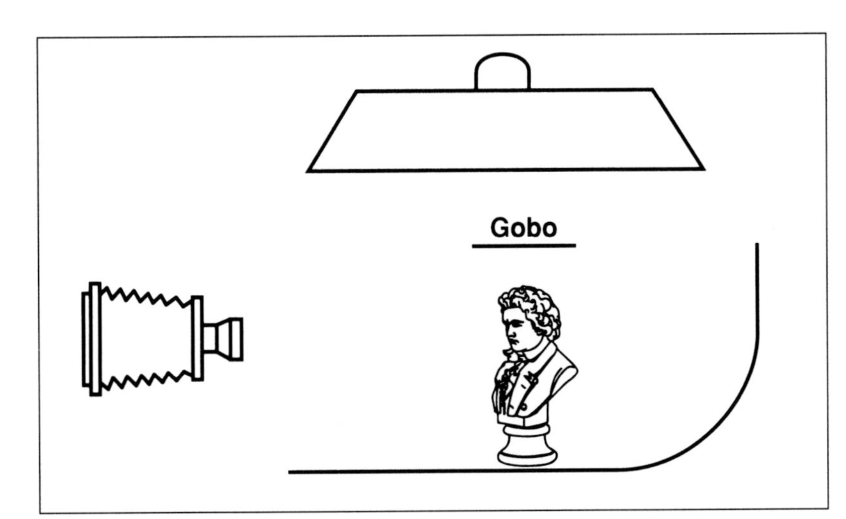

9.13

◀ *One good lighting arrangement for a white-on-white subject.*

1. Light the Subject from Above. Lighting from above places the front of the subject slightly in shadow but fully illuminates the tabletop. This readily establishes the gray subject and white background we want. In most cases, the camera sees good distinction between the sides of the subject and the background without any further adjustments. Figure 9.14 is the result.

▶ *There is good differentiation between the Beethoven bust and the background. However, the top of the head has vanished.*

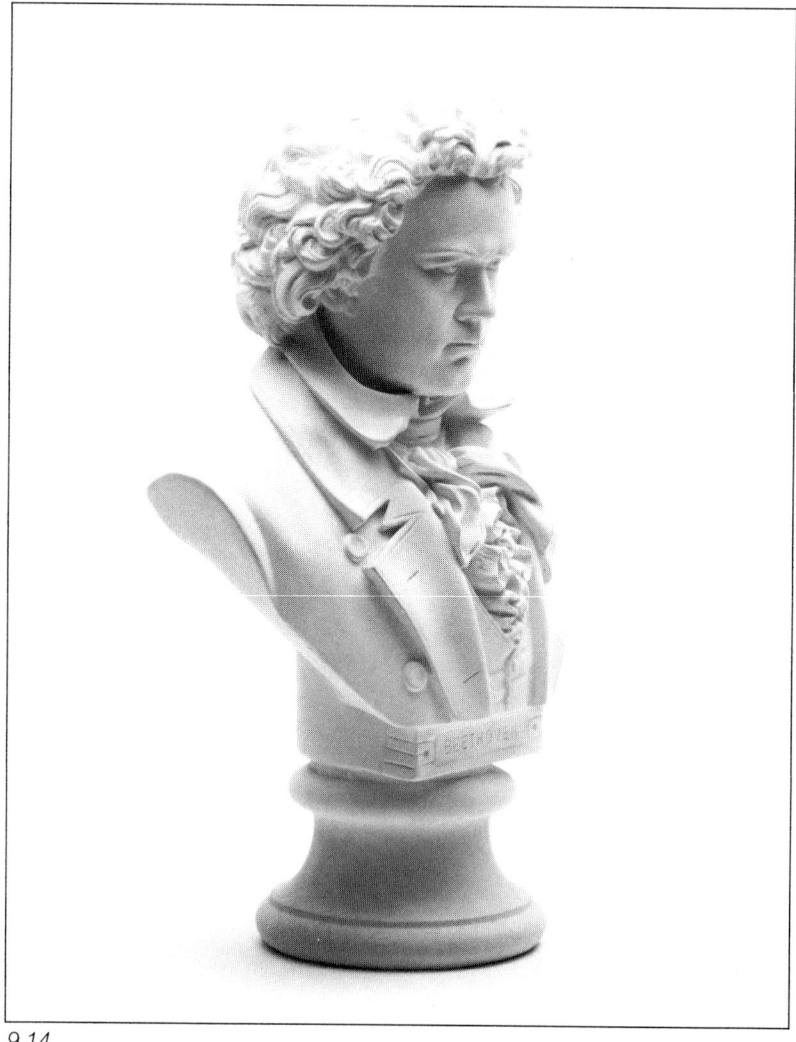

9.14

Notice, however, that such an arrangement also fully illuminates the top of the subject. The loss of tonal distinction in that area means we have to do some more work before exposing the film.

2. Use a Gobo above the Subject. This step is almost always necessary. We place the gobo to cast just enough shadow on the top of the subject to bring its brightness down to a level similar to that of the front. You can see the improvement in Figure 9.15.

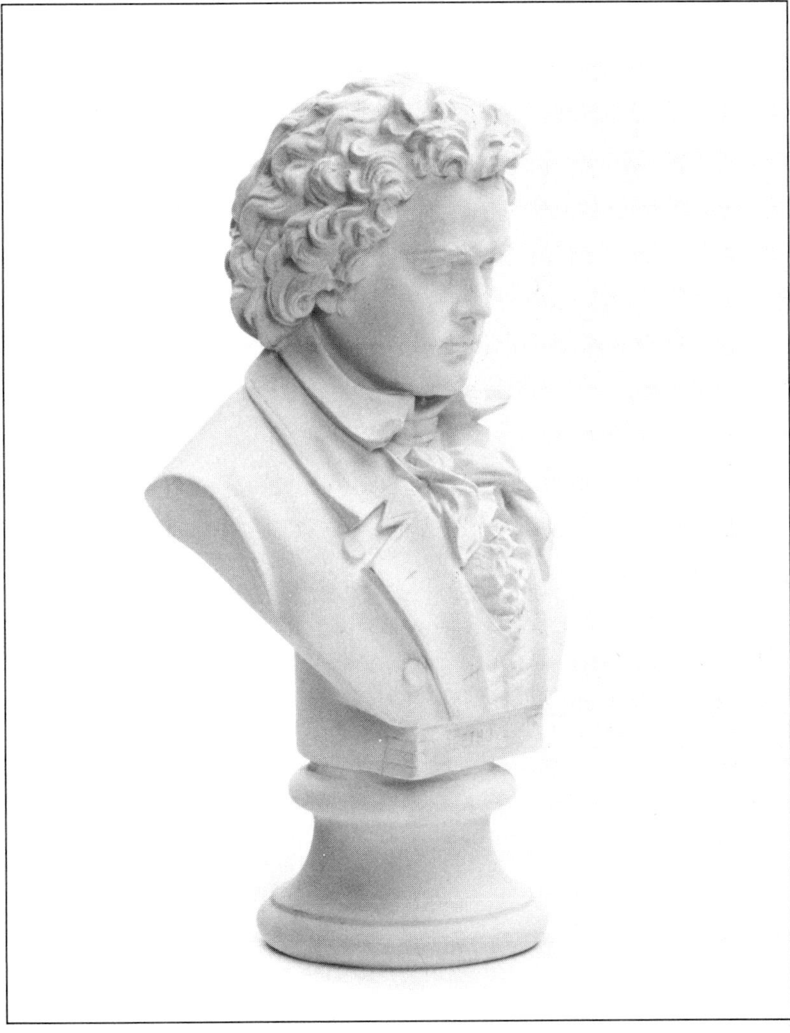

9.15

◀ *A gobo blocking light from the bust's head takes care of the problem we saw in the previous picture. The top of the head is now clearly visible.*

You may have been surprised that we did not discuss the size of the light in the previous step. As far as the subject is concerned, you can use a light of whatever size that looks good. However, we recommend a medium-sized light because it is likely to work most effectively with the gobo in this step.

The hardness of the shadow cast by the gobo is usually more critical than that of the subject. If the light is too small, we may not be able to get the shadow of the gobo soft enough to blend with the rest of the scene. A light too large may keep that shadow too soft to effectively shade the subject. Using a medium-sized light from the beginning reserves the privilege of experimenting with the gobo later.

If you have not done this before, you may not know how large the gobo should be or how far it should be from the subject. These things vary with the subject, so we cannot give you formulas. We can, however, tell you how to decide for yourself. Begin with a gobo about the size of the offending highlight. For ease of movement, hold it in your hand while experimenting. You can alter the size of the gobo and clamp it appropriately when you fine-tune the setup later.

The closer the gobo is to the subject, the harder the shadow of the gobo becomes. Move the gobo closer to the subject, then farther away, to see this happen. The edge of the shadow of the gobo needs to blend nicely with the edge of the highlight we need to conceal. The principle is exactly like dodging a shadow in a print. (However, this is much easier because we can see the result without waiting for a print to develop.)

The shadow of the gobo may become too light as you move it farther from the subject. If this happens, try a larger gobo. Conversely, if the shadow of the gobo blends well, but is too dark, cut the gobo smaller.

Finally, when the gobo position is right for the primary subject, look at its effect on the background. The gobo will also cast a shadow there. On most subjects, the shadow the gobo casts on the background will blend nicely with that of the subject and will not be noticeable. The gobo shadow will be softer on the background than on the top of the subject because the background is farther away from the gobo than the subject is.

If the subject is tall enough, the gobo may produce no perceptible shadow on the background at all. There will be a problem, however, with very shallow subjects. In an extreme case, such as a white business card on a white table, it is impossible to put a shadow on the card without shading the background equally. In those situations, we must either use one of the other backgrounds discussed later in this chapter or resort to masking or retouching after the photograph is completed.

3. Add Dimension. The white background on which the subject sits will provide a great deal of fill light. Unfortunately, this fill illumination will usually be too even to give the picture a good sense of dimension. Figure 9.15 is technically acceptable because the subject is reasonably well defined, but the bland uniformity of the grays makes it boring.

If the subject is very much darker than the background, we need to add an additional reflector to one side. This adds both fill and dimension. If the subject is only slightly darker than the background, we dare not further brighten it with fill. Instead, we usually add a black card, again to one side. This blocks some of the light reflecting from the background and produces a shadowed side to the subject. Figure 9.16 has a black card on the left, just out of camera range.

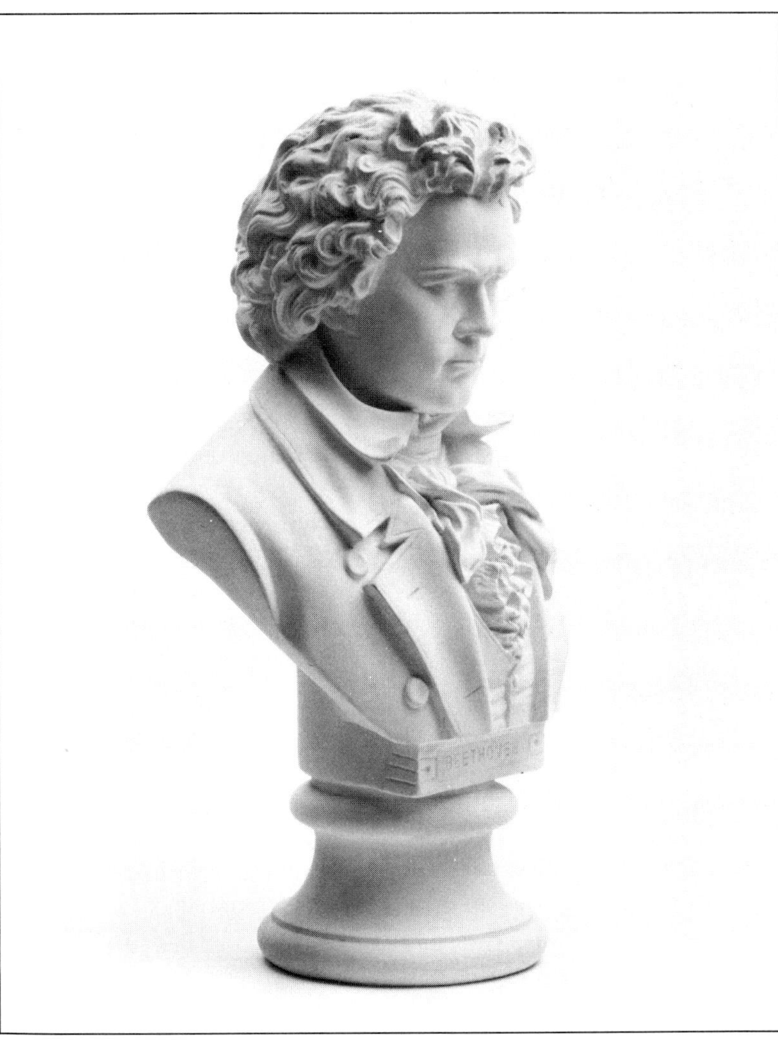

◀ *A black card on the left reduced the fill reflected from the tabletop, creating a sense of depth.*

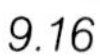

9.16

Using a Translucent White Background

If the shape of the subject is very flat, there is no way to shadow it without doing the same to the background on which it sits. One good solution to this problem is to use a translucent background that can be lit from behind. White acrylic is good for this purpose. As long as the subject is reasonably opaque, we can light the background to whatever brightness we please without affecting the subject. Figure 9.17 shows the lighting diagram.

► *A translucent background photographs "whiter" than a "white" subject.*

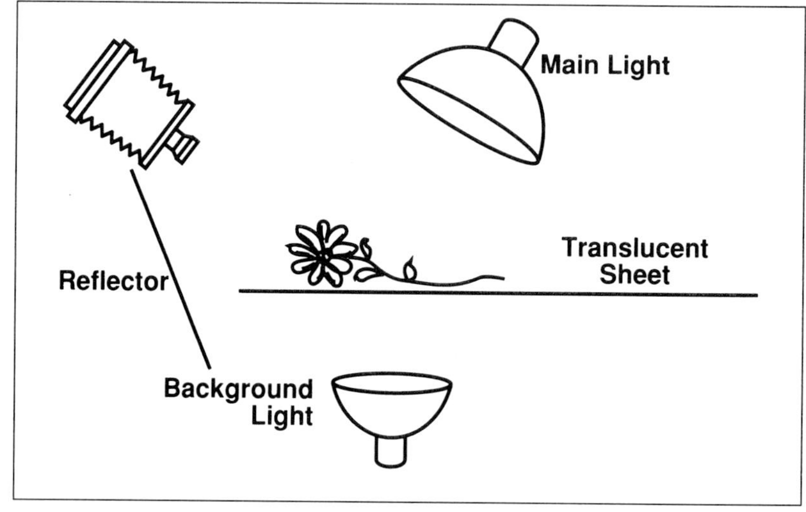

9.17

Figure 9.18 is a simple application of this technique. The subject is well differentiated from the background. Notice, though, that the illumination under the subject has erased any hint of a ground shadow.

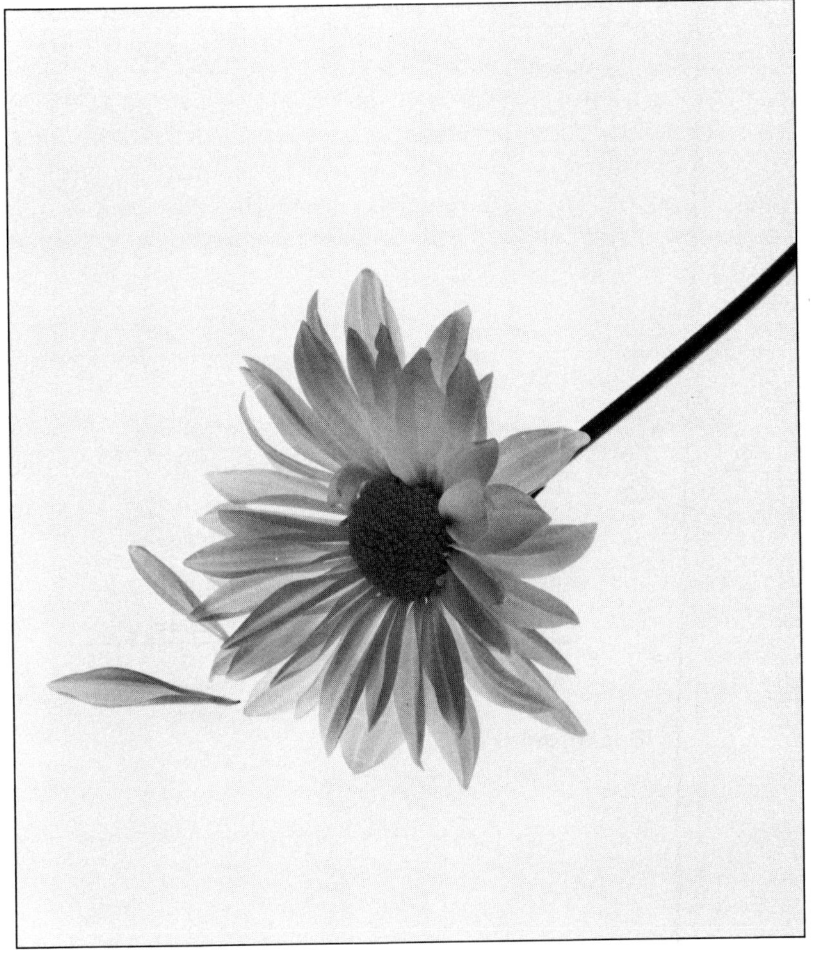

9.18

◀ *Light from under the flower eliminated any hint of a ground shadow in the print.*

After looking at this picture, we might be inclined to avoid this setup any time we want to preserve a shadow under the subject. This would be a mistake. One of the single biggest advantages to this technique is that it allows us to control the apparent shadow of the subject completely independently of the lighting of the subject. We admit this sounds like magic. Actually, it is just a magician's trick.

We begin the trick by turning off any lights we intend to use to photograph the subject. Then we set up a test light to produce a pleasing shadow. It does not matter whether this light is good for the subject, because we will not use it for that purpose. We intend to use the light to trace a pattern (as we did for the family of angles in Chapter 6 and the reflector behind the glass of liquid in Chapter 8).

Next, slide any opaque or semi-opaque paper under the subject. (If you move the subject in the process, go back to the camera to reposition it. Remember, critical positioning is unnecessary at this time.) Trace the shadow pattern on the paper with a pencil. Third, remove the opaque paper and cut out the shadow pattern. The final step is to glue the shadow pattern *under* the translucent background, as shown in Figure 9.19.

► *Manufacturing a ground shadow.*

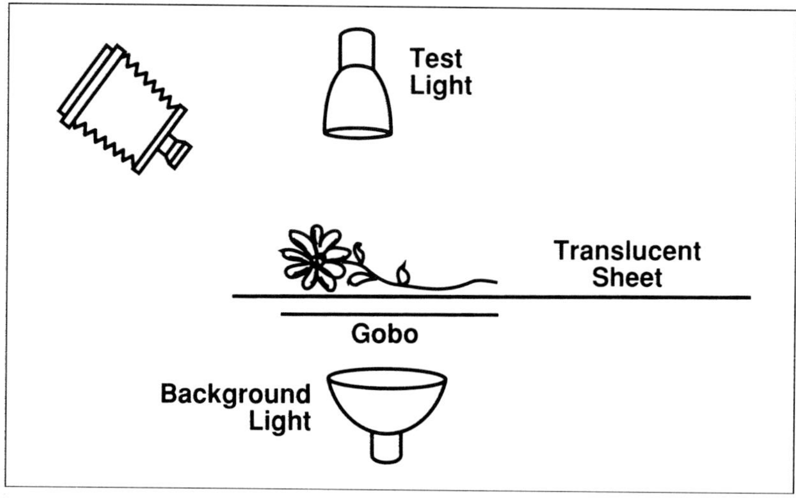

9.19

Now you can turn off the test light and light the subject in any manner you please. Figure 9.20 is the finished picture. The shadow under the blossom and the stem were not cast by the light illuminating the subject.

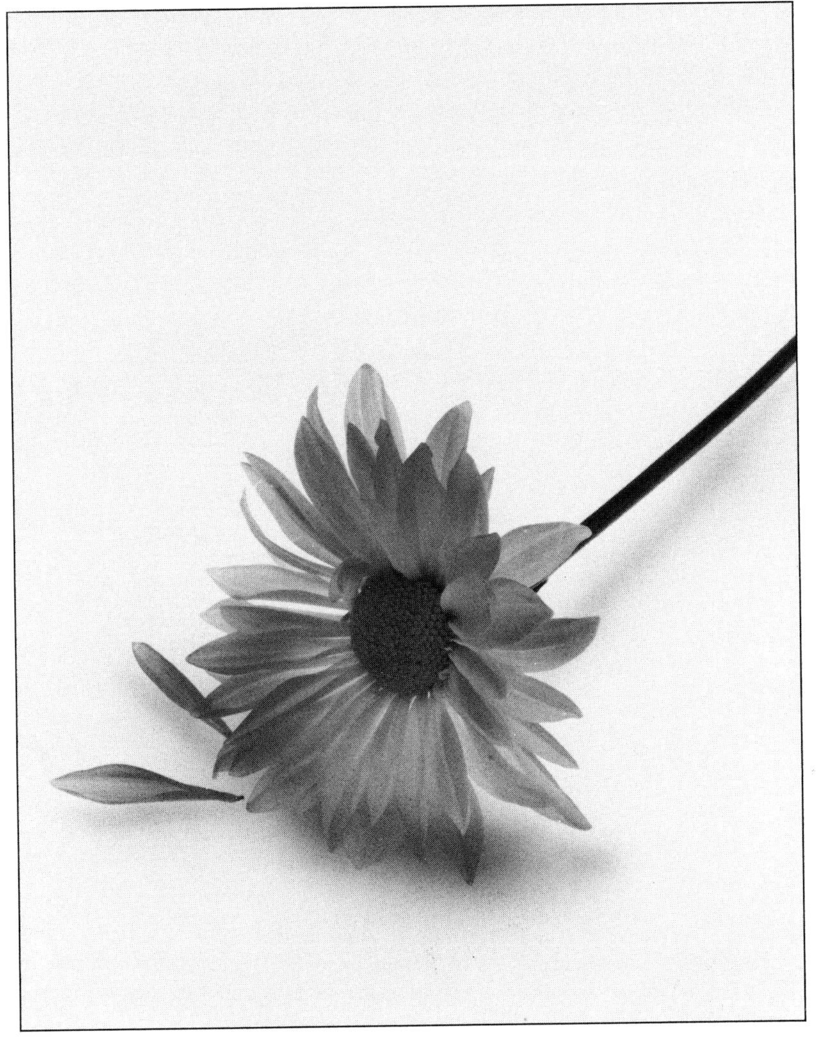

◀ *A gobo was placed under the table to produce a shadow that looks as though it was cast by the flower.*

9.20

Using a Mirror Background

Probably the easiest "white" background to use is a mirror. A mirror reflects almost nothing but direct reflections. Such reflections are likely to be much brighter than the diffuse reflections from a white subject.

We begin the arrangement with a light large enough to fill the family of angles that produce direct reflections on the entire mirror surface. (We determine where that family is exactly as we did with the flat metal in Chapter 6. You can look back at that section if you need a lighting diagram.) Since the light source must fill the family of angles defined by the entire background, this may turn out to be the largest light we will ever need for a flat subject.

The other special requirement for the light source is that it show no distracting texture. Remember that the light itself will be visibly and sharply reflected in the mirror.

No additional steps were needed for Figure 9.21. A light so large usually produces shadows so soft that no other light is required for fill. Furthermore, this is one of the few techniques in which the background can reflect much fill light *under* the subject.

► *A mirror reflecting the light source is another background that is "whiter" than the "white" flower.*

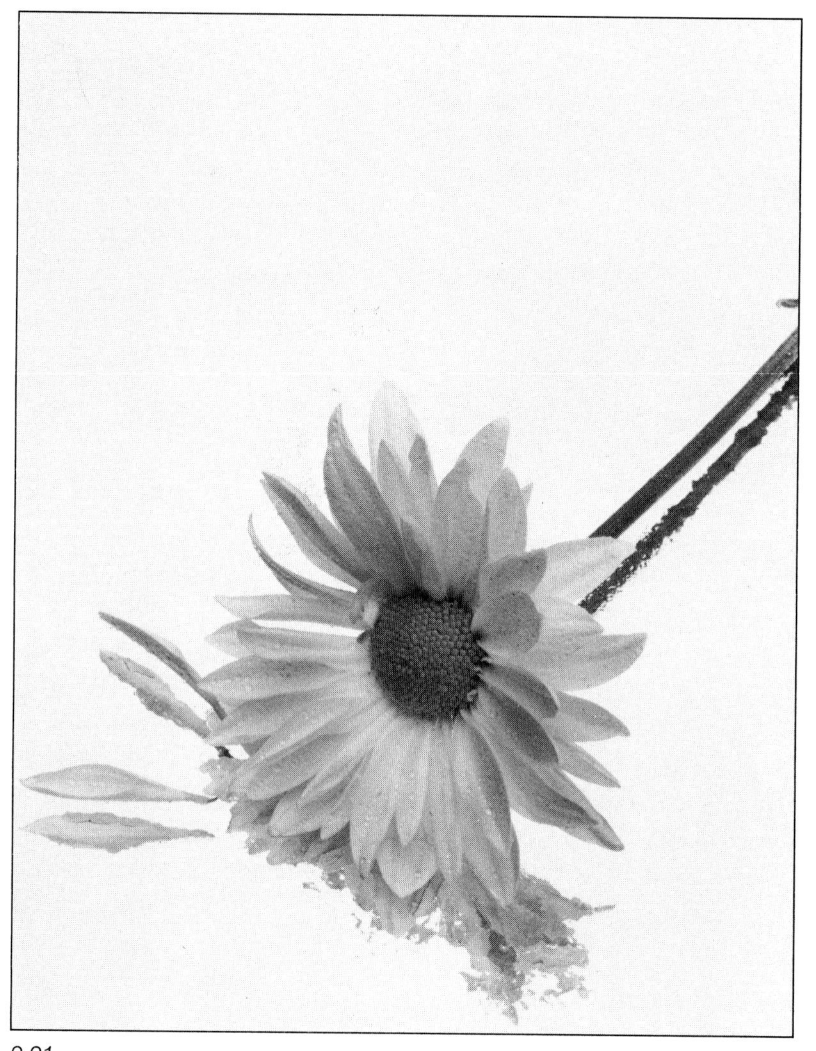

9.21

An occasional drawback to this technique is the reflection of the subject. It may be confusing, depending on the crop and on the shape of the subject. The water drops in this photograph are used to camouflage and break up that reflection. The other possible complaint is the lack of ground shadow. There is no way to obtain one with this setup. If you feel the shadow is necessary for your subject, then some other arrangement will be better.

In Any Case, Keep the Background Small

We have explained why direct reflections are usually not very important to white subjects. The few we see are generally helpful to add a bit of dimension, but compared with the diffuse reflections, they tend to be too weak to be major players in the lighting event.

The exception to this is direct reflection on the edge of the subject. Direct reflection in those areas is especially likely to make the subject disappear against the white background. To make matters worse, the white backgrounds in all of these arrangements are in exactly the position most likely to cause these reflections.

The most common solution is the same as the technique for keeping reflection off the edge of the glass in the bright-field method, as discussed in Chapter 7: Keep the background as small as possible. Sometimes we have a background much larger than the area the camera sees, and we do not want to cut it. In those situations, we either confine the light to the image area or surround the image area with black cards.

Another danger of white-on-white situations is camera flare. Large white backgrounds scatter a lot of light inside the camera. This flare will probably be so uniform that you will not see it, even when the general loss of contrast is significant. However, if you stay in the habit of keeping the white background only as large as it needs to be, you will not need to worry about the flare.

BLACK-ON-BLACK

Mastering white-on-white is a good step forward in the process of mastering black-on-black. Many of the principles are similar, but applied in reverse. We will point out some of these similarities, but we will emphasize the differences.

The major difference in exposure considerations is that tonal compression is likely to be worse in black-on-black situations. The major difference in lighting considerations is the increased visibility of direct reflection.

Are Underexposed Transparencies Acceptable ?

Underexposed negatives reproduce no distinction between grays that were very dark in the scene. All those grays record as clear film in the negative. There is no distinction left to print.

As you consider this, you probably also see that *overexposed* transparencies are useless for the same reason. A very light gray is rendered as clear film on an overexposed transparency and a still lighter gray is also rendered as clear film. Again, there is no distinction on the film and no account of manipulation can improve the defect.

So if you think overexposed transparencies suffer the same problem as underexposed negatives, you are right. Since this logic works so well we will take it a step further and see where it leads.

If the highlights in transparencies behave like the shadows in negatives, then we are tempted to assume that the shadows in transparencies behave like the highlights in negatives. And if there is almost always some highlight detail in an overexposed negative might we also expect to find some shadow detail in an underexposed transparency?

Unfortunately, the answer is no. Every film is a black-and-white negative *at the time it is exposed,* and it behaves like any other black-and-white negative at that time. (This is why most writers use black-and-white negatives for most examples in books like this one.) Both the reversal of the gray steps and the color are the result of processing. A transparency has "clear film" at *each* end of its gray scale at different times in its life.

Exposing Black-on-Black Scenes

The section on the film characteristic curve pointed out the compression of gray steps in both the shadow and the highlight steps. We also saw why overexposure exaggerates this problem in white-on-white scenes and why underexposure exaggerates it in black-on-black scenes.

Compression of the gray steps is not as bad in a white-on-white scene as in a black-on-black one. The shoulder of the characteristic curve does not become absolutely flat within any usable exposure range. If we overexpose a scene by many stops, the distinction between the highlight steps becomes poor, but it does not disappear. The distinctions still exist on the negative, and we can print them, although not excellently.

The problem is much worse in the shadow steps. Severe underexposure loses the distinction between the dark grays altogether. If a gray in the scene is dark enough to be represented by clear film on the negative, then a still darker gray in the scene will still record as the same clear film. This is the most complete compression possible. Since there is no difference between one clear film area and another, we cannot make a print that shows distinction between those steps, no matter how hard we try.

So good exposure is even more important in a black-on-black scene than it is in a white-on-white one. Sometimes the subject in a scene prevents ideal exposure. A dark secondary subject in a white-on-white scene and a bright one in a black-on-black scene are the most common examples of this. In those cases, remember that an overexposed white-on-white subject is often salvageable in the dark room; but an underexposed black-on-black subject almost never is.

The proper exposure of most black-on-black scenes requires increasing the exposure. This is true for the same reason that we tend to reduce exposure in white-on-white scenes. In both cases, we want to move the extreme gray steps closer to the straight-line portion of the negative characteristic curve.

The amount that we want to modify the exposure is also similar: two and a half stops. This means we expose that much more than what a gray card reflection reading or an incident reading tells us. Or we can accomplish about the same thing by simply pointing a reflection meter at the subject and exposing as it says, without any compensation.

This is a satisfactory shortcut to more sophisticated metering techniques *if* we remember the potential problems it can create. These, too, are similar to those for white-on-white subjects.

First, this method will overexpose secondary light-gray subjects in the same scene. We have seen why this is not as bad as underexposing secondary dark-gray subjects in a negative of a white-on-white scene. Of course, "not as bad" does not mean "good." We have to weigh the benefits and sacrifices before we expose the film.

Second, remember that if the shot requires a transparency, the client is likely to look at the original film, not at a corrected print. A negative needs to record maximum detail, but a transparency needs to record as much detail as possible and still look "right." Transparencies do need exposure increases for black-on-black subjects, but seldom as much as two and a half stops. Bracketing between a normal exposure and a two-stop increase produces an image that is both technically and psychologically acceptable.

Photographers hate to be told to increase exposure. Too often, light is expensive or unavailable. These difficulties increase whenever we need more of it. Therefore, we again want to finish our exposure discussion with an observation that will make you feel better about accepting our advice. Black-on-black scenes produce the least grainy negatives. Faster films with coarser grain are less likely to be objectionable for these subjects. If you want to use a faster film, instead of more watts, feel free to do so!

Lighting Black-on-Black Scenes

Black-on-black scenes require special attention to exposure to record as much detail as possible on film. However, increasing the exposure of a black-on-black scene works only if there are no secondary white subjects in danger of overexposure. Even without any white subjects, increased exposure of a black-on-black scene sometimes does not *look* right in a transparency, even if it records more detail than a normal exposure. Although good exposure is essential, it is not enough. The manipulation of exposure and of lighting help one another to record the scene well. Now we will look at the lighting principles and techniques.

Like "white-on-white," "black-on-black" is an accurate description of a scene only when we acknowledge it to be an abbreviation for a longer description. A better description would be "a scene composed mostly of dark grays, but with some blacks in it also."

Like all scenes, lighting black-on-black scenes requires that we reveal depth, shape, and texture. Like white-on-white, the lighting of black-on-black scenes needs to move some of the exposure steps in the scene to the middle of the density scale in the negative. This is how we overcome the tendency for very light or very dark similar tones to become identical in a photograph.

White-on-white scenes produce a great deal of diffuse reflection; this is what makes them white. Conversely, black subjects are black because of their lack of diffuse reflection. This difference in diffuse reflection is important mainly because of what it implies about direct reflection.

The greatest single difference between lighting black-on-black and white-on-white scenes is that most black-on-black scenes allow us the full use of direct reflection. White subjects do not necessarily produce less direct reflection. Instead, whatever direct reflection a white thing does produce is less noticeable because the diffuse reflection is so much brighter by comparison. By the same token, black things do not produce any more direct reflection. However, the direct reflection they do produce is more visible because those reflections have less competition from diffuse reflections.

So the rule of thumb for lighting most black-on-black scenes is to capitalize on direct reflection whenever possible. If you have mastered lighting metal, you know that we usually do the same for those cases. (Direct reflection makes the metal bright. We rarely want to photograph it to appear dark.) Therefore, another good rule for black-on-black is to light it like metal, regardless of the actual material.

Generally, this means finding the family of angles that produce direct reflection and filling that family of angles with a light source or sources. (Chapter 6 describes how to do this.) We will talk about specifics in the rest of this chapter.

Subject and Background. We can only photograph a scene composed of grays, not a truly "black-on-black" one. This means that either the subject or the background needs to be dark gray, not black, to keep the subject from disappearing.

Figure 9.22 is a black subject on a black background. Notice that we have lit it so that the background is absolutely black. Doing this meant that we also had to keep the subject from being absolute black. Rendering the subject as a dark or middle gray keeps it distinct from the background and preserves its shape.

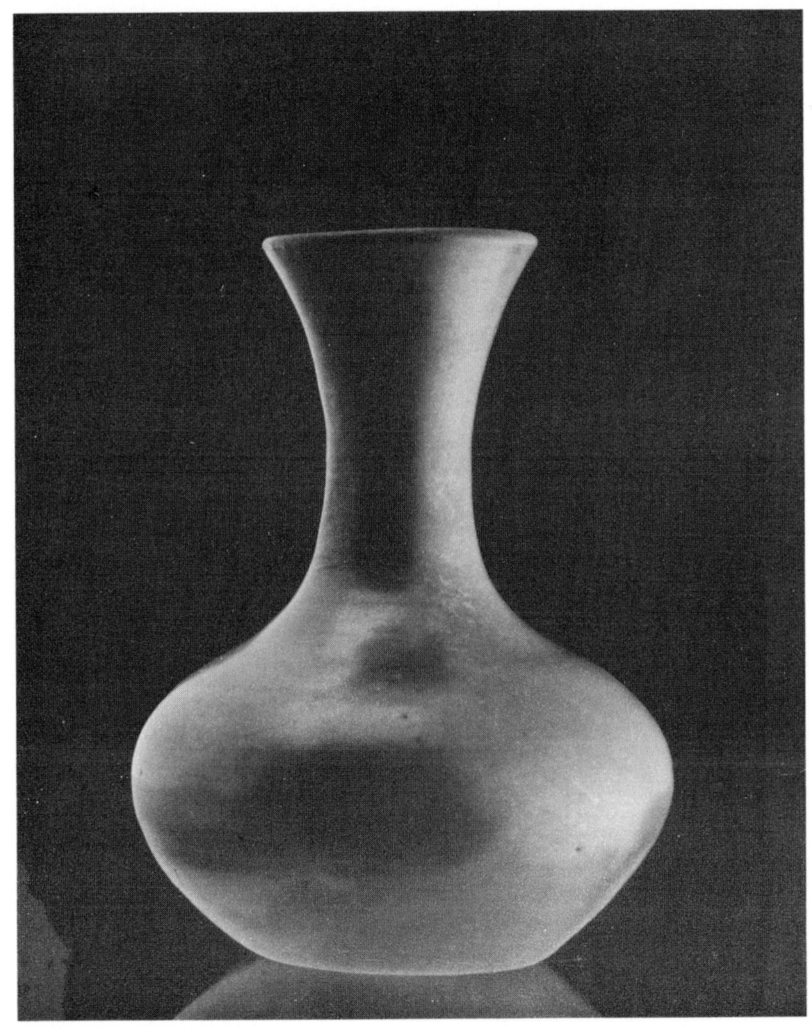

◀ *The brain interprets a gray subject, such as this pot, against a black background as a "black-on-black" scene.*

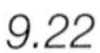

9.22

A black subject on a dark-gray background could maintain the same distinction. In either case, there is enough difference between the subject and the background to keep the subject from disappearing. However, illuminating the background causes additional problems. Figure 9.23 shows them.

► *The subject is black, and the background is dark gray. The brain no longer accepts the scene as black-on-black.*

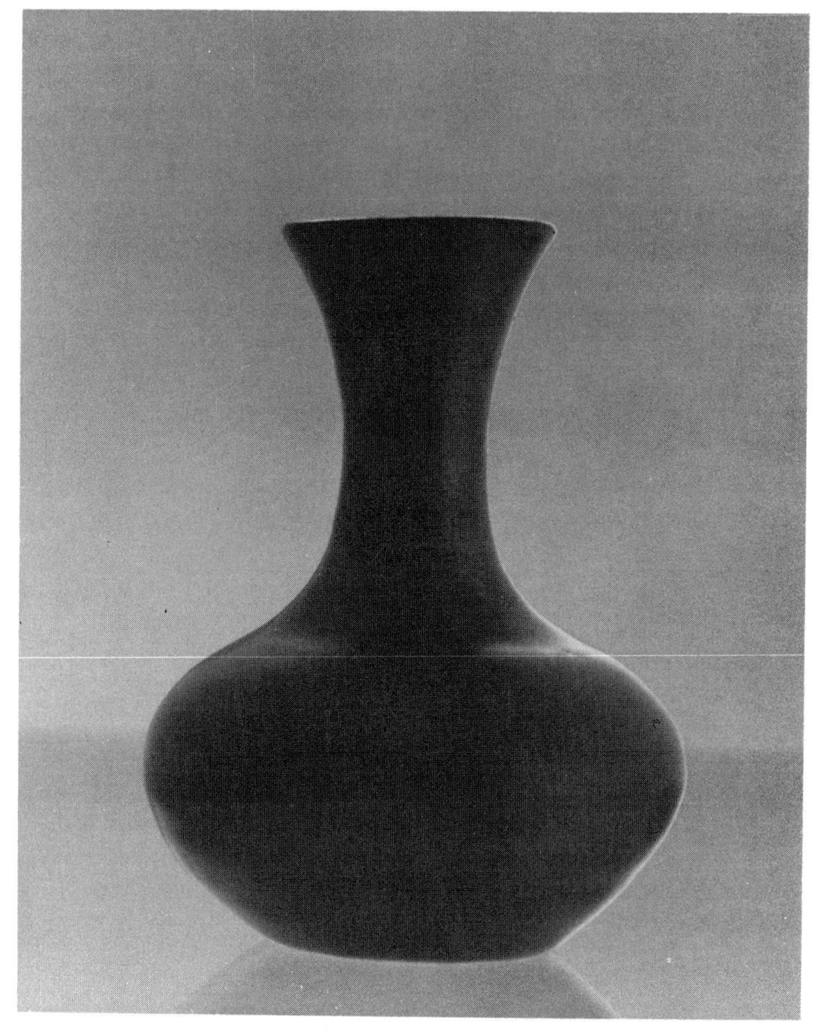

9.23

The background no longer looks black. We are psychologically willing to accept a dark-gray subject as black, but not a dark-gray background. This is almost always true for simple scenes that do not give the brain many other clues to decide how the original scene looked. The same is also true for many complex scenes.

This correlates with the earlier principle that human brains consider most scenes to be white-on-white only when the background is pure, or nearly pure, white. It also suggests similar action. If you just want to differentiate the subject from the background, keep either one of them black and make the other one gray. However, if you want to successfully represent "black-on-black," make sure the background is as black as possible.

You will see that this opinion influences almost every technique we are going to suggest. There is only one exception to this, and we will talk about that next.

Using an Opaque Black Background

Putting a black subject on an opaque black background is usually one of the worst ways of creating a black-on-black scene. We discuss it first because it is often the most available solution. Most studio photographers have black seamless paper handy.

Figure 9.24 shows the problem. (The lighting is a large overhead source like that used for a box in Chapter 5.) The paper background directly under the subject receives as much illumination as the subject itself. There is no easy way to light the subject any brighter than the background. We know that we need to render the subject dark gray, not black, to preserve detail. However, if the subject is not black, then the background under it cannot be black either.

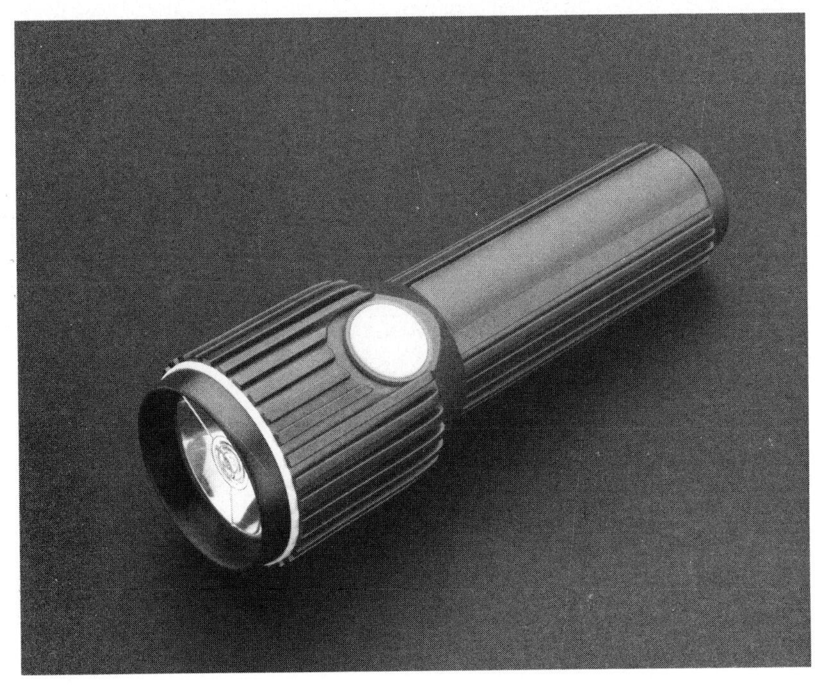

◀ *The black paper cannot be exposed dark enough to render it black if the flashlight is properly exposed.*

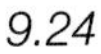

9.24

We could use a spotlight to concentrate the light on the primary subject, thus keeping the background darker. Remember, however, we want to produce as much direct reflection on the subject as possible. This requires a large light source to fill the family of angles that does that. Using large lights generally means using no spotlights.

We could also hope that a lot of the reflection from the background is polarized direct reflection. Then we could use a polarizing filter on the camera lens to block that reflection and keep the background black. Sometimes this works, but in most of those scenes the direct reflection from the subject is also polarized. Unfortunately, the polarizer is likely to darken the subject at least as much as it darkens the background.

The best solution is to find a background material that produces less diffuse reflection than the subject. Black velvet serves this purpose for most subjects. Figure 9.25 is the earlier subject photographed with the same lighting and the same exposure, but with black velvet replacing the paper.

► *With the same exposure, the black velvet is much darker than the black paper used in Figure 9.24.*

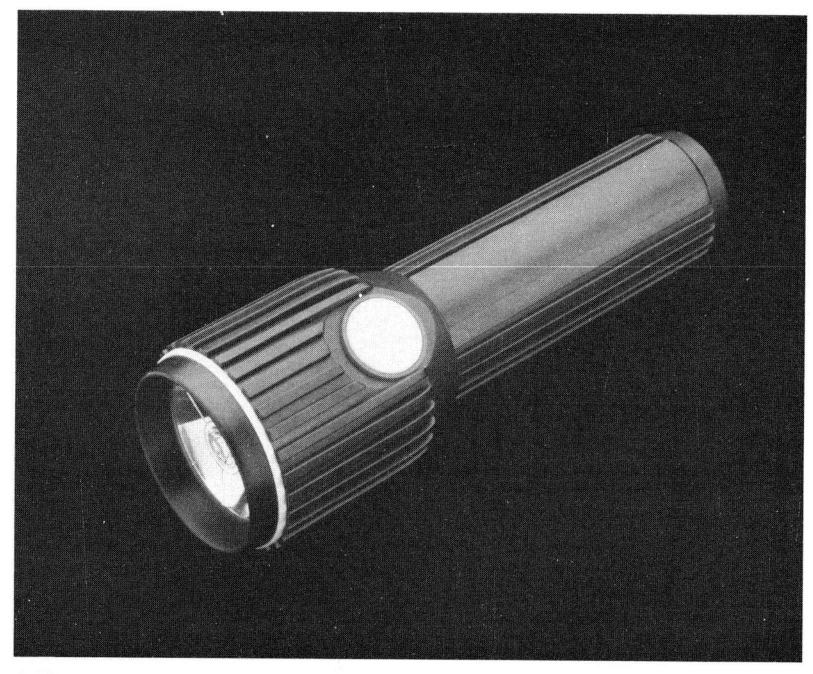

9.25

There are two possible problems to the black velvet solution. A few subjects are so black that even the velvet will not be blacker than they are. A more common problem is that the edges of the black subject merge with their own shadow. Fill light does not help much. Remember that the subject does not produce significant diffuse reflection, and the only place from which a light can produce direct reflection on the edges of the subject is located within the image area.

Notice that this problem is similar to the metal box shown in Chapter 6. We solved that problem with invisible light. Unfortunately, we cannot reflect very much light, invisible or not, from black velvet. That requires a glossy surface.

Using a Glossy Black Surface

In Figure 9.26 we substituted a black acrylic surface for the black velvet. Then we bounced a little invisible light from the glossy surface to fill in the sides of the subject. This works for almost any black subject. Or does it? Notice that the large light above the subject also fills the family of angles that produces direct reflection on the glossy acrylic. Therefore, the background is no longer black. Since you saw that so quickly, you probably also remember that we said earlier that the background had to stay black.

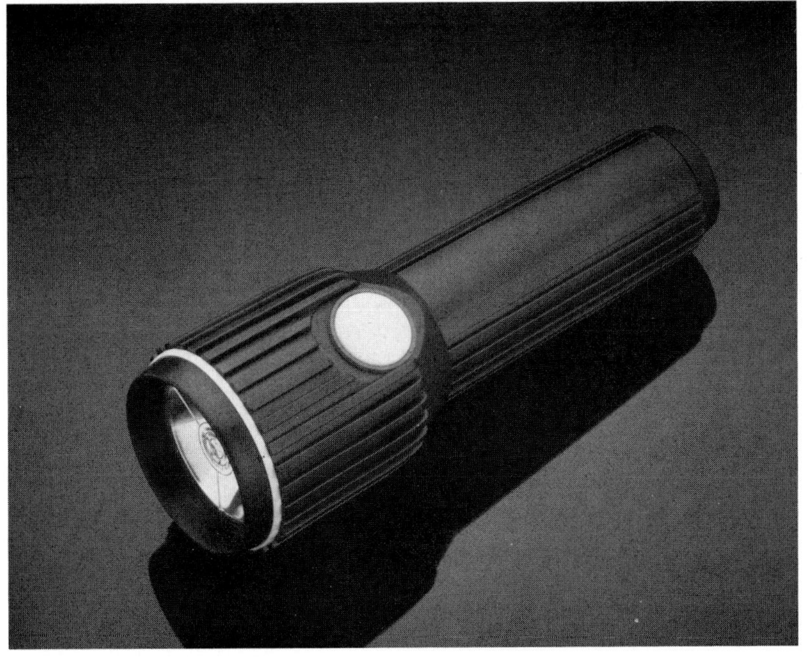

9.26

◀ *A black acrylic background. Notice the sharply outlined reflection of the flashlight. Is the scene black-on-black?*

We would like to talk our way out of this apparent discrepancy by pointing out that the brain needs to see a black background in *simple* black-on-black scenes. The subject, background, and *reflection* of the subject add up to a more complex scene. We maintain that the black reflection under the subject is a sufficient visual clue to tell the brain that the surface is black, but glossy and reflecting light. So this is still a black-on-black scene!

This argument ought to convince most readers to let us get by with the gray background, but a few of you will be less charitable and insist that we keep our original commitment. We will do so with the next solution.

Keep the Subject Away from the Background

Suppose we place the subject far enough from the background that the lighting of the subject has no effect on the background? We can then light the subject any way we please and the background will remain black.

This is easy if we crop the bottom of the subject out of the picture. This allows us to put the subject on any convenient support and keep the visible background as far away as we please. However, if the entire subject has to show, we have to support it with trickery.

Amateurs assume professional photographers do this with string. Sometimes we do, but too often the string needs to be retouched. (String might *occasionally* escape undetected in a brief motion picture or video shot, but it is likely to be apparent in a high-quality still.) Retouching a black background is usually not difficult. However, doing no retouching at all is even better, so we will suggest some other ways.

In Chapter 6 we invisibly supported the metal box on a sheet of glass. Then we had to use a polarizing filter to remove the polarized direct reflection from the glass surface. This did not affect the metal because direct reflection from metal is rarely polarized.

The glass table will not work for most black subjects. Much of the direct reflection from a black subject is likely to be polarized. If we use a polarizing filter to take the reflection off our table surface, we will probably turn the subject black, too.

The least detectable invisible support is a rod through the background. Careful positioning allows the subject to hide its own support. Figure 9.27 was made in this manner.

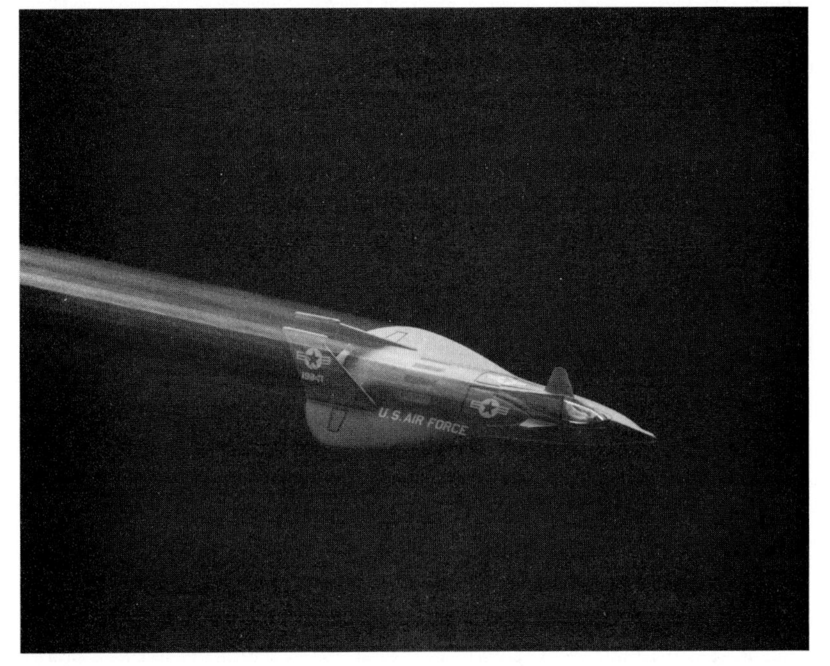

◀ *By suspending the model far enough from the background to keep light off the background, we kept the deep black we wanted.*

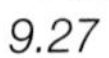

9.27

Figure 9.28 diagrams the setup. Variations on this theme can use whatever support rod suits the subject. Photographic booms make good support rods because they often have a screw end that can be inserted into a hole drilled in the subject. A wooden board screwed to a frame behind the background can support a heavier subject. Metal plates and angle irons from the hardware store can attach to the wood to make a thin, invisible support under a subject too expensive to damage by direct attachment.

► *A rod supports the subject from the rear. In this position it cannot be seen by the camera.*

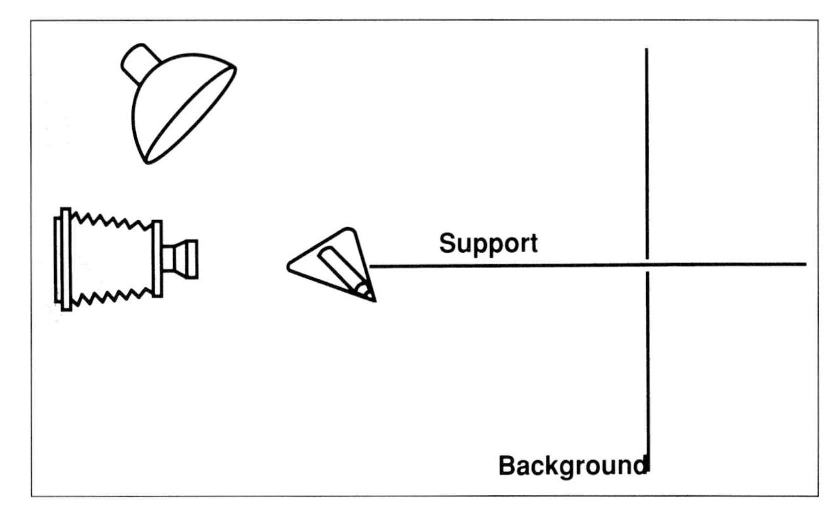

9.28

We choose to introduce invisible support rods here because they make the best solution to some black-on-black problems. Consider applying the idea to any other scene where independent lighting of the subject and background is useful.

NEW PRINCIPLES?

We have introduced very few new principles in this chapter. Instead, we have talked mostly about basic photography and basic lighting (plus a few bits of magic and chicanery).

White-on-white and black-on-black subjects do not require many special techniques. Such subjects do, however, require the basics, applied meticulously. This may be true of photography in general. Professional development may not be so much a matter of learning new things, but of learning and relearning the basics, and combining them in more perceptive ways.

One of these basics is that light behaves like light, and none of our piety or wit can ever make it do otherwise. We like to say we control light, but often all we can really do is to cooperate with what it wants to do. This is true of any light, in the studio or out of it.

You will hear more of this in the next chapter.

Chapter 10

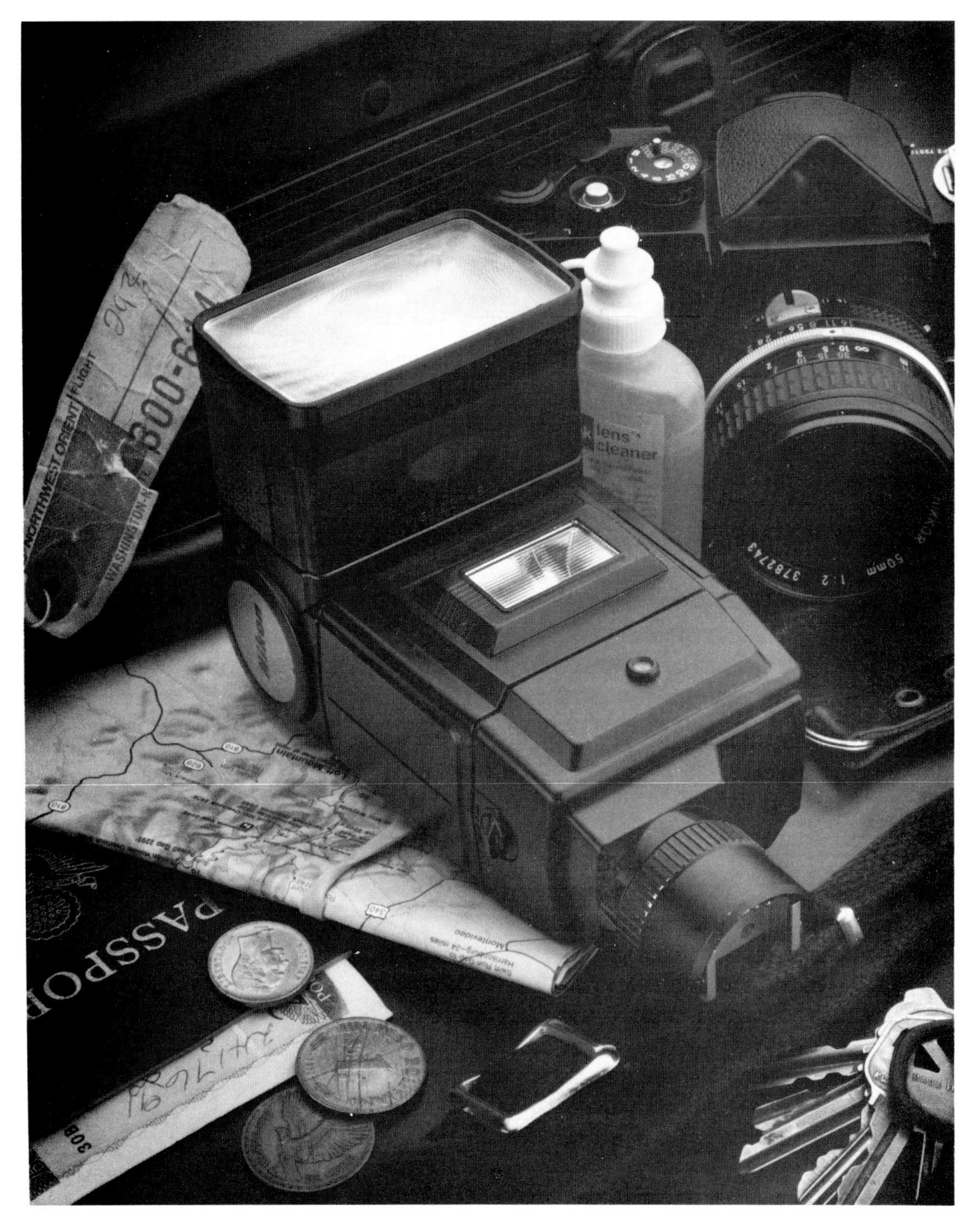

Traveling Light

While some photographers choose to spend their entire careers locked away in their studios, most of us venture into the world at least some of the time. We usually have to bring our lights with us too.

The primary challenge of location lighting is to make the photographic light work well with the existing light. For example, video and motion picture photographers have to cover their lights with blue gels to get a good color match if they use those lights to supplement daylight. We will discuss some other problems and solutions for unmatched light colors in this chapter.

Still photographers usually avoid the color match problem by using electronic strobes that produce light of nearly the same color as daylight. This, however, presents new problems. We cannot see the effect of the brief flash. Even using studio strobes, the modeling lights are too dim to accurately represent how the strobe light compares with the ambient light. Most of this chapter will deal with the special techniques needed for location strobe lighting.

CHOOSING THE RIGHT STROBE

In Appendix 1 we discuss the different kinds of strobes that are available. We will look at some examples of location assignments for which each type is best suited.

At the heavy—frequently very heavy—end of the gamut there are *studio strobes*. The term *studio* does not mean that such strobes always stay there. When you need to shoot 4 x 5-inch film of the twenty-five members of a board of directors sitting around an enormous conference table, you need plenty of light. Only studio strobes can provide enough watt-seconds to meet such large-scale, high-quality demands.

Of course, studio strobes are cumbersome on location, and even more so if the location lacks electrical power and we have to carry a generator. Fortunately for the tired backs of photographers, most location assignments do not require studio strobes. Most jobs can be adequately handled with portable units.

Next down the portability scale are the *heavy portable strobes*. Battery-powered, these are less powerful than their studio counterparts, but they can be carried around with comparative ease. Averaging from 100 to 400 watt-seconds, the power packs of such strobes are supported by shoulder straps and attached to the flash head by a power cord. These often produce a pleasing quality of light that can rival that of studio strobes.

Lightweight portable strobes, often weighing less than one pound and rated at as much as 100 watt-seconds, offer a high degree of portability and enough light for many 35mm photographs.

The portable strobe you choose depends on how much light you need and how fast you have to work. For example, if you are shooting a wedding, you may choose a heavy portable unit with a large battery and a large reflector. You will probably be using a medium-format camera, requiring more light to maintain depth of field. The more flattering quality of light such strobes produce is likely to sell more prints. If, on the other hand, you are covering a fast-breaking news story with high-speed film in a 35mm camera, a lightweight strobe mounted right on your camera may be perfectly adequate and much more manageable.

GETTING THE EXPOSURE RIGHT

Studio photographers often work under such consistent conditions that they can use the same exposure they did the day before without thinking about it. Determining exposure can be more difficult on location. Ambient light varies. The brightness of reflective walls and ceilings differs from one location to another. The distance to those reflective surfaces depends on the size of the room.

There are three basic ways of coming up with the right exposure using strobes: Let the strobe do the work, use a flash meter, or calculate.

Letting the Strobe Determine the Exposure

Automatic strobes read the light reflected from the subject, then quickly turn themselves off when they think they have seen enough light to expose the film properly. Several manufacturers offer automatic strobes specifically designed for use with particular camera brands. These *dedicated* units tend to maximize the ability of the camera and strobe to work together. One of the most important features that dedicated strobes offer is the option to use *through-the-lens metering.*

In addition to ease of operation, the chief advantage of automatic strobes is that they account for the room environment. If you use one in a large gymnasium, then take it into the coaches' office, it will make the proper exposure adjustment to compensate for the strobe light reflected from the walls of the smaller room.

The disadvantage of automatic strobes is the influence of light or dark subjects. Like any other averaging light meter, they overexpose dark subjects and underexpose light ones. This is no fault of the excellent electronics. The strobe simply has no way of knowing whether it is looking at an average subject with an abnormal amount of light or an abnormal subject with an average amount of light. If you photograph a white-on-white or a black-on-black subject, remember to compensate, either by an experienced guess or by one of the following methods.

Using a Flash Meter

As we mention in Appendix 2, a number of different flash meters are available. While the details of their operation vary somewhat, they all calculate the proper aperture at which the lens should be set for any given combination of ambient light and flash.

We use flash meters and we like them. Such meters are a useful accessory for any photographer who uses strobes. However, they have too many disadvantages to depend on them entirely. Like any other sophisticated equipment, they can break when we need them most, especially after they have been knocked around in a camera bag on the way to a location assignment. However, a bigger disadvantage is that on many location assignments, photographers often find themselves with too little time to work and too much bulk to manage. Flash meters worsen both problems.

We do not want to discourage you from using flash meters. We do want to encourage you to be able to do without one when you must.

Calculating the Exposure

The quickest way to calculate an exposure using a flash is by using a *guide number.* You can find the guide number in the literature that comes with the flash if you trust the manufacturer. Otherwise, you can calculate it yourself. Figure 10.1 shows how to use a guide number and gives an example of how to do it.

► *An example of how to calculate the proper flash exposure using the guide number.*

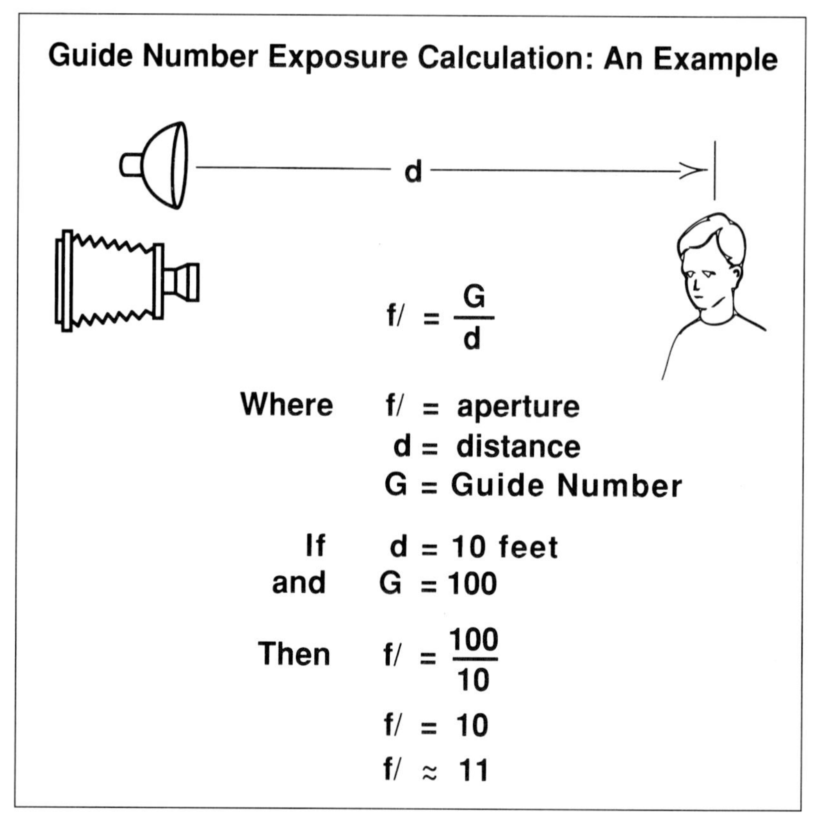

10.1

In this particular case, the subject is standing ten feet from the strobe and the photographer is using a film with an ISO rating of 100/21. When used with this film, the flash has a guide number of 100. Using the formula shown, *guide number/distance (of flash to subject) = aperture,* the aperture works out to f/10. Thus the lens is set to f/11, the closest even f/stop to the one the exposure formula gives.

The guide number assumes the flash is mounted on or near the camera. The greater the angle from the camera to the subject to the flash, the lower the usable guide number becomes. For example, if the strobe is at a forty-five-degree angle to an average subject, the guide number drops to about seventy percent of its normal value. This means you need to open up one stop. Keep these numbers in mind to estimate the exposure compensation when the flash is very far off camera and the subject is close. (We could give you a trigonometric formula for a precise guide number adjustment when the flash is off the camera. But the whole point of using a guide number is to save time, not to take more time with unwieldy computations. Furthermore, variation in the shapes and the surfaces of subjects completely eliminates any potential gain in accuracy.)

You may use a guide number based on either feet or meters, depending on which unit you have learned to estimate better. If you buy a strobe with a guide number based on meters and you prefer to use feet, multiply the manufacturer's guide number by 3.3. Divide by the same factor to convert a guide number based on feet to one based on meters. Either way works as long as you do not use one measurement unit with a guide number based on the other.

At this point, however, a note of warning to the unwary is due. There seems to be an international conspiracy that demands that strobe manufacturers inflate the guide number of their equipment. Even the honest makers are unable to control the variation in flash tubes and capacitors from outside suppliers well enough to guarantee that every strobe will be up to its rated power. With that in mind, let you, the buyer, beware! *Always* run a couple of test rolls through to determine the true guide number of any strobe you buy. That is the only way to be sure of the output of any strobe.

If you decide you do not like the manufacturer's published guide number, you can calculate your own. To do so, you need to bracket the exposure until you get one good photograph. Note the distance to the subject and the aperture that produced the proper exposure. Then use this rearrangement of the formula to determine your own guide number:

$$G = f/ \times d.$$

The only flaw in the guide number method is that it does not account for light reflected from walls and ceilings. Small white rooms can produce more exposure than the guide number predicts by reflecting extra light onto the subject. Large rooms and dark rooms produce less exposure for the opposite reason. Unfortunately, there is no precise way to calculate such effects. You have to base exposure adjustments on experience with your strobe. Fortunately, the effect of room reflection is seldom more than one stop. This means that if you lack the experience to estimate the necessary adjustment, a slightly wider bracket will cover the error.

You will also notice that the guide number does not consider the ambient light in the scene. This is no problem. If the existing light level is high enough to significantly affect exposure, we can deal with it with good precision. We will see how later in this chapter.

GETTING MORE LIGHT

More often than not, photographers want more light than they can have. This tends to be especially true of location assignments because mobility and available electrical power often preclude carrying adequate equipment.

There are times when all that really counts is having enough light to get the picture. We have all been up against such situations. We know before we even release the shutter that the lighting will produce harsh, high-contrast results, but, due to situations beyond our control, such lighting is the best we can get.

Some time ago we accompanied police officers working in a busy precinct. They worked at night and when things happened, they happened fast. There was no time to think the shot through, no time to put the flash in another spot. As most of the action took place on the street, there were no ceilings or close-by walls from which to bounce a light. The only alternative was to use a flash mounted on the camera.

When the action started, the only thing we had time to do was aim and shoot. Under such circumstances, it would have been foolish to worry about the "quality of the light." All that counted was having enough light to record the scene on film.

Another time one of us went to shoot pictures of a rare jungle wildlife species. As in the busy police precinct, many of the animals became active at dusk (near water holes). Once again, all that really mattered was being able to light up the scene well enough to get the shot.

The list of such situations could go on. Examples could be drawn from almost any kind of photography. But no matter how diverse such situations may be, the common thread is that being able to put enough light into the scene determines whether a picture is possible at all. Quantity means more than quality.

The first thing you can do to provide as much light as possible is to use just plain common sense: Take the brightest light you can use practically. Less obvious is that this does not simply mean using as many watt-seconds as possible. Some strobes have more efficient reflectors than others; others offer interchangeable reflectors. Efficient reflectors can multiply light output without increasing weight.

Focused Flash

You can also use accessories to focus your flash on distant subjects. Figure 10.2 shows a commercially made flash focusing lens. This kind of unit has won wide acceptance with many wildlife photographers. It consists of a fresnel lens that is held in front of a powerful lightweight strobe. In addition, a flashlight may be mounted in the unit to help with focusing at night.

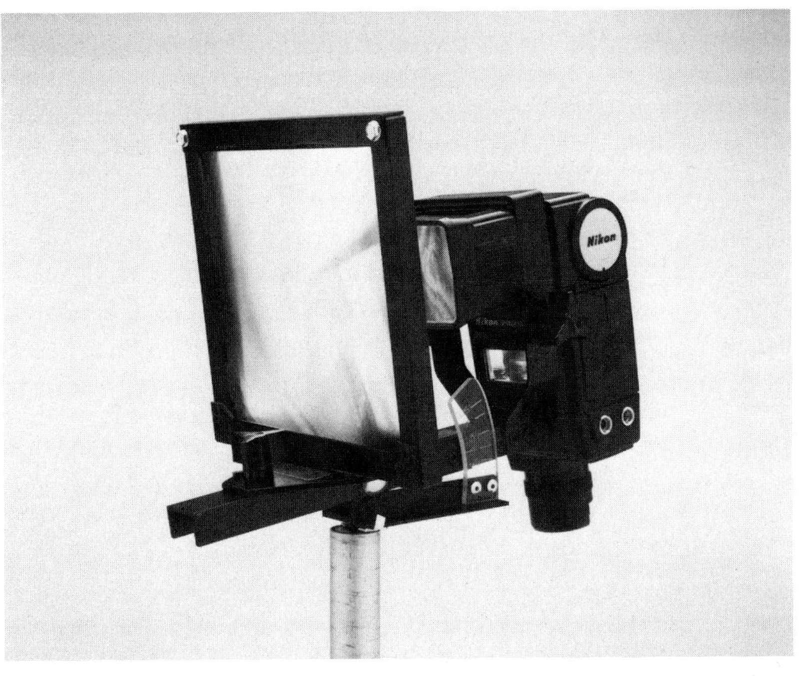

◀ *Commercially made flash-focusing units are a favorite among wildlife photographers.*

10.2

The fresnel lens focuses the light into a powerful, far-reaching beam. With such a unit it is possible to photograph animals and other such subjects at a far greater distance at night than it would be with the flash alone.

You can also use an enlarger condenser lens to make an effective flash focusing lens. Such apparatus is bulky, but it is far less so than a strobe that produces equal brightness without it. We once made one to photograph speakers from the balcony of a large auditorium. We determined the most efficient distance from the flash head to the condenser by moving a light bulb back and forth until its rays were properly focused on a distant wall. Then we clamped the whole assembly to a wooden base with large hose clamps.

Multiple Strobes

Several portable strobes together produce as much light, but allow more flexibility than a single studio strobe. We can use them separately as a multiple-light setup, as larger lights might be used in the studio; or we can group them as a cluster to behave as a single very powerful strobe. In either case, only one strobe needs to be triggered by a synch cord attached to the camera. Instead of synch cords, the others are usually equipped with light-sensitive triggers called *slaves*. This minimizes the number of cords to hide in the scene.

You can best maximize flexibility without limiting your speed of operation if your portable strobes are identical. When all of the strobes have the same power, it is easier to calculate the combined guide number for a multiple strobe arrangement used as a single source:

$$G_C = \sqrt{N} \times G_1.$$

where G_C = the combined guide number, N = the total number of strobes, and G_1 = the guide number for one strobe.

It pays to calculate the guide numbers for any combination of strobes you might use. Keep the list on a card in your camera bag or taped inside the battery pack of each strobe.

Multiple Flash

You can also flash the same strobe several times. This works well as long as the subject stays still and the camera is mounted on a sturdy tripod.

You could calculate a guide number for multiple flashes with the same formula we gave for determining a guide number for multiple strobes in the previous section. If you like this approach, you can let *N* represent the number of flashes you want to use, instead of the number of strobes.

More often, photographers use the standard guide number to calculate the aperture to use for a single flash. Then they multiply the number of flashes by two, for each stop they want to close down.

The basic exposure calculation for such a shot is simple. All you have to remember is that two flashes of the strobe provide twice as much light as one. Suppose maintaining depth of field required shooting at f/11 but your strobe only produced enough light for f/8. All you would have to do is flash it twice. Four flashes would allow shooting at f/16, eight flashes would allow f/22, and so on.

Multiple flash works best in nearly total darkness. Then the shutter can be left open for the entire duration of the exposure. Moving the camera is unlikely if you do not have to touch it. However, if the ambient light is bright enough to compete with the strobe, you will have to use the shutter to trigger each flash. Leaving the shutter open long enough to complete the sequence of flashes can allow the ambient light to overpower the effect of the strobe.

A little later in this chapter, we will discuss how to figure ambient light into your calculations. For now, however, it is worth mentioning that the presence of ambient light does not complicate multiple-flash exposure calculations. Once you decide the aperture and shutter speed that produces a good mix of strobe and ambient light for a *single* flash, you can close down the aperture, but keep the same shutter setting regardless of the number of flashes. As you repeatedly use the shutter to trigger the flash, the total shutter time adds up to the correct amount, regardless of the adjusted aperture.

A variation of multiple flash is called *painting with light*. This means moving the strobe to a different position with each flash. If the flash is aimed at the same small subject each time, a small strobe begins to behave like a large, soft one. This can improve the quality as well as the quantity of light. For any aperture, you can calculate the number of flashes as we did in the preceding example. Just keep in mind that the effective illumination drops whenever the flash position is *too* far off camera. (Remember that about one stop is lost when the flash is at a forty-five-degree angle to the subject.)

The other method of painting with light involves pointing the strobe at a different part of the scene with each flash. This is good for illuminating areas that would otherwise be too large for the single strobe to light evenly. For example, we had to shoot a picture of bats hibernating in a large cave. The cave interior was dark brown and far too big to be lit evenly by a single flash. Our solution was to mount the camera on a sturdy tripod, open the lens, and then flash the strobe at different areas of the cavern. When we were through, we had a picture in which the entire cave was visible, an impossible task with just one flash of a single strobe.

This second method of painting means that each area of the scene gets a single flash. Therefore, exposure needs to be calculated using the guide number for a single flash, rather than with the compensations we use in other multiple-flash situations.

Very often painting with light uses a combination of these two basic methods. In such cases, exposure calculation becomes difficult. Tests are the only fully reliable way of coming up with a reliable exposure. Use Polaroid or shoot and process a test roll before exposing the final picture.

IMPROVING THE QUALITY OF LIGHT

The previous section offered some suggestions for obtaining enough light using the limited equipment available for many location assignments. The other problem common to most easily transportable location lighting equipment is obtaining lighting that *looks* good. Now we will move from quantity to quality.

Location lighting tends to suffer from two basic defects: illumination that is too hard and illumination that is uneven. The hard lighting is caused by the need to use small strobes for portability. Uneven lighting is the result of needing to illuminate larger areas with fewer lights.

Fortunately, there are two relatively simple techniques that can be used to produce a quite acceptable quality of light with many portable strobes. These are *bouncing* and *feathering*. Both help to even out the light in a scene and to reduce unwanted shadows.

Bounce Flash

Portable flashes are, by their very nature, small light sources, and small light sources produce hard-edged, unattractive shadows. One way to soften these shadows is to bounce the light from a wall or ceiling, as shown in Figure 10.3. The ceiling becomes the effective light source. Since the ceiling is a much larger light source, it makes the shadows in the scene far softer and less noticeable.

► *Bouncing the strobe light from ceiling or a wall enormously increases the effective size of the flash. This causes shadows to become much softer and lights the room more evenly.*

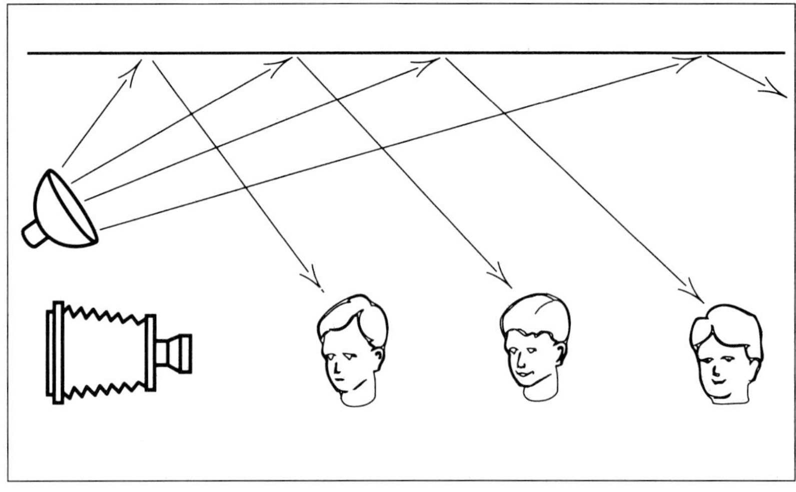

10.3

While bounced light is far more attractive than direct flash, it does have one major drawback: efficiency. One reason for this is that the light has to travel farther. The distance from the strobe to the ceiling to the subject is farther than a direct path from the strobe to the subject. Furthermore, part of the light is absorbed by the ceiling. All this adds up to less light where you need it.

With the use of a guide number, the adjustment for the increased distance the light must travel is easy. Just remember to base the calculation on the distance up to the ceiling and back down to the subject, instead of the distance from the strobe to the subject.

The amount of light lost by absorption and scattering varies according to how the ceiling is painted and what its texture is. In most situations, however, compensating by two stops is adequate. If, for example, you are working in a situation in which you would normally shoot at f/11, the proper exposure is probably f/5.6. Open up a bit more for darker ceilings. Bracket whenever you are in doubt and when you are shooting transparencies.

If the ceiling is very high or if the subject is close to the camera, a ceiling bounce will cause dark shadows in the subject's eye sockets. Many photographers minimize this defect by using small bounce cards, as illustrated in Figure 10.4. They are attached to the strobe by a rubber band or tape.

► *A small bounce fill card on the flash will reduce the facial shadows caused by bouncing light from the ceiling.*

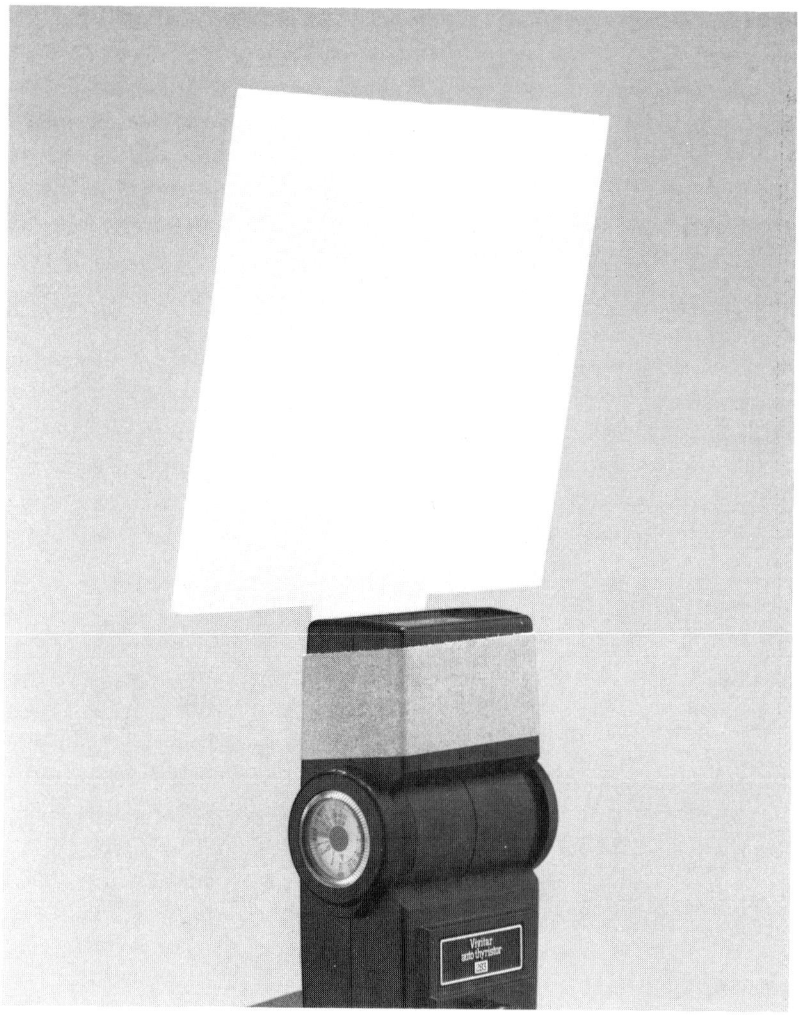

10.4

Notice that the card bounces some of the light directly onto the subject's face. The rest of the light is bounced from the ceiling. The combined result is a more evenly illuminated picture.

Figures 10.5 and 10.6 show the same scene shot with and without a bounce card.

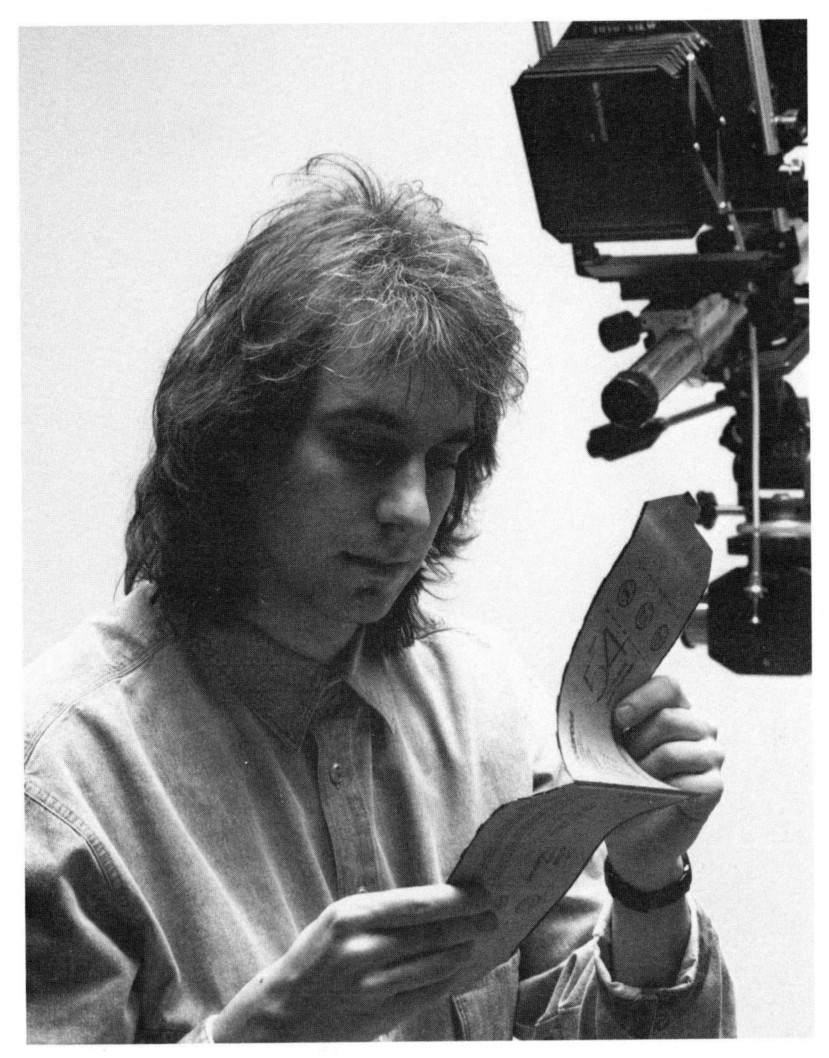

◀ *Without a bounce fill card, bouncing the strobe light from the ceiling causes very unflattering shadows.*

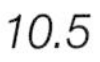

10.5

► *Look at how much lighter and less objectionable the bounce fill card makes the shadows.*

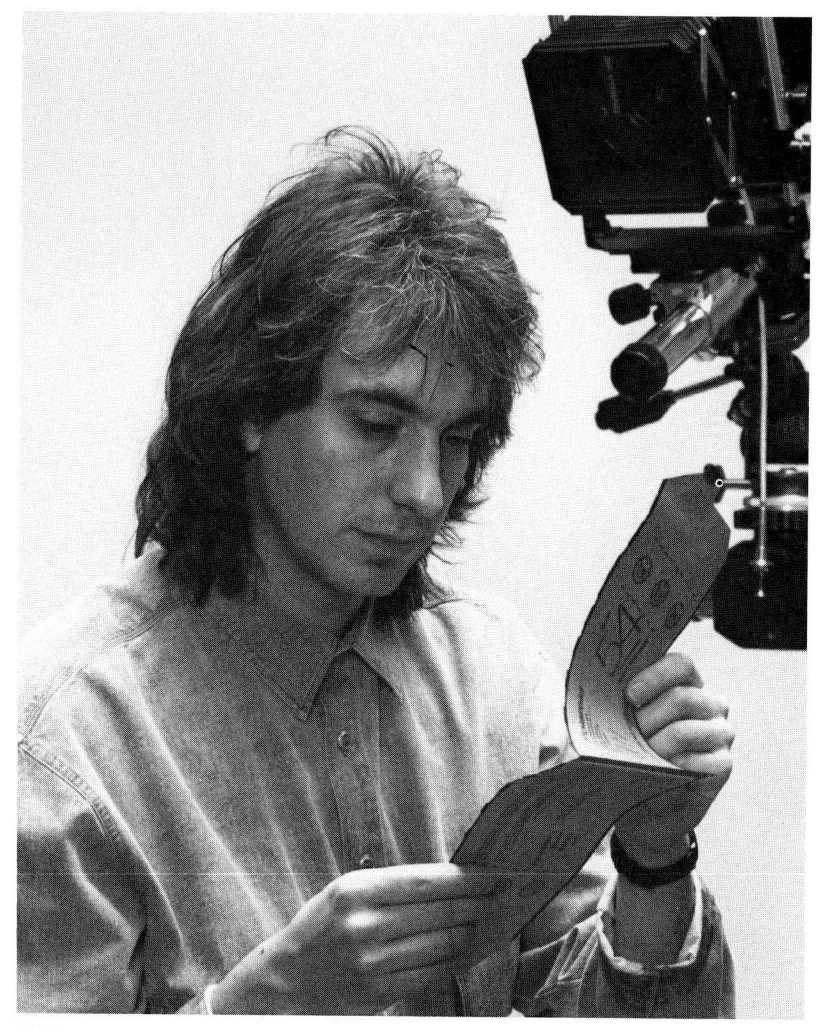

10.6

Any reflector that is useful in the studio is also likely to serve as a good bounce card on location. You can bounce strobes from them and use them to reflect ambient light into a scene. The only special requirement is that they be transportable. Some reflectors collapse or fold for this purpose. The most common example is the lighting umbrella.

Bigger reflectors are often useful outside the studio because many of the subjects are larger. However, the bigger the reflector is, the harder it is to transport. The most creative solution to this dilemma comes from a photographer we know who once rented large trucks and parked them so that their sides acted as fill cards. Even if you think this tactic is extreme, remember it if you decide to buy a van, and consider a white one.

Feathering the Light

Feathering a light means aiming it so that part of the beam illuminates the foreground and another part lights the background. Figure 10.7 shows how this technique can be used.

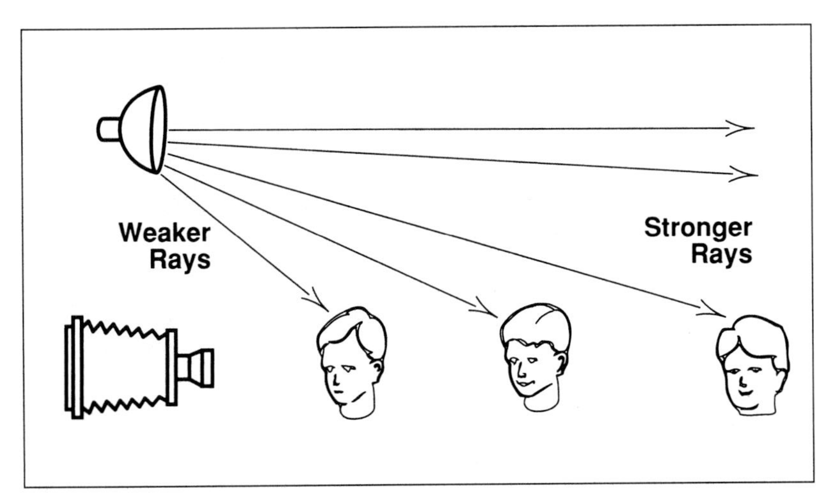

10.7

◀ *Feathering the strobe light. The success of this technique depends greatly on the design of the strobe reflector.*

Notice that the strongest rays of light are emitted from the center of the strobe head. If the strobe is held at the proper angle, these will illuminate the rear of the scene. The light rays that spill out of the sides of the reflector are far weaker. They illuminate things that are closer to the camera. With a little practice, it is fairly easy to learn how to hold the strobe to achieve the desired degree of feathering.

How well feathering works, or whether it will work at all, depends on how the flash head is constructed. Some of the larger portable strobes are made with large-diameter, circular reflectors. These usually scatter a great deal of light in directions other than toward the subject. Such units can almost always be feathered well.

On the other hand, many lightweight strobes have smaller flash tubes in efficiently focused reflectors. These direct a higher percentage of the light toward the subject and waste very little in other directions. Such a beam is far less well suited to feathering. What this means is that the only way to find out how well a unit can be feathered is to try it out.

There is still another lesson to learn from Figure 10.7. You will notice that the flash is being held as high as possible. This is done to position it so that any shadows its light casts will be as unobtrusive as possible. The higher the light is, the lower the shadow will be cast. Thus, if a subject is standing near a wall and the flash is held high, the shadow will fall where the camera cannot see it.

Figures 10.8 and 10.9 were made of the same subject with the strobe in two different positions. In Figure 10.8, the flash was held low, at about camera height. Notice the very pronounced and distracting shadow on the wall that this lighting produces. Now look at Figure 10.9. The photographer made this picture holding his flash as high above his head as possible. The shadow has disappeared.

▶ *Holding the strobe too low causes distracting shadows on the wall.*

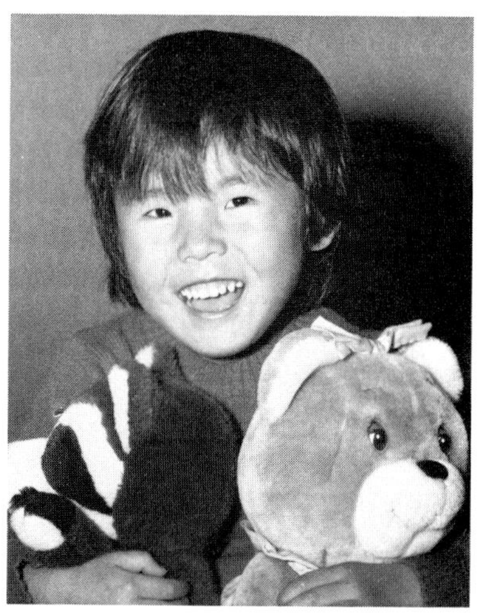

10.8

▶ *Holding the flash high enough causes many distracting shadows to disappear.*

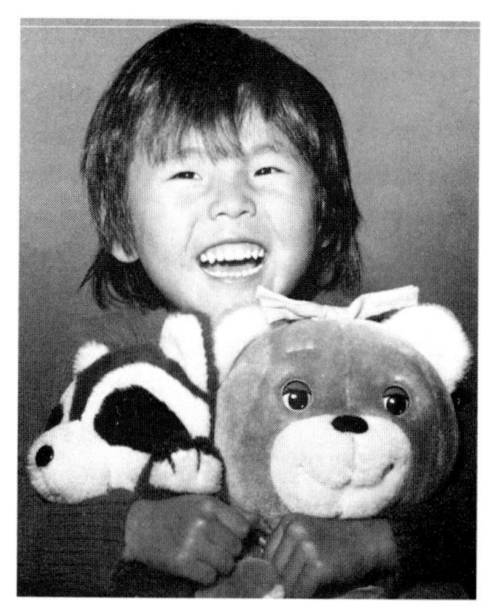

10.9

LIGHTS OF DIFFERENT COLORS

Photographers in the studio carefully control the color temperature of their light. All lights usually have the same color balance. Adding other lights with gels or lights of another type is a deliberate attempt to alter the color, not a whim or an accident.

Photographers working on location may not be able to carefully control the color temperature of the light. The existing light in the scene often does not match any standardized photographic color balance. It may be impossible to get rid of the existing light. Even in an indoor location in which the existing light can be turned off, it may be essential to leave it on for enough light to illuminate a large area. This nonstandard color has unpredictable consequences if photographers do not anticipate problems and take steps to deal with them.

Why Is the Color of the Light Important?

Lights of different colors in the same scene have little consequence on black-and-white film. All the colors in the scene are recorded as various shades of gray. As long as the light is reasonably "white," slight variations in light color affect the gray tones too subtly to bother most viewers. However, when we are using color film with light sources of different colors, we have a serious problem. The problem is inherent in the way in which the color films record the images that are exposed upon them.

No one color film works well with all light sources. We must choose the film to match the source. In addition, at times we must use filters to alter the color of the light. Films are manufactured for two standard color balances, *daylight* and *tungsten*.

Tungsten Film. Tungsten film is manufactured to reproduce the colors of a scene most accurately if that scene is illuminated by tungsten bulbs. These tend to be relatively orange. Tungsten film compensates for this large amount of orange. Used with tungsten lights, it produces picture colors that are close to natural. This means the film sees colors similarly to the way our eyes see them.

If, however, we were to use a tungsten-balanced film outside to shoot a picture that was illuminated by daylight, the resulting color would be very nonstandard. Instead of looking "normal," the entire scene would appear to have a blue tint.

Daylight Film. Daylight films are manufactured to produce standard picture colors in a scene that is illuminated by daylight. Such light is rich in blue. Looking at the sky on a clear day will show us this. Daylight films compensate for this, and they give the most accurate color reproduction when they are used with either daylight or electronic flash. If they are used with tungsten light, daylight films produce pictures that look orange.

Nonstandard Light Sources

Photographers consider daylight and two slightly different colors of tungsten light to be "standard." All of the others are nonstandard to us. Unfortunately, "nonstandard" does not mean "unusual" or "rare." Other lights are quite common. We will use a few of them as examples. These do not approach a complete list of nonstandard sources, but they show the dangers well enough to keep you alert to the potential problem in any location assignment.

Fluorescent tubes are the nonstandard light source photographers encounter most frequently. The light produced by fluorescent tubes presents photographers with a special problem. Not only is it nonstandard, it comes in many different colors. Film makers publish tables of recommended filtration for each of their films exposed under each common type of fluorescent tube.

However, age changes the color of fluorescent tubes slightly. Furthermore, people replace burned-out tubes with new ones of another type. After a few years, a single large room may have several different types of tubes. Filtration that is good for any particular type of tube may not be as good for the mix. As a result, it is all but impossible to predict the color of the picture.

As a rule, the light from these tubes tends to have a strong green cast. This can produce some particularly unpleasant nonstandard colors when either tungsten or daylight film is used. People, in particular, tend to look awful when they are photographed under fluorescent lighting.

Nonstandard tungsten light is more common than either of the photographic standard tungsten color temperatures. Ordinary tungsten bulbs are significantly more orange than photographic bulbs, and they get more so as they age. The difference is enough to matter whenever color balance is critical.

Nonstandard daylight does not surprise most people. We all know that sunlight is much more red at dawn and dusk. What surprises most of us more is learning that daylight can be very nonstandard, even in the middle of a bright day.

Figure 10.10 illustrates two different kinds of daylight. The house on the left has direct sun coming through a window onto the subject. Such direct light from the sun will be slightly warm. It will have a noticeable red to yellow color bias. On the right, we see a different "daylight" situation. This time the subject is being lit by light that comes from the blue sky rather than the sun's direct rays. This light is decidedly cool. It has a good deal of blue in it.

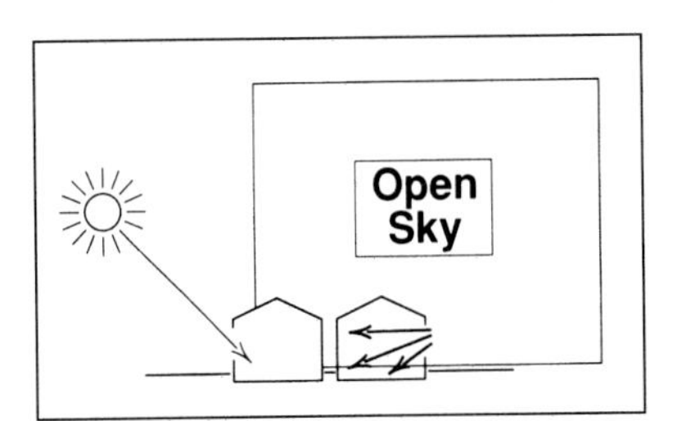

◀ *The direct sun striking the house on the left is warm colored, noticeably biased toward yellow. Light reaching the house on the right comes from the blue sky, and it will have a much cooler, blue-biased color.*

10.10

Both of these subjects are illuminated by what is called *daylight.* The only problem is that the "daylight" is very different in each of them. Each produces a picture with a very different color balance. The cause of the problem is that each subject lacks part of what we accept as standard daylight.

When photographers use the term *daylight* we mean light that is made up of a *combination* of rays that come *directly from the sun* and those that come to us from the *sky* around it. In the preceding example, each subject was lit by only one of the two parts of that combination.

Another common cause of nonstandard daylight is foliage. Subjects shaded from the direct sunlight may still be illuminated by the open sky. This causes the same blue shift we saw in the subject on the right in the preceding example. This problem is compounded by green leaves filtering and reflecting whatever sunlight does reach the subject. In extreme cases, the result looks more like fluorescent light than daylight.

Once again, the color error may not be significant in many cases, but we have to think about the importance of accurate color in each scene and decide whether the problem needs a remedy.

Do the Colors Mix?

There are two basic situations that we encounter when working with different colored light sources. The first of these happens when we use what we will call *unmixed color*, the second with *mixed color*. As you will see shortly, unmixed and mixed color present quite different challenges, and they are handled in different ways.

Mixed color lighting is just what the name implies. It occurs when the rays of light with different color balances *mix or blend together* to produce a color balance different from that of any single light source.

Figure 10.11 shows how light sources can mix together in this way. Fluorescent tubes provide the ambient illumination. A strobe is bounced from the ceiling.

▶ *Mixed strobe and fluorescent illumination produces evenly colored light.*

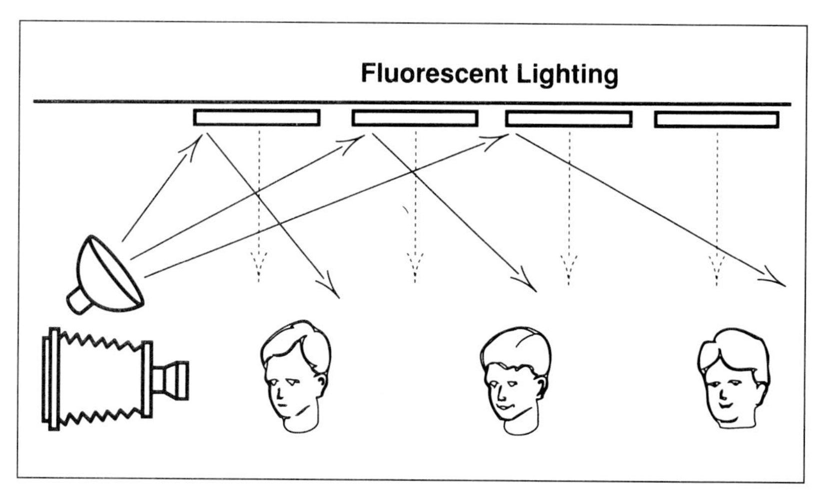

10.11

The bounced strobe illuminates the scene much as the fluorescent tubes do. The light rays from the flash tube mix with those produced by the fluorescent tube. The result is a fairly even illumination throughout the scene by light of a different color balance from either the flash or the fluorescent tubes alone.

Unmixed color is diagrammed in Figure 10.12. The scene is the same, but the strobe is now directed at the subject, not the ceiling. This is a common example of a scene that is illuminated differently by each of the two light sources.

▶ *Using the flash as shown here will produce a picture in which different parts of the scene are illuminated by very differently colored light. This can cause serious problems in color photography.*

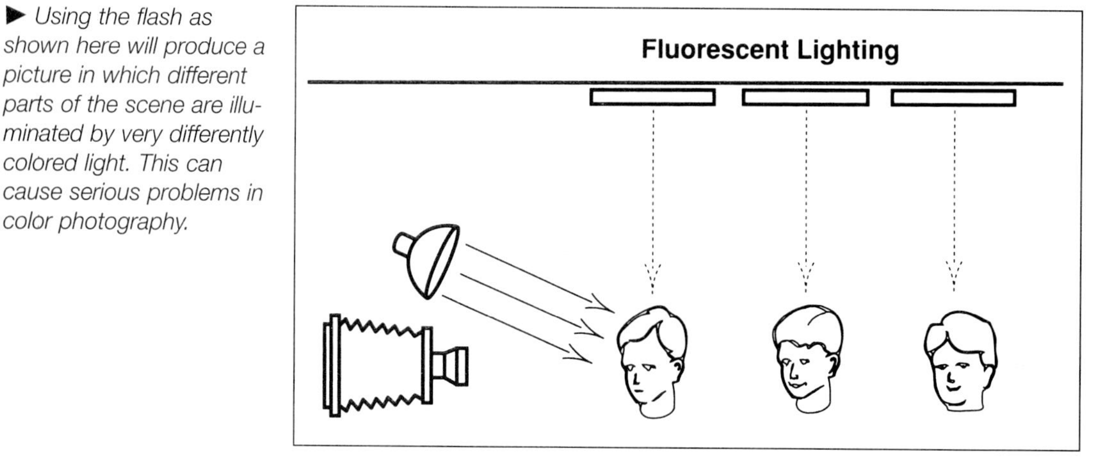

10.12

Notice in the diagram that the bulk of the scene is lit by overhead, fluorescent bulbs. However, the foreground subject and his immediate surroundings are lit by the flash.

The result is two very differently colored areas in the picture. The foreground subject and his immediate surroundings will be illuminated by the relatively blue "daylight" from the electronic flash. The rest of the scene will, however, receive the green light from the overhead fluorescents. The problem is that the film we are using can be balanced for only one light source.

Sometimes unmixed lighting can occur when we do not expect it. In Figure 10.13, the wall behind the subject is not significantly farther from the strobe than the subject himself. We might expect to have the same mix of strobe and ambient light on everything in the picture.

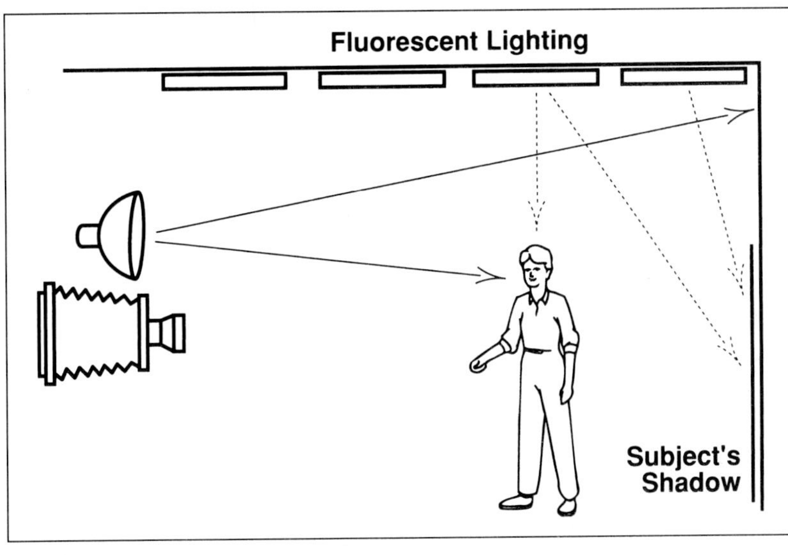

◀ *Because the fluorescent light illuminates the shadow that the strobe casts on the wall, the shadow will be green in a color photograph.*

10.13

Notice, however, that the strobe and the fluorescent light come from different directions. The strobe casts a shadow on the wall, but the fluorescent light illuminates the shadow and makes it green.

The Remedies

Both mixed and unmixed light situations are common, and it is important to be able to handle both of them. We use a slightly different remedy for each.

Correcting Mixed Colors. Mixed color situations are relatively easy to handle because the improper illumination that results from them is *uniform throughout the scene.* In other words, the entire scene is lit by light that has the same color balance. The color balance of the whole picture will be wrong, but all parts of the scene will be wrong in the same way.

Correcting Color While Shooting. It is this uniformity of error that makes the problem so simple to correct. All we have to do, in most cases, is to use the proper filter over the lens. This will correct the color balance of the light before it reaches the film. The result will be a picture that has the correct color balance and in which colors within the scene reproduce in a standard, or realistic, way.

Now, having said how easy everything is, we will tell you about the hard part. The trick is knowing what filter to use.

A color meter will do the job if you are mixing two continuous sources such as fluorescent and tungsten, but it will not tell you the combined color of fluorescent and strobe. The only accurate way to select the proper filter is by test exposures. Test exposures are time consuming and often a serious inconvenience, but they are the only way to be sure the color correction is right.

In fluorescent light try CC30M. Evaluate the result, then go back and shoot the final film with a different filtration if necessary.

What if you do not have time to reshoot? Use your best guess on filtration and call that film final. The nice thing about mixed color is that errors are almost always correctable in reproduction if you take simple precautions as you compose the image. We will talk about them next.

Correcting Color After the Picture Is Shot. Because any color balance problems are uniform when mixed colors are used, it is relatively simple for color separators, print makers, and slide duplicators to make any required color adjustments. This gives you a very useful safety margin should you fail to get the proper correction when you are shooting the picture. The color balance may not be quite as good as a picture that was shot right to begin with, but it is likely to be good enough that an experienced viewer cannot tell the difference without a side-by-side comparison of the two.

One caution is due. Beware of those scenes that include a light source or the mirror reflection of one. These extremely bright areas record in the picture as white highlights, regardless of the color of the light producing them. These highlights will then take on the color of whatever correction is used to remedy the rest of the scene. The only way to avoid this problem is to use the proper filter when shooting the picture or to compose it so that it does not contain any such troublesome highlights.

Correcting Unmixed Colors. No filter on the lens can correct unmixed color. Whatever correction is right for one area is wrong for another. Trying a compromise filtration value between the two produces just that: a compromise in which nothing in the scene is quite right.

Making the Sources Match. The best way to cope with unmixed color sources is to filter the lights to match each other as closely as possible. The objective of this is to get all of the light sources to be a *single* color, but not necessarily the *right* color. Then, if necessary, place a filter over the camera lens so that the color reaching the film is right.

Thus, if we were faced with situations such as those in Figure 10.12 or 10.13, we could cover the flash with either a CC30G filter or a theatrical gel that approximates it. [Color compensating (CC) filters are expensive, and their optical quality is unnecessary over the flash.] Either would add enough green to make the strobe light approximate the color of the overhead fluorescents. Then the entire scene would be lit by light of at least similar color.

Next, we could place a CC30M filter over the camera lens. (We *do* need that optical quality here.) It would block the green from the light, thus giving it a color balance near that of daylight, for which the film is balanced. The result would be a picture in which all the colors in the scene would be reproduced with a high degree of accuracy.

The filter values we suggest are common examples. The specific filtration varies with the scene. As was the case earlier, the only really satisfactory way of determining exactly what filters to use over the flash and on the lens is by trial and error. Shooting test film is never convenient, but in complex lighting situations it is the only way of being sure that the color balance is perfect.

Filtering the Daylight. Remember that windows are light sources and that they can be filtered like any other light source. Motion picture and video photographers do this routinely, but still photographers tend to overlook the possibility.

Consider a scene in which a room is lit by tungsten photographic lights and by daylight coming through open doors or windows. A quick solution would be to use blue gels on the photographic lights to make them match the daylight. Then the scene could be shot on daylight film. However, our lights are probably weaker than the sun, and we would prefer not to dim them even more with the light absorbed by the filter. A better solution would be to put orange gels on the outside of the window, then shoot on tungsten film. This accomplishes the same balancing of light colors, but better balances the intensity of the two sources.

Correcting Errors in Reproduction. If the color is unmixed, this alternative is only a last resort. If, for example, you are making a color print, there is no single filter that will work for the entire scene. This is true for the same reason a filter on the lens cannot solve the problem. You may be able to improve the scene by burning and dodging the print with different corrective filtration in different areas, but the process can be tedious.

Retouchers can apply corrective color to selected areas. We can also fix local color error by digital image processing. Either one costs extra time, money, or both.

LIGHTS OF DIFFERENT DURATION

Photographers often use photographic light and existing light together so that one source is the main light and the other is the fill. Measuring the relative brightness of the two is easy if both lights are continuously turned on. This is true, for example, if the two sources are sunlight and tungsten.

However, if the photographic light is strobe instead of tungsten, comparing its brightness with the daylight is more difficult. The daylight is "on" continuously, but the strobe lights for only a fraction of a second. We cannot see the relationship between the two.

Figure 10.14 shows a common outdoor shooting situation in which strobes are useful. Only one view avoided the non-Civil War power lines and automobiles, and that composition put the soldier into a backlit position. A normal exposure was far too dark.

▶ *The best composition called for the model to be backlit. However, with a normal exposure, this arrangement produced a picture that was far too dark.*

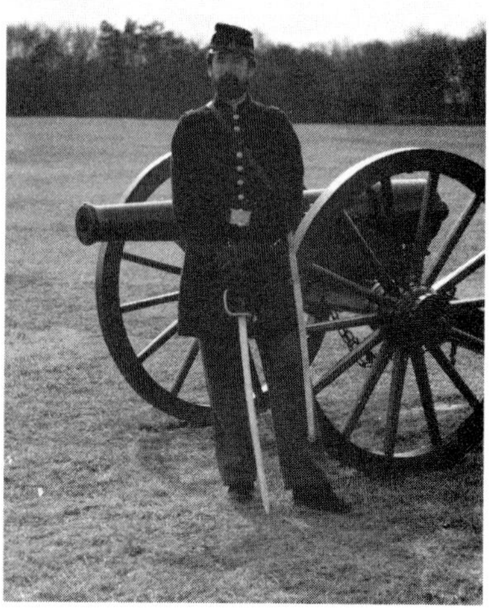

10.14

There were two ways in which we could have corrected this picture. One would have been to increase our exposure substantially. This exposure correction would have lightened the soldier, but it also might have caused the background to be seriously overexposed.

Our other alternative would have been to use a strobe to fill in the shadow. Figure 10.15 shows the result of such lighting.

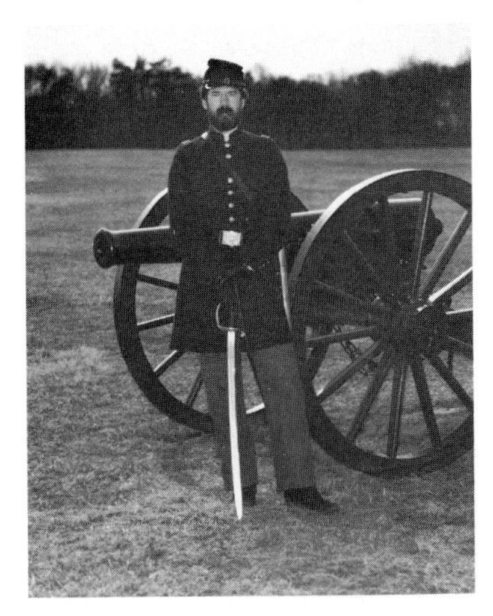

◀ *A fill flash produced an exposure in which both the subject and the background are properly exposed.*

10.15

The fill flash did just what we wanted it to do. It allowed us to produce a picture in which both the background and the subject are properly exposed. Granted that the use of a fill flash was a good idea in this situation, the next question is how to calculate the proper exposure for the picture. How were we able to select an exposure that took into account *both* the *ambient daylight* present in the scene and our *strobe output?* Keep the following points in mind:

- In situations such as our example, the strobe exposure will be determined almost exclusively by the aperture. The flash is too brief to be significantly affected by shutter speed.
- The ambient light exposure will, on the other hand, be determined by a combination of both the aperture and the shutter speed.

These principles can be applied in three basic ways. They all work, but some are better than others. The one you use depends on the amount of time you have. You will have to use a fast method to photograph a political leader dashing to the limousine after his fraud indictment. You can use the ideal solution for a room interior intended to be the cover of a furniture catalog. Often you will compromise between the fast solution and the ideal solution.

The *fast method* requires a little advance thinking.

1. **Memorize the Aperture** determined by your guide number for an average subject distance.

2. **Take a Light Reading** immediately before the assignment. Notice the aperture the meter gives for the shutter speed you want to use. (For most "fast" assignments, you will use a 35mm SLR and the shutter speed will be the fastest one that synchronizes.)

3. **Compare the Apertures** given by the guide number and by the light meter.

4. **When it Is Time to Shoot,** determine the exposure by the method that indicates the smaller aperture.

If the guide number indicates the smaller aperture, ignore the effect of the ambient light. Readjust the aperture according to the guide number as the distance to the subject changes.

If the light meter indicates the smaller aperture, forget about the guide number. Leave the aperture and shutter speed set unless the ambient-light level changes. Switch over to using the guide number to calculate the aperture if you get close enough to the subject for the strobe to provide most of the illumination.

The fast solution will overexpose the principal subject, but never more than one stop. This is acceptable for negative film. Bracket reversal film with frames using less exposure rather than more.

The fast solution may also underexpose the background, possibly by several stops. The more powerful the strobe is, the more likely this is to happen; but you are not likely to be using a 4800 watt-second studio strobe for a journalistic assignment. You are more likely to have a very portable, low-powered strobe. Therefore, ambient light is usually the principal illumination. This makes background underexposure less frequent. The fast solution produces the best pictures you can get under less than ideal circumstances.

The *ideal solution* produces the best pictures you can get. The ideal mix of strobe and ambient light depends on the subject and on personal taste. Personal taste cannot be scientifically calculated, so the best way to find the ideal mix is with Polaroid testing.

1. Begin with the Fast Solution. In an ideal situation, you are likely to have very powerful strobes, so you will usually determine the initial aperture by the guide number. Make a test shot at that aperture. Use a shutter speed twice as fast as your meter indicates for that aperture in the existing light.

2. Readjust the Shutter Speed to get the ambient exposure right. Use a longer time if the background is too dark, a shorter time if you want the background still darker. Make another test.

3. Re-evaluate the Principal Subject and Readjust the Aperture if the principal subject looks too dark or too light, and continue testing and fine-tuning until the mix is pleasing.

However, the ideal way is too tedious for some situations, and many photographers use cameras that are not practical for Polaroid film. So you may prefer the following method instead.

The *compromise solution* produces an equal mix of strobe and ambient illumination without any testing. You will find this is very close to the ideal in most situations. With a little preparation and practice, it is almost as fast as the fast solution.

1. Multiply the Strobe Guide Number by 1.4. Use this new guide number to calculate the aperture. (If there were no ambient light, this would cause an underexposure of exactly one stop.)

2. Multiply the ASA Part of the ISO Rating by 2, or increase the DIN part by 3. Set this value on a light meter and read the subject. (If there were no strobe, this would also produce a one-stop underexposure.)

3. Use the Aperture Calculated in Step 1. Use the **corresponding shutter speed** indicated by the meter for that aperture.

For example, to make Figure 10.15 we did the following:

1. Multiplied the guide number of 150 for the flash we were using by 1.4 for a new guide number of 210.

2. We then divided this by the distance at which the flash was located from the model, which was ten feet, for an answer of 21. This we rounded off for an aperture of f/22.

3. We then doubled the 100 ISO to obtain a new ISO of 200.

4. After setting our light meter for this new ISO of 200, we metered the background and noted that our light meter showed that the shutter speed of 1/125 of a second corresponded to the aperture of f/22 that we had calculated in step 2. We, therefore, set that as our shutter speed.

This amount of calculation seems too cumbersome for many situations. The event we want to photograph may be over before we decide the exposure! But we avoid that problem by making most of the adjustments before leaving for the assignment. Memorizing the adjusted guide number and resetting the film speed on the meter in advance leaves little to do at the location.

The logic of this method is easy to see if we remember that "one stop underexposure" is the same as "half the required exposure." The subject gets half the needed exposure from the strobe and half from the ambient light. Since two halves make a whole, the resulting exposure of the foreground subject is normal.

Notice, however, that the background receives less exposure than the subject because it is farther away from the strobe. A background subject slightly behind the main one will be only slightly underexposed, but a background subject an infinite distance away will be one stop underexposed. This usually produces a pleasing picture. The foreground is usually more important, and having more illumination there is more likely to help than hurt.

Sometimes, however, the background may seem too gloomy with one-stop underexposure. If you are afraid this might happen, you can reduce the uncertainty by the way you bracket.

For example, doubling the exposure time will increase the background exposure by one stop, but it will only increase the foreground exposure by slightly more than a half-stop. So bracket by changing the shutter speed if you are uncertain of the best strobe/ambient-light ratio.

On the other hand, if you know from experience with similar scenes that an equal mix of strobe and daylight is right, then bracket by changing the aperture. This will vary the general exposure without affecting the ratio.

Whatever the solution, match the film, the strobe, and the camera carefully. If you are using a leaf shutter, the choice of film and strobe is less critical. Leaf shutters synchronize at any speed. For this reason, they offer better control over combined daylight and strobe. However, location photography is exactly when the portability of a 35mm SLR with a focal-plane shutter is most useful. Using a fast film may force you to use a shutter speed too fast for the strobe to synchronize. Choose a slower film whenever ambient conditions are bright.

This is also another reason to use a strobe as powerful as you can afford and can carry. The powerful strobe allows smaller apertures, which, in turn, permit you to regulate the daylight exposure with the slower shutter speeds necessary for synchronization.

IS STUDIO LIGHTING POSSIBLE ON LOCATION?

Yes, of course it is; but it may require much more work to achieve it. Control is more difficult. Habit and experience sometimes will not substitute for calculation. Testing and reshooting are sometimes the only way to get the best results. Whatever it takes to get those results, we hope this chapter helps you to achieve them.

However, good pictures require more than good lighting. When we have even less control over the subject than we do the light, speed and spontaneity can count more than technical virtuosity. The success of the picture depends on being able to record the critical instant, not the instant just after it. So we also hope you can use some of the shortcuts in this chapter to get the picture before the picture gets away.

Either way is good at the right time and place.

This is the most important message in this book. There is no "correct" way to light a scene, just as there is no decidedly "right" camera or "proper" film to use. Good photographers have a toolbox of ideas and techniques. They pick from that toolbox according to the task of the moment.

We will not mind if you never light a single subject exactly as we have in our examples, but we do want you to have our toolbox of ideas to use as you please. Help yourself.

Appendix I

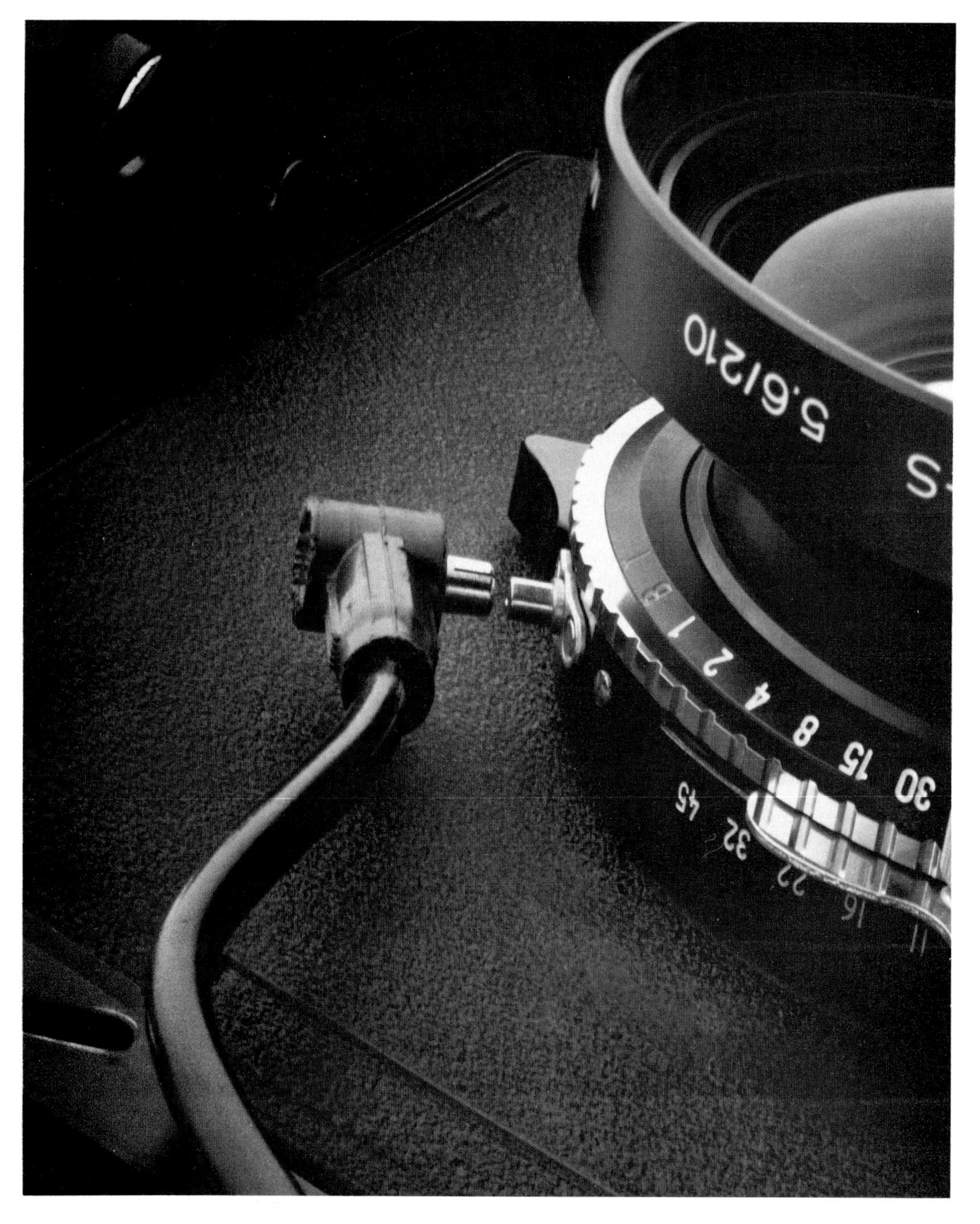

Let There Be Light

Let there be light! That is the first requirement of photography, and today's photographers have a wide range of available equipment to get it. Some, such as some of the tungsten lights that we will discuss shortly, are relatively simple and inexpensive devices. Others, like the more advanced studio strobes, can represent a huge investment.

We hope you do not let the glitter and cost of the best lighting equipment exaggerate the apparent importance of such hardware. This is a book about lighting, not lighting equipment. We hope that photographers who use only sunlight will find the principles as useful as those who work in elaborately equipped studios.

On the other hand, those who do work (or aspire to work) in the studio find they need to learn a great deal more about lights and accessories than other photographers need to know about the operation and maintenance of the sun! And they need most of this knowledge before they even begin to experiment with the lighting techniques. So we have to talk about the equipment, even if it is the least important part.

This appendix and the next are an overview of virtually every basic type of lighting equipment, from the more essential, to the less essential, to the trivial. (Because even the trivial is potentially essential for a particular task, sooner or later.)

Our emphasis will be on lighting equipment for still photography. This allows us to present the material with a much smaller vocabulary. Still photographers use the same lights and the same concepts, but not the number of unfamiliar terms that video and motion picture people do. If you are a novice, mistaking a scoop for a broad does no harm as long as you know how to make the lighting look right with whatever instrument you have in your hand. If you are learning cinematography, there are good books devoted entirely to naming the species and subspecies of cinematic lighting equipment. We do not need to duplicate their efforts. We are more interested in how the light behaves.

Before we get to the specifics, however, we want to make one more key point. Necessity is the mother of invention! While it would be lovely to own all the equipment that we would ever need for any picture, such an ideal is rare. We realize that many readers are just beginning to buy equipment, and we intend to address the issue of cost throughout this chapter and the next.

Professional photographers buy whatever equipment pays for itself. If an item is only rarely useful for their particular specialty, they are more likely to improvise than to buy. This is equally true for photographers with the largest and with the smallest gross receipts.

So almost every day the typical working photographer wishes for a piece of equipment that he or she does not have. With imagination, however, photographic and nonphotographic equipment can be adapted to do something completely different from the intended purpose.

Best of all, the materials needed for this innovation are often inexpensive. The average hardware store is filled with cheap parts that can extend the capability of whatever equipment you have. With a few simple tools you will often be able to put together a lighting setup that serves a specific need as well as the most sophisticated and expensive store-bought gear.

In one respect, the vast variety of lighting equipment that is now available is a real boon. It means that the tools exist to do just about anything that we want done. At the same time, the huge assortment of lights on the market also complicates life, especially for beginning photographers. With such competing factors as cost, the availability of service and accessories, weight, light output, portability, and probable use all influencing the decision, it is no easy matter to decide which lights are the best buy.

With that in mind, we would like to make two suggestions. First, try out lighting equipment before you buy. Use is the only real test. A set of strobes may sound just fine in the catalogue, but when the time comes to use them you may, unhappily, find that they are less than you expected. But you can rent such equipment by the day, at low rates, in most major cities. If you have a credit card, the rental houses can ship equipment to even the most remote rural area within 24 hours. In addition, many dealers routinely apply at least part of the rental fee to the purchase price.

Second, talk to other photographers who do the same kind of work you do before buying major equipment. Their experience, both good and bad, can save you time, energy, and money when the time comes for you to buy your own gear. If your friends are happy with whatever brand of equipment they are using, we suggest you buy the same. This is especially true of studio strobes. Then, if a particular project requires an extra head or power supply, you can borrow it from your friend with the assurance that it is compatible with the rest of your system.

CONTINUOUS LIGHTS

Continuous lights are always "on" when they are in use. Sunlight is the only common source that is truly continuous. Others flicker fifty or sixty times a second, depending on the electricity in the country in which you are working. But the flicker is so slight that human eyes and still cameras (and, for most such lights, motion picture cameras) cannot see the flicker.

Sunlight

Sunlight is the most commonly used continuous light source. It is the only light that is both bright and inexpensive. Many photographers consider it to be the most beautiful light. Unfortunately, it is difficult to control. Getting it into the right position can take months. Modifying its effect may require waiting for more or less cloud cover.

Any "white" light source may have a slightly different color from another. Photographers measure the *color temperature* of white light in *degrees Kelvin.* We abbreviate degrees Kelvin simply as "K."

Daylight is one of the three *standard color temperatures* for which films are manufactured. Mid-day light from the sun in a clear sky is 5500K. This is the most "cool" standard color temperature, containing more blue and less yellow and red.

Tungsten Lights

The most common example of a *tungsten light* is the incandescent household bulb. More specialized tungsten lights are standard in the motion picture and television industries. Relatively simple, inexpensive, and easy to use, they are also the starting point for many still photographers. Many different types and designs are available. Some of the lower priced ones are of limited use. Others surpass the more sophisticated electronic flash, even for some still applications.

The Advantages. Besides the cost advantages, tungsten lighting gives a photographer the best view of the appearance of the scene before making the exposure. Not only is the quality of the light constant (unlike a flash), but also photographic tungsten lights are bright enough to permit seeing the subject well, even in the ground glass of a large-format camera with the lens closed to a small aperture.

Some Problems. The problems inherent in tungsten lights are greater in the amateur-quality equipment but exist to some extent in all of it.

One of the biggest disadvantages of tungsten lights is their heat. Models soon swelter under their glare, and delicate subjects such as flowers can wilt away to nothing in seemingly no time at all. Conventional tungsten lights have another drawback. Compared with strobes requiring a similar amount of electrical current, they do not produce much light. This is less of a problem for motion picture and video photographers whose (usually) smaller image size provides adequate depth of field at wider apertures. But tungsten lights often present still photographers with choices of either too little light or too much heat and too much electrical demand.

The most bothersome difficulty presented by amateur tungsten lamps is probably their lack of consistent color. Depending on the type, new photographic tungsten bulbs give off light of a color temperature of either 3200 or 3400 degrees K. These are the other two photographic standard color temperatures. This means that tungsten is a "warm" light, and it contains more yellow, orange, and red than sunlight.

As these bulbs age, their color temperature changes. This is due to a tiny amount of residue from the burning filament coating the inside of the bulb. It is not unusual, for example, for a bulb starting with a color temperature of 3200K to drop to 2400K or less after just a few weeks of use. Sometimes, especially when we shoot black and white, a change of even this magnitude does little harm. However, when color is critical, color temperature shifts less than this can be disastrous.

Some Simple Tungsten Equipment. Figure A1.1 shows a very simple and inexpensive tungsten light source. It consists of a reflector-type bulb fitted into a spring-clip socket. Such a light is about as unsophisticated as we can buy. Nevertheless, used wisely, it can provide good results.

► *This tungsten equipment is inexpensive, but it can still produce good results.*

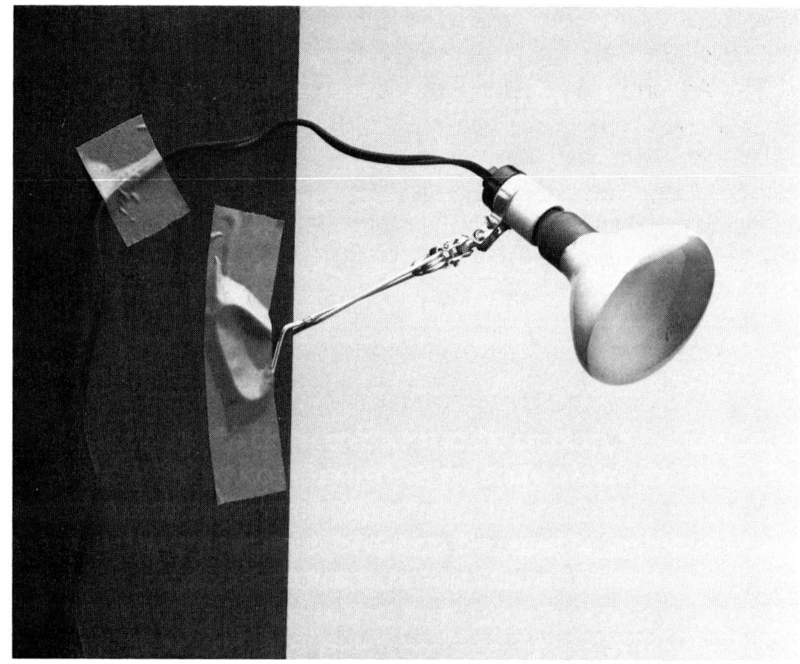

A1.1

Figure A1.2 shows another kind of basic tungsten lighting. The light is a spun aluminum dish reflector with a photoflood bulb installed. A light like this is adequate for many simple applications.

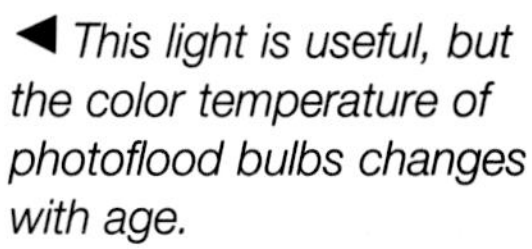

◀ *This light is useful, but the color temperature of photoflood bulbs changes with age.*

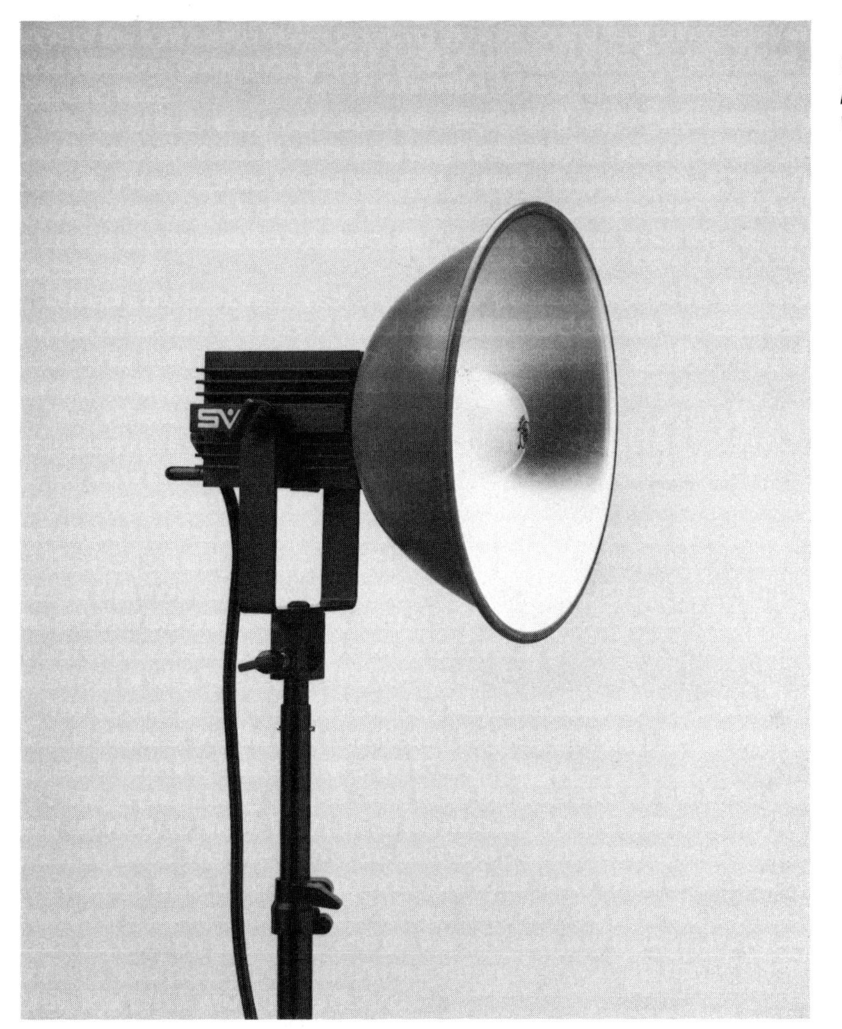

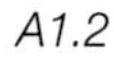

A1.2

Professional Tungsten Lights. So far, the lights that we have discussed have been inexpensive and low-powered affairs. That all changes with a light such as the one shown in Figure A1.3. It is a moderate-duty, professional-quality "quartz" light. This sort of equipment is brighter and more expensive than the lights we have discussed so far. The important difference is in the bulb.

► *Quartz lights can produce more light and have stable color temperature.*

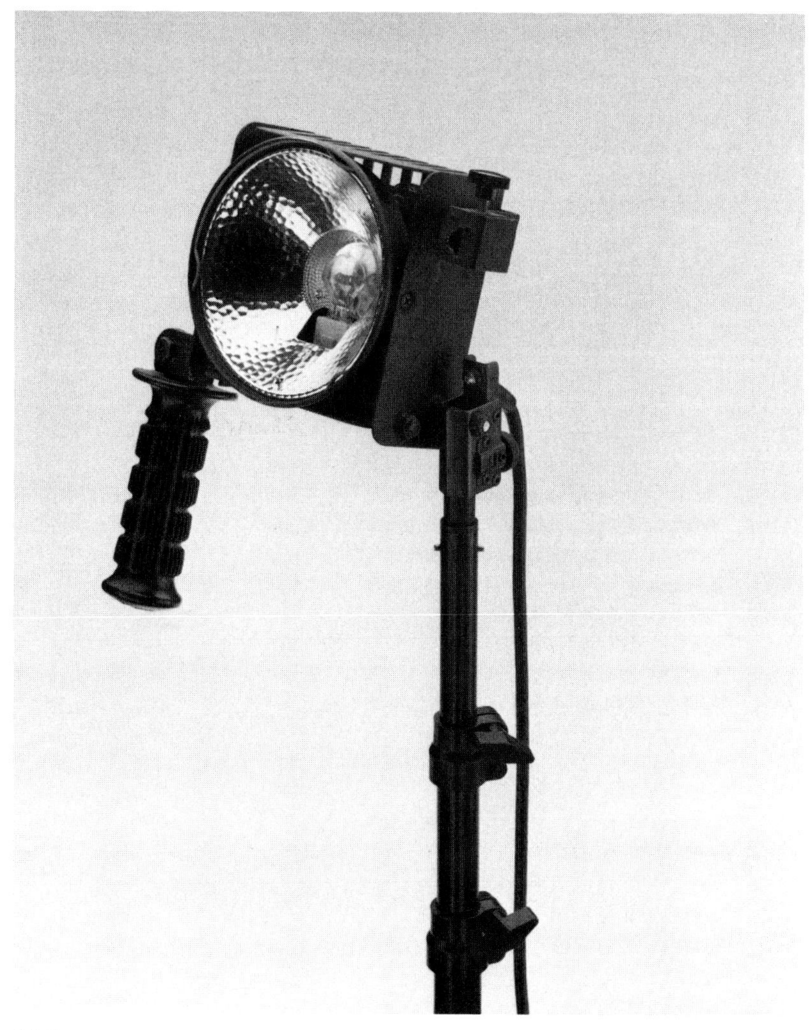

A1.3

Called *quartz-halogen lights,* these bulbs are filled with a halogen vapor such as iodine, and they have large filaments enclosed in quartz glass. Quartz lights are more efficient than household tungsten bulbs: Typically they are between 50 and 100 percent brighter than a standard tungsten bulb of the same wattage. Throughout the life of the lamp, there is almost no change in either its brightness or its color.

Even though quartz lights produce less heat than conventional tungsten, the glass envelope of the lamp gets hotter. This is because the lamps are smaller and, therefore, the glass is much closer to the hot filament. The quartz glass can withstand the heat without shattering (usually) or melting. This allows manufacturers to produce small but very bright bulbs. The added heat cleans filament residue from the glass and prevents the change in color temperature.

Other Continuous Lights

Alternative sources of continuous light offer more light, but some have other disadvantages.

Carbon arc lights use no bulbs at all, but produce a small continuous spark across an air gap.

HMI, CID, and CSI are all abbreviations based on the types of filament and gases used in the lamps: Hg (mercury) medium-arc iodides, compact indium discharge, and compact source iodine. *CID* and *CSI* are not commonly used in still photography and, in the United States they are less common even in video and motion picture production. The disfavor shown toward these sources is due partly to their nonstandard color or increased flicker, but also to the fixed habits of users. As the lights improve and the potential users become aware of them, those habits could change abruptly.

HMI lights have seen a marked increase in acceptance and may eventually replace quartz as the preferred continuous source. They are much brighter than even quartz lights of equal wattage, and their color approximates that of daylight. These qualities make them potentially superior sources for use along with sunlight by motion picture and video photographers. Unfortunately, HMIs are costly. Still photographers, who do not need continuous sources, will find even the most expensive strobe systems more affordable.

Designs for Continuous Light Sources

Photographers who use continuous lights usually have a selection of several different types to light the subject with different patterns and amounts of brightness. The two basic kinds of lighting equipment using quartz-halogen bulbs are spotlights and floodlights. *Floodlights* are assembled with reflectors that spread their rays over a wide area. *Spotlights* use reflectors and lenses to focus their light on a small area. Both of these can be classified into several subcategories based primarily on reflector size and shape, but the general classifications include the important distinctions.

We logically think of focusing light and diffusing light as mutually exclusive, but the fresnel light does both (Figure A.1.4). The *stepped fresnel lens* focuses the light, but not very sharply. A fresnel lens has the curved surface "stepped" in the manner shown in Figure A1.5 to reduce weight. Such lenses never approach the quality needed in cameras and enlargers, but they are more than adequate for most lighting applications. This is the most versatile design among the continuous sources.

► *Broad lights like that in the center spread their rays over a wide area. The fresnel light in the front allows focusing the light on a small area or, unfocused, spreading it over a large area. The general-purpose light at the top has adjustable focus like the fresnel, but less precision.*

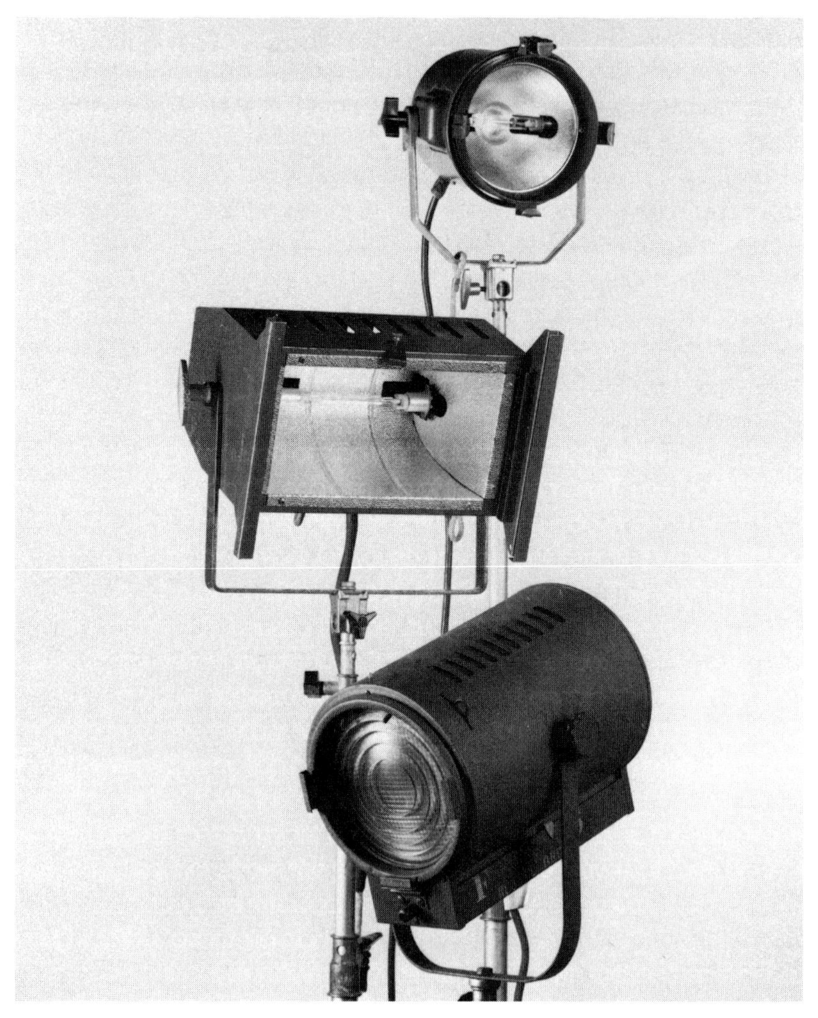

A1.4

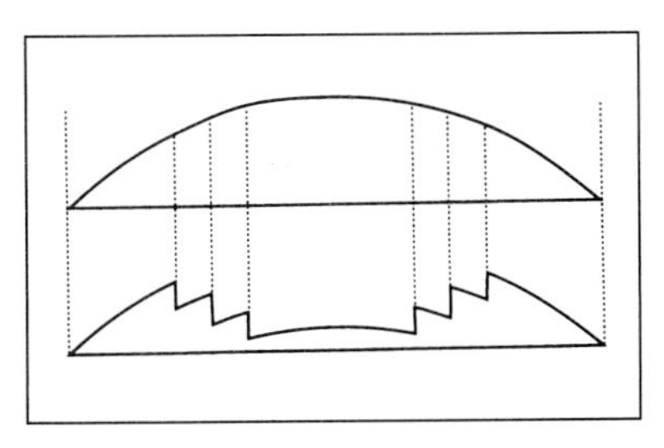

◀ *A fresnel lens is "stepped" to reduce weight. Such lenses partly focus and partly diffuse the light.*

A1.5

The light in the center of Figure A1.4 is called a *broad light* because it lights a broad area. Its reflector design makes its lighting pattern roughly rectangular. A light with a similar purpose but with a round reflector, shown in Figure A1.2, is called a *scoop.*

Expense and portability prevent some photographers from having as many flood lights *and* spotlights as they would like. For them, manufacturers have come up with what is generally called a *multipurpose light*. These lights are not made with a fresnel lens. Instead, they have either a movable reflector or movable bulb socket. This arrangement allows their beam to be either spread out over a broad area or concentrated on a small subject. The light in Figure A1.3 and that in the back of the group in Figure A1.4 are examples.

The wattage of tungsten lights is often abbreviated as "K," meaning "thousand watts." "K" also indicates color temperature (in degrees Kelvin), and people unfamiliar with lighting sometimes find this confusing. The numbers are so different, however, that is easy to decide which "K" someone is talking about. It would be unreasonable to imagine that a 2K broad, with a color temperature of 3400K, could ever have a color temperature as low as two degrees Kelvin or a wattage as high as 3400 thousand (3.4 million) watts!

FLASH

A flash is turned "off" except at the instant of exposure. This greatly reduces electrical requirements and heat buildup, but it makes it more difficult to anticipate how lighting will look in the picture. Flash is used by most still photographers. In motion pictures, it is used only for some high-speed applications.

Flashbulbs

For many years, flashbulbs were the only "on-camera" lights available to photographers. Today, they are rarely used by professionals. However, some amateur cameras still are equipped to use them. The basic workings of a flashbulb are simple. When fired, an electric charge causes an oversized filament to burn. This produces a burst of bright light that lasts for perhaps 1/50 of a second. The flash burns the filament away, and the bulb is then useless.

Although flashbulbs are now rare in professional work, there are times when they can come in handy. Their more simple apparatus allows more light with less weight than a strobe light. One of our associates wished to photograph inside a large cave. The underground "room" that he wanted to picture was so large that no strobe system he could carry into the cave could possibly illuminate it all. His solution was to strategically place several dozen flash bulbs around the cave and wire them together so that they would all flash simultaneously.

Strobes

Strobes are the most important of the electronic wonder tools that have revolutionized photography. Harold Edgerton invented the first practical strobe in 1931. Since his pioneering experiment, an ever-increasing variety of amazingly sophisticated electronic flashes has come to the market. Today, we can select strobes that range in size and power from small, portable flashes that easily attach to a 35mm camera to giant studio units that use thousands of watt-seconds of power. Some have less electronic sophistication than many of the simplest telephones, while others rival the intelligence of a desktop computer.

Regardless of their size and power, all strobes work in more or less the same way. Similar to a flashbulb, when a strobe is triggered it sends a large electrical current through a *flash tube* in a very short time, often less than 1/2000 of a second. The passage of this high-powered "spark" causes xenon gas inside the flash tube to glow brightly, producing the flash of light that we use to illuminate our pictures. Since nothing is burned, the flash tube is usable for thousands of flashes. Between the flashes, the strobe accumulates an electrical charge from a wall outlet or a battery. The time needed to accumulate a sufficient charge for the next flash is called the *recycle time.*

Although the color temperature of the light varies somewhat between different strobes, all approximate standard daylight. For that reason, they are used with daylight film. If a precise color balance is critical, any error can be easily corrected by filters.

In the United States, strobe power is measured in units called *watt-seconds;* in Europe, the measurement is *joules.* (The two are interchangeable: one watt-second equals one joule.) The physics behind these terms are unimportant to applied photography. The only thing you need to remember is that the higher the number of watt-seconds *directly* relates to the amount of light the strobe provides. A 2400-watt-second unit is, for example, twice as powerful as one rated at 1200 watt-seconds.

Ideally, a professional strobe would be powerful and lightweight, and also would have a fast recycle time. Unfortunately, present technology does not offer all of these features in a single package. If strobe designers fully deliver any two of these features, the equipment is likely to be deficient in the third. With that in mind, we will discuss some of the different kinds of strobes that are available.

Strobe Power Versus Light Output

Strobes are rated by three basic measurements: watt-seconds (or joules), beam candle power seconds (BCPS), and guide numbers. These are all useful. Any of them may be more important than another, depending on how we intend to use the strobe.

Watt-seconds measure the power used by the power supply, not the amount of light coming from the strobe head. The light getting to the subject is also influenced by such factors as the efficiency of the reflector on the strobe head and whatever diffusion material may be in front of it.

BCPS is a true measure of light output, with all elements of the system taken into account. As an extreme example of the distinction between the two measurements, consider an 800-watt-second strobe head with 10,000 BCPS. If we cover that strobe head with an opaque wrapper, the power consumption (watt-seconds) is not changed, but the light output (BCPS) drops to zero.

Guide numbers are based on BCPS *plus* the light sensitivity of the film. A photographer with a single strobe at a single power setting uses a different guide number with each change of film, assuming the films have different ISO ratings. (We discuss guide numbers more in Chapter 10.)

Strobe manufacturers put much effort into the design of their reflectors. A strobe head with a highly efficient reflector may light a subject several times as brightly as another head with the same power but a less efficient reflector. These manufacturers continually feel frustrated by photographers who pay too much attention to watt-seconds, because that measurement ignores their efforts to produce more efficient strobe heads.

Unfortunately, when we place a diffusion sheet in front of a strobe head, or put the head in a soft box, we undo much of the efficiency in the design of the strobe. This is particularly true if we decide to use one of several brands of soft boxes that require us to remove the strobe manufacturer's metal reflector entirely in order to fit the head into the soft box. One maker's 2400-watt-second strobe begins to behave much more similarly to someone else's brand rated at the same power, even if the two claim drastically different BCPS ratings.

Which type of rating is more meaningful? We might get several different, but equally valid, answers, according to which photographer we ask. Here are some examples:

Case 1. A commercial photographer routinely switches from one strobe reflector to another on the same head, then bounces the light out of an umbrella, uses a grid spot, or modifies the light in any of several other common ways. Since keeping track of sixty to eighty possible BCPS ratings is impractical and unnecessary, watt-seconds becomes a more useful measurement than light output.

Case 2. A photographer shooting 35mm film for a newspaper may routinely use a strobe with no modification to supplement ambient light. This person is likely to be more interested in a BCPS rating that is as high as possible and does not care whether that rating comes from greater absolute power or a more efficient design.

Case 3. Another photographer who specializes in wedding pictures uses a single type of film nearly 100 percent of the time. Here the guide number is a more useful measurement. Not only does it allow comparing one strobe with another, but it also allows predicting the lens aperture that a particular strobe might allow in a typical working situation.

Case 4. Two photographers are writing a book about general lighting principles. They have no idea what specific sorts of things the reader may decide to do with a strobe. So they decide to use watt-seconds for most examples, because that measure remains constant for a given strobe at a given power setting under any circumstances.

Lightweight Portable Strobes. Figure A1.6 is a typical lightweight portable strobe. The power of most of these small, on-camera strobes is less than 100 watt-seconds. Strobes such as this one consist of the strobe itself plus the batteries that power it combined into one unit that is small enough to attach directly to a camera. Because of their portability and extraordinarily sophisticated design, these strobes have revolutionized flash photography.

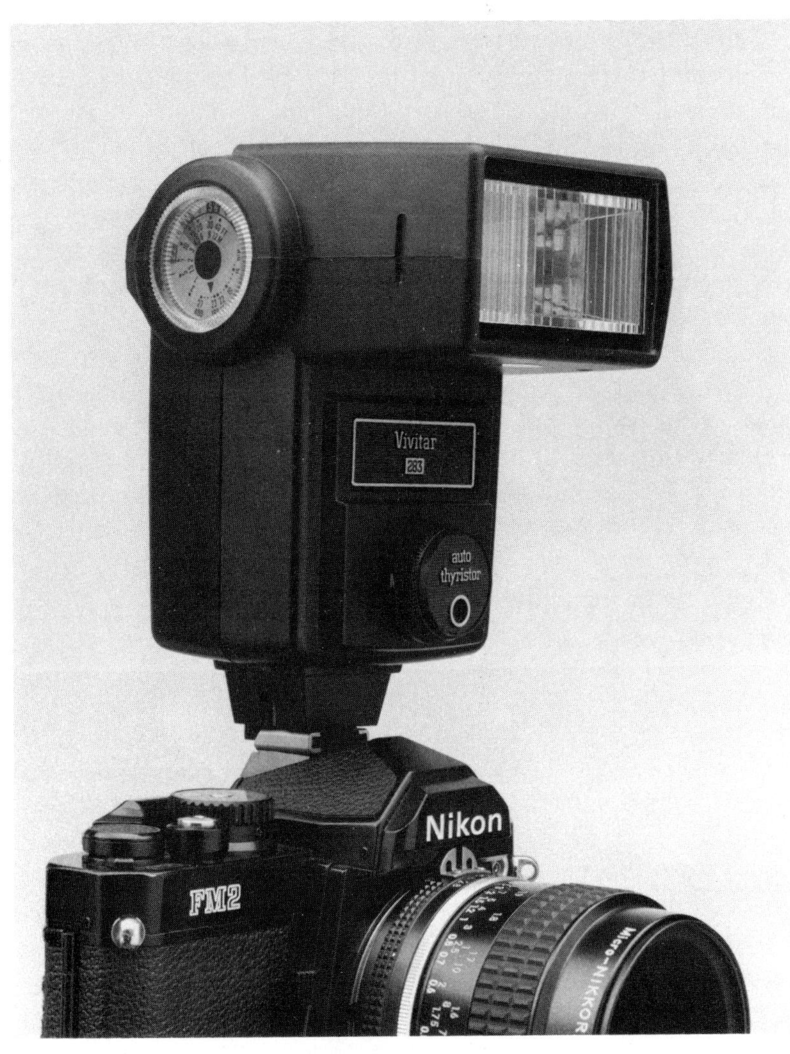

◀ *Small strobes, usually 100 watt-seconds or less in power, are ideal for photojournalists and others who need speed and mobility.*

A1.6

As useful as such small strobes are, they do have their drawbacks. Many of them tend to recycle slowly. All are low powered. To compensate for this lack of power, the smaller strobes are usually manufactured with very focused reflectors. By concentrating the light into a narrowly focused beam, such a strobe can be usably bright despite the low battery power. While ingenious, this solution causes uneven illumination of the scene when we use wide-angle lenses. It also tends to produce harsh, unattractive lighting.

Fortunately, it is easy to *bounce* the light from these small units off ceilings and walls. This results in a huge increase in the effective size of the light and a substantial softening of the shadows. Small flashes can also be used with umbrella reflectors. Umbrellas are among the most important of the lighting accessories.

Unfortunately, bouncing the light in either of these ways often wastes enough of the limited light output to force the photographer to use higher speed, coarser grained films. Small strobes are most useful for journalistic work. These photographers often need to be lightly equipped for mobility, and news reproduction usually obscures the difference between fine- and coarse-grained films. Small strobes are also good for nature, scientific, and medical documentation if the subject is small enough to allow placing the strobe so close to the subject that it becomes, effectively, a large, powerful light.

Because lightweight strobes often lack the power we need, we often carry several and use them together. Slave triggers (see p. 310) fire them all simultaneously.

Heavy Portable Strobes. These medium-power, fast-recycling strobes fill the gap between the small portable units and large studio strobes. Figure A1.7 shows a common example of such a flash.

► *Medium-powered, fast-recycling strobes fill the gap between the small units and large, heavy studio units.*

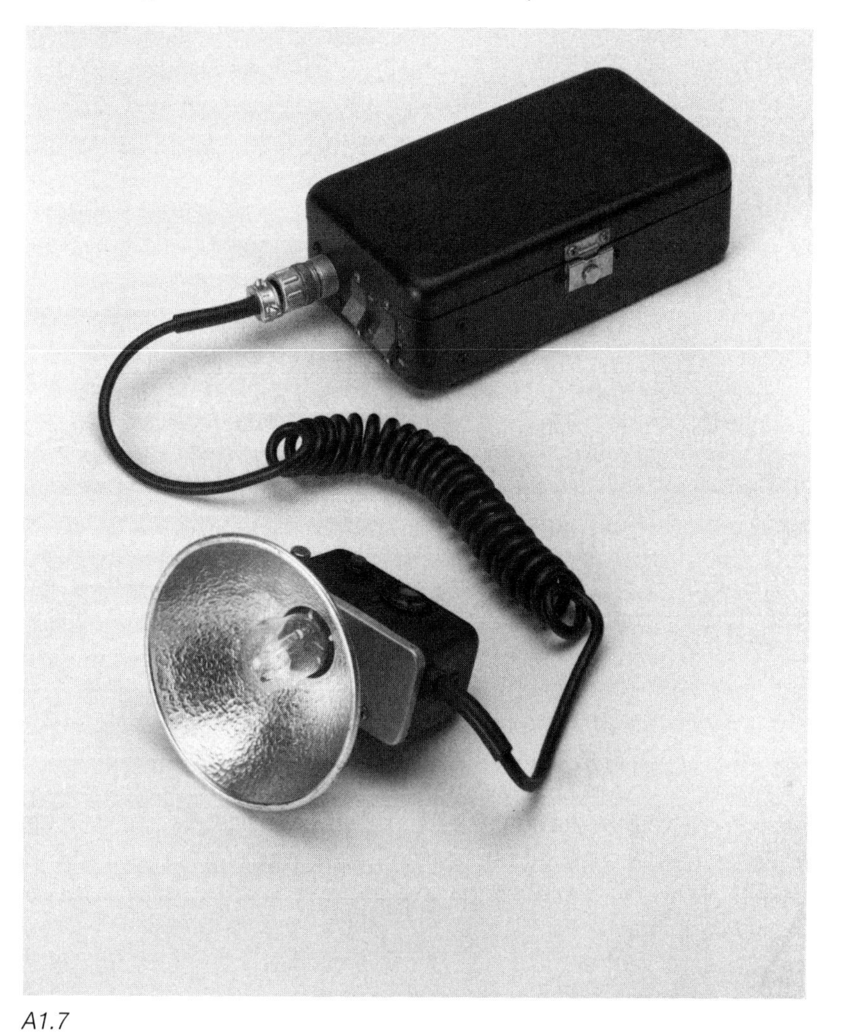

A1.7

Such strobes are powered by large battery packs that generally provide from 100 to 400 watt-seconds of power. Because of their weight, these are supported by shoulder straps and are connected to the flash head by a power cord.

Surprisingly, even though these heavy units are more powerful than the smaller, lightweight strobes, they often do not put a great deal more light on the subject than their smaller cousins. This is because of the way in which their reflectors are designed.

The reflectors that come with larger portable strobes tend to scatter a good bit of the light around the room rather than concentrating it directly on the subject as the smaller ones do. Some of this scattered light may then reflect from the walls and ceilings back to the subject, as shown in Figure A1.8. When this happens, it helps to fill troublesome shadows. This results in more pleasing pictures than those usually produced by smaller strobes. In the hands of a skilled photographer, a heavy portable strobe can produce pictures that look as though they were made with a roomful of lights rather than a single light source.

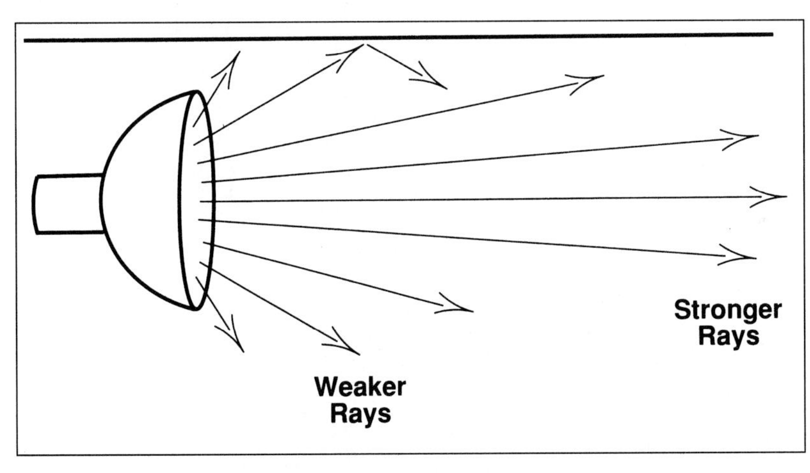

A1.8

◀ *The reflectors on larger portable strobes may scatter light to produce very attractive results.*

Because of the pleasing lighting these strobes produce, they are a great favorite among many wedding photographers. They are also frequently used by portrait photographers working outside the studios.

Although the standard reflector design of most of these strobes uses the light inefficiently, many of them offer interchangeable, more efficient reflectors. With such reflectors, these strobes become many times brighter than their smaller siblings, albeit with a sacrifice in the quality of the light.

Studio Strobes. Studio strobes are heavy and cumbersome. They must have an electrical outlet nearby. Nevertheless, their high-power and fast-recycling make them the workhorses of commercial photography (Figure A1.9). Because of their importance, the following section will explain them in some detail.

▶ *High-powered, fast-recycling studio strobes are the workhorses of commercial photography.*

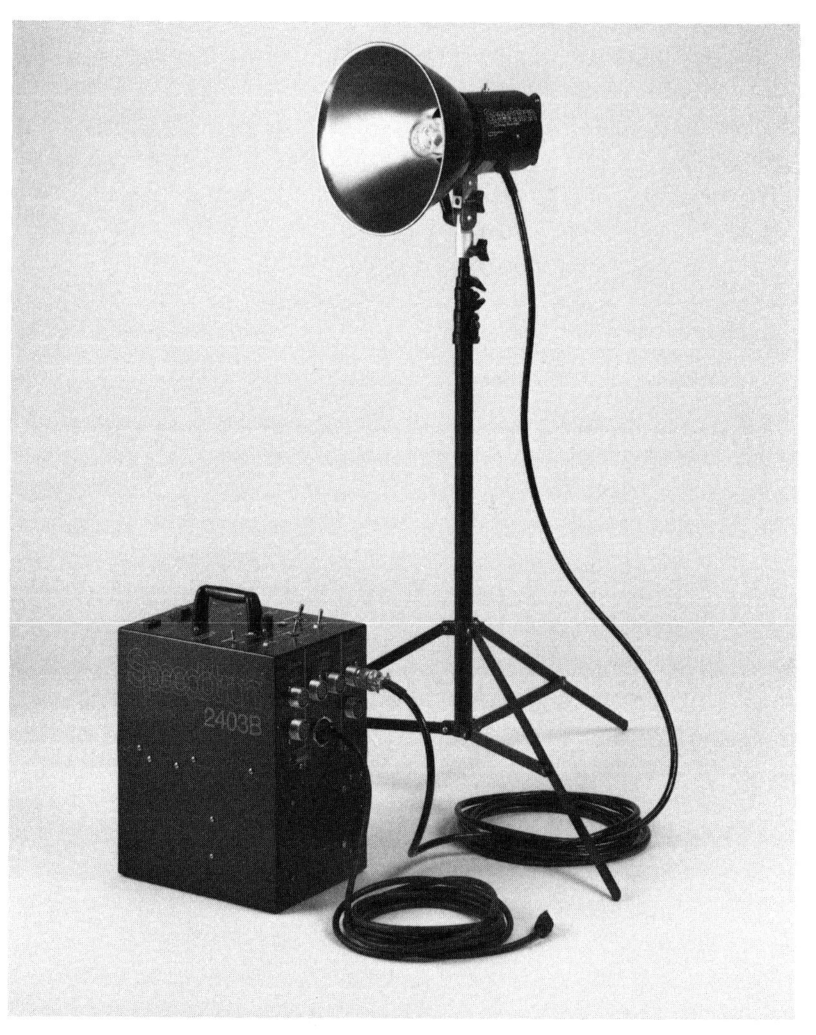

A1.9

The duration of the flash produced by most studio strobes is somewhere between 1/250 and 1/1000 of a second. The average flash duration is longer than that of most of the smaller strobes, but still brief enough to get reasonably sharp pictures of people in motion.

The brief flash means that it takes very little electrical current to produce a lot of light. In addition, because they give off far less heat, strobes are much more comfortable for models, and as any experienced photographer will tell you, a happy model is a better model. Finally, because the light of a strobe head is electronically controlled, its power can be changed without significantly affecting its color balance.

Studio strobe systems are made up of two main components: a head and a power supply. The *head* contains the flash tube and provides the light, and the *power supply* provides the energy that the head needs to operate.

The Head. Studio strobe heads have two types of lamps: a modeling light and a flash tube (Figure A1.10). The modeling light can be left turned on constantly. It allows the photographer to view the scene while setting it up. The flash tube is illuminated for only a brief instant. It provides the brilliant light needed to take the picture.

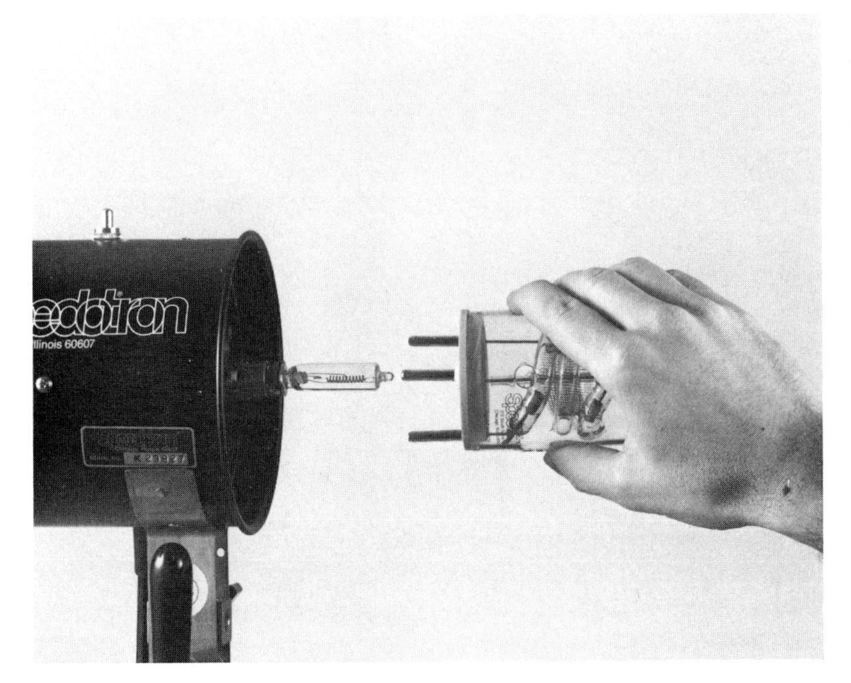

A1.10

◀ *Studio strobe heads have two kinds of lamps: the modeling light, which is on continuously, and the flash tube.*

Many flash heads also contain built-in cooling fans. Those manufacturers that do not routinely put fans in their flash heads usually can supply them as an accessory. These fans are important if you wish to cover the front of your flash heads with snoots, grids or diffusion material of any kind. These all restrict air flow. The resulting heat buildup can damage the equipment and sometimes cause a fire.

Most manufacturers offer several kinds of reflectors to fit their flash heads. Every reflector shown in Figure A1.11 fits the studio strobe head shown in the earlier photographs. These allow a single flash head to be used in different ways. A mere change of the reflector may, for example, change a small light source into a big one. It can also modify the angle of illumination to light either a large or a small area.

► *Interchangeable reflectors for a studio strobe head.*

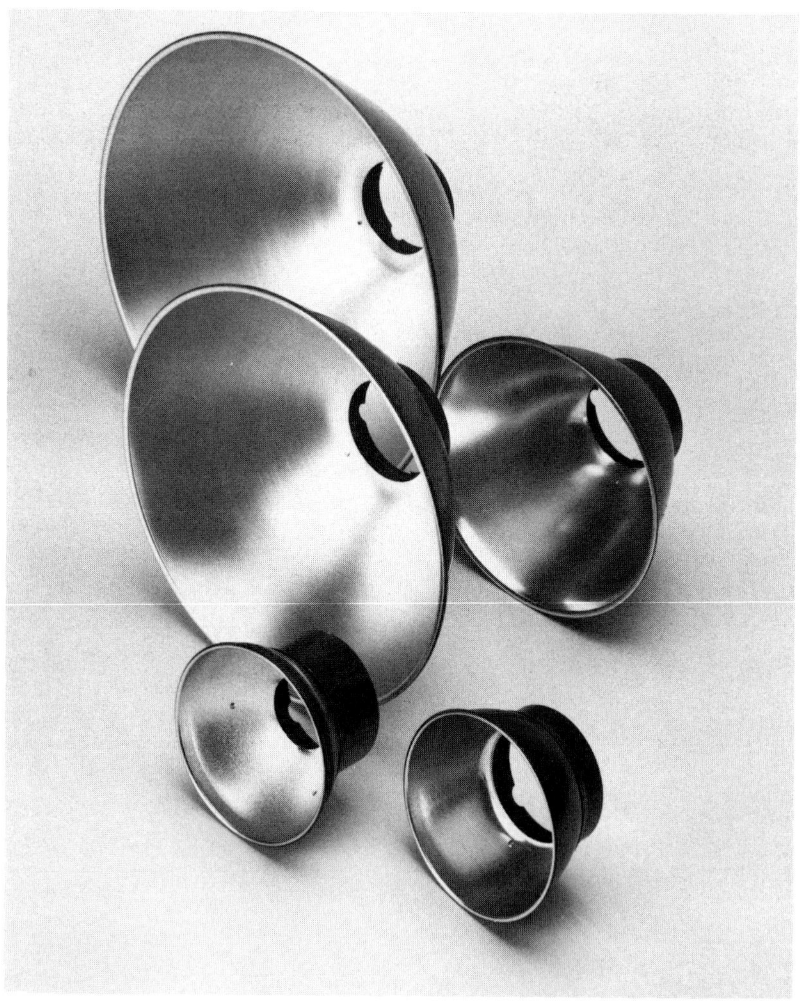

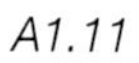

A1.11

It is possible to obtain strobe heads of different power and different lighting patterns, just as it is for quartz lights. In practice, however, most photographers standardize on just one head design. This is partly because the ability to interchange reflectors and to adjust power supply makes a single type of head more versatile. Cost imposes an additional limitation. The higher price of strobe heads makes it more economically effective to buy a single versatile head, plus accessories to modify it, instead of several specialized heads.

However, at times specialized heads can prove very useful. Examples include a *quad head* and a *bitube head.* Figure A1.12 shows a quad head.

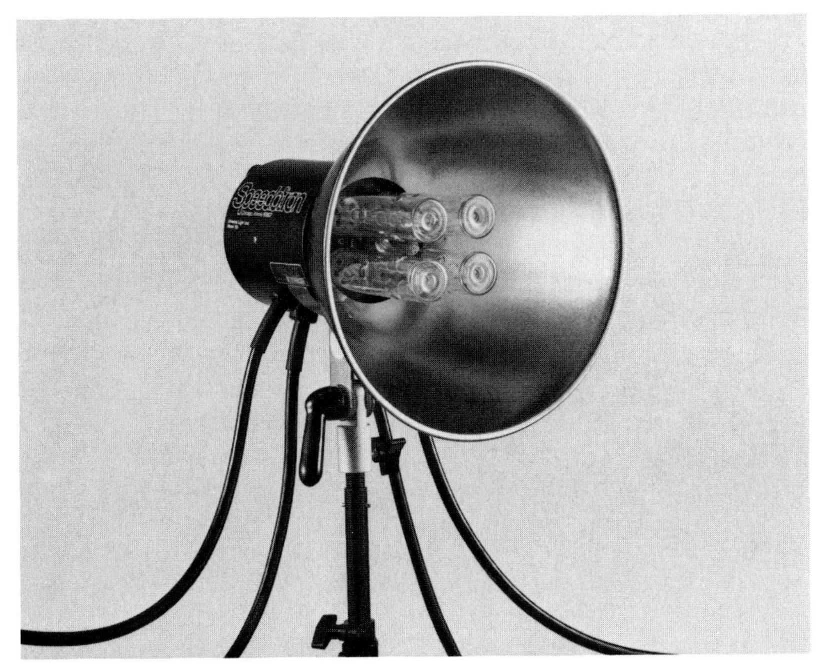

◀ *Multiple tubes allow enormous light output from a single head.*

A1.12

Multiple tube heads allow the photographer to connect each flash tube to a separate power supply. Such an arrangement is capable of providing a tremendous amount of light. Alternatively, all tubes can be plugged into one power supply. The result of this is the short flash duration that is ideal for making sharp pictures of moving objects.

The Power Supply. The power supply is the heart of a studio strobe, and the amount of power that it can provide is the single most important consideration when evaluating any system. The smallest studio strobe that is likely to be of common use to a commercial photographer must produce at least 400 watt-seconds. The largest power supplies likely to be in most studios are rated at 4800 watt-seconds. Most photographers have several power supplies, together providing 5000 to 10,000 watt-seconds. At the upper end of things, there is no limit to the number of watt-seconds that a photographer might need. For example, someone who specializes in cars or furniture groupings might routinely use a 50,000 watt-second system.

A few studio strobe systems have the power supply built into the flash head (Figure A1.13). Such systems have the advantage of being compact enough to pack and carry around. This makes them particularly popular with photographers who specialize in location portraiture and annual reports. The relative portability of these lights does have drawbacks, however. They cannot be built to provide much power because, if they were, they would be far too heavy to mount on light stands. Furthermore, their power cannot be directed from one head to another. Photographers can turn down the power in any one of the heads, but we cannot route that power to another head where we would prefer to have it.

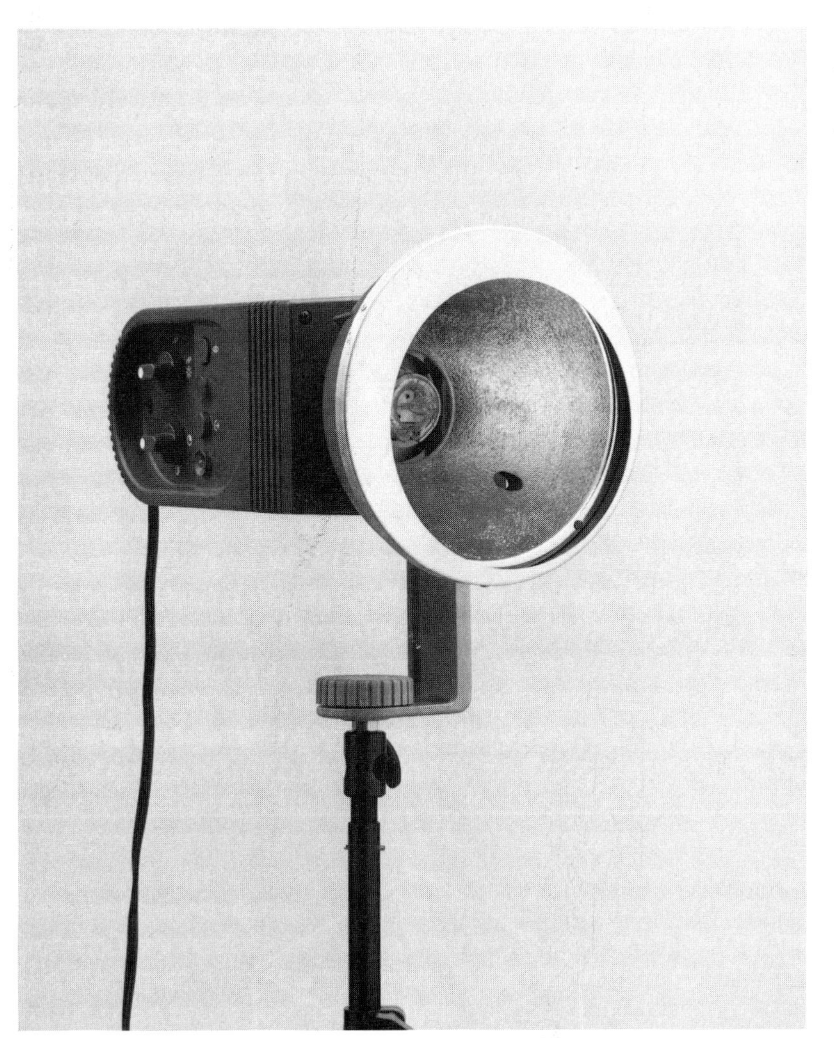

◀ *Some studio strobes are manufactured with the power supply built into the flash head.*

A1.13

Building the power supply and the head as separate units allows one to design more powerful systems with lighter weight heads. Such a design also allows the power supply to be much more versatile. The power supply shown in Figure A1.14 can distribute its power among as many as six heads. Or we can put all of its power into a single head. We can even use the combined power of four such power supplies in one quad head.

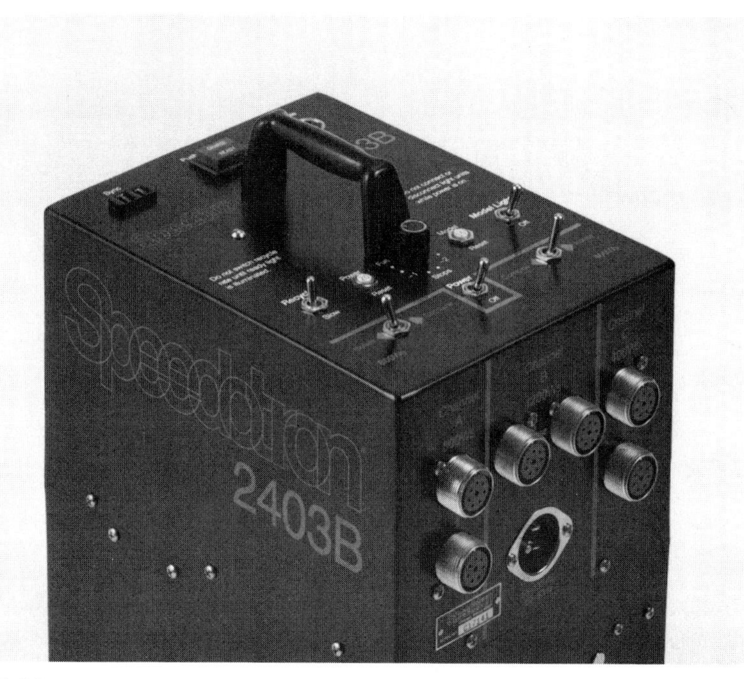

► *This studio strobe power supply has several outlets for attaching heads to different power channels. It also features significant power flexibility, controlled by switches.*

A1.14

How Cameras Control Strobes

Regardless of the kind of strobe you use, it must be synchronized to your camera. That is to say, the strobe and the camera must be linked together, or synchronized, so that the flash goes off within the exact time period that *the shutter is completely open.*

Types of Synchronization

Cameras use two different methods of synchronization, depending on the type of shutter.

Focal-Plane Shutters. Nearly all 35mm single lens reflex cameras have focal plane shutters. Figure A1.A shows how they are synchronized to work with a flash.

A focal-plane shutter makes an exposure by carefully controlling the movement of two curtains marked *A* and *B* on the diagram. When the shutter is released, curtain *A* opens and light exposes the film. Then, after a carefully timed interval, curtain *B* closes, ending the exposure.

Most cameras with focal-plane shutters will only synchronize with flashes at relatively slow speeds such as 1/60 or 1/80 second. At higher shutter speeds, curtain *B* begins to close *before* curtain *A* is fully open. *In a high-speed exposure, there is no time when both curtains are fully open.*

If we use a strobe with a focal-plane shutter set at a high speed, part of the scene will be cropped by the shutter curtain. Fortunately for those of us who are prone to forget such details, many modern 35mm cameras automatically set themselves to the fastest speed that will synchronize when they are connected to a strobe.

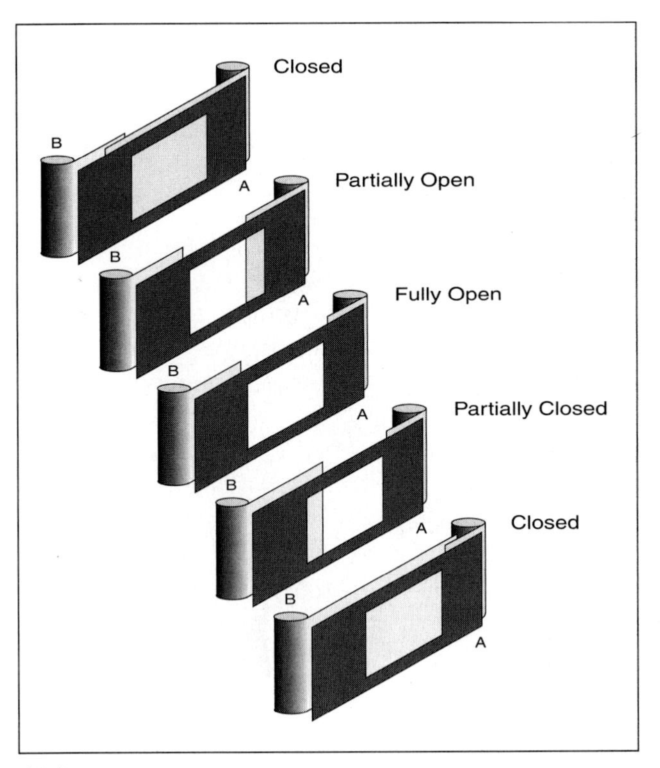

A1.A

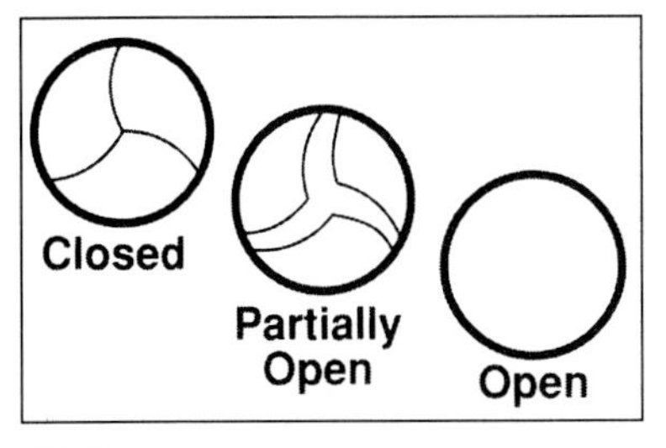

A1.B

▲ *Focal-plane shutters. At faster shutter speeds, curtain* **B** *begins to close before* **A** *is fully open.*

◀ *Leaf shutters control exposure time by opening and closing all their blades simultaneously.*

Leaf shutters. All contemporary large- and most medium-format cameras are equipped with leaf shutters, sometimes called between-the-lens shutters. Figure A1.B shows how such shutters work.

Instead of regulating exposure time by opening and closing of two curtains in sequence, leaf shutters have several blades that open and close *simultaneously.*

This means that at any shutter speed there is always an instant when all shutter blades are fully open. Therefore, leaf shutters will synchronize with strobes at any speed.

Most such systems also allow their power to be distributed at different levels, or *asymmetrically,* between heads. For example, such a system can be easily adjusted to send fifty percent of its power to one head, while the remaining fifty percent is divided between several other heads. Such a flexible power routing helps to simplify complex lighting setups immeasurably.

System versatility also allows a beginning photographer to start with a minimal system and add to it over the years without having components become obsolete. This does not always mean staying with one manufacturer's products. Some major brands of heads can be used with other power supplies with minor and inexpensive modification of the wiring.

Triggering the Strobe. A power supply is usually triggered by the camera shutter. This is done by connecting them with a *synch cord.*

Slave triggers allow the photographer to use more than one power supply at a time. Slave triggers are photoelectric switches. They automatically trigger the power supply into which they are plugged when they sense the light from another strobe. Thus, the light produced by one strobe head can trigger other power supplies. There is no limit to the number of power supplies that can be used together when using slave triggers.

Photographers also flash their studio strobes with the test switch. This is particularly true in those frequent cases when they are working in the dark with the shutter open. If their subject is stationary, they can fire the test switch several times to produce multiple flashes. The combined exposure is many times that of a single flash from the same system.

Remote controls require either a radio or an infrared transmitter attached to the camera, plus a receiver at each power supply.

The most elementary of these devices simply flashes the strobe. They serve the same function as a synch cord but eliminate the clutter caused by the cord. These systems are particularly useful for such subjects as room interiors or in studio setups with the strobes mounted on overhead rails, where it might be difficult to keep the synch cord out of camera sight.

Slightly more sophisticated systems have a transmitter with several different frequencies. This frequency selection allows a photographer to (a) tune the receivers on several different power supplies to different frequencies and control them independently, and (b) tune the whole system to a "clean" frequency if there are other electronic devices producing spurious signals in the immediate vicinity. Some of these systems also allow programming the number of flashes in a multiple-flash photograph. If the remote control has both of these capabilities, it allows the photographer to program one power supply to flash five times, for example, and another three times. This permits finer control of the total illumination from any given strobe than the power selector on the power supply usually allows. These remote controls work with any strobe.

The most sophisticated remote controls also allow the photographer to adjust the power setting on the power supply and to turn the modeling lights on or off. These work only with power supplies by the same manufacturer. At the time of this writing, only the most expensive strobe systems offer such an option. However, with the decreasing cost of sophisticated electronics, such controls may be common to most studio strobes by the time you read this.

MAKING THE LIGHTS DO WHAT WE WANT

Good control requires many other tools besides the lights themselves. Novice photographers often underestimate the importance of these other tools because they are usually simple and inexpensive compared with the sophisticated studio lights.

Of course, photographic lights are useful only when we can control them. This makes the more simple tools as important as the lights themselves. We will talk about some of these accessories in Appendix 2.

Appendix 2

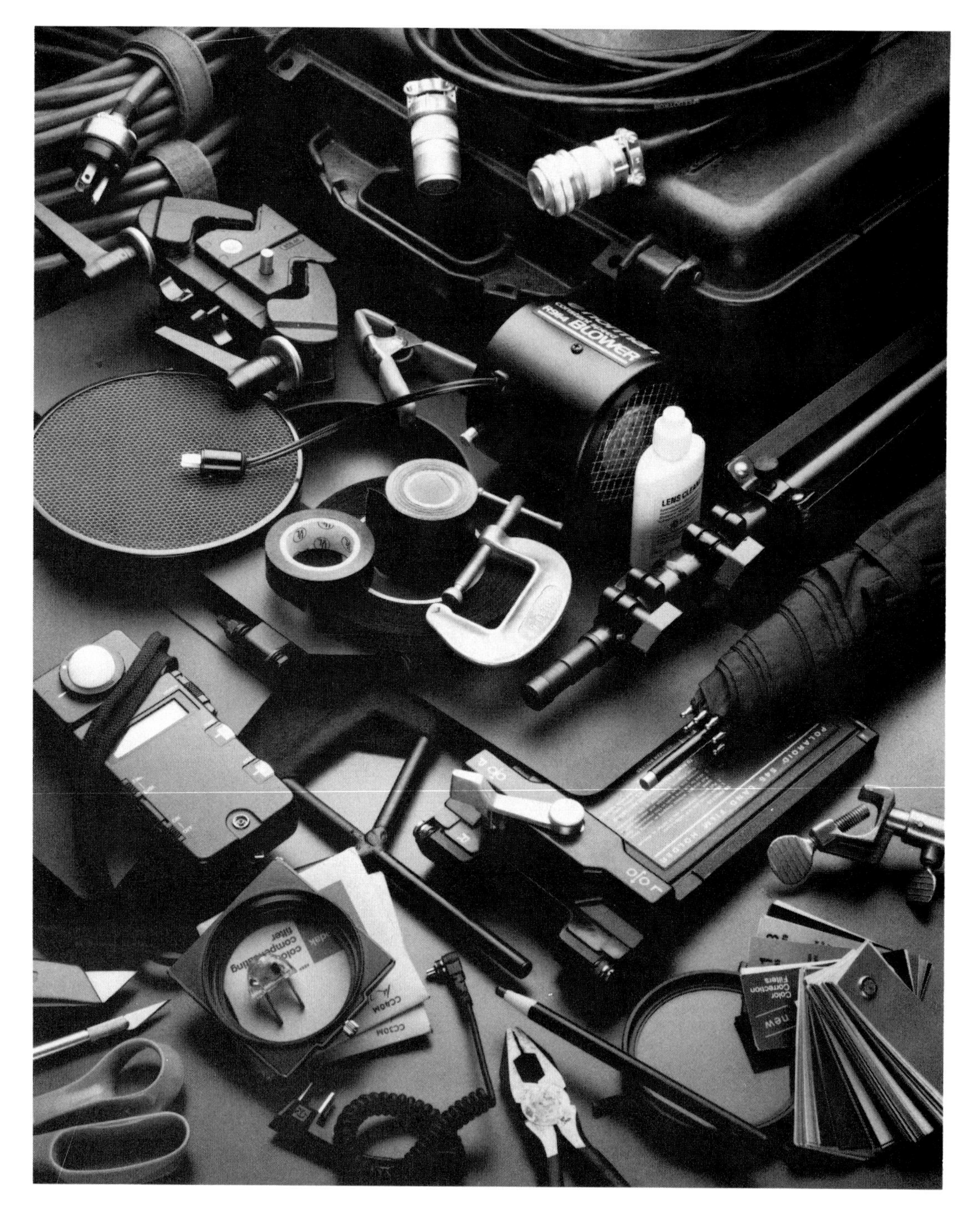

The Complete Toolbox

Good lighting requires additional tools to measure and control the light. For many photographers, lights are only a small portion of their lighting equipment. The additional tools are their most useful ones. Other photographers may need only a bracket to attach a strobe to a camera. The tools you need depend on your type of work.

Few photographers need every tool we are going to discuss in this appendix. We all, however, need to know about every available tool. Understanding how and when each of them is useful enables us to decide what to buy, what to borrow or rent, and what to make to use our time and budget as efficiently as possible.

LIGHT MEASUREMENT

All light meters convert light energy into electrical energy, which is easier to measure. They then have an electrical meter with a scale marked in f/stops and shutter speeds, rather than volts or milliamps.

Beyond these basics, the operation of different types of meters varies greatly. Each design is superior in some ways, but no single meter is best for all purposes. Meters of any particular basic design may have attachments or adapters that can give them some (not all) of the capability of a meter of another basic design. Understanding different light meters enables a photographer to choose the best meter for a given need or to make the best use of an existing one.

We are going to discuss some of the relevant capabilities that are important in choosing a meter. Notice that having any one of these capabilities may not necessarily exclude another. A flash meter, for example, is likely to be an incident meter also. Some other capabilities tend to be mutually exclusive: In-camera meters and spot meters, for example, are always reflection meters.

Incident Meters versus Reflection Meters

Incident light is the light falling on the subject. *Reflected light* is the light that bounces off the subject. Meters can be built to measure either. Some, such as the one shown in Figure A2.1, can measure both.

► *The diffusion dome on this multipurpose meter is set for incident light readings.*

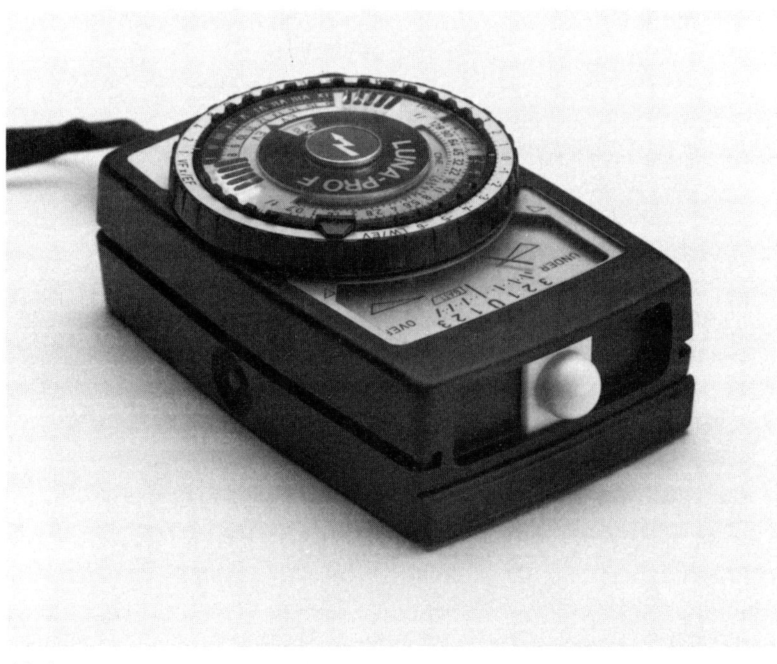

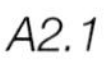
A2.1

Figure A2.2 shows how to use an incident meter.

► *An incident measurement. Place the meter close to the subject, then point the meter dome between the light source and the camera.*

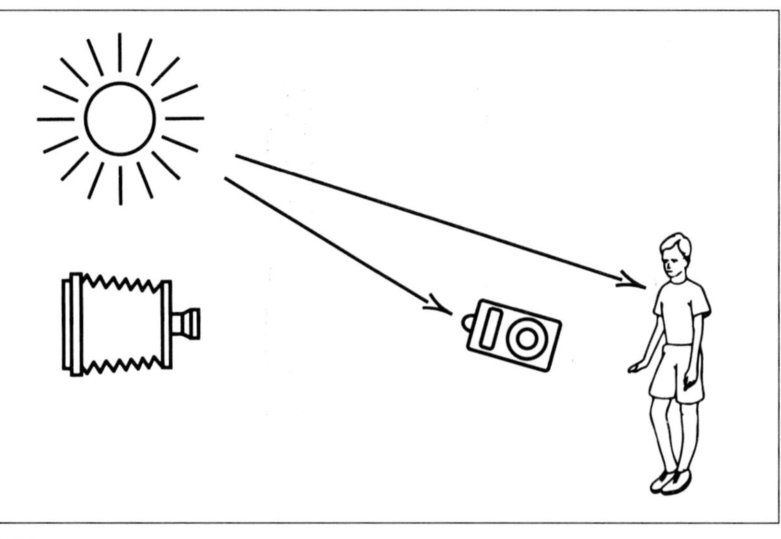

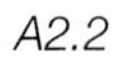
A2.2

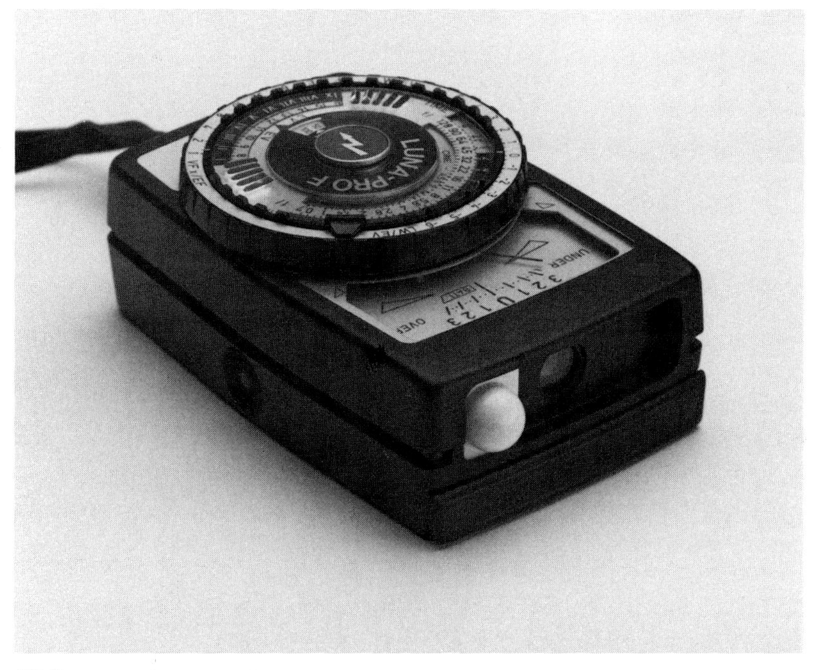

◀ *The multipurpose meter with the diffusion dome moved to the side to take a reflected-light reading.*

A2.3

A white dome usually covers the light-sensitive cell in an incident meter. We place the dome at an angle between the direction of the light source and the camera. The meter is close to the subject so that it receives the same light as the subject.

Incident meters are easy to use because they are not fooled by the tones in the subject. Because they read only the light falling on the subject, incident meters will indicate the same exposure for a light-gray or a dark-gray subject. This will usually be the correct exposure. An incident meter is ideal for a less sophisticated photographer or a photographer in a hurry.

However, the very advantages offered by an incident meter are also the disadvantages. Photographers sometimes want different exposures for different subjects in the same light. Because the incident meter does not read the subject, it takes such judgment out of the hands of the photographer.

The solution is to read the light reflected from the subject. This allows more creative control, but requires more thought by the photographer.

Reflection meters should, as Figure A2.4 shows, be pointed at the subject rather than at the light. The meter needs to be as close to the subject as practical without casting a shadow on the subject.

▶ *A reflective reading requires placing the meter as close to the subject as possible without casting a shadow on the subject.*

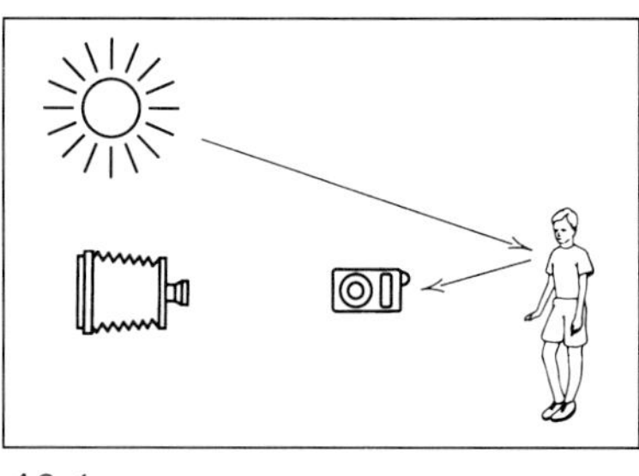

A2.4

Some photographers use a reflection meter to read a standard *eighteen percent gray card* instead of the subject they intend to photograph. In such cases, the reflection meter shows the same exposure as an incident meter. A reflection meter, with a gray card, is almost as easy to use as an incident meter (Figure A2.5). But the photographer can always put away the gray card and read the subject itself whenever more sophisticated measurements are needed.

▶ *A reflection reading of an eighteen percent gray card is the same as that of an incident reading.*

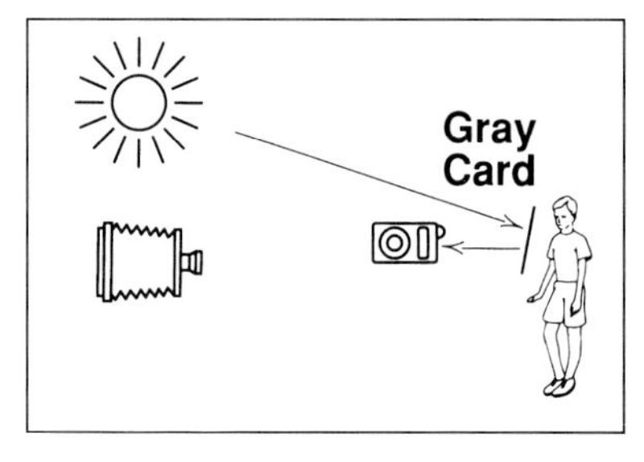

A2.5

Averaging Meters versus Spot Meters

The reflection meter we have just seen is *an averaging meter*. This means it looks at a large subject area and averages together any light and dark areas in the subject. Most reflection meters work this way. This is why such meters should be held close to the subject to avoid reading extraneous areas. If a subject is too far away, it may not be possible to get the meter close enough to read just the important area. Or if the subject is too small, it may be impossible to get the meter close enough without casting a shadow on the subject.

A *spot meter* is the answer to such problems (Figure A2.6). It has a lens in front of the light-sensitive cell to restrict the angle of view. The meter also has a viewing system similar to that in a camera so that the photographer can look through the meter and see exactly what the meter is reading.

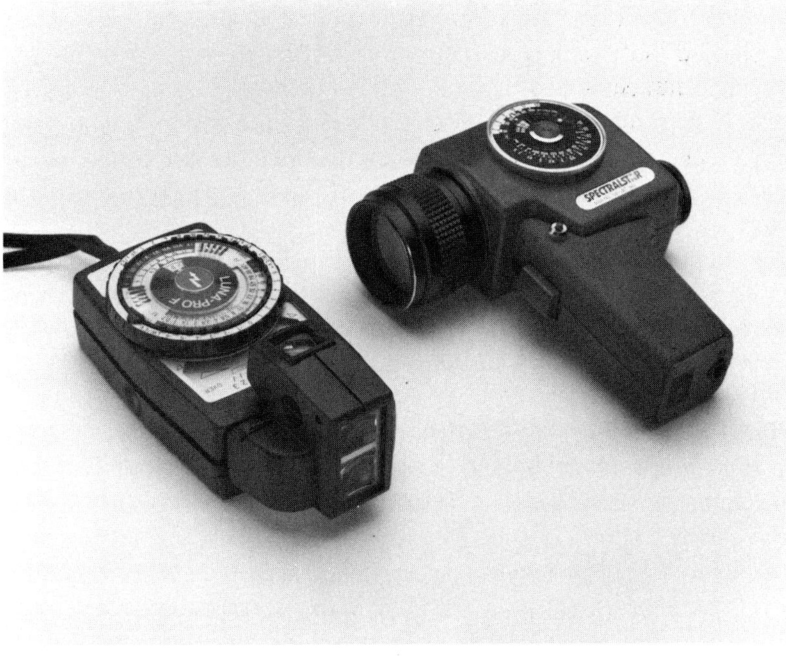

◀ *A spot meter and a multipurpose meter with a narrow-angle attachment.*

A2.6

A spot meter can measure the light reflected from a small subject, a distant subject, or small areas within a subject.

The spot meter offers the photographer creative freedom and technical control over exposure. However, many are heavier and take up more space in the camera bag than other meters.

Hand-Held Meters versus In-Camera Meters

Although all meters could be considered to be *hand held,* the term normally refers to meters that are not built into the camera. All meters we have examined so far have been hand-held meters. This does not suggest that every photographer needs a hand-held meter. Much of what we have said is also true of meters in cameras.

In-camera meters are always reflection meters. However, if the camera is pointed at an eighteen percent gray card, the measurement is identical to that of an incident meter.

The meter in the camera may be either an averaging meter or a spot meter. It may also be center weighted. *Center-weighted meters* are a compromise between averaging and spot meters. The best of them are supported by an internal microprocessor and have highly sophisticated programming that allows them to look at the four quadrants of the image, plus the center, and to base exposure on a reasonable guess about what sort of subject is in the scene.

Such meters are generally preferred by amateurs and by professionals who must work quickly in journalistic situations, because center-weighted meters almost always produce usable exposures. However, such meters may be more difficult to use for professionals who need very precise exposure control because the photographer cannot accurately determine exactly what the meter is measuring or how much it is weighting the regions within the area.

Both averaging and center-weighted camera meters can be used as spot meters. All you have to do is to put a long enough lens on the camera. Read the relevant part of the scene with the longer lens, switch back to any other lens to shoot the picture, and set the exposure manually.

Flash Meters versus Continuous Meters

A continuous light meter offers a measurement that varies with the fluctuating brightness of the light. If clouds move in front of the sun while we are making a continuous reading, we will see a corresponding drop on the meter dial or liquid crystal display (LCD). A flash meter, on the other hand, (a) does not show us any reading at all until it sees a *very* rapid increase in brightness, and (b) continues to display that measurement until we reset the meter.

Besides measuring a single flash, good flash meters will also account for the effect of ambient light accompanying the flash and for the cumulative exposure of a multiple flash. The latter capability is convenient, but it is not essential. As long as we know the correct aperture for a single flash, it is easy to quickly calculate the number of flashes we need at any other aperture.

For many photographers, the choice between flash and continuous meters is easy. For example, a portrait photographer who always uses a strobe needs a flash meter, and a video camera operator who always uses quartz lights needs a continuous meter.

The decision is more difficult for the vast number of photographers who have some of both needs. Some meters have both capabilities. However, those that work well as flash meters may not read continuous light at all if it is dim. Furthermore, the multipurpose meters that make good continuous meters sometimes cannot accurately measure very powerful studio strobes. Fortunately, electronic improvements continue to make meters more truly multipurpose every year.

How Many Flashes

Commercial photographers often need to use apertures from f/45 to f/90 to get adequate depth of field with large-format cameras. The expense of studio strobes can make it difficult to afford enough light to expose at such apertures, especially when light is wasted by absorption by diffusion materials. Keep in mind, the ability to close down just one stop requires doubling the cash investment in lights!

Any photographer can immediately see the advantage of increasing the number of flashes used to expose a static scene instead of buying extra strobes. Many, however, do not immediately see how to determine a reasonable exposure.

The principle is the same as the one that tells us we can get more exposure from a continuous light source with a longer shutter speed. Using two flashes instead of one, for example, gives us the equivalent of a one-stop exposure increase. Using four flashes is equal to a two-stop increase.

Notice that multiple flashes allow bracketing in precise steps. We do not have to double (or halve) the exposure with each step of the bracket the way we might if we were changing the shutter speed. We could, for example, expose three sheets of film using four, six, and nine flashes. This degree of exposure control offers yet another reason for using multiple flashes. In fact, photographers who have more than enough light to make the exposure in a single flash sometimes deliberately select lower power to benefit from this added control. (Of course, we could also change the aperture by a fraction of a stop. But remember, in this case we do not want to open the aperture, for fear of losing depth of field.)

Just remember that equal exposure steps mean multiplying or dividing, not adding or subtracting! Consider what we would get if we exposed three sheets of film using four, eight, and twelve flashes. Each step in the bracket is four flashes more, or less, than the next one. But the eight-flash sheet of film is a full stop more than the four-flash sheet, while it is only a little more than a half-stop less than the twelve-flash sheet!

Try multiplying or dividing the number of flashes by 1.4 instead. Suppose you determine, by flash meter, Polaroid, or guide number, that seven flashes is probably right. Try an extra exposure using five flashes ($7 \div 1.4 = 5$). Then give the next shot ten flashes ($7 \times 1.4 = 9.8$).

We chose 1.4 for this example because it is a factor of almost exactly half of a stop. If your needs are less critical, try multiplying or dividing the basic exposure by 1.6 instead. That is about two thirds of a stop.

Color-Temperature Meters

Color-temperature meters measure the ambient light to decide what filtration to use on the lens or the lights to compensate for light that is not one of the standard color temperatures.

These meters are a useful accessory for any photographer who uses available light on location. They are less useful for studio work because studio lights are usually very close to standard color temperature. Even on location, such meters have limited use with strobe lights. They can read the ambient light, but not the color of the combined ambient, plus strobe, illumination.

Polaroid Camera Backs

Even the most sophisticated in-camera metering systems have only limited ability to "think" about the scene. Using a meter to obtain technically precise exposure requires practice and training on the part of the photographer. Furthermore, a technically precise exposure may not deal with psychological preferences. We sometimes want other than "ideal" exposure or lighting contrast for a reason no more definite than, "I like what I like." The complexities multiply when we realize that the client may also have purely subjective preferences that we need to satisfy.

It is impossible to fully appreciate these psychological factors simply by looking at the scene; we need to look at an *image* of the scene. Polaroid test shots are the only way to quickly get an image that approximates the one we intend to shoot on conventional film.

Polaroid film magazines are available to fit most professional still cameras. These produce the most useful test images because they allow the Polaroid to be exposed from the same camera viewpoint, through the same lens, using the same aperture as the final photograph.

Unfortunately, Polaroid magazines for 35mm cameras are less practical because it is difficult to quickly switch from Polaroid to conventional film in midroll. Most of them produce Polaroid images too small to evaluate easily. Others, with built-in optics to magnify the image, make it almost impossible to produce a Polaroid with the same depth of field as the final shot. Still photographers using 35mm, along with motion picture photographers, may prefer to use a separate high-quality camera just for the Polaroids.

POSITIONING DEVICES

Lights are only part of a lighting setup. In any professional studio, we are likely to find a maze of stands, booms, clamps, cables, pulleys, and other assorted gismos and gadgets. Many of them are used, in one way or the other, to position lights. In this section, we will review equipment made for that purpose.

Light Stands

It is hard to overstate the importance of good light stands. Absolutely nothing is more disconcerting than to have a shooting session rudely interrupted when an inferior stand collapses and tumbles over, smashing our best, and, of course, most expensive flash head in the process.

High-quality light stands last for years. That makes them less expensive than second-rate equipment. Buy the best stands your budget will allow. Then, later, if you purchase heavier lights, or add booms and soft boxes, you will have stands that are sufficiently robust to support them. Never needing to replace light stands saves money in the long run.

This does not, however, mean that every stand that you own has to be the absolute top of the line. It does mean, however, that each stand you buy should support at least a slightly heavier light at a slightly greater height than you think you need. Eventually, you will accidentally kick that stand. Then you will appreciate the safety margin.

Check the construction of any stand before you buy it. Do the legs open wide enough to provide stability? Do the set screws loosen easily when you want, but stay set when the stand is in place? Are there any obvious weak points, plastic parts that need to be metal, aluminum parts that should be steel?

Finally, consider buying fully integrated, modular lighting "systems." The advantage of buying stands that are a part of such a system is that all the various components that are a part of it can be easily fitted together into a wide array of different lighting configurations. This compatibility can make your job a lot quicker when you have to set up for a complex shoot.

Booms

Booms are an important lighting accessory. Portrait and commercial photographers need to suspend such things as lights, diffusion screens, and gobos above their subjects. One of the best ways of doing this is to use booms such as those shown in Figure A2.7.

▶ *Booms allow convenient light positioning. Some maximize that convenience, plus stability; others can be disassembled for portability.*

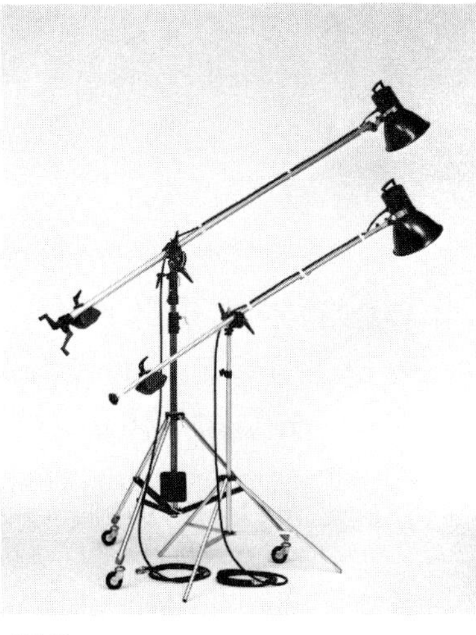

A2.7

Some boom assemblies are sold as boom and light stand combinations. These usually cost less than the boom and the stand bought separately.

Many booms have controls to adjust the angle of lights at the opposite end. Such control is a great convenience, but it also makes the boom more expensive and more difficult to disassemble and transport to a location outside the studio. If you do much location work, or if you are making an initial investment in studio equipment, a less elaborate boom will usually prove satisfactory.

Remember, "less elaborate" does not mean "low quality." As with light stands, it pays to buy a sturdy boom. Poorly manufactured ones cannot take much heavy use, and most of them soon break.

Rail Systems

In the studio, the most convenient and elegant method of mounting lights is to suspend them from a system of overhead rails. Keeping stands and cables off the floor and out of the way makes still photography faster, more efficient, and safer. Such systems are almost essential for studio motion picture and video productions, because the movement of the talent and the cameras requires still more usable floor space.

The most simple rail systems use ordinary iron pipe, plus inexpensive clamps to attach lights and accessories. This is adequate for setups that do not require frequent modification. More elaborate systems allow lights to glide across the track on rollers for quick modifications of portrait and fashion lighting, where the photographer may be expected to do a large number of very different pictures in a single day. The best systems add motors to move the lights remotely so that no one has to take the time to climb a ladder and adjust each light by hand.

Since rail systems are expensive, many photographers consider them appropriate for only the high-budget studios. However, a combination of overhead rails, plus common light stands, can be a good equipment mix for any studio operation. If you have a single large soft box that does not require extensive movement for your most routine work, a minimal rail system for that one light may be more convenient and less expensive than an adequate boom.

Clamps

You can never have too many clamps around a photographic studio! When your entire setup appears to be tottering on the verge of collapse, the well-placed clamp saves the day.

Two of the least expensive, the *C clamp* and the *spring clamp,* serve most purposes. But your work will also probably require one or two unreasonably expensive photographic clamps to hold something just the way you need it. Figure A2.8 shows some clamps designed for photographic use. Be aware that if something needs clamping, someone has probably designed a clamp for it.

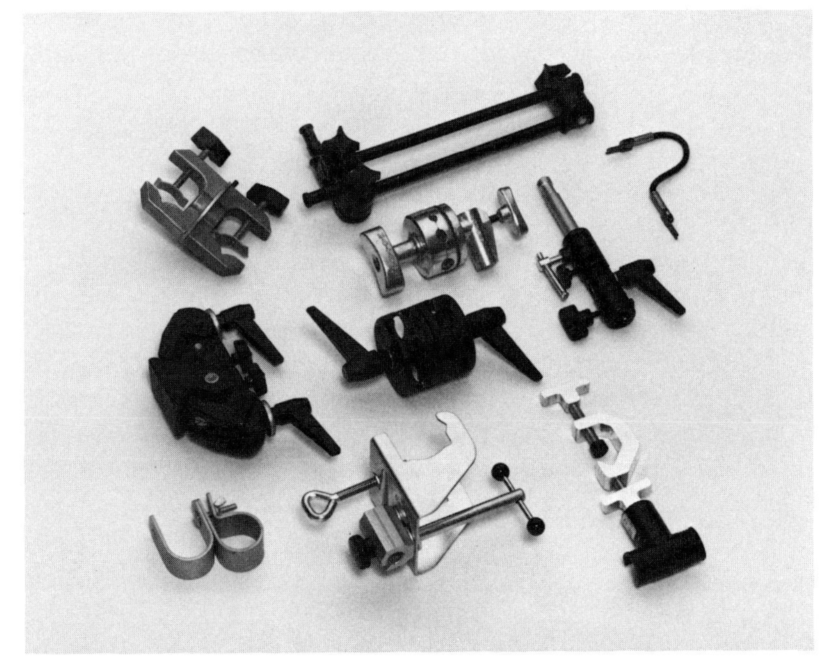

A2.8

◀ *Many different kinds of clamps are useful to photographers. Here we see a few of the many available types.*

DIFFUSION MATERIALS

Photographers often want to change the size of the light source they are using. As we saw in Chapter 4, the size of a light determines how hard or soft the shadows will be. In addition, experienced photographers also know that the size of the light may determine the size of the highlight.

However, lights are expensive, and large ones are cumbersome to carry around when working in the field. As a result, few photographers have all the different sizes of lights they need. Instead, they have learned how to manipulate the *effective* size of their light sources. They have learned, in other words, how to make a small light source act like a big one. One of the most common ways of doing this is to use a *diffuser*.

Figure A2.9 shows a diffusing sheet in use. Here the diffusion material is a plastic especially manufactured for the purpose. Unless the color balance is critical, tracing paper, a white shower curtain, a bed sheet, or similar translucent material could diffuse the light as effectively.

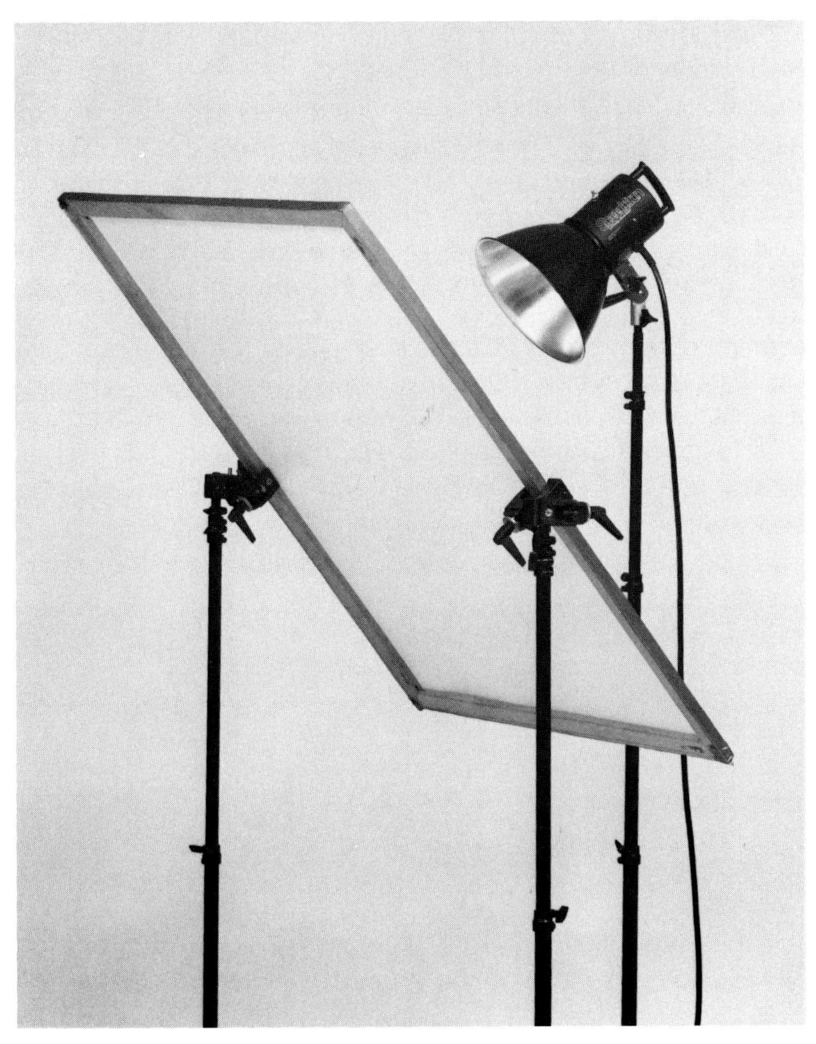

◀ *This simple, inexpensive, but very effective diffuser was made by attaching a sheet of frosted plastic over a wooden frame.*

A2.9

We made the diffusion sheet frame from the stretchers that painters use for canvases. These are especially good for our purpose because they are inexpensive, are easy to assemble, come in many different sizes, and are readily available at art supply stores. They can also be easily taken apart. That makes them handy on location.

When working outside with large diffusers, one always faces the problem of wind. Just a light puff can turn a diffuser into a sail that may well blow down all but the most secure setup. One way of reducing this problem is to make your outdoor diffusers from the same sort of plastic screen that gardeners use to shade plants. Because such a screen is porous, wind exerts less pressures on it than it would on a solid surface. This makes it easier to work with outside. Such screens are available in many different sizes and are often sold with grommets along their edges, making them easy to lash to a frame.

The kind of PVC pipe that one buys in home repair stores makes good outdoor diffuser frames. It is lightweight, inexpensive, and easy to assemble and take apart. Aluminum tent poles, tubing, and fittings also come in handy for frame building. They are available at camping and hardware stores.

SOFT BOXES

All simple diffusion sheets have one major drawback in the studio. They allow light to bounce off their rear surfaces, bounce around the room, and light the subject in ways we do not like. One way to prevent this is to use a *soft box* such as the one shown in Figure A2.10. Such a soft box acts as a light "cage." It prevents any of the light reflected from the back of the diffusion material from spilling out into the studio.

► *Soft boxes, such as this one, duplicate the lighting of diffusion screens, plus keep extraneous light in.*

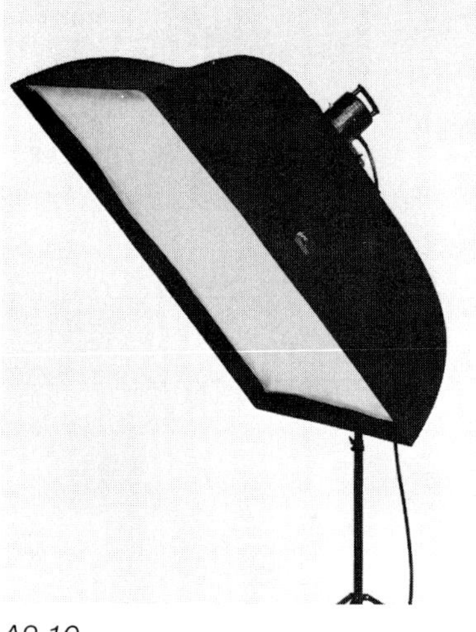

A2.10

It is a simple matter to build a perfectly adequate soft box, and most photographers used to do just that. In recent years, however, the commercially manufactured ones have improved enough to become popular. The most useful of these are made of fabric stretched over a frame. Such boxes are light and easy to disassemble. This makes them ideal for location work.

An overhead soft box with more than one light in it is called a *bank light.*

REFLECTORS

Reflectors are another simple but useful photographic tool. Umbrellas and reflective cards are the most common and most useful kinds. Like diffusers, reflectors can increase the size of a light source. Bouncing the light from a large card increases the effective size of the light source many times.

Reflective cards are especially useful as a source of fill lighting. Many photographers consider one main light, plus a reflector card, adequate for most scenes.

Any lightweight, rigid material that is quickly cut makes a good reflector card. Foam core is used most often. Since reflector cards are not expensive, it is worth keeping a large collection of different sizes and surfaces. Leave some white and cover others with silver mylar, aluminum foil, gold paper, and some of the textured silver plastics made specifically for the purpose.

Commercially manufactured reflector cards duplicate the homemade ones, but they are more durable. Many are easily collapsed for transportation. One particularly ingenious design uses a flexible plastic hoop to support a piece of white or silver cloth. Twisting the hoop folds the reflector to half the diameter. Untwisting it produces a usable diameter, but without the visible seams common to more rigid collapsible reflectors.

The classic collapsible photographic reflector is an umbrella such as the one shown in Figure A2.11. We use them in much the same way as we use reflector cards. Because they are light and fold into a small package, they are easy to pack and carry around.

► *Umbrellas are the classic collapsible photographic reflectors.*

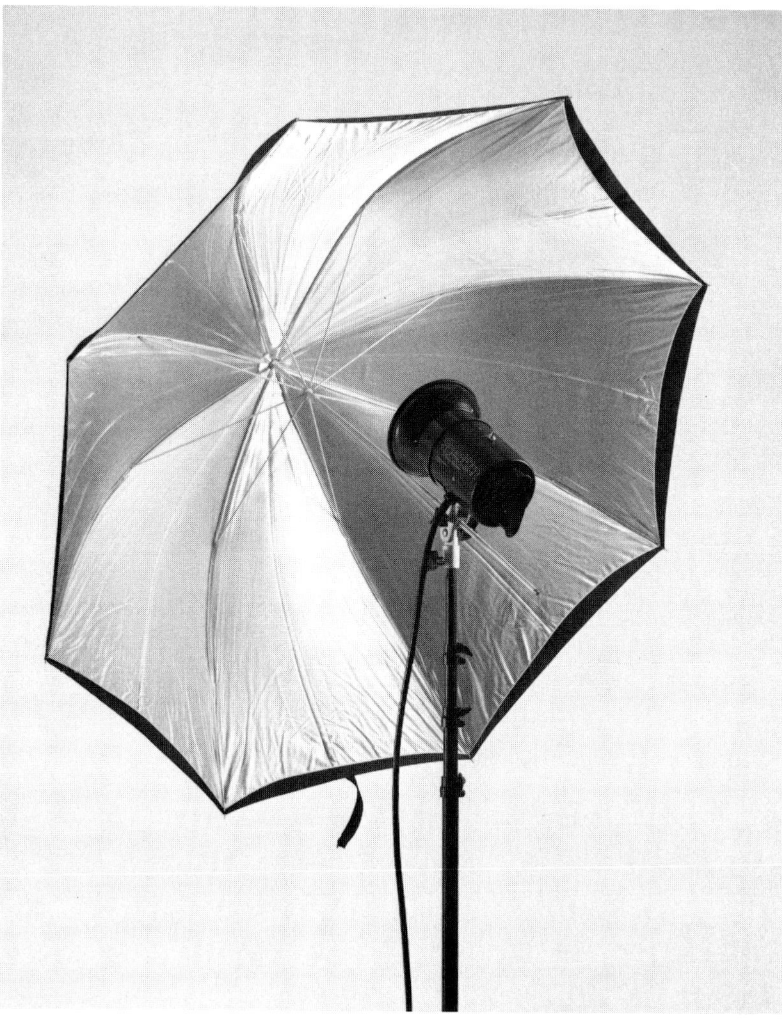

A2.11

The smaller the light is, the more likely we are to want to soften it. The auxiliary reflector shown in Figure A2.12, resembling both a bounce card and an umbrella, is intended specifically for small strobes.

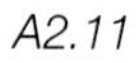

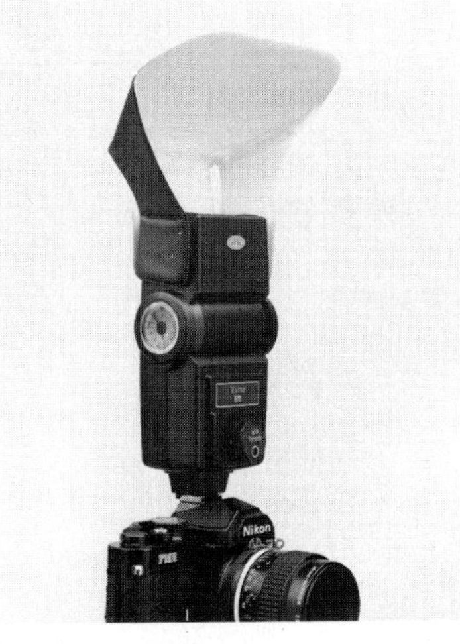

◀ *A reflector that enlarges the effective size of a small strobe.*

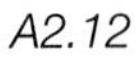
A2.12

LIGHT BLOCKERS

Photographers routinely need to block light to prevent it from reaching part of the scene. Figure A2.13 shows one of the ways they do this. In it we see a *gobo,* a black card that *goes* between the light and something else. This commercially manufactured gobo, along with its positionable arm, can shade areas in a medium-sized set. Still life photographers more often use a small piece of cardboard, cut to size and taped to a wooden dowel.

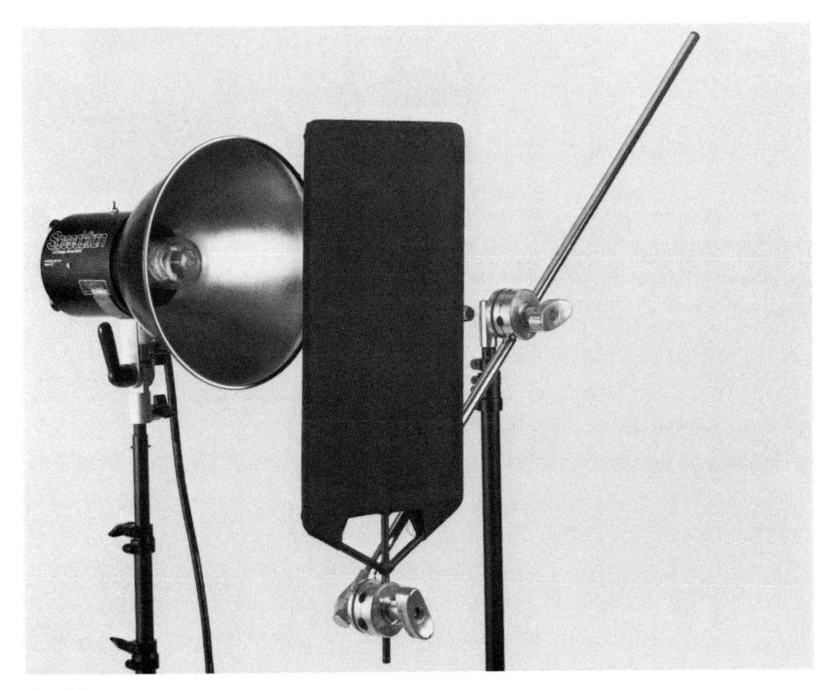

◀ *Gobos provide a convenient, easy-to-use way of keeping unwanted light rays out of a scene.*

A2.13

A variation on the same idea as the gobo uses wire screen to block only part of the light. These devices are called *scrims.*

Barndoors like those shown in Figure A2.14 can also block light from part of the scene. Barndoors are fast and convenient to use because they require no extra stands or clamps. However, we cannot change the distance between a barndoor and the lights to which it is attached. Therefore, the effect is less controllable than that of a gobo. Barndoors are nearly useless on very soft lights.

► *Barndoors are useful in controlling where light will and will not fall. However, being attached to the lights they control makes them less flexible than gobos.*

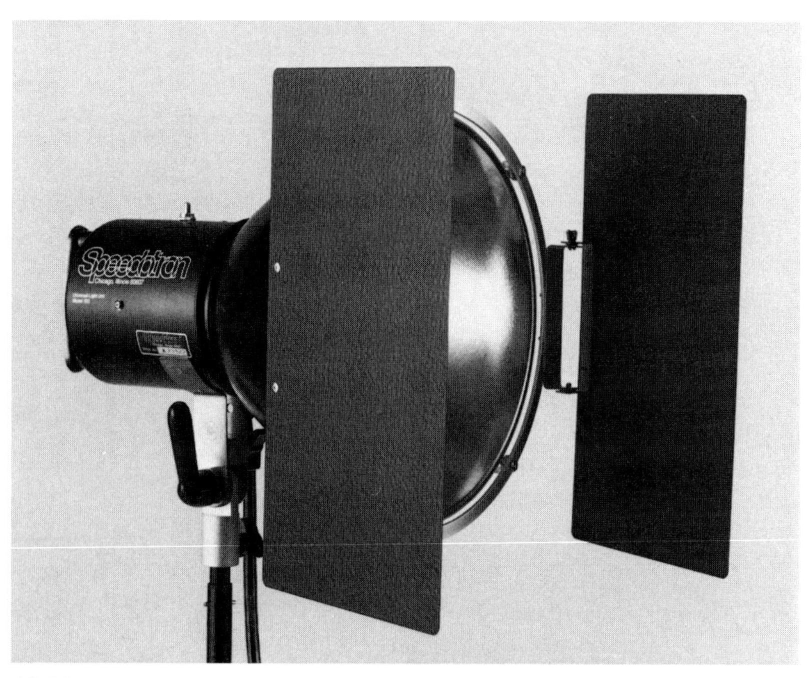

A2.14

SPOT DEVICES

Photographers often want to focus a lot of light on one small part of a scene. As we pointed out earlier, this is no trouble if you are using tungsten lights. It is easy to position a small quartz-halogen bulb in a head so that a reflector or a fresnel lens can focus the light.

However, building strobe fresnels and spots is not so easy. The difficulty of placing a modeling light *plus* a large flash tube at the optically correct location behind the lens makes most strobe spotlights low-powered, likely to overheat, or overly expensive. Given these difficulties, a few strobe spots and spot attachments such as the one shown in Figure A2.15 work surprisingly well.

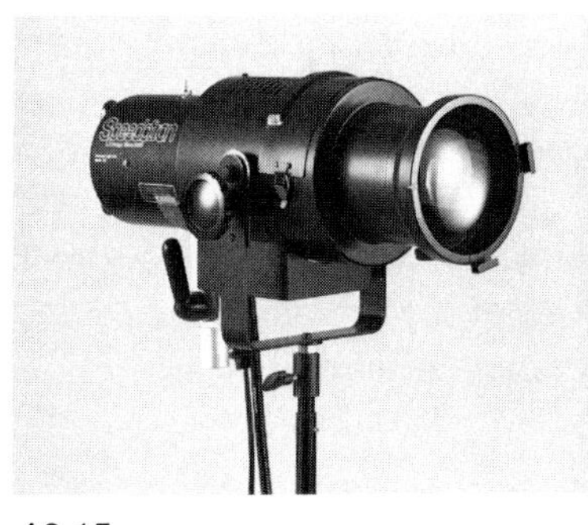

◀ *Spot attachments focus the strobe on a small area.*

A2.15

The problems with strobe spotlights lead most photographers to use devices that block all but a narrow beam of the light coming from a standard flash head. Because they block light, rather than focus or concentrate it, such devices waste light. However, the light that is not lost behaves much like a spotlight. The most popular of these light-blocking devices are snoots and spot grids.

A *snoot* is a tube that fits on the front of a light. It allows only the center beam of the light to reach the subject (Figure A2.16). Snoots are available in different lengths and diameters. These measurements determine the size of the spot of light that they produce.

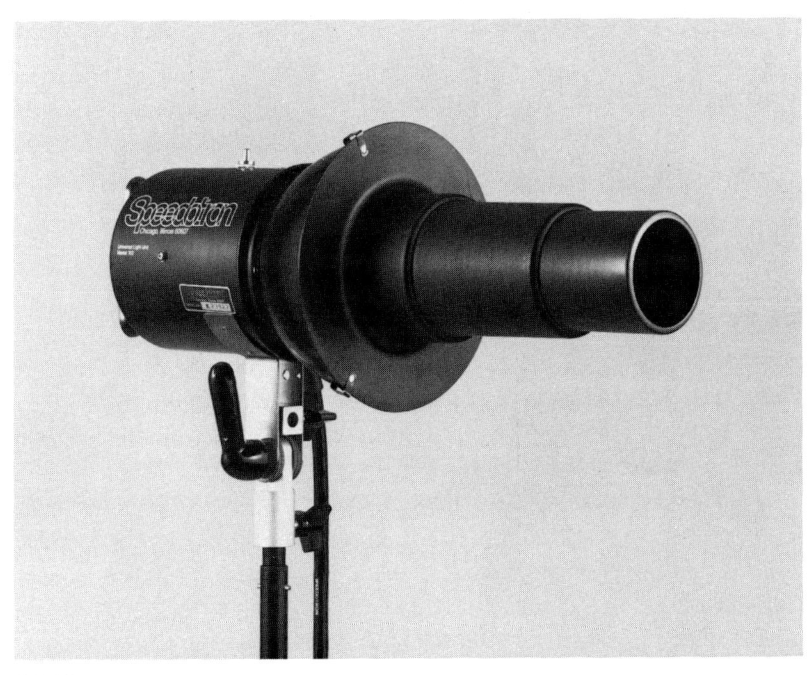

◀ *Snoots allow only the center beam to reach the subject.*

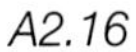

A2.16

Many photographers make their own snoots out of black paper. This works reasonably well, but it is a serious fire hazard. A better solution is black aluminum foil, available from some photographic and theatrical suppliers.

A *spot grid* is a metal honeycomb attached to the front of a light. It works in much the same way as hundreds of tiny snoots (Figure A2.17). Because they waste less light, grids are more efficient than snoots. On the other hand, because they are difficult to manufacture, they are also substantially more expensive.

► *Spot grids have an effect similar to snoots, but they are both more effective and more expensive.*

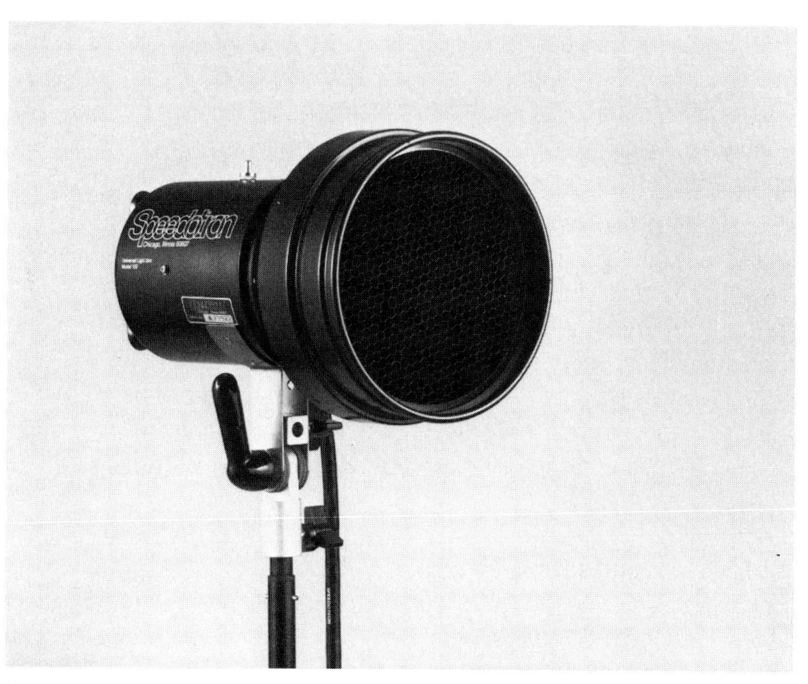

A2.17

FILTERS

There is a wide assortment of materials to attach to lights to alter their color. Whether you need them depends both on the type of work you do and on taste.

Most filtration materials are made of dyed plastic. The dyes inevitably fade with exposure to the light, and this can be a problem if very precise color is required. Others, called *dichroic filters,* use a precise internal molecular structure to alter the light color and require no dyes in manufacture. Dichroic filters never fade, but they cost many times as much as comparable *dye filters.* For most purposes, photographers find it more economical to use dye filters, discarding and replacing them as needed.

Many colored filters are used for no other reason than the fact that the photographer likes them. The colors of these filters range from very strong primary colors to very slight pastels, which have little perceptible effect on the light. They can duplicate any effect from a firefighter standing near the flashing light of the fire engine to the subtle golden highlights and slightly blue shadows found in a day at the beach.

Other filters serve a precise technical need. These include color-correction filters, color-compensating filters, ultraviolet filters, and polarizing filters.

Color-Correction Filters

Color-correction filters are available in large sheets and rolls to cover photographic lights and windows. Some make the color of a photographic light match that of available light on the location. These are most commonly used by video and motion picture photographers who want to use an incandescent light to lighten dark shadows in a daylight scene. Still photographers are more likely to use strobes that approximate daylight without filtration. However, aging softboxes can shift the color of a strobe. Putting a weak color-correction filter in that softbox is a fraction of the cost of replacing it.

Sometimes, using color-correction filters alone may only approximate accurate color balance. The ideal filter is often a step between available colors. Even if the nominally ideal color is available, manufacturing variations may mean that the filter we actually buy is not quite the color we need.

Color-Compensating Filters

Color-compensating filters allow the most precise control. Photographers usually call them *CC filters* for short. These filters are made with great precision, and their cost precludes buying them in sheets large enough to cover most lights. Fortunately, their optical quality is good enough that we can put them on a lens. As long as we do not stack more than two or three of them, they will not degrade the best optics.

Most photographers put the filters in front of the lens, but putting them behind the lens produces less flare, if the camera design allows it. Most photographers simply tape the filters to the lens, but holding them flat in frames designed for that purpose can offer a slight optical improvement.

CC filters are made in the three additive and the three subtractive primary colors. Most photographers use the subtractive primaries: cyan, magenta, and yellow. Others buy the additive primary colors: red, green, and blue. Few photographers use both the subtractive *and* the additive primaries. Either system works. Buy the one that suits the way you think about color.

We can obtain each filter color in several standard densities, rated by number. For example, a light yellow filter might be labeled CC05Y, a medium magenta is CC20M, while CC50B is an example of a dense blue.

Unfortunately, CC filters also reduce exposure and we need more light to compensate for that. The greater the density of the filter, the more the required exposure adjustment. Figure A2.18 shows the required compensation in f/stops.

Color Compensating Filters
Exposure Increase

Yellow (Absorbs Blue)	Exposure Increase in Stops	Magenta (Absorbs Green)	Exposure Increase in Stops	Cyan (Absorbs Red)	Exposure Increase in Stops
CC05Y	—	CC05M	1/3	CC05C	1/3
CC075Y	—	CC075M	1/3	CC075C	1/3
CC10Y	1/3	CC10M	1/3	CC10C	1/3
CC20Y	1/3	CC20M	1/3	CC20C	1/3
CC3OY	1/3	CC3OM	2/3	CC3OC	2/3
CC40Y	1/3	CC40M	2/3	CC40C	2/3
CC50Y	2/3	CC50M	2/3	CC50C	1
Red (Absorbs Blue and Green)	**Exposure Increase in Stops**	**Green (Absorbs Blue and Red)**	**Exposure Increase in Stops**	**Blue (Absorbs Red and Green)**	**Exposure Increase in Stops**
CC05R	1/3	CC05G	1/3	CC05B	1/3
CC075R	1/3	CC075G	1/3	CC075B	1/3
CC10R	1/3	CC10G	1/3	CC10B	1/2
CC20R	1/3	CC20G	1/3	CC20B	2/3
CC3OR	2/3	CC3OG	2/3	CC3OB	2/3
CC40R	2/3	CC40G	2/3	CC40B	1
CC50R	1	CC50G	1	CC50B	1 1/2

From **Kodak Filters for Scientific and Technical Uses**, Eastman Kodak Company, 1985

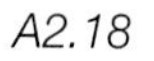

A2.18

If you do not have an exposure compensation chart when you need it, you can also determine the necessary exposure correction by a light meter reading of a white or gray subject with the CC filter placed over the meter. This method may be less accurate because the meter is more sensitive to some colors than others.

Notice that some combinations of CC filters produce neutral density. CC10Y, CC10M, plus CC20M is the same color as a single CC10M, but the neutral density wastes light. There is nothing wrong with such a filter package if you unexpectedly need a CC10M and do not have it. However, if you find yourself routinely using such a package, it is worth buying the right filter.

CC filters can be used to judge a test transparency. We view the test shot through various CC filters to find the one that gives the best color, then use that filter over the lens on the next occasion. We get very good color balance if we test each batch of film we buy, label the film box with the preferred filtration, then freeze the film to keep age from causing further color shift.

Ultraviolet Filters

Most strobes emit a significant amount of ultraviolet light that is visible to film but not to humans. This can cause the picture to be more blue than the subject appears to the eye.

This problem is so common to strobes that many manufacturers build the ultraviolet filter into the glass envelope covering the flash tube. It is unnecessary to buy additional filters to cover strobes with these tubes.

Such flash tubes are superior, but not so much that this, by itself, should determine the choice of strobe. It is more important that each strobe in a studio match the color of the others. If you do not own a strobe, consider buying one with built-in ultraviolet filtration. If you are buying an additional strobe, you should probably buy one like whatever you already have.

Also be aware that any diffusion warms the light somewhat. This is because the lower frequency rays penetrate the diffusion material more readily than the higher frequency ones. Using UV-corrected flash tubes *plus* diffusion can cause a stronger color cast than using uncorrected flash tubes.

Polarizing Filters

Polarizing filters intended for use on lights are identical to those designed to attach to the lens, except they are laminated in layers of plastic instead of optical glass. This keeps both their weight and their cost manageable, although they are many times the size of lens polarizing filters.

In some situations, these filters can be powerful tools for controlling lighting. Additionally, the way they affect the light can teach a great deal about light and lighting in general.

CASES

Lighting equipment is expensive and easy to break. Bang it around in the trunk of a car or drop it on the floor and there is every chance in the world that the light will light no more! This brings us to those vital but often underrated items: cases.

If you work entirely in the studio, the cardboard box in which the equipment was originally packed may be adequate protection. But for location work, sturdy, well-built cases are a must. Some lighting manufacturers offer a line of cases to fit their own gear. There are also many "universal" cases on the market.

Before buying a case, check its construction details carefully. Do the handles seem to be well attached? Does it come with a sturdy carrying strap? Does it look like it will dent easily? Can you arrange the interior compartments in the way you want? Do the carrying straps go all the way around the case or are they merely stitched on? Does it have good locks? Does it close tightly? Is it reasonably dust tight and watertight? A good case costs less than a cheap case if the cheap case allows broken equipment.

RISK MANAGEMENT

We should not leave a discussion of lighting equipment without noting that such tools are potentially dangerous. Almost every experienced photographer has, at one time or another, had to deal with flying glass, fire, electrical shock, or a simultaneous and unpleasant combination of these. Most accidents involving lighting equipment are simple nuisances, but others are fatal. Almost all are preventable.

Heat Buildup

Fire is a real hazard whenever we are working with diffusion materials. This is especially true if they are made of some particularly flammable material such as tracing paper. Never attach such materials directly to quartz lights. Even if you are using a strobe with a low-wattage modeling light, never leave a light covered by a diffuser unattended too long.

In extreme cases, we have seen the subject of the photograph catch on fire when the light was too close. Be especially careful of spotlights, which concentrate the light, and of black subjects, which absorb a great deal of light and therefore produce heat.

Handling Quartz-Halogen Lamps

Never touch a quartz-halogen bulb with your bare hands. If you do, there is a very good chance that the oil that rubs off your fingers will cause the bulb to crack, or even explode, when you turn it on. The falling glass will be hot enough to ignite flammable materials. For this reason, always use gloves or paper when you touch one of these bulbs.

Electrical Defects

Any photographic light is likely to develop an electrical defect with enough use. The combination of high current and high temperature sooner or later breaks wires, burns insulation, and melts solder connections. Any of these defects can allow a wire to come into contact with the light housing. Most light housings are made of metal. So are the stands to which they are attached. The potentially fatal consequence of this is that the entire setup becomes "hot."

Lethal accidents caused by this type of defect are so easy to prevent that they should never happen. All that is required is a *grounded electrical circuit.* A grounded circuit will blow a fuse or a breaker, instantly, when the defect occurs. This shuts off all current, and electrocution is impossible. An ungrounded circuit may allow a defective light to continue working perfectly with no indication of trouble until someone touches it.

Most of the lights discussed in this appendix are to be used with grounded circuits. That means that they are manufactured with standard three-prong plugs. Always use them as the maker intended by plugging them into properly grounded three-hole sockets. Never, under any circumstances, shortcut safety by using a two-prong adapter and plugging them into an ungrounded circuit.

Another common hazard is extension cables. These are sold with the maximum allowable load labeled on them. Always make sure that the rated wattage or amperage of the cable is as high *or higher* than that of the light. Never plug more than one light into a single extension unless the rated current load for the cable is at least as high as the *combined* rating of the lights.

Be aware that longer cable lengths require higher wire gauge. Two perfectly safe cables plugged end-to-end may have a gauge too low for the combined length.

Falling Lights

The sturdy stands we recommend in this appendix reduce these types of hazards considerably. Here are some ideas to further minimize risk. They are particularly useful when working on location, where people unaccustomed to photographic equipment may be walking around the set.

In Figure A2.19, we attached a cloth bag filled with sand to the light stand. The extra weight adds stability. Collapsible water bottles and clamp-on lead weights also are available from photographic retailers. Cheap plastic bottles, such as old milk bottles filled with water, also work *if* you keep them away from power supplies and *if* the lights are grounded.

► *Ballasts, such as this sand-filled bag, add stability to light stands.*

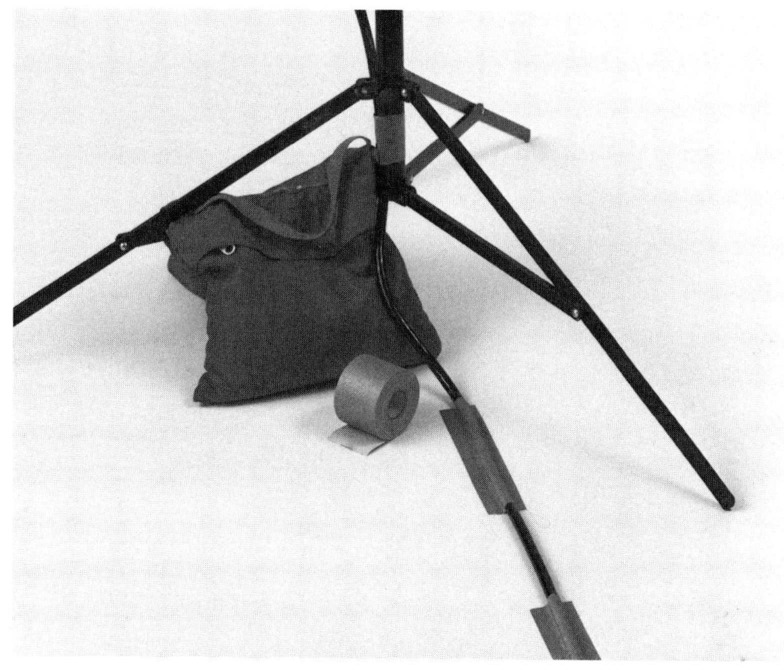

A2.19

Notice also that the light cable is attached to the base of the light stand. This means that if anyone trips over it, the stand is more likely to slide along the floor than fall over. Finally, notice that the cable is taped to the floor, making it difficult for anyone to trip over it in the first place.

Index